.

Paardeberg
Lord Roberts' Gambit

Martin Marais

Published in 2014 by Lulu.com Publishing

ISBN: 978-0-9574011-4-3

A CIP catalogue record for this title is available from the British Library.

Cover Image: Paardeberg
Copyright © Matt Coburn

In memory of the men, women and children of all creeds
who gave life or limb in the struggle that was the
(Second) Anglo-Boer War

To
Frans Johannes Marais
A great story teller who I like to think
would have enjoyed this one

Acknowledgements

I offer my thanks to Matt Coburn for creating the artwork for the cover of this novel. Further examples of Matt's work can be seen and purchased at www.theartcircus.com.

Thanks also to Sarah Bury for casting her editorial eye over the manuscripts and for mentoring me through the process of writing this novel. Any remaining grammatical and spelling errors are entirely my own, as I could not resist tinkering!

Thanks also to Margaret Marais for reviewing the final versions of the manuscript.

Finally, thanks to my family for their forbearance with the obsession that writing this novel became.

Contents

Maps

The Lesson

Let us admit it fairly, as a business people should,
We have had no end of a lesson: it will do us no end of good.

Not on a single issue, or in one direction or twain,
But conclusively, comprehensively, and several times and again,

Were all our most holy illusions knocked higher than Gilderoy's kite.
We have had a jolly good lesson, and it serves us jolly well right!

This was not bestowed us under the trees, nor yet in the shade of a tent,
But swingingly, over eleven degrees of a bare brown continent.
From Lamberts to Delagoa Bay, and from Pietersburg to Sutherland,
Fell the phenomenal lesson we learned – with a fullness accorded no other land.

It was our fault, and our very great fault, and not the judgment of Heaven.
We made an Army in our own image, on an island nine by seven,
Which faithfully mirrored its makers' ideals, equipment, and mental attitude
And so we got our lesson: and we ought to accept it with gratitude.

We have spent two hundred million pounds to prove the fact once more,
That horses are quicker than men afoot, since two and two make four;
And horses have four legs, and men have two legs, and two into four goes twice,
And nothing over except our lesson – and very cheap at the price.

For remember (this our children shall know: we are too near for that knowledge)
Not our mere astonied camps, but Council and Creed and College
All the obese, unchallenged old things that stifle and overlie us
Have felt the effects of the lesson we got – an advantage no money could buy us!

Then let us develop this marvellous asset which we alone command,
And which, it may subsequently transpire, will be worth as much as the Rand.
Let us approach this pivotal fact in a humble yet hopeful mood
We have had no end of a lesson, it will do us no end of good!

It was our fault, and our very great fault and now we must turn it to use.
We have forty million reasons for failure, but not a single excuse.
So the more we work and the less we talk the better results we shall get
We have had an Imperial lesson; it may make us an Empire yet!

Rudyard Kipling

Foreword

The Second Anglo-Boer War (to give it its British title) has held a fascination for me for a number of years, especially the Battle of Paardeberg, as, arguably, it was the turning point of the war.

What intrigued me was why Lord Roberts, a man of reputed enormous compassion towards his men, put them through such torment in a forced march of over one hundred miles across African semi-desert and, more importantly, why General Cronjé responded in the way he did. It was the decisions and actions of these two men during the prosecution of this particular battle that were to change the direction of the war.

Detailed records of the thoughts and decisions of these men and the reasons for the actions they took do not survive, even in the many reports and books, including autobiographies, written after the war.

I then read the novel *The Killer Angels* by Michael Shaara, a splendid telling of the American Civil War Battle of Gettysburg. The story is told from the viewpoint of those who took part in the battle. Shaara's novel inspired me to attempt to understand the thoughts, values and convictions of those involved in the Battle of Paardeberg and to write down their story. This novel is the result, for, to quote General Jan Christiaan Smuts, *the interest is not so much in the war as in the human experience behind it.*

Martin Marais
July 2014

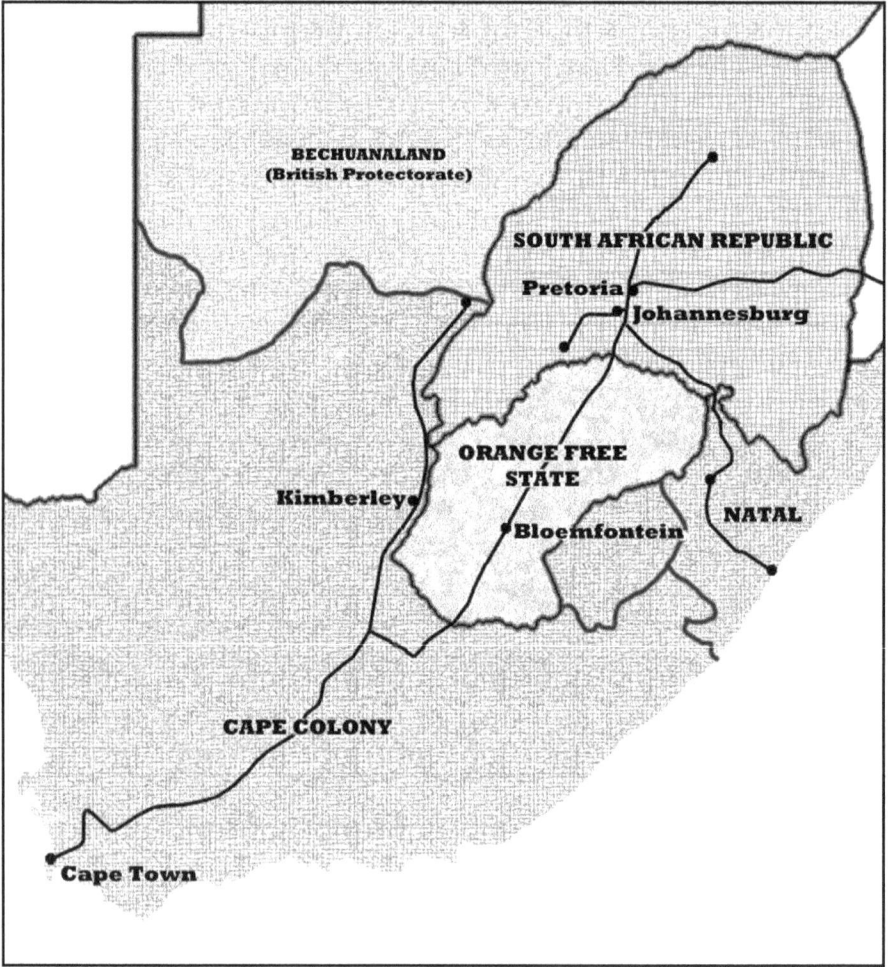

Map 1: Southern Africa 1899

Historical Context

The Dutch East India Company (VOC) was established in 1602. The Netherlands' Government granted it a monopoly to the spice trade in East Asia and it dominated European trade in that market during the seventeenth and eighteenth centuries. Its charter also gave it powers to wage war, imprison and execute convicts, negotiate treaties, mint money, establish colonies and enslave indigenous peoples.

In 1649, a decision was made to establish a refreshment station on the southern tip of Africa to supply VOC ships *en route* between East Asia and the Netherlands. In 1652, an expedition of ninety Calvinist settlers established the station at the Cape of Good Hope.

The settlers were apathetic towards developing and improving the station and in 1685 a commission was set up with the aim of attracting more progressive settlers to the settlement. This coincided with a resurgent persecution of Protestants (known as Huguenots) in France. Large numbers fled their country to settle in other parts of the world, including the Cape. By the end of 1689, Huguenots made up nearly twenty per cent of the white population at the station at the Cape of Good Hope. The Huguenots were soon fully integrated into the Dutch community, aided by shared religious beliefs and a VOC policy that schools taught exclusively in Dutch.

Increasing dissatisfaction among the settlers with the governance by the VOC eventually evolved into an aversion of imposed government and libertarian viewpoints that became characteristic of the Dutch farmers (Boers). Seeking to escape the governance of the VOC, the Boers migrated farther and farther east, away from the seat of government in Cape Town. The Company attempted to continue controlling these Boers by placing magistrates in the new settlements they established. In 1780, it declared the Great Fish River as the boundary to the colony. The new boundary was established partly in order to avoid conflict with the Bantu tribes that were advancing southwards down the east coast of Southern Africa.

In 1795, the Netherlands fell to Napoleon Bonaparte and the British sent their army to Cape Town to secure the colony against the French. Taking advantage of the situation, the Boers of the frontier districts in the east of the Cape Colony established independent governments at Swellendam and Graaff Reinet. In response, the

British sent an army against the Boers and returned the towns to the Cape Colony. However, the Boers subsequently rose in revolt in 1799, and again in 1801. In 1803, the colony was returned to the Batavian Republic, a Dutch vassal state of the French. By 1806, resurgent hostility between the British and French led to another British occupation of the colony and in 1814 the Dutch government formally ceded sovereignty of the Cape to the British.

To strengthen its position within the colony, the British Government encouraged its own citizens to settle in the colony and large numbers arrived through Port Elizabeth in 1820. The Boer community, especially those along the eastern frontier, became increasingly dissatisfied with the situation and between 1830 and 1840 a *Great Trek* took place in which an estimated twelve thousand Boers left the Cape for the South African interior.

These pioneers, or Voortrekkers, entered a land that had been subjected to many Bantu wars, forced migrations and famines – a period known to the indigenous people as the *Difaqane* or *mfecane*. Its effect was to greatly weaken their social structures, creating conditions that allowed the Voortrekkers to displace them with little effort, the exceptions being the Ndebele, the Basotho and the Zulus.

The Voortrekkers first halted near present-day Bloemfontein and established a Boer republic. However, following disagreements among their leadership, various Voortrekker groups split away, with some continuing north across the Vaal River and others east across the Drakensberg mountain range into Zululand.

The latter came into bloody conflict with the Zulu Nation, but eventually the Zulu king, Mpande, allowed them to establish the Natalia Republic in 1839. In 1843, the Republic was annexed by Britain and most of the Boers left for the Transvaal to join the Boers who had settled there. The Boer territories of the Transvaal and Orange Free State were officially recognised as independent by Britain in 1852 and 1854, respectively. Their independence was also recognised by other nations, including the Netherlands, France, Germany, Belgium and the United States of America. In 1857, they united to form the South African Republic.

In 1877, Britain annexed the South African Republic on the basis that annexation would avoid a war between the Boers and the Zulus and also because the Republic was bankrupt. The Boers viewed this as an act of aggression and the episode culminated in the First Anglo-Boer War, or the War of Independence, of 1881. The British were defeated at the Battle of Majuba Hill (27 February 1881) and sued for peace. One consequence of the war was that the Transvaal and the Orange Free State reverted to two separate, independent sovereign states, the former being known as the South African Republic.

In 1886, the discovery of huge reserves of gold within the Republic caused a gold rush and thousands of prospectors and others entered the country. They subsequently became disgruntled about the manner in which they were treated by the Republic's Government. Their discontent played into the hands of those expounding British imperialist and expansionist views, most notably the Prime Minister of the Cape Colony, Cecil Rhodes. As tensions increased, it became inevitable that war would result, and ever more apparent to the Orange Free State that its position of neutrality was untenable.

War was declared on 11 October 1899.

The Cast

Major Friedrich Wilhelm Richard Albrecht is a German national who, prior to joining the Oranje Vryijstaat Artillerie Corps (OVSAC), served in the 4th Prussian Guard Artillery of Berlin. He is a veteran of the Franco-Prussian war (1870–71). In November 1880, he was appointed captain and commanding officer of the OVSAC. Under his competent leadership, the OVSAC underwent considerable improvement. In 1885, he replaced the uniform of the Free State artillery from one based on the British Royal Artillery with one of a Prussian style, imported from Berlin. By the beginning of the (Second) Anglo-Boer War, Albrecht has been promoted to major. He is one of a small number of foreigners of officer rank in the Boer army.

Sergeant Alfred Atkinson (26 years old) is a sergeant in the 1st Battalion, the Yorkshire Regiment. He was born in Armley, Leeds, Yorkshire, and is the son of James Harland Atkinson, a shoeing smith in the Royal Artillery, and Margaret Mansfield.

Brigadier General Robert George Broadwood (38) joined the 12th Royal Lancers in 1881 and spent most of his early military career in North-east Africa. As a lieutenant colonel, he served under Lord Kitchener in the Battle of Omdurman in Sudan (1898), where he was placed in charge of a contingent of Egyptian cavalry on the British right flank. He was commended for his adept leadership. Broadwood is the commanding officer of the 2nd Brigade in the Cavalry Division led by Lieutenant-General French.

Johannes Petrus Coetzee (15) is a Cape Boer from Cradock.

Doctor Arthur Ignatius Conan Doyle (39) was born in Edinburgh. He was a physician, writer, sportsman and adventurer. Although a prolific writer, he was most noted for his stories featuring the detective Sherlock Holmes. Conan Doyle is in Southern Africa serving as a volunteer doctor with the Langman Field Hospital.

General Pieter Arnoldus Cronjé (65) was born in the Cape Colony but raised in the Transvaal from an early age. Known as Oom Piet,[1]

Cronjé made his reputation as a general in the War of Independence (First Anglo-Boer War) by besieging the British garrison at Potchefstroom, for which he gained the title "The Lion of Potchef-stroom" from his countrymen and "The Tyrant of Potchefstroom" from the British. He commanded the force that rounded up Jameson and his men, who had entered the Transvaal in January 1896 as part of an attempted *coup d'état*. He is the general commanding the Western (Cape) theatre of the war and initiated the sieges of Kimberley and Mafeking. He is a national hero with a reputation for considerable personal courage.

Lieutenant-General John Denton Pinkstone French (46) joined the Royal Navy in 1866, the Suffolk Artillery Militia in 1870 and was commissioned as a lieutenant in the Hussars in 1874. He took part in the Sudan expedition to relieve Major-General Gordon in 1884. In the Second Boer War, he initially served under General Buller on the Natal front and led the cavalry to success at the Battle of Elandslaagte on 21 October 1899. Subsequently ordered to the Cape, he was one of the last people to leave Ladysmith before that town became besieged by the Boers. He has the local rank of lieutenant-general and is the commanding officer of the Cavalry Division.

Colonel Ormelie Campbell Hannay (51) entered the army as an ensign in the Argyll and Sutherland Highlanders in 1867. He served during the latter part of the Anglo-Zulu War and then in various posts in England and India. He is a colonel of the 1st Battalion, Argyll and Sutherland Highlanders, and a commander of the mounted infantry.

Major-General The Right Hon. Lord Horatio Herbert Kitchener, GCB, KCMG (48) was born in Ireland. Eager to see action, he joined a French field ambulance unit in the Franco-Prussian War, but was reprimanded because his service in the war violated British neutrality. He was commissioned into the Royal Engineers in 1871 and served in Palestine, Egypt and Cyprus as a surveyor. He served in the Nile Campaign (1884-85) as an intelligence officer and was severely

---

[1] The term Oom (Uncle) was used as a sign of respect to one's superior officers in the Boer army. Neef (Nephew) was the reciprocating term used by those of senior rank to their subordinates.

wounded in the jaw during a skirmish. In 1896, he led British and Egyptian forces up the Nile and defeated the Sudanese at the Battle of Omdurman in 1898, near Khartoum. He was created Baron Kitchener of Khartoum and Aspall in 1898. Kitchener arrived in South Africa with Lord Roberts in December 1899. Although holding the title of Chief of Staff, he is, in practice, second-in-command to Lord Roberts.

State President Stephanus Johannes Paulus Kruger (74), known as Oom Paul, was born in the Eastern Cape Colony to a farming family. As a child, he took part in one of the earlier departing parties of the Great Trek. He is deeply religious and a founding member of the traditionalist Reformed Church in South Africa. Kruger began his military service as a field cornet, eventually becoming Commandant-General of the South African Republic. He was a member of the commission that drew up the constitution for the Republic. He has been a Member of Parliament since 1874 and President of the Republic since 1883, being re-elected in 1888 and 1893.

General Hector Archibald Macdonald (45), known as 'Fighting Mac', was born near Inverness, Scotland, to a crofter/stonemason and a dressmaker. At school, he took it upon himself to stop bullies terrorising the meek. He worked on his father's farm until the age of 15, when he became an apprentice draper and joined the Merchants' Company of the Inverness Highland Rifle Volunteers. Aged 17, he enlisted with the Gordon Highlanders and was stationed in India. He took part in the Roberts' Afghan Campaign. In 1881, the Gordon Highlanders were sent to South Africa and he took part in the Battle of Majuba Hill, where, after a fist fight with the attacking Boers, he was taken prisoner. In 1888, he was transferred to the Egyptian army and during the Battle of Omdurman, while commanding a force of three thousand men against twenty thousand Dervish; he averted disaster by protecting the exposed rear of Kitchener's forces. His actions at Omdurman earned him promotion to full Colonel. In January 1900, Macdonald arrived in South Africa to take command of the Highland Brigade.

Fredrick Abram Marais (31) is a Cape burgher from Langkloof.

Lieutenant-Colonel William Dillon Otter (56) is a Canadian who began his military career in the non-permanent militia in 1864 and saw his first action against the Irish Republican movement, the Fenian Brotherhood, which attacked British interests in Canada. He joined the first Canadian Permanent Force in 1883 and, in 1885, led a Canadian force in the Battle of Cut Knife against the Cree Indians. He was appointed as the first commanding officer of the Royal Canadian Regiment of Infantry in 1893. Otter has the reputation of being something of a martinet, mainly because of his desire that the young Canadian army should not compare badly with the British troops.

Major Michael Frederic Rimington (40) joined the Dragoons as a lieutenant in 1881. His first posting was to South Africa where, in 1884, he took part in the capture of the small Boer republic, the United States of Stellaland. He returned to Britain with his regiment in 1890, but was back in South Africa in 1899, where he was appointed to raise a force of irregular mounted scouts, known as Rimington's Guides.

Field Marshal The Rt Hon. Lord Frederick Roberts, Baron Roberts VC GCB GCSI GCIE (67) is one of the most successful British commanders of the Victorian era and known affectionately as 'Bobs'. He was born in Cawnpore, India, the second son of General Sir Abraham Roberts of Waterford, Ireland. He entered the army of the East India Company in 1851 and served in the Indian Rebellion (1857), winning the Victoria Cross. He served as a senior officer in the Second Afghan War (1878–80), during which he made his famous march on Kandahar to relieve a British brigade besieged in the city. He marched ten thousand men three hundred and ten miles in twenty-two days and gained a complete victory over the enemy. In 1881, he was sent to South Africa to take command during the First Anglo-Boer War, but the war ended on the day of his arrival. He returned to India and was appointed Commander-in-Chief throughout India. He left India in 1893, for Ireland, as Commander-in-Chief of British forces. Roberts published his autobiography, *Forty-One Years in India*, in 1897. In 1899, he was posted to South Africa as Commander-in-Chief, replacing General Sir Redvers Buller. During the journey to South Africa he learned of the death of his son, Frederick, killed in action at the Battle of Colenso.

Major-General Horace Smith-Dorrien DSO (46) is a graduate of the Sandhurst Royal Military Academy. In November 1878, he was posted to South Africa as a transport officer and served in the Zulu War (1879) and was one of less than fifty British soldiers to escape from the Battle of Isandlwana (22 January 1879). He was nominated for the Victoria Cross for helping others to escape, but a bureaucratic failure meant he never received it. He subsequently served in Egypt (where he met Kitchener) and India. He returned to South Africa in October 1899. He is the commanding officer of the 9th Brigade.

Captain Daniël Johannes Stephanus Theron (27) was born in Tulbagh in the Cape Colony, but as a child moved to the Orange Free State and then to the South African Republic. He began his career as a school teacher, but later gained a degree in law and started his own law practice. He became involved in politics and infiltrated pro-British associations, where he was able to gather intelligence about the *coup d'état* planned by Jameson. He founded a bicycle corps, used for scouting and relaying messages between Boer units (the use of bicycles made more horses available to the commandos). He is responsible for reconnaissance and intelligence in the Boer army.

Lieutenant James Vipan Maitland Watermeyer (31) is an officer in the Kitchener's Horse, a colonial mounted unit established in February 1900.

General Christiaan Rudolf de Wet (45) was born in the Orange Free State. He is a farmer, with farms in both the Orange Free State and the South African Republic. He also owned a wagon haulage company, running goods to the gold mines of Johannesburg. De Wet fought in the War of Independence (1880–81) as a field cornet, taking part in the Battle of Majuba Hill. He was a member of both the South African Republic and Orange Free State parliaments. A progressive politician, he encouraged the establishment of railways in the two Republics. At the start of the (Second) Anglo-Boer war he joined as a private, fighting in the Natal campaign. When his commando's commandant fell ill, de Wet was elected as his replacement. Soon afterwards, President Steyn of the Orange Free State appointed him General and transferred him to the Western (Cape) Front under General Piet Cronjé.

Wednesday 11 October 1899

President Stephanus Johannes Paulus Kruger

Stephanus Johannes Paulus Kruger, State President of the South African Republic, was angry. Not with the crowd of people in front of him. No, he was not angry with them. They were the victims of the calamity that had fallen on his nation. He was angry with a foreign queen living in a palace thousands of miles away who had laid claim to his country.

He stood on the tailgate of an open wagon, leaning on his brolly and adjusting his old top hat to give himself time to recover from the exertion of climbing on to the wagon. Taking out his fob watch, he looked at its yellowing face. Hmm, he noted, six o'clock. So they had been at war for an hour. Clenching his jaw in anger, he put his watch away, and from under the brim of his battered hat studied the men, women and children gathered before him. It was a good-sized crowd of two hundred, perhaps three hundred and, he reflected, it would have been more if he had travelled into town. But he could not be doing with towns, and anyway, the townsfolk would benefit from the fresh country air.

His gaze moved beyond the crowd to the haphazard scatter of Cape carts, with their horses still in harness, which had brought the towns-people from the settlements around Kruger's farm. They walked in that determined urban manner, the husbands supporting their wives' hands in the crooks of their elbows. The men sported smart, beige flannel trousers, white shirts with sombre bow ties and the obligatory fashionable, dark waistcoat and light-coloured felt hat. Their faces were adorned with neat, well-trimmed beards, which Kruger considered to be too fussy in appearance. The women wore white, or pale-coloured, flowing dresses that swished engagingly around their ankles, sending up small flurries of dust as they walked. Each lady entertained a flat, wide-brimmed hat, some set off with dried flowers, and all held aloft lacy parasols. Extending either side of the parents were two to three children, the boys beside their fathers and the girls alongside their mothers, all smartly turned out replicas of their parents, except for the younger children, who wore knee-length shorts or skirts that ended a few inches above the ankle.

Beyond the careless array of Cape carts stood the deliberate lines of covered wagons, lined up as though forming part of a defensive laager. These had brought rural Boers from farther afield. Kruger smiled nostalgically to himself as he remembered the years he had spent as a boy travelling in one of those contraptions during the Great Trek. Then he frowned, as his thoughts turned to bitterness when he recalled that, even as a child, he had been trying to escape the interference, tyranny and injustice of the English.

From the wagons had tumbled a very different folk compared to those from the Cape carts. Even before the wagons had been brought to a stop, hordes of rough-clothed kids had poured from them in search of friends not seen for months, or to hunt in small gangs to settle old scores from previous gatherings. Once halted, the women had disembarked. In their long, dark dresses and white bonnets, wives had been helped from the wagons by respectful husbands and had gathered in animated little clutches where they stood talking earnestly, sometimes with scandalised expressions as they swapped news and traded gossip. The elder matriarchs, in their heavy-duty, black dresses and bonnets, from which their knowledgeable, stern and wrinkled faces peered, had been settled into tight circles of trek stools, around which had flitted native servant girls offering refreshments. The teenage girls in their ankle-length skirts and white blouses had formed tight-knit, closed groups, the wings of their bonnets touching, to exclude all intruders, especially the annoying youths who hovered around them in various states of shyness and bravado. The full-bearded men, in their leather slouch hats, moleskin trousers, and cotton shirts buttoned to the throat and woollen jackets, had greeted each other enthusiastically, and then got on with the serious business of parking the wagons and releasing the cattle so that they could graze and recover from the strenuous task of pulling the wagons.

The veldt beyond the wagons was crowded with cattle, which were being eagerly marshalled by native boys to the best grazing, a difficult job at this time of year, when the grass was as unwholesome and brittle as the dried spaghetti Kruger had seen during one of his trips to Rome to galvanise support for the Afrikander cause against English aggression. The herders had plenty of choice, for the dry, dusty veldt extended in a huge sweep, the yellow grass eventually meeting the azure blue of the immense heavens.

Kruger stared across the landscape, beyond a large herd of spring-buck and zebra, to the broad horizon. He leaned forward slightly as the beauty and vastness of the land drew him in. It was his Land. It is our Land. And no one was going to take it from them this time. He watched a dust devil swirl across the landscape and brush past a stand of blue-gum trees, making them quiver and rustle in complaint.

He looked again at the multitude, which, now that the excitement of arriving and catching up with friends had subsided, had gathered in front of him. He appraised the men in their slouch hats and the women in their broad-winged bonnets and wide-brimmed sun hats. Before him stood as God-fearing and upstanding a people as one would find anywhere on God's Earth. Kruger sensed a solemnity developing in the crowd. Even the children seemed aware of the sombreness of the gathering, including the usually boisterous farm kids, who were now keeping close to their parents. A large bluebottle fly landed on his cheek. He brushed it away nonchalantly.

A tall, slim youth of about 15, standing at the front of the crowd, caught Kruger's eye. Kruger recognised him. My, Frans Marais has grown up into a fine young man, he thought. The youth stared back intently at Kruger from under a new slouch hat. He was with his family, his father standing tall and grim in his farmer's Sunday best, with his statuesque, big-boned wife beside him. Marie kept her sons close to her, placing restraining hands on the shoulders of the younger two. Kruger could see that the young man understood the importance of what he was about to say. He smiled at the youth.

"Frans, come here," he said, beckoning him forward.

Kruger noted with an inward smile the expanding chest and swagger of pride that the boy took on at being recognised by the President. The youth moved towards him, removing his new hat in respect, his shuffling feet raising small waves of dust. To get closer to him, Kruger slowly went down on one knee, leaning heavily on his brolly to support his ageing frame. He gruffly shrugged off the supporting hand of his secretary with a crotchety grunt and a mental tut. Just because he had had to be helped on to the wagon did not mean he was incapacitated. His smile returned as the boy drew near. Kruger beckoned him closer still.

"Frans, I have an important task for you."

"You do? What should I do, Oom Paul?"

"Can you pass me up a handful of sand?"

"Of sand, Oom Paul?"

"Yes Frans, as much as you can gather."

The boy stared at Kruger for a moment. The old face, framed by a white beard and shabby top hat, looked back at him and gave a tiny nod of encouragement. Frans returned his hat to his head, crouched down and scooped up a double handful of dusty sand. Standing up, he stretched his hands towards Kruger. Kruger reached forward with his right hand.

"Now carefully pour some into my hand."

The youth obeyed, slowly parting his hands so a thin stream of sand and dust trickled on to Kruger's open palm. Kruger noted the boy's hands. They were young and fresh on the back, but already the palms and insides of the fingers revealed the calluses of his farmer's life. How they contrasted with his own, which had grown soft as a consequence of the time he now had to spend in offices and meetings. It had been many years since he had turned his hands to the labours of farming, but he remained a staunch boer at heart.

"That's enough, thank you."

The sand stopped flowing and Frans turned his gaze back towards the old man's face.

"Now, very carefully place the rest back on the ground. What you have there is very precious. It is the land of the Afrikander."

Kruger regarded the youth as he crouched down again and gently deposited the sand, as though placing down a day-old chick. The young man stood up and Kruger nodded his thanks. Frans turned, and Kruger watched him walk back to his parents. They were probably wondering what that was all about. Well, it was time to tell them.

Kruger slowly straightened his unsteady frame, shaking off the assistance of his secretary, and raised the fistful of sand in front of him. A hush fell over the crowd. A light, warm spring breeze brushed Kruger's face and fluttered the wings of the sun bonnets. Kruger noticed a thin line of dust start to trickle from between his fingers, arching away from him in the breeze. Despite the heat and the greatcoat he wore, Kruger felt a chill run through his body. The trickle of dust seemed to be an omen – a warning of his land slipping from his grasp. Kruger flicked his hand over so that the fingers of his fist pointed to the heavens and he tightened his grip on the treasured dirt.

He stared at his hand. It was as old and as brown and as dry as the veldt itself. Prominent blue veins, with their life-blood, ran across it like the rivers that gave life to the veldt – the Orange, the Vaal and the Modder. But for all his age, his grip was still strong and its contents were safe within it.

Kruger let his eyes drift down to his people. The heat was stifling; sweat was obvious on the men's brows. The only movement was from the ladies gently fanning their faces. Kruger broke from his reverie and squared his shoulders.

"Ladies and gentlemen."

He paused. All eyes were on his fist with its cherished contents.

"I have here," he stretched his arm out straight and thrust his fist higher, "a most precious thing, a thing more valuable than my own life." He felt a tingling of the flesh and he wondered if others felt it. "There are only two things more precious than what is in my hand. And they are the Afrikander People and their independence."

Yes, he knew some felt it that time, like miniscule spiders crawling under the skin.

"And yet both our People and our independence are utterly dependent on what I hold in my hand. For I hold the land of our farms and of our homes, the *land* of our People. The land of the Afrikander. It is the land to which we were guided by the Almighty. It is the Promised Land given by Him to us. It is the land of our Republic."

Kruger started to tilt his fist and slowly release his fingers in order to pour away the soil, so that the people before him could see the land for themselves, but his grip tightened involuntarily. He stared at it. Then, with his free hand, Kruger fumbled inside his coat for his handkerchief and gave it to his secretary.

"Open it and lay it on my palm," he said hoarsely.

The man did as he was requested and Kruger respectfully poured the material on to the spotless white square of cloth. He carefully folded the handkerchief around the soil and, taking it, placed the small parcel into the left inside pocket of his coat. He said nothing; he did not need to. The people knew what he had done.

Kruger bowed his head and, letting his shoulders sag, announced: "Yesterday I entered my seventy-fifth year," his voice, although subdued, remained audible to all, "and, together with you, with God's benevolent guidance, I will soon see the dawn of a new century – an auspicious date for God-fearing Christians. Yet, at this providential time, when we should be preparing to celebrate this special anniversary of the birth of our Lord's only son, we find ourselves, a new and tiny nation, threatened by one of the greatest powers in the history of mankind. It has an empire so vast that their queen has styled herself 'Empress of India', empress over a nation halfway around the world from her palace and many times bigger than her own country. And now it seems that this woman also has a desire to be empress over us.

"This will not surprise you. It certainly does not surprise me. For my earliest memory is of the day I left the land of my birth, driven out by the English. I was too young to preoccupy myself with the reasons for leaving, but I understood that the English had arrived and taken the Cape. They treated us, the people of that land, unjustly. We were deprived of our slaves, without fair recompense, and the repeated raids by hostile natives and their stealing of our cattle went unpunished. Indeed, it was worse than that, for whenever the English army did intervene and we did recover our cattle, they were simply appropriated by the English 'in payment for their services'.

"Is it any wonder that we Afrikanders declared that we could not live under such unjust governance? And I, at the age of ten, together with over ten thousand other burghers, left the land and homes of our ancestors for a wild and unknown country. You know how God's hand guides us, and how He led us to this Promised Land, a land of independence, a place where we could be free from the tyranny of outside interference. Even the blindest heathen and the greatest unbeliever must acknowledge that it was God that gave this land to us. And with our blood, sweat and tears, we have established our own independent republics. This land is now part of us: it is in our hearts."

Kruger rested his hand over his heart and the small packet of soil inside his pocket.

"But still the English could not resist interfering. When diamonds were discovered in the South African Republican town of Vooruitzigt, the English simply took the town and its diamonds from us. They renamed the town Kimberley and incorporated it into their Cape Colony. And English greed did not stop there!

"When we allowed English citizens into our nation to take advantage of the benefits of *our* railway from Pretoria to Delagoa Bay, they petitioned their Government to support their excessive exploitation of our nation and their Government simply annexed our state – in *flagrant* contravention of the convention by which they recognised the full independence of our Republic. This hostile act was conducted against our independent sovereign Government, which had on *no* occasion given *any* cause for such violent action to be taken against us. When the English stole our sovereignty that time, back in 1877, we were in no position to defend our rights or our independence. We stood unprepared against a superior power. We had but fifteen rounds of ammunition per man.

"And then the English imposed an illegal and unjust tax upon us, and stole the goods of innocent people to auction in forcible payment of the illegal tax. It was an act that no free people could forbear. And so the War of Independence was forced upon us in 1881. But, with our God strengthening our hearts, we went bravely to face greatly superior numbers. Our heroic General Cronjé and his brave burghers showed the English the nature of our people – that we will *not* be plagued by their unwanted governance. And we gave the English a very bloody nose on the 27th of February 1881 at Majuba Hill.

"That day will always be remembered in the name of God, for we placed our hopes in the Lord and He delivered us from the English. They sued for peace and, magnanimous in victory, we agreed a just resolution. We won back our independence and we showed them that we will not relinquish what we cherish.

"And then...," Kruger paused, and whispered thickly, ".. disaster!"

The people craned forward to hear him.

"Gold! Gold was discovered in the heart of our country. Do you know what gold is?" he cried. "When you return home read the Book. It will tell you what gold is. Look in Ezekiel. There you will find that gold is an unclean thing. It will not deliver us or the English from the wrath of the Lord. It cannot satisfy hunger or fill stomachs.

"The gold reserves that exist within the bowels of our land are unprecedented in their volume and purity. Even the American discoveries are dimmed by what we own. At the time of its discovery many were overjoyed and foresaw a new and brighter future for our Nation. But our great General Joubert prophetically predicted that instead of rejoicing, we would be better to weep. He said: 'This gold will cause our country to be soaked in blood. For every ounce of gold found, we will cry rivers of blood.' To our great sorrow, we have

9

been shown the truth of that potent man's words. As it says in Lamentations, 'How the gold has grown dim!'

"There is no doubt that it is the presence of gold within our borders that has caused us to be in the precipitous position in which we find ourselves today. It is quite certain that had no gold been found in our Republic, no matter how great the influx of Englishmen and no matter how varied and manifold their complaints, the English Government would not have lifted one finger in their defence. So the bounty of our country has made us victims of the greed of others.

"And there is one man who has been most tempted by our gold, and who can be credited with our present perilous state. Of all men, this devil has the greatest desire for gold and the status that it brings. And this man is the former Prime Minister of the Cape Colony, that spawn of Satan, Cecil Rhodes. For him, the end always justifies the means; for him, the desire for gold *is* the end to justify *all* means. In his search for gold, he has been unscrupulous in annexing one territory after another, and now he has turned his burning eyes on us.

"In the face of this imperialism, your Government has tried every measure to avert war. In the negotiations that proceeded today, we have been yielding and compliant. And we are not the only ones who have been charitable in pressing for a just conclusion to this matter. Our friends in the Orange Free State, and their President Steyn, have intervened on many occasions and made every effort to avoid war. And so it is with exasperation and great sadness that I have to tell you that the English Government has ignored our last letter setting out a just, fair and Christian solution. In spite of all the concessions, all the patience, and all the indulgence of the Republics, since five o'clock this afternoon we are at war with England and its empire."

Kruger studied the crowd. He saw a youth punch Frans Marais enthusiastically on the shoulder. Kruger felt his throat tighten and a hollow sensation grow in the pit of his stomach. How many of his people would be lost this time? In previous wars, the numbers killed had been small, but this time he sensed it would be different.

Frans' mother had also seen the reaction of his friend and although her son was a now young man, and was as tall as her, she placed a protective arm around him and drew him closer to her. Her expression was pensive, her lips drawn in a tight line and her brow furrowed. Kruger saw the shadow of grief pass briefly over her features. She would put on a brave face in public, but Kruger knew that during the coming night, in the privacy of her bedroom, she would weep in fear of the safety of her men. That was the way of the Afrikander mother and wife. Her husband placed a comforting arm around her shoulders, but she knew he would go to war. He had his land to defend.

"So the English lion has roared again. Britannia has launched her pride against us, but she should not forget that we Afrikanders shoot lions as soon as we are old enough to hold a gun. The English will not find a people better at shooting lions than us Afrikanders. And this time we have ammunition sufficient to meet every man's needs. We may only be farmers, lawyers and teachers, but we are a proud people, we have determination, we have right on our side and we have God's hand guiding us. *And* we have already shown England that we are able to defeat those who threaten our freedom and independence. We have belief in our God. He will guide our bullets against those who would impose themselves upon us against His will.

"We may be two small nations facing overwhelming numbers, but this time the world is watching. Germany, Holland, France and the United States of America all understand the hypocrisy of the English. This time we have allies who will come to our aid.

"But I must warn you that England has not only dispatched forces from her own shores, her soldiers will also come from all her dominions. She will pour troops into Southern Africa. If we are to control our destiny, we must strike first. Tomorrow we will advance into the English colonies of the Cape and Natal, so that when the tortoise sticks out its head, we will be ready to catch hold of it.

"England may claim to rule the waves, but the Good Book tells us that it is God who rules the raging seas, and when the waves rise He will still them. He will scatter His enemies with a strong arm. So it shall be in Southern Africa. We have no watery seas, only calm oceans of grass, and it is us who rule the veldt. And when the thousands of enemy assail us, let us offer up our prayers to the Lord and put our trust in God. He is with us. The decision rests with Him and *He* will decide. Therefore, I say that I take my stand at God's side and on His word alone."

Kruger paused. He glared at the crowd massed before him, he squared his shoulders and, shaking his dusty fist towards them, he growled, "This time, when I say war, it will be war to the bitter end."

Friday 22 December 1899

Doctor Arthur Ignatius Conan Doyle

Doctor Arthur Ignatius Conan Doyle settled back into his dining chair, at the same time lifting the glass of Irish whiskey to his lips. As he did so, his eyes drifted around the table and he studied each of his dinner guests through the swirling cigar smoke.

To his left sat Mam. She wagged her finger down the table at *The Times* hack, Leopard Amery, as she informed him of his mis-understanding of the Irish issue. Next to her sat the unsavoury Bryan Waller, who had attached himself to Mam some time ago and whose attention, for some inexplicable reason, she encouraged. Opposite Conan Doyle sat his wife, Touie. He paused to study her face, searching for the shadow of her bride's beauty that her long illness had stolen from her. Touie must have felt his scrutiny, for she drew her eyes from her mother-in-law and looked at him. She smiled and her eyes sparkled; they, at least, had not lost any of their allure. He smiled back fondly. The perfect hostess, Touie turned her attention back to Amery, who sat on her left, and who was defending himself against the accusations being flung at him by the forthright Mrs Doyle of his misrepresentation of the Irish situation in *The Times*.

Conan Doyle considered the charmless man. He was a friend of Touie's and Conan Doyle had only agreed to invite him because she had informed her husband that Amery had been present at the departure of Field Marshal Lord Roberts to Southern Africa a few days previously.

Finally, Conan Doyle's eyes fell on Jean, sitting to his right, the wonderful Jean, or Miss Leckie, as he called her in polite company. His eyes soaked up her features, which were making a splendid show of appearing to be absorbed by the conversation about the history of the troubles in Ireland.

"Arthur!"

Conan Doyle snapped his eyes towards the voice. They met the impatient stare of his mother. He cocked an enquiring eyebrow at her.

"The Boer war? Leo is interested in your views on the Boer war."

Conan Doyle turned his gaze upon the man.

"My, that is a big question, Leo. But I am more interested to hear about your trip last Sunday to see Lord Roberts off."

Amery smiled. "I must say it was quite an occasion. I am sure that you, Arthur, are used to a certain amount of accolade from the public, but the reception Lord Roberts received was quite astonishing."

"Well," said Waller mischievously, "he *is* going to save us from General Buller's tomfoolery, isn't he?"

"That he is," Amery shot back hotly. "It is difficult to understand how Buller, one of our best generals, has been put to the sword so effectively by a bunch of farmers, but Roberts is a man of considerable military experience. I could extol the virtues of the man, but in order not to bore these dear ladies with the complexities of military tactics and strategies, I shall refrain."

Out of the corner of his eye Conan Doyle saw his mother bristle, but he kept his attention on Amery, who continued.

"However, I suggest that if you read Roberts' autobiography you will understand that he is precisely the right man for the job."

"Yes, Bryan," Mrs Doyle intervened, her voice crackling with indignation. "I also recommend the book to you. *I* found it most enlightening." She threw Amery a glare, the man coughed, and she added, "Especially for those with an interest in empire-building."

Conan Doyle quickly stepped into the awkward silence that threatened to descend over the table.

"Do carry on Leo," he encouraged.

"Ah-hem, apologies Mrs Doyle, the point I was attempting to make was that our friend here," he nodded at Waller, "is missing the point. The accolade is not for what he is about to do, but for what he has already done. For one so compact in stature, Lord Roberts is a giant among men."

"For sure!" Mrs Doyle exclaimed. "You would expect nothing less from an Irishman!"

Amery blinked at her in bewilderment.

"Mam, will you please let Leo continue."

Conan Doyle smiled supportively at Amery, and Amery smiled back wearily.

"Yes, I would think that Bobs, as he is called," Amery looked at the women, as if imparting to them a small piece of information of more domestic interest, "is precisely the man we need to put the Boer back in their place."

"And some putting back they will require," Waller threw into the conversation. "For a people that everyone seems to agree is extremely ignorant and narrow-minded, the Boers appear to be *singularly* minded in roughing up our soldiers. Since their invasion of our colonies they have succeeded in besieging three British towns." Waller listed them on his fingers, "Ladysmith, Kimberley and ummm… ?"

"Mafeking," Conan Doyle helpfully interposed.

"Yes, Mafeking. And they have caused us no end of trouble."

"Indeed," agreed Amery begrudgingly.

"Indeed? Unquestionably indeed!" voiced Mrs Doyle. "Except for a small victory at Elandslaagte, our generals have, this month, suffered three ignominious defeats in the space of one week. General Gatacre suffered humiliation at Stormsberg, Lord Methuen at Magersfontein and now we hear General Buller has been beaten back at Colenso. Is it any wonder those seven days are *already* known as 'Black Week'."

Amery looked at Mrs Doyle in surprise; she smirked back. "I am able to read, Leo, even *The Times*, though I wonder why I do!"

"I understand that Lord Roberts' only son was killed at Colenso?" It was Touie's gentle voice that broke into the conversation.

"I'm afraid so," professed Amery. "A terrible tragedy. Lord Roberts will be devastated, as will his wife of course. But his family has a long tradition of military service. Lord Roberts is himself the holder of the Victoria Cross. So he will play the part of the pro-fessional soldier and put aside this personal tragedy to focus on the job in hand, that of defeating the Boer invaders."

"Leo, it is difficult to understand how an army of farmers can have been so successful against the might of our Empire, especially as I am informed that militarily the British are most effectual in every way." said Miss Leckie.

"Yes," interjected Touie, "I have read in the papers that Lord Wolseley has admitted that the Boers have turned out to be much better soldiers than expected. And they appear to be surprisingly well trained and equipped, including having superior rifles and artillery to us. Can this be true?"

"They have certainly given us our blackest week in a generation and the most disastrous one for the British army during the reign of

Her Majesty. But you must not concern yourselves. Lord Roberts and his chief of staff, Lord Kitchener, will soon have the situation in hand."

"This General Kitchener, Leo, what do you know of the man?" asked Miss Leckie.

"Ha, I know that he is called 'K' by his men," retorted Waller. "And some say the K stands for chaos."

"K for chaos?" Miss Leckie turned to Conan Doyle, "but that does not make sense. Chaos is not spelt with a 'K'."

"Indeed, my dear," returned Conan Doyle, "but unfortunately many of our gallant men are somewhat lacking in education and phonetically chaos does start with a 'K'." He shrugged his shoulders in exaggerated amusement.

Waller laughed, "Lords Roberts and Kitchener – that will be the long and the short of it."

The two younger women looked bemused. It was Mrs Doyle who enlightened them.

"A more incongruous pair you are unlikely to find. Bobs is a sociable, neat, dapper little man, well into his sixties, While K is tall and gangly and, I am told, of a haughty predisposition. A rather distasteful man seems to be the general consensus. And, I am sorry to declare, of Irish stock, although being from Kerry explains much."

"Yes," said Amery, pleased to be in agreement with Mrs Doyle, if even on such a trivial matter. "Kitchener, in contrast to Roberts, is reputed to have little interest in human comforts, both for himself and for the rank and file."

"Was he with Lord Roberts in Southampton?" asked Miss Leckie.

"No," replied Amery, "The *Dunottar Castle* will stop at Gibraltar to pick him up."

"And then we'll show those damned Boers, what's what, hey?" mocked Waller.

Amery glared across the table at him. "That is the plan. Foremost, this war offers Britain the opportunity to make right the calamity of Majuba Hill in 1881. Ever since our misfortune on that day the Boer has been rather full of himself and has been actively hostile to all that is British. They have, on every possible occasion, used that escapade to humiliate us and to turn the loyalty of the Cape Dutch against us. The Boers use it as a rallying point against the British in the Cape

Colony, and it serves their wish to sweep us from Southern Africa. The evidence for this is clear in many respects. For example, why do they have a four-coloured flag? They have only one state, if you can call it that, and yet their flag has four colours. It is obvious that there is one colour for the Transvaal and one for the Orange Free State, and one each for our colonies of Natal and the Cape! That this is absolutely the case is shown by their unpardonable invasions of both those colonies. In respect to these outrageous invasions alone, the British case for retaliation is indisputable."

"The Boer," he continued, "are a people that is suspicious and jealous of anything they do not understand. They have no literature, save the Bible. They are an old-world community, with manners and traditions that are preserved from the seventeenth century. Their utter isolation from the soothing influence of civilisation has resulted in their culture becoming retrograde rather than advanced. To allow such people to attack our Empire without retribution is untenable.

"But their greatest fault is that of forcing the servitude of Englishmen to the Dutch. It is the principle upon which their republic is based and is counter to our own principle that all men are equal before the law and that all civilised races stand precisely on the same footing. Let us not forget that the British have long been faithful to the noblest call of duty and the highest instincts for aiding the cause of progress. Our cause, which is the cause of God, is that of liberty." Amery sat back and threw an arm casually over the back of his chair, confident that his case was won.

Conan Doyle could see his mother gathering her thoughts for the counter-attack. He intervened quickly, aware that he would only postpone her from expressing her views.

"The Boers have at least taught us one lesson," he quipped, "that it only needs a brave farmer with a modern rifle to make a soldier." Trying to maintain the initiative, he added more seriously, "It is clear to me, as it should be to every man in England, that it is not a wine glass that one must grasp for the health of the Empire to be honoured, but a rifle. It is the duty of every male citizen of the Empire to serve our Queen and country. As you know, Leo, I have written to *The Times* advising the Government to call upon all riding and shooting men to defend the honour of our country in this time of need. And of course, having offered the opinion that all able men should volunteer, I was honour bound to be the first to do so."

"You have volunteered, Arthur! Well done." Amery raised his glass to Conan Doyle.

"I attempted to, but was foiled at the first hurdle," Conan Doyle replied sourly. "It was the army itself that thwarted me, in the form of some self-important buffoon behind a desk who sneered at me when I tried to enlist."

"Really?" Amery seemed genuinely surprised.

Waller sniggered as he drew on his cigar, looking gleefully through the cigar's smoke at Conan Doyle.

"The fool made some disparaging remark about men of a certain age," Conan Doyle mumbled into his glass. Replacing his glass on the table, he declared, "It seems to me that the one obstacle preventing us patriotic fellows from making a valuable contribution to the war are those laggards of the recruitment office."

"Ha!" guffawed Waller, smoke erupting from his lips. "Do not believe a word of it, Leo! The main stumbling block to Arthur fulfilling his patriotic duty is his own little mam." Waller turned to Mrs Doyle, "Is that not so, my dear?"

Mrs Doyle flushed, "I merely said…"

"Come, come, Mary, dear. Do not be *so* economical with the truth!" Waller's eyes sparkled mischievously. He turned to Amery.

"Leo, you have been served nothing thus far by your host's dear mother compared to what poor Arthur endured on the day he announced his intention to volunteer for the war. It was a sight to behold. Wee Mary with her Irish passion all stirred up, standing foursquare in front of her bear of a son." Waller squared his shoulders, looked upwards into the imaginary face of Conan Doyle and in a parody of an angry Irish accent continued, "'How dare you?' Mary stormed," Waller said, emphasising each word with a jab at Conan Doyle's imaginary chest. "'How dare you volunteer for that miserable excuse for patriotism? It is a deplorable war and I shall not have you involving yourself in it'. To which Arthur replied, 'But mam, it is you, with your patriotic Irish nationalism, who has given me my sense of patriotic duty'."

Waller had told this story many times, but it improved with the telling. He leaned towards Amery.

"Mary hesitated for an instant and then scowled at her son. 'That is irrelevant. Why, look at you. Your very height and breadth will make you a simple and sure target for those Boer marksmen!'"

Waller fell into a trembling heap of mirth, and a ripple of laughter ran around the table that increased as Mrs Doyle also laughed at the ridiculousness of her argument. But Waller had not finished. Stifling his laughter, he continued.

"'Fear not, Mary,' I said. 'To allay your fears I have advised Arthur about the baobab. I hear they are the highest and broadest trees on the veld and I have recommended that he should hide behind one at every opportunity'."

This was met with further hilarity. As the laughter subsided, Amery looked at Conan Doyle.

"So, Arthur, what will you do?"

"You will be pleased to know, Leo, that I have found a solution which reconciles my sense of duty with my dear mother's desire to preserve my being. I am to serve my country as a medico."

"That is an excellent idea, Arthur," responded Amery enthusiastically, "I am sure your medical skills will be in great dem…" Amery caught Mrs Doyle's eye and quickly took a different tack, "…erm, will be a most welcome contribution to the war effort."

Mrs Doyle gave Amery a steely stare.

"Of course that is all by the by," she said. "The point is we would not be having this conversation were it not for the fact that Britain wishes to impose its will on a people who have toiled with infinite pain to make a home for themselves in their dry, brown veld, which is as dear to them as our beloved green countryside is to us. Therefore, it is no surprise that they do *not* wish to hand it over to us."

"Mary, if I may, I must point out that there is no body of opinion in England which desires the annexation of the Transvaal, or the Orange Free State for that matter. And yet annexed they will have to be for want of a little pliability upon their part."

"Mam," Conan Doyle said. Mrs Doyle fixed her eyes on her son. "I will admit to having had grave doubts about the merits of the war before it started. However, since the Boer invasion of our colonies I am now sure that it is a righteous war. It is generally accepted that the Boers have been very irritating in this matter and to a large extent deserve their misfortunes. War is a horrid thing, I most certainly agree, yet the Boer is a most stiff-necked race to deal with, and they have brought this situation upon themselves."

Amery, encouraged by Conan Doyle's support, spoke. "Mary, we should remember the undisputed facts. The majority of the population of the Transvaal is made up of non-Boer people, or 'Uitlanders' as the Boer call them, and of these, the larger part is British. Their industriousness furnishes nine-tenths of the taxation of Kruger's republic and yet they are harassed and oppressed in every way. They are compulsorily taught Dutch in schools. They are not allowed to attend public meetings or to serve on any juries and, indeed, they cannot rely upon the impartiality of the courts. But, most crucially, after fifteen years of campaigning, they still have no vote. One cannot, in this day and age, exclude over half the population of a country from the franchise. We must not forget that England is the guardian of these people as well as a paramount world power. She cannot allow herself to be pushed around so."

"Fiddlesticks!" retorted Mrs Doyle. "You should not delude yourself. There is only one reason for British interest in the Boer republic and that is gold! The excuse of protecting that swarm of humanity, including no doubt the rabble of society that has descended on the republic, is but a means to an end. It is inexcusable that we have been pushed to war through greed for a base metal. And it is astonishing that an entire nation can be led down that dire path by the greed of a single individual, by whom I mean Cecil Rhodes. *That man* should have been hobbled years ago and should certainly be so now, before he causes any more damage."

"Mary, dear," chortled Waller, "Rhodes has many peculiar characteristics, but his strongest is that he bears any form of restraint very badly."

"Be that as it may, is it right to lose so many young lives for such an unjust cause?"

All eyes turned on Amery. He felt the pressure of having to justify the inevitable loss of British lives.

"I would agree if matters were as simple as your arguments portray, Mary, but it is curious how narrow-minded the Boers are. They would actually rather let the gold alone than mine it. So who can blame the influx of Uitlanders who wish to work the gold? It is normal for there to be such great interest in the precious metal. The justification for war is not the greed for gold, but to protect those who would work the gold."

Conan Doyle intervened to relieve his guest from the attention he was receiving.

"We should remember that the situation has now moved on and whatever the rights or wrongs of the case, the moment the Boers invaded Natal the merits of the quarrel became merely academic."

"And," added Amery, "their invasion of Natal and the Cape Colony surely makes it obvious that they have prepared for this war for many years, while our own state of unpreparedness shows that we have not. From this, it is clear to me that we have had no sinister designs on the republic. In contrast, one has to ask what old Kruger is trying to do. He seems to have become irrational. He is so anxious to preserve the independence of his nation that he has taken the very steps that will imperil it."

Conan Doyle nodded in agreement, "I do think that within the last few months Kruger has set us increasingly in the right."

"Ha!" retorted Mrs Doyle, "I would declare that it is from our Government's endeavouring to whip the small South African nations for being in the way and for the want of benevolence on our part that they have been pushed into an impossible position. *That* is why we find ourselves at war."

Amery lent forward, demanding the attention of all at the table. "I am afraid there is now no turning back. We are at war. And after the debacle of the First Anglo-Boer War, I sincerely hope there will be no peace this time until we have secured their absolute surrender. And, I believe, the British public will demand nothing less."

Sunday 11 February 1900

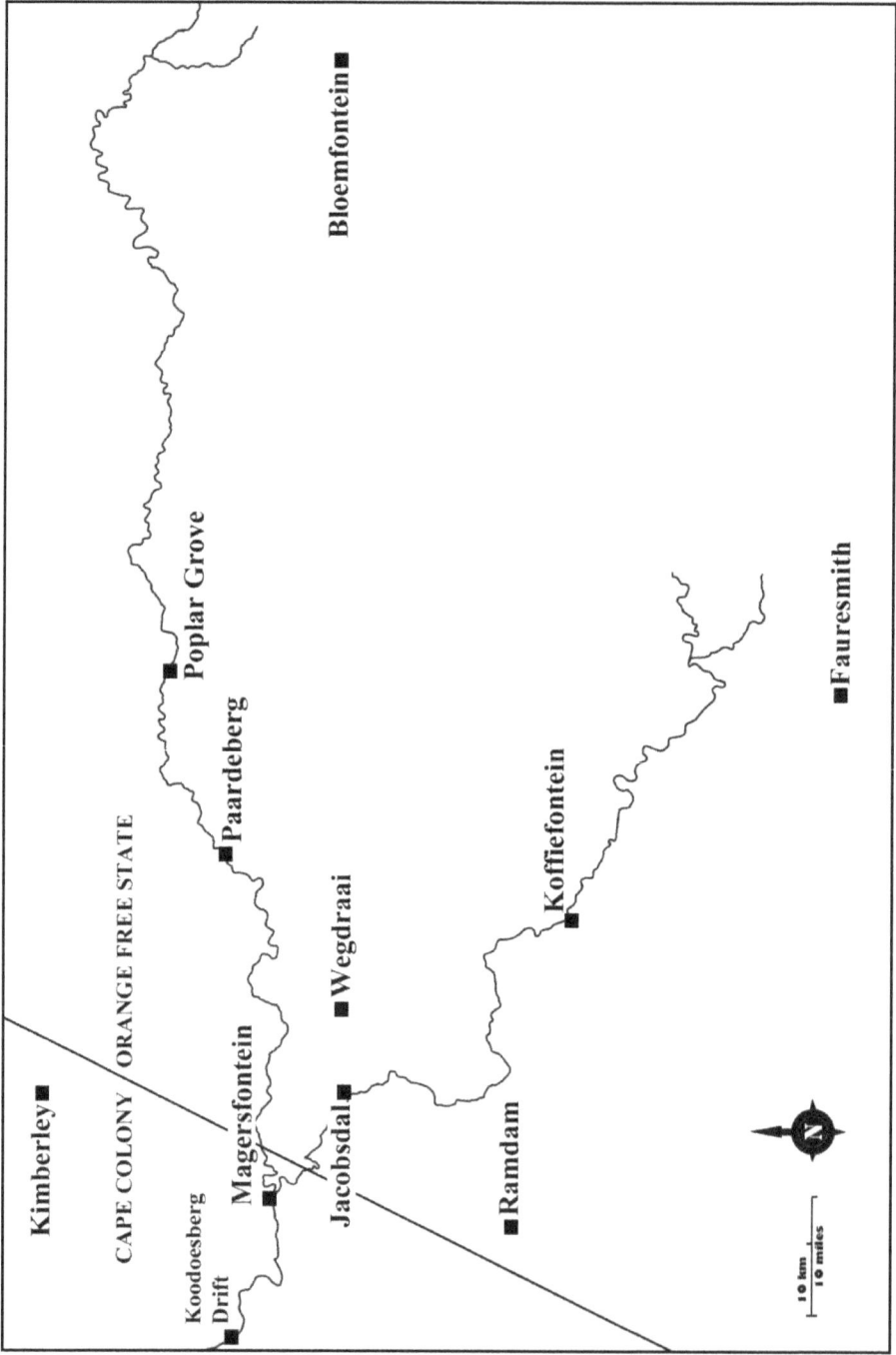

Map 2: Paardeberg and its environs

Field Marshal Sir Frederick Sleigh Roberts

Field Marshal Sir Frederick Sleigh Roberts looked intently at the chess pieces in front of him. The lantern resting on the scarred wooden table cast long shadows across the board. Watching the two men at their table, and an incongruous pair they made, chaprasi Chet Singh took a particular interest in the small, immaculate military officer. Roberts sat smart and erect, scrutinising the chess board with a career soldier's clarity of purpose. Opposite him sat a brown bear of a man, a casually smart society-type with a slouching civilian attitude, his suntanned hand stroking his walrus moustache as he stared at the increasingly desperate situation of his pieces. Singh could not prevent an inward smile as he saw Field Marshal Roberts, Commander-in-Chief of all the Imperial forces in South Africa, build up his relentless attack. Singh watched and waited for that final move of the knight down the right flank.

Once one understood what was happening, it was obvious, and Singh had seen the move many times in the past. However, to the uninitiated the move was underhand and devious in the extreme and Lord Roberts was able to use the same strategy under the guise of different tactics repeatedly before his opponents began to appreciate how the move developed.

Lord Roberts' opponent, Dr Arthur Conan Doyle, glared at the board. He could see that something was amiss, but could not disentangle the threads of danger that had been thrown around his pieces. Finally, he seemed to decide on a move, but hesitated and withdrew his hand, and then, like an uncertain god playing with a human life, he picked up the piece and cautiously moved it. A certainty seemed to flow over Conan Doyle's face. He had defended himself against a move on his rook and was threatening Roberts' queen. It was a good move. Conan Doyle sat back in his rickety wooden chair with a sense of relief. His right hand remained on the heavy wooden table, his fingers playing around a deep gouge in its surface – most likely caused by a bayonet.

Having watched Roberts for a short while, Conan Doyle's eyes ran around the low-ceilinged kitchen of the small, squat farmhouse that they occupied at Ramdam. He took in the jumble of wrecked wooden chairs piled up in one corner, from which his and Roberts' had been rescued by Singh. Through the broken window behind him, he could hear the night-time sounds of Africa, the crescendo of arguing crickets, a hyena laughing maniacally somewhere in the bush. A cold breeze suddenly rushed in through the shattered window, breathing icily against the nape of his neck. It sent a shiver down his spine and he looked thankfully at the cheerful fire blazing in the kitchen hearth. Above the fireplace, in the white-washed wall, a Boer had scratched into the plaster, 'Remember Majuba, boys!' Underneath was scored a reply, 'Don't worry, we don't', probably by a member of Rimington's Tigers, the unit of irregulars that had been ordered to secure Ramdam Farm with its precious water supply. Conan Doyle assumed they had been ordered not to destroy the farmhouse, because otherwise, as was their usual approach, it would have been burnt to the ground. As it was, they had made a good attempt at trashing it, for as well as the chairs, other furniture and broken crockery lined the walls, to where it had been roughly heaped prior to the Commander-in-Chief entering the building.

While Conan Doyle looked around the room distractedly, Singh watched Roberts. The little man did not move. He sat like a neat khaki statuette. Singh could see the concluding moves of the game. He knew Lord Roberts would win. There was no escape for the doctor. But Roberts remained motionless. Singh relaxed minutely from his attentive stance. Roberts noted his change in attitude, but remained impassive, except for the cock of an eyebrow. He continued to stare at the board. His eyes prowled over it, looking at each piece in turn. Noting the threat to his queen, he checked the pieces again. He reached over and moved the knight in a rather careless way, and Singh let out a long, but inaudible, breath, relaxing further.

Roberts glanced slyly at Conan Doyle, but his opponent missed the expression. His eyes were now glued to the board. He was confused, dumfounded. How had Roberts missed the threat on his queen? His own move had been canny, but not that unsubtle. Conan Doyle stared intently at the board. His previous unease returned and grew. Then he saw it. Mate in one! No? It was impossible! His eyes rushed around the board, hunting for the escape route, but there was none. He scrutinised the board, sat back, leant forward and scrutinised it again. There was nothing to be done.

"Well, I'll be damned!" He looked at Roberts. "That is the damnedest, sneakiest move I've ever seen."

Roberts smiled embarrassedly. "Sorry old chap, my favourite move. A cavalry attack down the right flank! Singh," he glanced up and gestured to the man, "calls it Roberts' Gambit."

"*Lord* Roberts' Gambit," Singh demurred.

Conan Doyle stared down at the board again and, taking his king, he laid it down.

"Congratulations, and my compliments on a brilliant campaign."

He took up his reclining king into an admiring hand.

"I must also compliment you on your superb chess set. Ivory, I believe?" he said, examining the exquisite detail of the king in his hand.

"Yes, from India, and the black pieces are Indian Blackwood. They were presented to me by my general staff when I left India for the last time, supposedly to retire from active service!" Roberts laughed at how the hand of fate took control of one's life. "The set is a very prized possession. The board itself is from home, Irish yew and ash."

Conan Doyle felt a sense of pride rise in him at the thought of sharing a common heritage with this great man. It appealed to his sense of irony that the 'most popular man in England' should be an Irishman. How Mam would burst with her own Irish pride if she were present to see the tableau of her son sitting with *the* Lord Roberts. He slowly caressed the piece in his hand between thumb and finger, sensing the smooth, cool surface against his skin.

"Beautiful," he murmured.

Both men dropped into a contemplative mood, Conan Doyle reflecting on his recent defeat by his illustrious foe and his family back home, while Roberts' mind drifted to those matters that should surely be preoccupying his mind – the small matter of a war to be fought and won. Singh stepped forward, breaking the spell.

"May I offer you another whiskey, sirs?"

Without waiting for a response, he topped up the two glasses in front of the men. Conan Doyle took up the glass with an appreciative nod towards Singh and lifted it towards the lamp. Although he was Scottish-born, his conviction was that there was nothing to beat Bushmills Irish whiskey, from the oldest distillery in the world. Scotch had been the downfall of his father and he never allowed a drop of it to pass his lips, but this Irish liquor was different. Its nose was soft and spicy, its palate luxurious satin with a finish of liquorice and oak. It was magnificent!

Conan Doyle was about to compliment his host on his fine whiskey when Roberts raised his own glass.

"To Her Majesty, Queen Victoria."

"To Queen Victoria and to victory," Conan Doyle smiled at his play on words.

"To victory," repeated Roberts, thoughtfully, "and tomorrow it starts."

"Yes, tomorrow it starts – the road to victory."

"I wish I could be allowed your certainty."

"You doubt our success?"

Roberts looked at Conan Doyle. "All the time, sir," he said and then, as if to himself, "All the time."

Conan Doyle stared back at Roberts in astonishment. This man was a hero, a national treasure. He was adored throughout England as the man who ruled in India and who had conquered Afghanistan. How could he, at this moment, at the very start of the campaign, have any doubts? On the evidence of his chess alone, surely it would be a well-planned campaign. How could he doubt his ability, and that of his army, to bring the campaign to a victorious conclusion? He had at his disposal the best army on the globe. The army had created and maintained an empire such as had never been seen before, nor was likely ever to be equalled. It could not fail against an army of farmers.

"Sir, I fail to understand your uncertainty." A patriotic tone rang in his voice.

"It is simple, Arthur."

Conan Doyle noted the sudden change to informality and in the tone of Roberts' voice.

"That will be all, thank you, Singh," Roberts said.

With a smart snap to attention and a bow, Singh exited the room, quietly closing the door behind him. Silence. Even the previously insistent rasp of the crickets in the darkness outside seemed to hush in anticipation.

"Arthur, I have read your patriotic letters to *The Times* and *The Gazette*, and I welcome their content and their tone very much. We need the great British public to believe in ultimate victory, for if the public does not believe in the cause, then my job becomes untenable. This is especially true in our modern society. We have a press that wields considerable influence over what the public understands and over public opinion. We have almost as many correspondents covering this war as I have medical staff tending to my wounded." Roberts smiled, "And I note and I am pleased to see that you cover both roles. There are journalists from virtually every country you can name, both our friends and our enemies. These latter will be spinning a web of misinformation about our activities in South Africa and it is, therefore, of vital importance that we get true and accurate details to the people at home so that they can have confidence in the cause. Often, as in your letters, this will require a certain amount of jingoism and flag-waving," Roberts added quickly, "This is by no means a criticism of you, sir, for what you say is good and very helpful."

Roberts paused. He studied Conan Doyle. He had not expressed the views he was about to divulge to any man. Why should he trust the man in front of him more than any other? Did he understand? Roberts looked into the grey eyes that were returning the scrutiny. They reflected back a Victorian gentleman whose belief in British honour was impeccable and in whom discretion was the better part of valour. Roberts relaxed.

"However, the truth of the matter is that war is not a simple game. It never has been and it never will be. Chess, for many, would appear to be a complex game and in many respects it is damnably complex. However, once mastered, it is simple. It consists of learned strategies and remembered tactics. But," Roberts looked Conan Doyle directly in the eyes, "chess is not a matter of life or death. For those politicians who stay at home, keeping out of harm's way, it is easy to forget this. They decry the risks and belittle the dangers. They are not the ones who risk their lives, and few of them deliver their sons to the slaughter. Even I, although I am here with the troops, no longer risk my life. Oh, I did in the past, and I would do so now if I was allowed to, but I am considered too valuable to be in the firing line. All I can do is plan, and hope that what I plan does not cause the needless deaths of those who necessarily have to follow my orders. And if what I plan seems foolish to the ordinary soldier, he will still proceed, even in the full knowledge that his sacrifice will be for nought. The worst of it is that men will die believing I have failed them and that, but for me, they could have lived and fought another day.

"The British soldier is an extraordinary person. Many of our colonies have provided men of almost similar calibre. So there is a great burden on me. I hold in my hands the destiny of these extraordinary men: do they to live or do they die? To many of those self-promoting oafs at home, war seems to be no less than playing a chess gambit. But that is very far from the truth. How many men am I prepared to sacrifice to win this ridge or that hillock? What is the price I am willing to pay in the lives of men and the sorrow of mothers, wives and children? They have no choice in these decisions. Even those brave fellows who volunteer for special missions do not really decide on their fate."

Roberts glanced at Conan Doyle, "I cannot remember the last time I asked for volunteers. For me, it is a sign of failure. It is a sign that the main campaign is not going to plan. I do not claim to be always successful in my campaigns, but I do not wish to encourage men to choose their own demise. You will know that my son, Freddy, was killed recently at Colenso. He volunteered. And he died. He won the Victoria Cross and I am unspeakably proud of him, but he died. His mission was to rescue guns that had been placed – I would say misplaced – too close to the enemy. The gunners had been shot to pieces and the guns were in danger of being lost. It was the right thing to do – to retrieve the guns. The embarrassment of losing the guns would have been testing in the extreme on regimental pride. It had to be done. But the campaign had gone off course, so volunteers had to be called upon. They took the risk and paid the consequences."

Roberts fell silent. Conan Doyle sat as still as granite. This was not a time to speak; this was a time to listen. He looked at Roberts, sympathising with him, but encouraging him to continue. Roberts looked down at the forces on the chessboard.

"Do you know our army in Southern Africa will be the largest force I have ever commanded in a career of nearly fifty years' service to Her Majesty? And by the time all the reinforcements arrive from Britain, and from our colonies, I shall command the greatest force ever to have been marshalled under the Union Flag. You may find that an interesting fact, but I find it astonishing! It is astonishing because we have transported the greater part of our army and those of our colonies to go to war against a militia of farmers with no formal military training and who fight in their Sunday best, and whose numbers include men older than myself and some little more than children. But they have 'a cause' and, by God, they have taken that cause to heart. They shoot with a Christian zeal and then melt away like spirits before our soldiers can get anywhere near them. This is a different kind of war, different from any I have fought before and from any that has been fought by the British army. So far, we have not performed well and have been taught no end of a lesson."

Roberts fell silent again, this time for what seemed an eternity. He stared again at the chess pieces where his knight occupied the right flank of the board: Lord Roberts' Gambit. God in heaven, he thought, it had better work this time! He looked up and at Conan Doyle as though noticing him for the first time that evening.

"Thank you, sir. You are an excellent listener."

The formality had returned; the need to unburden his thoughts had been accomplished.

"And thank you, sir, for your confidence," murmured Conan Doyle.

Roberts smiled grimly. "I believe you will be discreet in your writings about this evening."

"Entirely discreet, sir."

"Then I bid you goodnight, sir. I suggest you get some sleep for tomorrow will be the start of a trying few days and I have no doubt that your surgical skills are going to be in great demand."

Roberts stood up, shook Conan Doyle's hand and walked slowly out of the farmhouse and into the night.

The cold air closed in on Roberts as he left the building and a shiver ran over his body. He was instantly joined by Singh, who carried a lantern. Roberts waited to allow his eyes to adjust to the darkness. The cold air was heavy with the tang of eucalyptus from the blue-gum trees that towered above the house. The crickets had greeted him stridently, but they could not mask the sounds of the great army in whose midst he stood: the snores of sleeping men, the lowing of cattle and the stamping of horses' hooves. He remembered the countless times that he had been here before – a man in charge of sleeping innocence that, once woken, was transformed into an instrument of death and destruction. His eyes roamed up to the dome of blackness above him. It was studded with a chaotic mass of stars, chaotic because he did not recognise any of the constellations. He looked to his left, but the comforting Northern Star was absent. Turning to his right, he could easily make out the distinctive Southern Cross. Too fussy, thought Roberts, a single point of direction was what one required. And that was what he needed to deliver now. He dropped his eyes to Singh and gestured the man onwards.

Following Singh, who held the lantern high in front of him, Roberts walked towards his wagon. He had previously requested his senior officers to gather there so that he could set out his plan to them. Roberts mulled his situation over in his mind. One could argue that the plan had a classic simplicity, but the counter was that it contained some classically simple dangers. Nonetheless, everything was now in place; he and Kitchener had spent weeks putting things in order. Kitchener had done an extraordinary job. Roberts wondered where on earth Kitchener had managed to get hold of two thousand wagons, twenty-two thousand oxen and mules and fourteen thousand horses, and with more horses still to come from Argentina and Australia. But, even that number might still not be enough to service the four thousand cavalry and three thousand five hundred mounted infantry as well as draw one hundred and twenty guns and the monstrous number of supply wagons.

A second shiver went through Roberts' body, this time accompanied by a chilling sweat that was not caused by the cool air. Those wagons were critical to the success of the campaign. Roberts knew that feeding twenty-six thousand infantry plus the cavalry and other mounted troops as well as their mounts, and the five thousand native drivers would be a constant weight on his mind. Would the eighteen thousand infantry he planned to leave behind be sufficient to guard the rail link and supply route from the Cape? They would have to do as they were all that could be released. The seven thousand men of Methuen's 1st Division at Magersfontein also needed to be kept in place to ensure that the Boers remained in their trenches for as long as possible. The flanking movement he planned depended on it. That left three divisions of infantry and one of horse to be force-marched across a virtual desert.

Speed! The whole enterprise relied on speed. He needed to make this absolutely clear to the generals. Speed to get from one source of water to the next in the shortest possible time. Speed to secure the river crossings. Speed to ensure the element of surprise. That surprise relied on the 1st Division keeping Cronjé busy at Magersfontein. General Macdonald's recent demonstration attack at the ford at Koodoesberg Drift demonstrated the speed at which the Boers could mobilise to reinforce a position. It was extraordinary how fast those compact Boer ponies could move. His own forces needed to match their speed. General French and his cavalry would have to do their part. It was the infantry that concerned Roberts in particular. 'Horses have four legs, and men have two legs, and two into four goes twice', Roberts allowed himself a wry smile as the words of Kipling's poem drifted into his mind.

It reminded him of something he'd said to Conan Doyle. What was it? Ah, yes, 'This is a different kind of war'. How true! He had never engaged an adversary so well equipped with the most modern weapons. This 'little war', as some in London had called it, was going to be bigger than they thought. It had already ruined the reputation of General Buller. Roberts doubted that the general would ever recover from the damage his character had suffered. From this point on, Roberts declared to himself, those under *his* command would only have their reputations enhanced by their actions in this 'Little War'. And the British *would* win the day.

Having thus reassembled his thoughts, Roberts entered the lean-to tent attached to the side of his wagon that served as his office and prepared to explain his plan.

Before him, around a campaign table, on which a hand-drawn map had been laid out, stood five men. One was Major-General Horatio Kitchener whom Roberts had got to know well during their journey, by ship from Gibraltar to Cape Town and in the subsequent time they spent planning the defeat of Cronjé.

He knew none of the others personally, and only two by reputation. Standing in the centre was Lieutenant-General John French, the commanding officer of the Cavalry Division. He was actually no more than a colonel; his current rank was a local one, but it made him the most senior officer after Roberts. In many ways he reminded Roberts of his younger self. Like Roberts he was of a compact stature and very confident of his abilities. Roberts had heard of his exploits against the Boers in Natal, where he had won the only notable British victory at Elandslaagte. However, he differed from Roberts in that he had a legendary foul temper. He was also one of Wolseley's men, that other British Field Marshal who had shown such bad character when Roberts, rather than himself, had been chosen to lead the South African campaign.

Another of Wolseley's men was also present, Lieutenant-General Thomas Kelly-Kenny, commander of the 6th Division. A stout Irishman of medium height, he was the only officer in the British army of more advanced years than Roberts. In previous conversations with him, Roberts had perceived an over-cautious approach to military tactics, which concerned him.

Roberts did not know the other two officers, Lieutenant-Generals Henry Colvile and Charles Tucker, the commanders the 9th and 7th Divisions respectively. In complete contrast to Kelly-Kenny, Colvile was tall and as shapeless as a stick. There seemed to be nothing distinguishing about Tucker, except a bulbous moustache that hid his mouth and made his West Country accent even less intelligible.

Looking around the group of men, Roberts did not feel inspired by what he saw. He reflected on his request for more of his own officers from India, but this had been denied him. Needs must, he concluded. At least he could count on some of his lower ranking officers, such as 'Fighting Mac', which reminded him, he must catch up with Hector Macdonald some time.

"Gentlemen, I have brought you together to explain my strategy for dealing with General Cronjé and to give you my final orders. It is a simple plan. We are to trap Cronjé between our forces at Magersfontein and divisions we are to place behind him to the south of Kimberley.

"General French, you are to take the cavalry and race towards Kimberley, followed by the infantry. The critical tactic is speed. We need to cross the barren landscape between ourselves and Kimberley with the utmost speed. And two rivers need to be crossed, the Riet and the Modder."

Roberts gave French a knowing look. To date, the Modder had been the friend of the Boers and an enemy of the British. The Highlanders had already been cut to pieces on its banks and General Methuen was presently held up by the river, along which the Boers were entrenched in an impenetrable position, dug deep into its banks.

"Speed is of the utmost importance if we are to ensure that we do not give the Boers warning. If we do not succeed, we may have another bloodbath on our hands. Both rivers have to be crossed and secured before the Boers can do it. It is a race, but we will have the advantage. I have taken all necessary precautions to convince Cronjé that Methuen and the 1st Division are to make another frontal attack on his current positions. But he is a wily old devil. We should not under-estimate him.

"Therefore, in detail, the 1st Division is to remain at Magersfontein under Methuen. They are to keep the Boers occupied and make all the signs of building up numbers so that the Boers stay in their current defensive position. I have ordered your divisions' tents to be taken there and pitched as you will have no immediate need of them. You will be sleeping under the stars for the duration. The cavalry and the 6th, 7th and 9th Divisions are all to move forward and around the left flank of the Boers.

"General French, your cavalry will move the fastest and so will form the vanguard. You will march due west to cross the Riet River at the ford at Waterval Drift," Roberts traced the line of the march with his finger on the map in front of him. "You will then swing north towards Wegdraai, where, I am informed, there may be some water, and then continue on to the Modder River to capture and secure the ford at Klip Drift. There you will await the 6th Division, before moving on towards Kimberley, where you will position the cavalry to the west of the town to prevent any attempt by the Boers to escape through that route.

"General Kelly-Kenny, your 6th Division is to follow General French closely, guard the fords on the Modder River until relieved by the 7th, and then extend your division northwards between the river and Kimberley, in so doing placing yourself behind the Boers' present position.

"General Tucker, your 7th Division is to follow and guard the fords at Rondeval Drift and Klip Drift on the Modder River to prevent the Boers from crossing the river. In addition, you are to send a contingent to remove the Boers from Jacobsdal, where I shall set up headquarters. Finally, General Colvile, your 9th Division is to be held in reserve in the vicinity of the farm at Wegdraai.

"General French, there is an extra task for you, which is to relieve Kimberley. This is a distraction and an annoyance, but a necessity. Rhodes is making an interminable noise about being abandoned in Kimberley, and he has friends in high places and in the press. However, on the positive side, in taking Kimberley there will be an opportunity to capture the Boer guns that are besieging the town."

Roberts looked at each man in turn before he continued.

"Gentlemen, this campaign will be a severe challenge to our men and horses. We are expecting an astonishing amount from them. We will require them to march for several days at speed and with minimal rest across semi-arid terrain with scant water, save two muddy rivers. General French will lead the largest cavalry division to have been put into action by the British Empire and the largest that has ever had to work as a single unit. And all of you will be jointly commanding the largest deployment of infantry in the history of the British army. While the men will rejoice in this opportunity of maintaining their regimental traditions, the demands of leading your divisions will be enormous. And one of the biggest challenges will be ensuring that the supply wagons keep up with the troops. However, General Kitchener and I have spent the last month arranging the logistics to ensure the transport of supplies will proceed smoothly.

"I have no doubt that you will all do us proud. Remember, speed is everything to the success of this campaign. Once we have subdued Cronjé and his Boers, the door will be open to the Orange Free State and Bloemfontein, and then to Pretoria and the South African Republic. And so we shall conclude the war."

Roberts looked around at his attentive audience.

"Any questions, gentlemen?"

Silence prevailed.

"It is a plan of classic simplicity, sir." said Kitchener.

Roberts smiled. "Indeed. Well, thank you, gentlemen. General French, prepare to leave before dawn. The rest will follow as soon as practicable. Goodnight and good luck."

The generals saluted and started to troop out of the canvas shelter. Roberts looked down at the map, running his finger along the route of the march, as though reassuring himself that the distances to be covered were possible.

As French was about to leave the lean-to, Kitchener stepped in front of him. Kitchener towered over him and glared down his angular nose with piercing blue, predatory eyes. French took an involuntarily step back and was instantly angry with himself for doing so. His action reminded him of frequent encounters with his Latin school-master at Harrow, who had had the same overbearing presence, the same arrogant attitude. He scowled up at Kitchener, returning a hard, level stare into those unblinking cobra eyes. It was Kitchener who spoke first, in a stern, school-masterly tone, but quietly enough so as not to attract Roberts' attention.

"Sir, the cavalry is to reach Kimberley even if they leave half their strength on the road."

French's scowl turned to a look of astonishment. He felt the heat of hot blood spreading across his face. He felt he was about to explode.

"Of course," snapped French, just able to contain himself, "It shall be done within five days!"

He stormed out into the darkness. He was livid. He was enraged. He was… he was… apoplectic. French stopped suddenly, his hands opening and closing into fists. Why, that trumped up Egyptian! How dare he question a senior officer? *How dare he?* Kitchener did have a substantive rank of Major-General, compared to French's Colonel, but in South Africa, French fumed, his local rank made him Kitchener's superior officer. The insubordinate bastard! French thought of complaining to Roberts, but then a contrary thought struck him. Kitchener was one of Roberts' men and a complaint was unlikely to be pressed. Those buffoons in Government should have appointed Wolseley as Commander-in-Chief, not that self-indulgent little Indian, Roberts. Good God, if Roberts held Kitchener in high esteem, then French had grave doubts about his judgement, *and* about the successful outcome of this war. In a paroxysm of fury, he strode off towards his cavalry.

Monday 12 February 1900

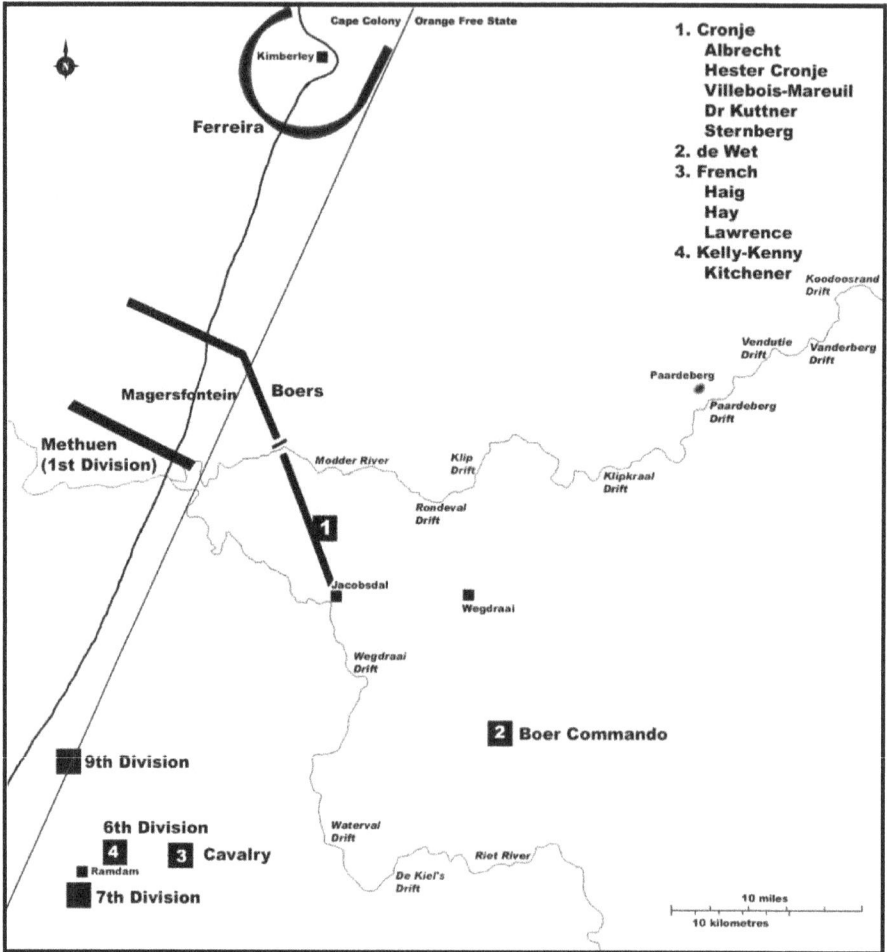

Map 3: Morning of 12 February 1900

Major Friedrich Wilhelm Richard Albrecht

Major Friedrich Wilhelm Richard Albrecht rode purposefully through the disorganised camp of tents and trek wagons towards the green tent of General Cronjé, the soft plop of his horse's hooves raising small puffs of dust. The burghers had risen and, in various states of dress, were seeing to their ablutions with much coughing and clearing of congealed throats. Their native servants were preparing breakfasts over smoky fires fuelled with dried cow dung.

Ahead Albrecht could now see his destination. In front of the tent sat Cronjé on his low, tripod trek stool. He was hunched in his customary greatcoat, this time done up against the early morning chill. His slouch hat was jammed on his head. In his hands he cupped a large mug of steaming green coffee, from which he sipped absent-mindedly. He was staring into a pot in which his breakfast of boiled mutton was cooking over a small camp fire. Next to him sat the diminutive Mrs Hester Susanna Cronjé, who chatted away at her husband, frequently interrupting herself to snap orders at a native tending to their breakfast. It was such a domestic tableau that it was almost possible to forget that only a few miles away a desperate battle was raging in which men were losing their lives.

Mrs Cronjé was the first to notice Albrecht's approach. She stood up and stepped closer to Cronjé, bending to whisper in his ear.

"Here comes the Free State Clotheshorse!"

"Shoosh, Hester," Cronjé reprimanded. "Friedrich is a proud man who takes easy offence at ridicule."

But she was right. Albrecht did look like a mixture between a flunky and a railway guard, especially with that ridiculous shiny black hat with all its sparkling metalwork and brass ball on the top.

"Just as well he is on our side," Hester whispered, "for he would make a striking target for your riflemen."

She moved around to stand behind her husband, and Cronjé smiled broadly at Albrecht as he drew near.

"Good morning, Major," he called. "How are you this beautiful morning? No doubt you are looking forward to giving those English yet another bloody nose."

43

Albrecht

Albrecht dismounted, jarring his back slightly as he did so. These wretched Boer ponies! They really were too short for proper military service. If only the larger European horses could cope with the harsh conditions in South Africa, things would be so much more comfortable. Albrecht nevertheless returned Cronjé's smile.

"Yes, General, if the British continue with their present tactics, we will give them another lesson in how to conduct war. For myself, I am well and I see you are in good spirits."

"Indeed I am. The English are contained both here and in Natal and will soon have to surrender as they did in '81. Their public will not allow their commanders to sustain such high losses, and their politicians will have to capitulate again. It will not be long now. Please sit." Cronjé indicated the stool recently vacated by his wife.

Albrecht sat down, removing his pickelhaube and resting the shiny black helmet on his thigh.

"Good morning, Mrs Cronjé. How are you this morning?"

"I am very well, thank you, and delighted, as ever, to see you on this lovely morning. Will you join us for breakfast?"

"Thank you, but no. I shall have breakfast at the hotel, as usual."

"Ah, yes. At the 'gentlemen's club'," said Cronjé with a twinkle in his eye.

"At the hotel, yes," repeated Albrecht.

In the easy silence that followed, he looked at the pair in front of him, Cronjé sitting like a big circus bear upon a stool too small for his bulk, his wife standing behind him with a possessive hand resting on his shoulder. It was as if they were posing for a photograph, an impression enhanced by their stillness and their silence. Albrecht broke the silence.

"So, General, what are your orders today?"

He knew the answer already, but felt obliged to ask.

"Well, Major, we sit tight in our trenches, wait for the English to advance and shoot them until they retreat again. You continue your part of disabling their guns with your own and lobbing a few shells into the advancing troops for good measure. I know it seems rather simple and is tedious, but it works, and until the English change their tactics we need to continue in this vein. Any questions?"

"No, General, not about what we do at Magersfontein."

"But you do in respect to something else?"

"Yes, General, if I may. It is about our flanks."

"I suspect I know what you wish to say, but this is not the Prussian army, as you know. This is a democratic army and as an officer of the Orange Free State you have the right to discuss our strategy. You need not be so coy. Please continue."

"General, there are reports of large British reinforcements moving towards the front."

"Yes, there are."

"More recently, reports indicate a massing of cavalry at Ramdam."

"Indeed."

"This is a change from what the British have done in the past. They have left the railway."

"I hear what you say, Major, but I hardly think that going to Ramdam can be counted as leaving the railway. You could hit Ramdam from Graspan Station with one of your smallest artillery pieces. What is more infuriating is the fact that they have entered the Orange Free State. We have been formally invaded. But I think the main reason they have gone to Ramdam is because they need water. Have you seen the size of their horses?" Cronjé laughed. "In Africa, if you made horses that size stand in water they will soak it up like sponges. As you have seen for yourself, Friedrich, for you now ride one yourself, there are benefits in our little ponies." Cronjé gave Albrecht a wink.

"I agree, General. The British horses are unsuited to South Africa's environment and will require much attention, particularly in respect to water, but it is the new commander-in-chief who concerns me. Lord Roberts is a man with a considerable reputation and many years' experience of war."

"Indeed, Friedrich. And at least this time he made it to the battlefield. During the War of Independence he was only in South Africa long enough to disembark in Cape Town and board the next ship back to England. Still, I suppose he had a nice cruise; it was more than most soldiers get. So why is this little 'Bobs' causing you sleepless nights? You know, of course, that it is said that the queen herself was annoyed to hear that he was given the top post."

"Yes, I have heard that. But I believe that was more to do with the underhand and conspiratorial manner in which he was appointed, rather than a reflection of his skills as a military leader. We should not underestimate him. May I suggest that you read his autobiography, in which he…"

"My dear Major," Cronjé laughed loudly, "I have no need to read the writings of some little officer with such a high opinion of himself as to think anyone is interested in what he did with his life thousands of miles away. *This* is the only book I read." Cronjé lifted his well-thumbed copy of the Bible that lay on a blanket beside him. "This is the book to which you should refer. It contains all the knowledge I require. A single sentence in this book offers more understanding and a greater depth of knowledge than the entire book published by that self-promoting 'novelist', Roberts."

"I hear what you say, General. I only ask that we consider the new threat posed by this man. He has a great military brain. He is known for his skill in flanking movements and I suggest that the concentration of cavalry at Ramdam may be the start of such a manoeuvre on our left flank. Also, his men are said to adore him and will do anything he asks. They will endure great discomfort without complaint if he orders it – such as will be required for a march around our flank."

Cronjé regarded Albrecht sourly. "Do you imply that my own men do not adore me sufficiently?"

"No, of course not, General. I meant it in the context of the other British officers in South Africa. Your men voted for you to be their leader. There is no doubt of their respect for your military skills and prowess."

"Good, I am glad to hear it. Major, I respect your concerns and am pleased that you feel able to bring them to my attention, but let us look at the facts. The only concentration at Ramdam appears to be their cavalry and some support units. There is no evidence that the infantry is moving away from the front at Magersfontein. Indeed, the evidence suggests to me that they will attack there again and will continue to try to advance along the railway line to Kimberley. The English love affair with the railway continues, but their horses are such a drain on supplies that they have had to move them off their main line of attack simply to water the great lumbering beasts," Cronjé smiled at Albrecht, "I hope you are able to recognise the merits of my arguments, Major. Have no fear. We have beaten the English before. We have proved they are fallible. God is on our side.

He led us to our homeland, so why should he have a desire to remove it from us? My dear Albrecht, do as we do; put your faith in God and the Mauser."

"Yes, General. Thank you for listening. You are probably right, but we must keep an eye on the situation at Ramdam."

"Of course, Major. I have already asked General Christiaan de Wet to ride towards Ramdam and keep us informed of what is going on."

"De Wet is a good man. I commend your choice, General. I shall not delay your breakfast any longer."

Albrecht rose, lifting his pickelhaube by the balled spike. He snapped to attention smartly, dipped his head at Cronjé and bowed to his wife, who had remained standing behind Cronjé. She curtsied in return. Albrecht returned to his horse, mounted it and turned it towards the town of Jacobsdal where his breakfast was waiting at the hotel. Cronjé and his wife watched him trot off.

"So that's what the spike is for. It's a handle for lifting the hat."

"Shoosh," insisted Cronjé, looking at his wife sternly.

"I must say that for all his aloofness he does have impeccable manners." She smiled, winked at Cronjé and went to the fire to check the progress of their breakfast.

Cronjé watched the retreating man. He might have been a flunky in his taste in uniforms, but there was no doubt about his skill as an artillery man. It was not unusual for him to estimate the correct range of the English forces with his first shell. The English, on the other hand, tended to overshoot. Yes, it was a good thing that Albrecht was on their side.

Albrecht rode through the Afrikander laager towards the town. On the outskirts, he passed a small pile of stones. It appeared to be of little note, but it was already one of the 'must see' attractions in Jacobsdal as every stone had a name scratched on to it – the name of a burgher going to war. The battle they had gone off to fight had been one of the early confrontations of the war. Albrecht had to remind himself that they had been at war only four months; it seemed much longer. During that time the war had developed into one of attrition, a fact that concerned Albrecht. The Afrikanders had known they had the early advantage and had made rapid advances into the Cape and Natal, but it was soon obvious that they had no grand plan other than to shock the British Government into surrendering before too many reinforcements arrived in South Africa. Well, that opportunity had passed. From the reports coming in, the British had amassed the largest army in the history of human conflict. The Kaiser must be glowing green with envy.

Albrecht passed an elegant, white church. People were streaming in for morning prayers. He watched them as he rode past. If God is on the side of the righteous, then he could not do better than be on the side of the people of the Afrikander Republics, for a more religious people he had not seen. They put even the nuns at Lindow to shame. Albrecht smiled happily and sat upright in his saddle as he recalled one particular nun with whom he developed a rather close relationship. Maria would have been canonised if he'd had any say in the matter.

As Albrecht approached the hotel his mood was further improved by the smell of cooking emanating from the building – a squat, red-brick edifice surrounded by a white-painted wooden veranda that was crowded with tables. Most of the tables were occupied, mainly by war correspondents, but there were also a few foreign officers sympathetic to the Afrikander cause. The journalists called out to Albrecht.

"Any news?" they joked, for they knew there would none as the war in the Cape had ground to a halt. "Major, we are thinking about scooting over to Natal. Things seem to be more exciting over there!"

"Suit yourself," Albrecht mumbled.

Where had all these people come from? He had never seen so many news people at a war before. How was anyone supposed to keep military secrets with all these people telling the world about every plan or move one made? Albrecht avoided the clusters of correspondents and made for a table occupied by two military types. One was Major Villebois-Mareuil, a 51-year-old Anglophobic French officer who had made his way to South Africa to take part in the war. To Albrecht, it was clear that Villebois-Mareuil saw the war as an opportunity to avenge the diplomatic humiliation the French suffered at British hands over the Fashoda affair in Sudan in '98. Albrecht considered looking for another table, but Villebois-Mareuil spotted him and beckoned him over. Oh dear, thought Albrecht, as he resigned himself to another grilling. The other officer was Count Sternberg, a 31-year-old minor Austrian aristocrat and adventurer.

Albrecht was not quite sure what Sternberg was doing in Southern Africa, but it was as though he was there as a tourist. Also present at the table was a German doctor, Kuttner.

"Good morning all."

The men stood up, "Good morning, Major."

They shook hands and sat down. Before they could commence any conversation the hotel owner's wife came over with a plate of sliced cold ham, bread and coffee.

"Your usual, Major?" she enquired.

"Yes, thank you. What excellent service, as usual."

Albrecht smiled at the woman and watched as she returned into the hotel. It still struck him as strange, under the circumstances, being served by an Englishwoman. But the more interesting thing was what her Afrikander husband would do if the English did take Jacobsdal. Would he stay or would he return to Bloemfontein? Albrecht left the question unanswered and turned his attention to those whose table he had joined. As Albrecht expected, it was Major Villebois-Mareuil who spoke first.

"Major, have you given consideration to my proposal?"

"I have sir, and I'm afraid I am unable to find a place for you in the Orange Free State Artillery. It is much regretted, but that is the case."

"But why, sir? This is very disappointing. You have read my letters of reference. Are they not excellent? I have considerable experience with the Creusot guns that the Orange Free State Artillery uses – after all, they are French. And I am a veteran of the same war as you."

"Indeed, sir, but that is not the issue. The issue is that Afrikanders will not follow the orders of foreign officers, especially if they have not been elected to lead. I am sorry, there is nothing further I can do."

"But that is nonsense, sir. I was raised to the rank of Major by General Joubert himself, and I fought with General Botha at Colenso. Neither of them had this aversion to foreign officers to which you allude. Also, as you know, I have been specifically sent to Jacobsdal to advise General Cronjé. And what about you? You are also a foreigner, an Uitlander, so your arguments do not hold. In addition, many in your unit are Hollanders and Germans, and not Afrikanders. There must be some other issue at the heart of this."

"Sir, as you well know, I have been involved in improving the Orange Free State Artillery for the last twenty years and have created the most effective artillery regiment in Southern Africa. I think I have earned the respect of the Afrikanders. Secondly, if your *other issue* is an allusion to the Franco-Prussian war, that is indeed a pertinent matter as I doubt whether my German colleagues would be content to serve under a French officer. It would seem incongruous, having beaten the French so recently, to expect them to do so. Indeed, the well-documented involvement of the French in the barbarous seizing of the city of Blois will only make the situation more untenable." Albrecht saw Villebois-Mareuil bristle, but carried on before the man could interrupt. "I hear your conduct was exemplary during the battle, despite being badly injured, but that does not detract from the fact that certain elements of the French forces behaved despicably during that action. The decision is made. That is the end of it."

Villebois-Mareuil stood up sharply. He was scarlet with anger and trembling with indignation.

"Sir," he stormed, "the liberation of Blois was a master-class in how to recapture a city, and the brilliance of the French tactics is not to be belittled by the incompetence of the Prussian generals, nor the subsequent slanders they circulated to hide their own stupidity." He glared at Albrecht but seemed to be at a loss of what else to say. "Good morning, gentlemen," he said, looking at Sternberg and Kuttner, and pointedly avoiding Albrecht. With that, he left.

"He did not like that," noted Sternberg.

"You've upset him," said Doctor Kuttner mockingly.

"Oh, for goodness sake, the man is tedious. Every day it is the same question. I have had enough. I do not want some French adventurer messing around with my guns. Why doesn't he go and ask the English if he is so keen to shoot shells around?"

"Good meeting with Cronjé, then?" asked Sternberg with a knowing look.

"Hardly. The man would not see a flanking movement if it bit him on the arse."

"The English manoeuvre can hardly be called a flanking move-ment, at least not yet," observed Kuttner.

"True," agreed Albrecht, "but this Roberts is a whole new prospect. He is a sheep in wolves' clothing. The increasing bluster of the English at Magersfontein, the skirmish they initiated at

Koodoesberg Drift, and the build-up of troops at Ramdam. There is something going on."

"I agree," said Sternberg, "and have stated as much."

"To whom?"

"To Cronjé, of course."

Albrecht choked on his slice of ham.

"You did what?"

"I suggested to Cronjé that he might take action to counter a possible flanking movement by the British."

Kuttner looked wide-eyed at Sternberg and then burst out laughing. Albrecht stared at him in disbelief.

Between huge peals of laughter, Kuttner managed to splutter, "I bet that went down well. Goodness, I wish I had been there to see that!" He rocked in his chair, his shoulders shaking, and tears running down his cheeks.

"What happened?" asked Albrecht.

"He did not take it well."

Another huge laugh erupted from Kuttner. Sternberg noticed people turning to see what was going on. He leant forward so as to contain the conversation to their table.

"I don't suppose he did," grinned Albrecht.

"So, what did he say?" Kuttner managed to get out between laughs.

"He informed me that he had been fighting wars before my mother deposited me into this world and that I should focus on my role as a wordsmith for the papers rather than put my nose in where it had not been invited."

Kuttner was off again. "Priceless, absolutely priceless. I do admire your pluck!"

"Oh for heaven's sake, be quiet, Kuttner. Cronjé's behaviour was most unseemly. I am an officer of the Austrian army. It does not do to be treated with such disrespect. Cronjé really should listen to us. Albrecht, and others, agree with me about the danger of a flanking movement. Jacobsdal is the most vulnerable part of the Afrikander line. If the British roll this flank up, then there is nothing to stop them advancing to Bloemfontein, and there is no one in this town to stop the British taking it. "

Sternberg looked at Albrecht for support. Kuttner calmed down and fixed his attention on Albrecht.

"What the Count says is possible," agreed Albrecht, "maybe even probable, but what Cronjé believes is also possible. He is convinced that should the British attack Jacobsdal, he is perfectly able to mobilise men quickly enough to repel such an attack. It has to be said that it would be a fantastic feat for the English to march their army in sufficient strength across the desert to be able to roll up our left flank. But that does not mean it cannot, or will not, happen. And if there is an English officer who might achieve such a feat, then that man would be Roberts. All I can suggest is that we keep a very close eye on the situation."

Lieutenant-General John Denton Pinkstone French

Lieutenant-General John Denton Pinkstone French considered the khaki-clad men and their horses rushing down to the brown river in a desperate attempt to quench their thirst. He did not move to stop them. It was only ten in the morning but already the sun was fierce. The heavy early dawn mist had burnt away hours ago to be replaced by air that was threatening to be furnace hot. Although they had started at two o'clock in the morning, progress had been painstakingly slow. Even with the full moon casting its grey, cold light over the landscape, the ground was treacherous for the horses. Small animal holes and the round, concrete-hard anthills were an ever-present threat, and great care was required in moving forward. The ground was so strewn with burrows, anthills and other hazards that he had halted the division during the short period of pitch-blackness between the moon setting and the first light of dawn. French recalled the huge, red, African sun rising like a ball of molten lava, its immense size a portent of the heat it was to deliver during the day.

Although progress was slow, French was satisfied. They had reached their first objective: their crossing point on the Riet River at Waterval Drift. It offered the men and horses an opportunity to slake their thirst and take a well-deserved rest. But a tinge of unease troubled French and he turned to study the immense cavalcade behind him. Only the vanguard had reached the river and, obscured in a canopy of hot, dry, grey dust, the remainder of his force slowly trudged towards him. He worried about the number of horses that had already been lost – how many he did not know. Major Haig, his right-hand man, would give him the count later in the day, but the fact he had already started to lose horses was very concerning. This had been the easy part. Tomorrow would be far more difficult. But that was tomorrow's problem. Before then he had other difficulties to overcome: his first priorities were to get his men and horses across the river and fed, and to secure the opposite riverbank. He had not heard about the progress of his supply wagons and that made him apprehensive. Equally, he had not had any reports about the enemy. That was either good news or bad. He had a niggling feeling that it was probably the latter.

Sharing similar thoughts, but waiting for his comments, were his general staff: Colonel Charles Gore Hay, who had been made his Assistant Adjutant General by Lord Roberts, Major Douglas Haig, who he had wanted to be his Assistant Adjutant General and Captain Lawrence.

In many ways Haig reminded French of a younger version of General Redvers Buller, a man he much admired and who was leading the campaign against the Boers in Natal. Haig and Buller shared the same broad shoulders and heavy build and the same gruff face and serious look about the eyes. Haig also had the same haughty attitude that hid a hint of concern about his own abilities. It is good, thought French, for men to be aware of their limitations; it makes them consider things more deeply. The danger arose when it caused them to be over-cautious, and if Buller had one failing, French reflected, it was that he was too cautious. That was the principal reason for all his reverses on the Eastern Front in Natal. Of courage, both men had barrels full, although French recalled, with an inward smile, how he and Haig had flattened themselves to the floor of the last train to leave the besieged Natal town of Ladysmith as Mauser bullets flew around them like angry wasps. It would be a jolly story for them to reminisce over once the war was won. French considered his friend thoughtfully. He had never really got to the bottom of what motivated the man. Not only was he from the wealthy Scotch whisky dynasty, but he had also attended university – it was not a typical background for an officer in the British army. Still, he was a likeable and generous man, and a good friend.

French let his gaze drift to the mounted man next to Haig, Colonel Hay. Now there was a disagreeable man. He was another hawkish aristocrat from Roberts' ring. French frowned at the 46-year-old officer that had been imposed upon him by Roberts – to spy on him. With his straight, slim face he had much in common with Kitchener, but Kitchener was a socially inept man from the Home Counties, while Hay was a dour Scot. A movement to his right drew French's attention. It was Lawrence shifting in his saddle. Conscious of the scrutiny that French had been applying to Haig and Hay, Lawrence flashed a quizzical smile at French. French returned a knowing smile and then turned his scrutiny on the man himself, much to his discomfort. Here, in contrast to the other two, was a man of a different character. He was much younger and he sat his horse with youthful enthusiasm, always ready to canter off on some great adventure.

French's contemplation of his companions was brought to an abrupt halt by a shout from across the river. A couple of khaki horsemen were galloping towards the river as though their lives depended upon reaching it. He could not make out what they were shouting, but they were obviously agitated in the extreme.

"It's Major Weston," commented Lawrence from behind his field glasses. And then they heard the rifle shots. The approaching men forced their horses at breakneck speed down the steep riverbank, through the clinging, dry sand of the wide riverbed and on through the shallow, brown water of the river towards Captain Henry Majendie of the 4th Rifle Brigade, at whom they were bellowing. French saw Majendie yell urgent orders to the men around him and then splash across the river to the opposite bank, followed by two dozen riflemen. They reached the top of the steep-sided bank just as a small troop of Boers, firing as they rode, broke over the ridge from which Major Weston had galloped.

Majendie and his riflemen returned fire and the Boers turned and retreated behind the ridge. French watched them dismount and throw themselves sloppily to the ground, from where they continued firing on the British lines. Major Weston ordered more men across the ford to engage the enemy. A sudden explosion a short distance from French made his horse jump and spattered him with a shower of sand and stones. The situation was more pressing than he had appreciated! The enemy had brought forward guns. French sent for Weston to get a report on the situation.

"Sir, I believe there are some four to five hundred Boers to our front," Weston reported. "I did not have time to reconnoitre for guns, but it sounds like they have at least three – probably located about two miles north of the river, on a couple of koppies – that is, a couple of small hills."

"Yes, thank you, Major, I am aware what a koppie is. You are to send a battery of the Royal Horse Artillery to this locale immediately to return the favour on the enemy's guns. Also, deploy a section of Ripley's mounted infantry to support the riflemen on the northern bank. This drift must not to fall into enemy hands. But we must cross the river without delay, so while you entertain this small band of merry men, I shall divert the rest of the division towards the ford at De Kiel's Drift further upriver. Do you have that, Major?"

"Yes, sir. RHA and MI to secure this ford."

"Thank you, Major. Proceed."

Weston spurred his horse towards the nearest battery of artillery emerging from the curtain of dust. French turned to Lawrence.

"Captain, the general order is to continue towards De Kiel's Drift. I want the nearest brigade of horse to establish themselves on the banks before the Boers do."

French drove his horse into a canter, followed by Haig and Hay. He was soon joined by Brigadier-General Gordon and the 9th and 16th Lancers. As Gordon came alongside him, French looked across.

"Ah, General, it seems our Dutch friends have arrived at the same party as us. We need to secure the next ford on the river. But be careful with the horses. We are going to need them over the next few days so save them, but get to that ford as quickly as you can."

"Yes sir."

Gordon turned in his saddle and waved the Lancers on. They pulled away with an easy stride. French and his companions slowed their horses to a more leisurely pace.

"What do you think, sir?" asked Haig.

"Not sure yet. They do not appear to be in any great numbers, but we need a clearer idea of their strength. I would like to know who is leading them. Let's see if we can take some prisoners."

When French arrived at De Kiel's Drift in the company of Hay, Haig and Lawrence they were approached by a captain of the Rimington Rangers. French took an instant dislike to the man, as he did to most officers of the irregular forces, but he held a particular distain for the officers and men of the so-called 'Rimington Tigers'. As far as French was concerned, when units started giving themselves aggressive-sounding names it usually meant they had got above their station. In his mind, Rimington's men, in particular, assumed an attitude of considerable self-importance and contempt towards discipline and etiquette. They ignored rank and seemed to look down on others as though they had the right to judge them. They, who had only seen action against savages and farmers, gave no recognition of the years of experience of the professional officer.

As the man drew up beside him, French looked away nonchalantly and said, as if talking to a servant, "What's our situation, Captain?"

"Captain Charles Rankin, Rimington Rangers reporting, sir," came the response, in an attempt to receive a more respectful reception.

French did not alter his gaze and not making eye contact, repeated impatiently, "Yes, yes. What is our situation?"

"Sir, the Lancers have taken De Kiel's Drift without opposition. The Rangers are reconnoitring the area to the north of the Riet River, between here and Waterval Drift. We believe the enemy number about a thousand mounted infantry and they have only two guns. Their guns have been driven back and no longer dominate our positions either here or at Waterval Drift. The enemy have occupied a collection of koppies, which are small hills, across the river to the north-east of our position."

This time French ignored the education he had received about koppies. "What are our casualties?"

"Good, sir. Only a small number wounded, but none seriously, except for Captain Majendie. Unfortunately, his wounds are likely to be fatal."

French turned to Rankin. "Is that the fellow who saw off the Boers this morning?"

"Yes sir."

French looked away again. "A pity, the captain showed a lot of guts this morning. He had potential. Colonel Hay, please keep me informed of his progress."

"Yes sir."

French smiled at the man's stiff-upper-lipped acceptance of such a menial task.

"Sir?" asked Rankin. "Do you wish to drive the enemy from the positions they presently hold?"

"No."

The disappointment showed on Rankin's face. French turned to look at him. My God, he thought, these men really were up for getting one over the Boer. It must be something personal.

"No captain, I do not wish to be distracted from our main objective? I shall use a contingent of Hannay's mounted infantry to keep them occupied and off our flanks. Do we know who the Boer commander is?"

"Not for certain, sir, but the name 'de Wet' has been suggested."

"De Wet? Humph, never heard of him. Good. He is obviously some junior officer, so Cronjé seems not to have taken our action seriously. Speed, gentlemen, speed remains the imperative. Thank you, captain, carry on." Turning to his general staff, he said: "Gentlemen, we need to get everyone and everything across the river as an absolute priority. Major Haig, I leave that to you." And to Lawrence he said, the irritation audible in his voice, "Captain, find out what has happened to our supply wagons. I managed to keep them out of the clutches of Roberts and Kitchener, but I've not seen or heard anything of their whereabouts. The men have rations, but there is no grass for the horses in this God forsaken and drought-ridden place. The poor wretches have been driven hard and have not eaten since two o'clock this morning. We have already lost too many and we will lose more if we do not get forage to them immediately. Do whatever you must to get feed for our horses."

He paused, was that everything? It would do for now. "If you need me, gentlemen, I shall establish my temporary headquarters...," French scanned the dry terrain, which shimmered in the heat, and eventually pointed to a low ridge south of De Kiel's Drift, "...on that ridge. Thank you. You may proceed."

Accompanied by Hay, he then rode a short distance along the ridge to a cluster of large boulders on which to take lunch and to study the dusty progress of his cavalry division. He was duly joined by Haig and Lawrence. The sun beat down mercilessly on their shoulders. French left his hat on to get some relief from its glare.

Rock hyraxes had taken cover in what little shade there was, from where they cautiously watched French and his colleagues. The horses stood close by, their hooves cocked, dozing and their heads drooped as if they were melting in the heat.

Shading his eyes against the dazzling sunlight that seemed to reflect from every surface, French looked north, through the heat haze. He could make out the line of the river slicing its way through the landscape in a steep-sided, flat-bottomed valley, some five hundred yards across. Several deep, rain-washed gullies, or dongas, incised the steep banks and ran away from the river into the dry veld. The slow, brown river occupied only a small part of the river valley, meandering, dividing and re-joining across its sandy bed. Beyond the river, the African landscape stretched out before him, a never-ending sea of yellow, brittle grass, from which rose several randomly scattered, flat-topped hillocks, the koppies that seemed to be on everyone's mind. They reminded him of small replicas of Table Mountain, which he had seen when sailing into Cape Town. Except for the koppies, the landscape seemed to be as flat as a pancake, but French examined it in detail through his field glasses, looking for the low ridgelines, such as the one he currently occupied, that provided an opportunity for surprise attacks by small bodies of mounted men, much like the one they had experienced that morning. From this distance, however, it was impossible to make any out.

Sweeping slowly to his left, past herds of zebra and wildebeest, French studied the landscape through which his division had marched. The dust cloud that had hung over his men and horses was starting to settle now that his main force had passed through and was waiting to cross the river. In the distance he noted a second cloud of dust billowing from the veld. It marked the slow progress of the infantry and supply wagons as they ground their way across the shimmering landscape.

The scene fascinated French. A mirage made it look as though a vast sea stretched out before him. The canvas covered wagons seemed like a flotilla of squat, square-sailed barges. From them the fine, grey dust rose into the sky like a plume of steam rising from the silver water that boiled around them. In all his time in the Sudan, he had never witnessed mirages as clear and extensive as this one. For a while he watched the wagons and infantry struggle through the desert 'ocean' and then swept his glasses along the route they would take. The route was scattered with black mounds which dotted the mirage like wave-smoothed rocks emerging from the water. But these were not rocks upon which unwary barges might flounder, they were something more horrific. They were the lifeless forms of dead horses. Many, many dead horses. Already the white-hot sky was peppered with ominous black shapes as vultures circled above, many already sweeping earthward to settle and feast on the corpses.

Impatient to take his mind off the loss of the horses, French turned to Haig.

"Any news about our supplies, Major?"

"No sir." Haig looked at him grimly. "Orders had been given for the supply train to move out as soon as possible, but Roberts would not let it proceed before that of the 6th Division. He wishes the infantry's wagons to move out with the men, before ours do."

"God!" exploded French.

Infuriated by the incompetence of his commander-in-chief, he found it increasingly difficult to contain his anger. But it would not do to be seen to be openly criticising his senior officer, especially in the presence of Hay – that would be a career-limiting move! So French kept his criticism to himself. But the man was an idiot! It must be apparent to all that Roberts' idea to centralise the army's transport was already having disastrous consequences. It meant that the entire supply system fell under the control of one man who could not hope to fully appreciate the needs of individual divisions across such a vast swathe of land. Enormous lines of wagons, which did not allow any flexibility in delivering the supplies to those who needed them, were the result. And why had it been ordained that the infantries' supplies had to be moved out before his own cavalry's supplies? It was completely nonsensical. He suspected that it was probably because he had tried to keep his supplies out of the hands of Roberts and Kitchener. Wolseley would not have been so petty. And what on earth was taking the infantry so long to get here? It was a shambles! Not only did he not have supplies, but he could not advance from his position and leave the enemy to his rear without securing the ford first. French stood up suddenly.

"Idle minds, gentlemen. If you have finished lunch, I suggest we do a tour of progress at the ford."

Progress at the ford did not help to ameliorate French's bad mood. From the top of the high bank, it was obvious that crossing the river was going to be an extremely arduous process. The gun carriages sank to their axles into the soft sand, which then clung around the wheels like a vice. Double-spanning the horses did not help and men crowded around the artillery pieces, pulling, pushing and heaving. Inch by inch the canons moved forward to a general chorus of encouragement from the soldiers watching from both banks. French noticed that several were shirtless because of the heat.

"Captain Lawrence, get those idiots to put their shirts back on. How many have to suffer sunstroke before they learn the dangers of this African sun?"

French looked over his shoulder at the sound of approaching horses, the dust raised by their hooves glowing golden in the late afternoon sunlight. A group of officers had detached themselves from the infantry division and were making their way towards him. He recognised the tall, straight figure of Kitchener riding slightly ahead of Kelly-Kenny, the commander of the 6th Division. Some way behind them were the infantry, and behind them was the first of the supply wagons.

"Good afternoon, sir," saluted Kitchener.

"Good evening," returned French. "Any news about *my* wagons? I see that you have taken care of your own!"

"Yes sir. You will be pleased to know that they were ordered to move out at eight this morning."

"Eight o'clock!" French erupted. "That was six hours after I left Ramdam. Do you understand how long I have been kicking my heels at this damned ford? Seven hours! The horses are done in and they have not eaten properly for over fifteen hours. We have already lost scores of animals and I am in danger of losing many more at this rate. Do you understand what effect this will have on our progress? Was there not an explicit demand that speed was key to the success of this flanking movement? Is this what Lord Roberts calls speed?"

French glared into Kitchener's piercing blue eyes. On horseback, Kitchener lost the advantage of his height. He remained silent and let French continue his angry diatribe. "Is it Lord Roberts' desire, as well as yours, that we *do* lose half the horses on the way to Kimberley? This is outrageous!"

Kitchener stared back at French with cold blue eyes. He still said nothing. Hay spoke up.

"Sir, it is imperative that the men have their rations."

French turned in his saddle and glared at Hay. He was incensed. Was his insubordination encouraged by his being a protégé of the commander-in-chief or a consequence of his aristocratic arrogance?

"Sir, you will hold your tongue in matters concerning the priorities of the infantry over my cavalry. This is not the Horse Guards on some Sunday parade! If we lose our horses, we lose the initiative and we shall lose the war. You, sir, will go down to the ford," French pointed emphatically to the river where a cannon was axle-deep in the sand, "and ensure my vehicles get across before this lot," he gestured at the approaching infantry's supply wagons.

Hay hesitated and glanced at Kitchener.

"Colonel," French snapped, "I am the senior officer here! You will do as *I* order."

Kitchener broke eye contact with Hay. Hay wheeled his horse round and galloped down the slope towards the river, from where the increasingly frantic shouts of men and the noise of distressed draft animals could be heard. French turned on Kitchener.

"And you, General, you are to make sure that your wagons do not delay my cavalry."

Kitchener stared at French. He did not appreciate the tone but knew the short, Irish cavalryman held a field rank above his own.

"Yes sir, I have done so already."

French was taken aback. "You have?"

"Yes sir. I have directed the infantry and their supplies to this ford at De Kiel's Drift and your wagons to cross at Waterval Drift."

French pondered this information, and then angrily queried the logic. "But, General, my horses are *here*, at De Kiel's Drift?"

"Indeed, sir. So I have instructed the wagons to cross the river and then to make towards *this* ford." French ignored the impudent emphasis. "And I have come to inform you of the fact and suggest that once your men are across the river that you travel towards Waterval Drift and intercept the wagons travelling towards you."

French glowered at Kitchener. The man had got one over him. "Good. Nevertheless, I shall hold you responsible for any further loss of horses that we suffer. Good day."

After a perfunctory salute at his superior officer Kitchener turned his horse and trotted towards the infantry and its wagons. Kelly-Kenny followed.

Tuesday 13 February 1900

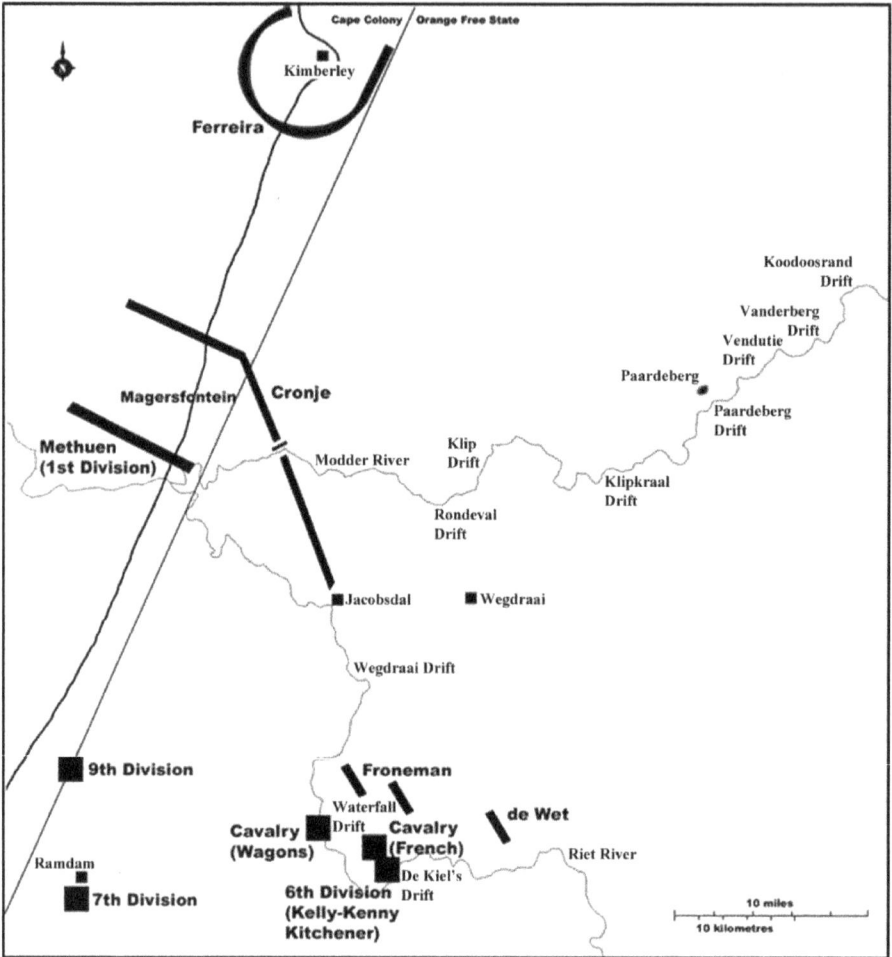

Map 4: Morning of 13 February 1900

General Christiaan Rudolf de Wet

General Christiaan Rudolf de Wet, his fashionable felt hat tipped back on his head to accommodate his field glasses, examined the apparent mayhem below him. It was still before ten o'clock, but already the sun was showing its intent of scorching the veldt again and the khaki-clad figures in his view were already starting to quiver as the cool morning gave way to the developing heat wave.

De Wet and his three hundred burghers showed no urgency in taking cover from the enemy. There was no need. The English army had shown a complete disregard for their presence on the kopje, which they had occupied before dawn. Even yesterday, any contact the English had made had been derisory, and de Wet knew there was nothing his tiny force could do to encourage more meaningful action and even if the English did attack he would have no choice but to flee, because of the inadequate size of his force. His commando, together with that of General Froneman, who occupied the kopjes overlooking Waterval Drift, numbered less than five hundred. In contrast, swarming over the veldt below them were at least five thousand English cavalrymen and thousands more infantrymen. The whole, broad sweep of the landscape between De Kiel's and Waterval Drifts was a chaotic sea of humanity, horses, mules and oxen. The sound of shouting men and lowing cattle drifted up to him on the warming air.

Beside him, some with their own glasses trained on the commotion below, stood General C.J. de Villiers, Commandants Grobler of Fauresmith and Lubbe of Jacobsdal, and his younger brother, General Piet de Wet of the Bethlehem Commando.

"What do you think?" de Wet asked no one in particular.

"There's a hell of a lot of them," came the concerned response from Grobler.

"Looks like total chaos to me," laughed his brother.

"Chaos, yes," agreed de Villiers, "but when they sort themselves out we are in trouble. They must have cleared every one of their colonies to find all those men and horses."

"Any suggestions on what we do?" enquired de Wet, still looking through his glasses. "They outnumber us and Froneman's forces by over ten to one."

"Well, they must be staying where they are today." Said de Villiers. "If they had planned to move on, they would have done so already. They would be foolish to start marching now, just as the day is heating up. The greatest concern for the English must be keeping their fancy horses in good shape, and they will be unlikely to cope with another long march without a rest. That will slow them down."

"I agree," said Grobler, and the other two nodded in agreement.

"Hmm," reflected de Wet. "You may be right, but we must not be complacent. We do seem to have something different here. It is the first time the English have moved so far from the railway."

"Yes, and as a result they are completely dependent on wagons for their supplies. That makes them vulnerable," commented de Villiers.

De Wet nodded. "They will also need a lot of water. So they will need to stay with the river when they do get going, in which case they could march upstream to Koofiefontein and on to Fauresmith. That would take them further into the Free State and to Bloemfontein. Or they could go in the opposite direction to Jacobsdal, to turn Cronjé's left flank."

"Or they could move directly north, via Wegdraai, to relieve Kimberley," de Villiers added. "But I agree, that would be an unlikely choice. It would take them away from the river and result in an unacceptable loss of horses. Even the English must realise that. They already have a trail of dead animals behind them from yesterday's march. To expect horses to undertake an even longer march across an even bigger expanse of waterless veldt would be foolhardy."

There were general murmurs of agreement.

"So which is it?" De Wet looked at his companions. They shrugged their shoulders in answer. "So all we can do is wait, watch and react. Yet regardless of what they do, there is nothing we can do with our current numbers."

"Of course we need more men," concurred de Villiers.

There was emphatic agreement among the other officers. De Wet's brother looked at him. "What was the result of sending Commandant Scheepers to General Cronjé to ask for reinforcements?"

De Villiers answered for de Wet. "He said: 'Are you afraid of a few English? Just go and shoot them and catch them when they run.' And then he laughed." De Villiers shook his head unhappily, "The Lion of Potchefstroom continues to use his heart and not his brains." The comment did not receive the same consensus as his previous remarks. Such disrespect towards their hero general did not go down well with many burghers and Lubbe came to Cronjé's defence.

"Oom Piet gave the Khakis a lesson in '81 and has done so again this time. We cannot presume to understand the situation any better than he does."

De Wet, thinking that the last thing he needed was to be distracted by a discussion about the merits of the commander-in-chief, intervened.

"Gentlemen, there is no doubt about Oom Piet's abilities and he has many things to consider, both in securing the line against Methuen at Magersfontein and in dealing with what we are facing here. The fact is that the general does not feel he can offer us any reinforcements, so we have to do the best we can. At present, that is to keep an eye on the situation and keep him informed. Hopefully he will be able to provide us with some additional men and guns later. Once it is clear what the English plans are, I shall ask him again. Until then, please ensure that we are aware of *everything* the English do. We shall reconvene after lunch, unless something serious happens before that. So please keep close at hand. Thank you, gentlemen."

As they turned to go de Wet caught de Villiers' eye and the man hung back.

"The situation is extremely serious," de Wet concluded to de Villiers, who nodded grimly in agreement. "I have lost count of the number of times I, de la Rey and others, including our foreign officers, have tried to convince Oom Piet of the danger of being out-flanked, but he will not be moved. Indeed, I believe my insistence on this issue is part of the reason he sent me away from his camp.

"Of course I understand his reasons. If we keep falling back, as we have been, we will eventually fall back all the way to Bloemfontein. I understand that completely. But now the English have come in through the back door and I believe that Methuen is no longer the key to this new English plan. Methuen has not made a direct attack on us for days now; he just keeps bombing us. The problem is that such bombing is the normal English tactic before a full attack, and so Methuen keeps Oom Piet preoccupied and the General feels compelled to keep up his strength on the Magersfontein front. But we have another problem. Even if Oom Piet did send us some reinforcements, how many could he spare? Even if he sent his entire commando of four thousand to us it may not be enough to hold these English back." De Wet swept an arm across the veldt at the ant-like army below him. "And it would mean there would be no one to hold Methuen back once he realised we had left Magersfontein. They seem to have us by the balls!" he exclaimed angrily.

De Villiers did not answer immediately, but looked towards the drift, over which an unending stream of horses, wagons and khakis were pouring. "It's not good," was all he could think to say. After a pause, he repeated, "It's not good at all. What to do, hey?"

The two men stood side by side staring out over their veldt, de Wet absent-mindedly tugging at his small, well-trimmed beard. The English had now been within the Orange Free State for two days. What to do was becoming an even more important question than which direction the English would take once they got moving.

The real concern to de Wet was the size of the English army. It had grown in number like a plague of rats after a good harvest, but then the English had the whole world from which to recruit soldiers – even the Canadians had sent regiments. De Wet assumed it was the English Canadians who are fighting rather than the French Canadians; after all, France took the Republics' side in this matter. Then again, so did Germany, but she had not sent any forces in support and the Republics had had to pay top-dollar for their Mauser rifles. So, de Wet concluded, the Republics were alone against half the world.

"Something is happening down there."

De Villiers' observation brought de Wet back to the English forces. There was now a definite pattern to the manoeuvres by the river.

"Can you fetch the others?" requested de Wet, and, taking up his glasses, he scrutinised the enemy troops on the veldt below him. They were definitely not going upriver, he noted. Both the cavalry and infantry were moving off together. How many would they leave behind to secure the drift? Maybe it would be possible to cut their supply lines? They must be aware of that danger. He doubted whether the Afrikander army would be able to take back the drift.

"My God, it's like a black mamba uncoiling itself."

De Wet looked up from his glasses. The others had joined him and it was his brother who had spoken. It was a good analogy, thought de Wet, a huge snake striking at the heart of its prey.

"Why are they leaving so late?" continued his brother. "This is madness. Just as it is starting to get hot they head out. The sun must have got to them."

"Crazy idiots," concurred Grobler. "They are fools, but that is to our benefit. They will wear their animals out. By the end of the day their horses will be no use to the cavalry. We must thank God that the suffering of those poor animals will strengthen our hand."

The group of men continued to watch their enemy from under their slouch hats. The general movement was in a downstream direction.

"At least Fauresmith is not the target," said Grobler with relief.

"So it's Jacobsdal then," interjected Lubbe grimly.

Grobler frowned in sympathy. "It may not be. They might still strike out for Wegdraai and Kimberley." But it was a forlorn hope. The English would not be that stupid, surely? "Wherever they do decide to go, we'll stop them before they get there," he said, with false confidence in his voice.

So, thought de Wet, it was clear to all of them that there was nothing they could do. But that was not good enough. No! He would not stand here and do nothing.

"There is no need for us to stay here. Piet, find Scheepers. Return with him to General Cronjé. Inform him that Jacobsdal is threatened. Ask him for reinforcements and guns so that we can delay the advance of the English. He will also need to strengthen the defence of Jacobsdal. Lubbe, tell Froneman to fall back and meet us at Wegdraai Drift; we need to join forces if we are to be effective. The rest of you prepare to leave. We have to follow the English and keep an eye on things, and harass their flanks as much as possible. Now go!"

De Wet watched as burghers, roused from their cooking fires, stuffed pieces of partly cooked meat into their mouths and stormjager cakes into their satchels and rushed around as they broke camp. Their disorderliness entertained de Wet for a few minutes, but could not distract him indefinitely from the more pressing matters on the veldt below. It was not an encouraging sight.

What did Cronjé expect him to do? He was sent to stop the English cavalry with only five hundred men. It was sheer madness to pit such a small force against this huge English army. It was like using a fly swat on a swarm of locusts. He had only asked for an additional one hundred and fifty men, and even that would have enabled a mere pin-prick in the flanks of the massed army seething across the veldt, but still Cronjé had refused. There were simply not enough burghers to match the numbers of English soldiers.

De Wet laughed out loud in frustration – "just catch them when they run!" The English did not look like they would be running away any time soon. There would definitely be no chasing the English today. Looking at the size of their army there would not be any chasing them in the future. Somehow the Afrikander army had to find some edge over the English. Maybe, if they could use the land to their advantage. He had been wandering the veldt since he was no bigger than a duiker. He knew its virtues and its dangers like the back of his hand. Every Afrikander did. They could strike and disappear like the morning mist in this vast land. There had to be a better way to beat the English and it had to be found.

But before then he needed time to convince Cronjé to fall back from Magersfontein to a new defensive position. He had to use his small commando to slow the English down. He must keep them out of sight. Hit and run. Target their flanks and disrupt their supply routes. He needed to keep the English constantly looking over their shoulders, and keep them worrying about their supplies.

De Wet strode purposefully down the kopje. He vaulted on to Fleur, his white Arab. He turned and glared at his men. They were ready. He nudged his heels into the horse's flanks and trotted away from the kopje and deeper into his beloved Orange Free State – that part which had not yet been soiled by the tramp of the English invaders. His commando followed.

Major Michael Frederic Rimington

Major Michael Frederic Rimington, darkly sunburnt, tall, lean and wiry, sat in his saddle with careless ease, as though perfectly part of his horse. He and half a dozen of his 'catch-'em-alive-o' irregular rangers occupied the southern, lower slope of a koppie. The hordes of regular cavalry inched northwards and passed them on either side of the koppie like a river eddying around an island. To the west, beyond one arm of the crawling cavalry and about a mile distant squatted a second koppie. Dark shapes silhouetted against the white early afternoon sky told Rimington that a cluster of mounted infantry was also occupying the slopes of that koppie.

Although the column inched between them at snail's pace it still sent an immense pall of dust into the sky that was visible for miles. To Rimington's frustration there was an additional towering column of black smoke that was billowing up into the hot atmosphere. The fire must have been started by some idiot discarding a lit match or burning cigarette. A warm breeze fanned the flames and drove them away from Rimington, but towards the cavalry. The flames crackled through the vegetation, leaping and dancing four or five feet into the air. Hares and other small mammals, which had lain low, hidden from the herd of passing cavalry, now broke cover to escape and insects swarmed from the grass in front of the fire, attracting birds which flittered about the flames snatching at their fleeing prey.

The horses, already suffering from heat exhaustion and a lack of water, were thrown into further distress by their fear of the fire. They shied away from it, pushing and shoving into neighbouring animals and causing disorder among the ranks. As a result, the cavalry was forced away from the flames and closer to the distant koppie.

Suddenly, a crack of gunfire echoed across the veld from the direction of the second koppie. Rimington took up his field glasses to see consternation among the mounted infantry posted on its slopes. He saw a man tumbled from his horse and then a second. The riders erupted into action. They drove their horses down the slope of the koppie towards the main body of the cavalry. As they dashed away a commando of Boers burst over the sky line, their Mausers snapping.

71

The Boers did not follow the mounted infantry, but pulled their horses up and proceeded to pour bullets into the British lines. Their behaviour was almost casual. They knew they were safe as long as the element of surprise caused mayhem within the British troops. Rimington watched as this new threat caused further havoc among the column of cavalry.

The horsemen involuntarily drew away from the attacking enemy, while from the opposite direction horses continued to shy away from the fire. The resultant chaos caused the distressed horses to panic and to rear and buck, throwing their riders. Above the crack of the rifles and the crackle of the flames Rimington could hear the terrified whinnying of horses, the howls of injured men and the shouted obscenities of those trying to establish order out of the confusion.

It was not clear to Rimington whether the men he saw falling had been shot or were simply thrown by their panicking horses. Eventually, an officer was able to make himself heard above the din of the terrified horses and disoriented men. Gesticulating wildly, he organised a counter-attack, and he and a dozen men galloped at the Boers. The sight of the approaching lancers proved to be a sufficient deterrent. The Boers turned and galloped back the way they had come, melting into the landscape as quickly as they had appeared.

Rimington frowned. It had been a wonderful piece of opportunism, he reflected, using the bush fire to limit the manoeuvrability of the cavalry. It was just the sort of thing he would have done in the circumstances, and was exactly the sort of tactic that the Boers should be adopting. They simply did not have enough men to win the big, set-piece battles against the might of the British army. Instead of getting bogged down in trenches, if they worked to their strengths of mobility and fleetness against their ponderous foe, then the British officers would really have something to worry about. That's when the British would realise that their current problems were nothing more than a Sunday picnic. Rimington knew the Boers were not stupid. They would learn, and then he knew mobility would be everything. Rimington leant forward to fondly pat the neck of his horse. "Then you will come into your own, my beauty."

But if the Boers did move into a more effective style of mobile warfare, the British cavalry would have no horses of any worth left to counter the change in tactics, because, for all General French's excellent skills in horsemanship and his constant fretting about the welfare of his horses, he was still pushing them beyond endurance. He must have lost over five hundred horses since the march had begun and they were only halfway to their goal. The situation was not helped by the fact that the supply system was extremely chaotic, and although prioritising the men rather than the horses was more humane, it was militarily short-sighted, especially against an enemy like the Boer, who valued their horses greatly. Rimington concluded that Roberts would come to regret the neglect of his horses.

The counterpoint, he acknowledged, was that Roberts really did care about the welfare of his men and was popular as a result. He had even made the trip to Waterval Drift overnight to congratulate them for reaching the ford so expeditiously. There was no doubt he was a charmer, and picking out the Highland Brigade for special attention – to remind them of the marvellous experiences they shared in India – was a masterstroke. The Scots would now give their all for him, and the other regiments would do their utmost to outdo the Highlanders. As a result, Rimington had no doubt, there would be a few posthumous Victoria Crosses sent to grieving families before the week was out. But they would not be blaming Roberts. No, he would be the hero who looked after the well-being of their fallen sons.

Rimington saw one of the cavalry horses in the column stumble and valiantly regain itself. The horses, on the other hand, suffered in silence and without official recognition or reward. Rimington contemplated the implications of the fact that the cavalry's supply wagons had not arrived at Watervall Drift until after midnight. He recalled French's fury and how he had refused to leave the Riet River until the horses were properly fed. As a result, the cavalry had not continued their march until the heat of the day was upon them and now they were also being roasted by a fire caused by some fool discarding his fag-end.

Damn, it was hot! He removed his slouch hat, wiped his wet forehead with his sleeve and then beat the dust from his hat on his thigh, and straightened the band of leopard skin that was wrapped around it. It was this band that gave his unit the nickname 'Rimington's Tigers'. Rimington replaced his hat and watched the cavalry horses struggling across the burning veld, heading towards the northern horizon that danced in the heat. At least, he thought, they had already completed twenty miles that day, which left another ten before they reached Klip Drift. The opportunity for taking on water at Wegdraai Farm was behind them. Now there was only sun and dust to keep them company and the occasional Boer commando to liven things up.

Lifting his field glasses to his eyes, he scanned the oven-hot, vibrating landscape. To the south he could just make out the town of Jacobsdal, which they had simply bypassed. A line of telegraph poles marched from Jacobsdal across the veld and over the shoulder of land occupied by Rimington and his men, and continued on to Bloemfontein, but the cable that had once connected them now lay useless on the ground. The man who had cut it scrambled down the pole and dropped on to the dusty ground. Rimington grinned. That would get the Boers in Jacobsdal excited. He imagined the shock on the face of the Boer telegraph operator when he realised they had been cut off from the rest of their world. Rimington waved his hand in front of his face to drive the flies away and turned to Captain Charles Rankin.

"Can't stop here all day. We have to reach the ford 'with all due speed'. Off we go, but preserve the horses."

He wheeled his horse round and moved off to the north at a determined, but easy pace.

Rimington consulted his watch. Three hours had passed since their last rest. Having gone scouting some way ahead, the Tigers had now returned to the main body of the cavalry. The dust-shrouded horsemen seemed to be moving even more slowly than before. He lent casually on the pommel of his saddle, watching the approaching group of dusty officers. In the front was the compact figure of General French. Rimington studied the general as he guided his horse between the concrete-hard anthills and small rocks scattered among the bone-dry grass. He had to agree that the old man led by example; there was no stopping him. Not for him to be dragged along in a covered wagon. No, he led from the front, and he would be as parched as his men.

"So what do we have, Major?" French asked without any preliminaries.

Rimington sat up, straightening his long, thin torso as he answered. It was always good to show some respect to these traditional types.

"Sir, we have a gang of Boers dug in on top of a koppie between us and the river, about five hundred men in all, with two guns, commanded by de Wet. He has chosen a good, tight spot, I'll give him that, but with sufficient men and a few guns we'll soon have him scuttling back to the other side of the river."

"De Wet, you say? Wasn't he the fellow who gave us a bit of stick down on the Riet River?"

"I believe it was, sir."

"Hmm, I can see that this de Wet has the propensity to be an irritation."

"Only a small irritation, I suggest, sir. If you wish, I could swat him off the hill for you."

"Tempting though that is, Major, we must not allow ourselves to be distracted from our main purpose, which is to take the fords across the Modder. May I see your map?"

Rimington drew up alongside French and handed over the weather-beaten parchment. French ran his dusty, but manicured, finger along the hand-drawn line of the Modder River.

"Here's what we'll do. We'll swing right on a decoy march east, towards Paardeberg. Once we've passed the koppies occupied by the Boers, General Broadwood will extend our lines to the north, towards the Modder River, but we will all continue marching in an easterly direction. We need to convince this de Wet that we are making for Paardeberg to secure the river crossings there. If he has any sense, he will retreat and defend those fords, because he knows that if we take them, we can cut off General Cronjé's retreat to Bloemfontein. Your part, Major," French looked directly at Rimington, who returned the look. French's face hardened. "Is to *allow* de Wet to get away. As soon as you believe he is committed to Paardeberg, let me know." French stopped and waited.

"Yes sir. Let you know as soon as de Wet is out of the picture."

"Precisely, Major. General Broadwood will then double-back with the 12th Lancers and capture Rondeval Drift, while I shall swing north again and take Klip Drift. Good, that's settled."

French turned to Haig.

"Major, issue the general order for a wheel to the right and inform General Broadwood of his orders."

75

French handed Rimington his map with a dismissive nod. As he moved away Rimington ended up next to one of French's officers.

"Are they doing any better with the supplies today, Lieutenant?"

"Can't say for the moment, sir. Some damned idiot set the veld on fire and burnt our telegraph cable back to HQ, so we've had to send someone back to find out. He's not returned yet, sir."

"Thank you, Lieutenant." Rimington pulled his horse away. He smiled ironically, so it was not only the Boer's telegraph operator who got a surprise today.

From his vantage point, Rimington and his men watched the trail of dust speeding across the veld. The plan had worked. A greater part of the Boer commando was racing towards Paardeberg. Although he could not make out the individuals, Rimington suspected that de Wet, being in command, would be with this larger contingent of men. He noted the fine white horse at the front of the commando. Judging by the size of the commando Rimington concluded that de Wet must have left some men to help guard the fords at Rondeval and Klip Drifts, but how many was the question. In fact, Rimington was generally surprised by the small number of Boers he had seen over the last two days. Ordinarily, they would be crawling all over the veld, if only to keep an eye on what was going on. He had come to respect the Boers' scouting skills, especially those of a certain Captain Dannie Theron, who was already making quite a name for himself.

So what was going on, he asked himself. It was impossible to hide the fact that tens of thousands of men, horses and wagons were tramping through the Orange Free State, but they had been opposed by no more than five hundred men and a couple of guns. The Boers must understand what was happening by now. Had the war reached the point of being a simple numbers game? Had they insufficient men to both occupy Magersfontein *and* keep French and the following infantry at bay? What was old Cronjé up to? Well, all would become clear soon. The intelligence from his rangers was that there was a large laager of wagons at Klip Drift and there were definitely Boers occupying the banks. How many was unknown, but they were well dug in. French was taking a bit of a gamble with his idea of rushing the Modder River.

Rimington

Rimington decided that the enemy's dust trail had progressed far enough to the east. He touched the sides of his horse with his heels. It was time to let General French know he could turn back towards the river.

Major Rimington lounged in the shade of a sallow tree on a carefully arranged stack of boxes that were labelled 'Biscuits' but, he had already discovered, contained Mauser ammunition. The brown Modder River lazily weaved its way through undulating sandbars to his right. Rimington watched the antics of a troop of vervet monkeys chattering in the branches above him. He sliced strips of meat from a piece of biltong he had liberated from one of the wagons that the Boers had abandoned as they had fled from their positions on the Klip Drift. In the face of the British charge, they had scarpered. With him sat Captain Rankin and others in an equally relaxed attitude, while around them cavalrymen from the regular forces busied themselves securing and improving the defences of their newly acquired position on the northern banks of the Modder River. In the end, crossing the river had been remarkably easy. Rimington was unperturbed that he had missed the fun of the charge; it had been an altogether disappointing affair.

The Boers had scattered like chaff in a breeze. But then there had only been a handful of them and they had continued firing until there was no option except to run. The most impressive aspect of the engagement was that the cavalry's horses had been able to gallop at all. Rimington's gaze fell on some horses feeding on forage taken from the Boer wagons. Of all the animals on God's earth, he mused, the horse has to be His greatest creation.

"He's got that look in his eye again," smirked Rankin. "Ye gods, if it was legal, I suspect you'd marry a horse."

This caused raucous hilarity from the other Tigers. Rimington laughed along with his men.

"All I can say is thank God the Boers travel to war with their supplies and know how to treat their horses. Old Bobs would do well to take leaf out of their book."

"They've only got one book." said Rankin. "*The Book*! And I don't remember anything in the Bible about how to care for horses."

"With care and respect, I think you'll find."

"Well said."

A silence fell over the men, until Lieutenant John James Roach said, "I'm off to see what else we can salvage from the wagons, before the foot monkeys arrive and take it all? Anyone coming?"

Rimington watched his men as they walked towards the wagons, joshing and pushing each other like mates on a county walk. But this was not a country walk. They were involved in something far more serious, as was evidenced by their khaki uniforms and slouch hats with their flash of yellow and black, and the chaos of the abandoned Boer camp, littered as it was with a tumble of broken cases from which spilled tinned meat, biscuits and thousands of bullets.

Wednesday 14 February 1900

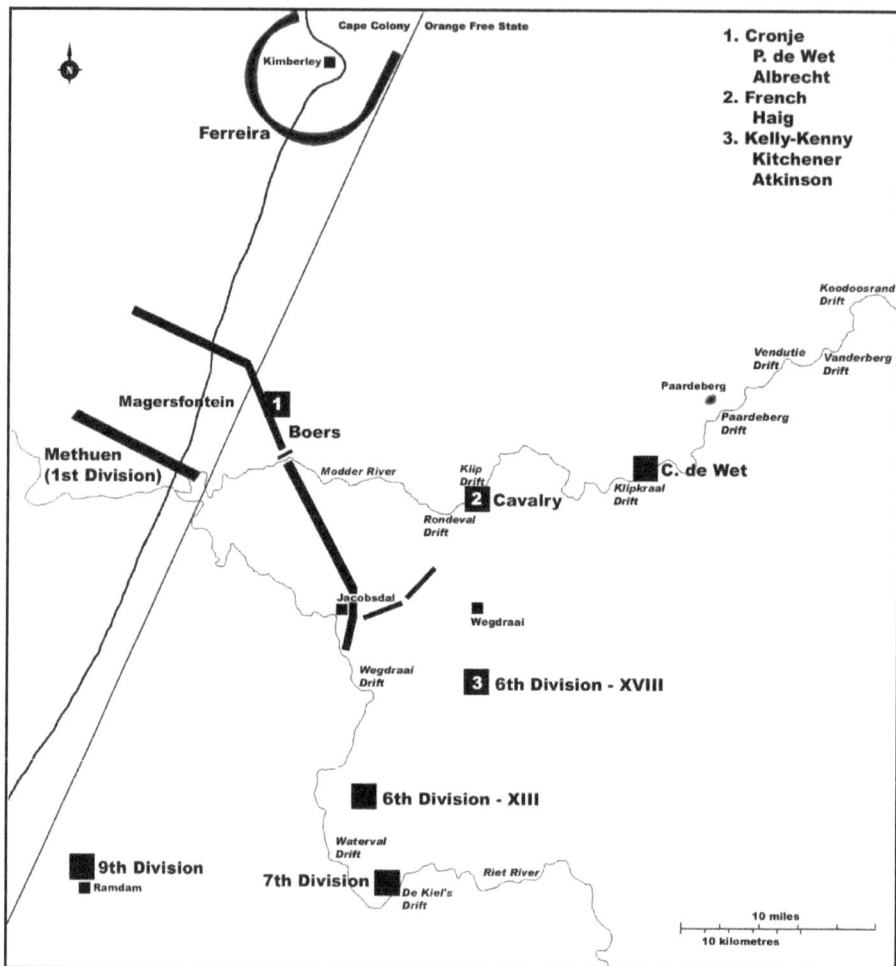

Map 5: Morning of 14 February 1900

General Pieter Arnoldus Cronjé

General Pieter Arnoldus Cronjé was in a foul temper. He sat on this three-legged trek stool scowling over his morning coffee, breathing in the aroma as it rose, hot, from his mug. On a separate stool, set between his knees, lay his Bible, open at the Book of Psalms. He glared at the words. They offered no comfort to him this morning. The coolness of the dawn was already burning off and the flies, which he could normally ignore, were starting to irritate him with their persistent buzzing around his head. He took a careless mouthful of his coffee, which scalded his mouth, and he slammed it down on to the ground, in turn scalding his hand.

"Samuel, you damn fool. Are you trying to kill me? Bring me some coffee that I am able to drink!"

"Yes, Inkosi."

Cronjé returned to his brooding. Those damned English. What the hell were they up to? What arrogance! Christiaan de Wet had sat astride their advance twice and they had simply ignored him – bypassed him as though he was not there. He had allowed the English to get round Jacobsdal and cut communication with Bloemfontein, and then he had ridden away and hid himself on some kopje while his brother Piet had simply let the English saunter across the Modder as if they owned the river.

He stared at the open book in front of him. He had not been able to concentrate on it at all this morning. It had offered him no insight, but that was hardly surprising because he was not in the right frame of mind. How could he be expected to hear the Lord's words while all those around him acted like idiots? He looked up at the sound of footsteps coming towards him. It was General Piet de Wet, the man who had abandoned the laager at Klip Drift and at whom, together with his brother, Cronjé's ire was directed. Seeing his approach did not improve Cronjé's mood.

De Wet removed his hat and clutched it in front of him.

"Oom Piet."

"Yes," came the growled response.

"The War Council has gathered."

"Has it?"

Not sure what the most placating response was, de Wet remained silent.

"I'll be there," Cronjé snapped with a dismissive wave of his hand.

De Wet turned and walked back to the cluster of men from which he had just come. Cronjé watched him walk away. A timid fellow, that de Wet, not one to perform well under pressure. Not like his brother, Christiaan, who was a leopard of a man. Cronjé had to admit, despite his current frustration with him, that Christiaan had a good military brain and he would fight to the bitter end. Cronjé was not so sure about Piet. He would need to make sure that Piet did not end up leading any situations where he might be placed in a difficult position. He would need to keep him to the back or in the centre and definitely away from the flanks – that would just be asking for them to be turned. As de Wet reached the group of men, they parted to include him in the circle. The heated conversation that had been going on continued with renewed vigour.

Conspiring against me? scowled Cronjé to himself. Thinking of voting me out? He would have none of that. Cronjé stood up, jammed his slouch hat onto his head and walked determinedly towards the gathered men. As he got nearer, he changed his scowl into a look designed to show them that he was the person in charge. The War Council became less animated as he approached and the circle opened for him well before he arrived. He stopped in the gap. His grey eyes roamed around the circle of men and he stared into the face of each man in turn. He was now calm and contained and he held the gaze of any man who dared to look him directly in the eye, eventually forcing them to break eye contact. *He* was in control of the meeting and they were to know it.

"Neef Piet," he looked suddenly at de Wet, "explain to us again what happened yesterday."

"Oom Piet, five thousand cavalry and mounted infantry, with twenty guns, crossed the Modder at Klip Drift and Rondeval Drift."

"And how do you know this?"

"I was there, Oom Piet."

"And so why are you here? Should you not be on the river bank holding the enemy back?"

Cronjé

De Wet looked at Cronjé in amazement. He had only stopped at Klip Drift briefly on his way from his brother's commando *en route* to see Cronjé. He had not been in charge of defending the drift. He had just happened to be there when hundreds of English had suddenly appeared and charged the Afrikander emplacement on the river. And although their numbers had not been sufficient to hold the river, he and the others had stayed and fired valiantly as long as it had been possible. Ultimately, however, they had been compelled to abandon the drift. In fact, some had stayed too long and had ended up being captured. De Wet went to answer, to defend himself, but stopped. He was being accused of cowardice, but to try and explain himself would infer that his actions needed defending, and may be interpreted by Cronjé as insubordination, incurring the wrath of the most respected general of the South African Republic. He did not have confidence that the others would support him should he attempt to argue with this great man. He felt a flush coming to his cheeks and he looked down so that the brim of his hat would hide his humiliation.

"There were too many," was all he could manage.

"Too many, hey? So, what's to be done?" demanded Cronjé. It was a rhetorical question. "I say we stay here. Why? Because the might of the English army is still in front of us, at Magersfontein. They shell us constantly, every day, morning till night. And just like every other time, they will eventually march towards us to their deaths. They have done it before. They will do it again. They are a professional army. They have manuals for everything. They are not taught to think. They are taught to do. And they do everything by the book!"

"But, Oom Piet this is different. They have marched five thousand cavalry over fifty miles around our flank in just two days. Now they are almost behind us. Surely, you agree this is different."

"Extravagant yes, but different no. This Roberts is a great showman. He marched an army across Asia and beat a band of Indians, and he thinks to deceive us by apparently using the same trick. But this is not Asia and we are not Indians. Five thousand horses, you say. But they are gentlemen's horses, bred for fox hunting and polo matches. If Neef Piet had stayed at the drift long enough, he would have seen that those horses were nothing but living skeletons; they will not be capable of walking, let alone charging and driving away well-armed Afrikander soldiers. What do you say, Neef Piet? What did their horses look like?"

"I did not notice, Oom Piet."

"He did not notice," repeated Cronjé sarcastically. "But *you* should know how the English fight," he continued. "This is not your first war against them. Both you and your brother were with me at Majuba Hill. We beat the English then with just a handful of old muzzle-loading rifles. But this, this is a different war. They are actually trying to win this one. So imagine their humiliation when we beat them again. It will be unbearable for them. The whole world knows about this war. When they lose, they will be the laughing stock of the world. 'Beaten by farmers!' Ha, it will destroy their empire! Yes, they are really trying to win this war. They're desperate and they will do anything. This is just a ruse and one that has been very expensive in horse flesh. And I shall not be fooled. Roberts' main forces are still in front of us at Magersfontein and if we move out of our trenches to attack those decrepit horsemen they will throw everything they have at our rear."

"Oom Piet, I agree that does make sense, but what of the infantry that is also marching from Waterval Drift?"

"Aagh, that is nothing but a sideshow. Nevertheless, I have strengthened our left flank at Jacobsdal with five hundred men. They are all I can spare as General de Wet still has a large number of my burghers, with whom he was supposed to stop the English crossing the Riet River."

"Five hundred does not seem many against the thousands that are marching on Jacobsdal."

"It is all that will be needed. As with their cavalry, the English infantry is being force-marched without water. But our men will be fresh and refreshed, and dug into trenches and hidden in buildings. By the time the English reach Jacobsdal they will be ready to surrender."

There was a general grumble of disbelief.

"Is it not so?" demanded Cronjé.

It was Albrecht who answered.

"General, the British soldiers are certainly being forced to march for miles in the heat and without water. Many will suffer and many will collapse from exhaustion, but it is unlikely that they will surrender. That is not their way. Their pride will not allow them to."

"That is true for the regular English soldier, but," countered Cronjé, "there are many irregulars, traitors from the Cape Colony and Uitlanders, who have fled our gold mines to fight for the enemy, and civilians from the English empire, such as Australians and Canadians. They will not be used to war, and they will panic as soon as they realise that we have a cause and we will not treat them any differently from other members of the enemy forces. Their panic will be contagious, and it will cause uncertainty in the ranks of the regular army. No army can fight if it fears part of its strength is liable to run away at the slightest opportunity."

"But still, five hundred?"

Cronjé snapped. "Tell me! What would you have me do? I have four thousand men to defend the western border of our Republics. I have fifty thousand men and horses in front of me trying to get to Kimberley and into our Republics. And now I have this ruse of a few tired men wandering around the veldt on my flank. If I take men from Magersfontein to defend my flank, I am weakened against the frontal attack. If we leave the protection of our trenches, we will be exposed to an attack from Methuen. I do not know where Christiaan de Wet has gone with five hundred of my burghers, and the commandant who should have stopped the English advancing over the Modder is standing beside me." Cronjé threw a sour look at de Wet. "So tell me, what am I to do?"

He glared at the men around him. Some looked at Albrecht, but he, being both a foreigner and a member of the Free State forces, knew his influence with this Transvaal general had run its course and would not be sufficient to turn the argument. De Wet also kept silent.

"We should withdraw and set up a new defensive line further along the Modder, or beyond at Poplar Grove, to prevent the English reaching Bloemfontein," came the eventual reply from another member of the Council.

"The English are not interested in Bloemfontein yet," retorted Cronjé. "Their first wish is to relieve Kimberley. Why do you think Methuen has been pushing us all the way up the railway line in the direction of that damned town? If we fall back along the Modder, the door will be open to Kimberley. They will stroll in without a shot being fired and the English newspapers will be crowing their triumph around the world. The impact on the Afrikander people will be disastrous. All our burghers will simply go home out of disgust. Entrenched at Magersfontein, we are at least keeping the main English forces at bay. No, we stay at Magersfontein."

Silence.

"Oom Piet?" It was de Wet who spoke.

"Yes!"

"With our leaving Klip Drift," de Wet started cautiously, "we now have no commandos between the English at Klip Drift and Kimberley."

"Yes," responded Cronjé acerbically, "that was why it was important to hold the drift!"

De Wet hesitated. "Are we to leave the English to simply march on to Kimberley then?"

"Of course not, that is the basis of my determination to stay at Magersfontein. I have not completely ignored their presence! But I am not concerned. The English have already destroyed their horses. They will not make it to Kimberley. To do so they have to find a way onto the plateau that sits between them and Kimberley. There are only two routes up to the plateau: one to the west, which will bring them towards us, and we will stop them, and one to the east via Paardeberg, but the distance will be too great for their horses. They will be dead before they can make it to Kimberley."

Albrecht now spoke. "Actually, General, there is a third, more direct route."

"There is?" Cronjé was surprised.

"Yes General. There is a wide, shallow valley that runs through the escarpment from the Modder River up onto the plateau near a farm, I forget its name, but it has a dam and therefore water. Unfortunately, the entrance to the valley is near Klip Drift. If the English wish to relieve Kimberley, this would be the most obvious route for them to take, assuming they are aware of it. And we have to assume that they are since they chose to cross the river at that point. If they do not know about it, they soon will. We should place some men in the valley to stop them getting through, if that is their plan."

"Oom Piet," interjected de Wet, "I would like to take some men and give that damn cavalry a lesson. If, as you say, Kimberley is so important to them, they may be stupid enough to drive their horses to death trying to relieve the town. We should sit across their path and stop them."

Cronjé gave de Wet a thoughtful look. "Yes, Neef Piet, they may just be that foolish." He calculated what he could offer. "Take eight hundred men and two guns. That should be enough to stop them. Place yourself across their path and give them a lesson on how well we can shoot."

"Thank you, Oom Piet." Looking at Albrecht, "Major, would you care to join me with some of your guns?"

"With pleasure," smiled Albrecht.

The two of them left, a departure that signalled that the Council was over, and the men broke away in twos and threes, leaving Cronjé to himself. He looked down at his hands, spreading them out and examining the backs of them and then his nails. He scraped out a bit of dirt caught under one nail. Looking up, he rubbed his nose between his finger and thumb. There was nothing else to be done. He was sure of that. He turned towards his tent, and his thoughts turned to Psalm 89, a psalm from which he often drew inspiration. He began to recite it quietly to himself as he walked.

"I will sing of the Lord's great love forever; with my mouth I will make your faithfulness known through all generations. I will declare that your love stands firm forever, that you have established your faithfulness in heaven itself. You said, 'I have made a covenant with my chosen one, I have sworn to David my servant, I will establish your line forever and make your throne firm through all generations.'"

Lieutenant-General John Denton Pinkstone French

Lieutenant-General John Denton Pinkstone French was reasonably satisfied. He halted his horse and sat back in the saddle, allowing the animal to reach down and pluck at the yellow grass. Together with Major Haig and Captain Lawrence, he had completed an inspection of their new camp at Klip Drift and here, at the western end of their position, everything seemed to be in place or would be so in due course. His engineers had adapted the Boer trenches to suit his requirements and were extending them so that they could be used to defend the camp from an attack.

He and Haig had been impressed by the sophistication of the Boer defences. Intelligent use had been made of the terrain. The steep-sided banks of the river and the deep, dry dongas running into the river were natural defences to which minor adaptation had been made to make them even more effective. But what had been particularly impressive were the trenches. These had been dug into the soft sand plateau above the Modder to extend their defences beyond the immediate environs of the river. From a distance, the line of trenches was difficult to see. The trenches were jar-shaped in cross-section, being no more than a long, narrow slit at ground level and widening with depth so that they provided quite spacious accommodation for the occupants within the protecting earth. They were deep enough to allow a man to stand with his head and shoulders protruding through the narrow opening. The spoil dug from the trenches was laid in ridges along the line of the trench, one to the front of the trench, in the direction of the expected attack, to form a low, protective parapet to shield the heads of the Boers, and in which they had channelled notches in which to rest the barrels of their rifles, and one to the rear of the trench, where the ridge of spoil was higher and more substantial. French concluded that this was to protect the Boers from shell blasts.

He realised that the cavalry had been fortunate to meet such little resistance when they had charged the enemy lines the previous day. The Boers had deserted their position very quickly, despite constructing trenches that indicated their intention of putting up a strong defence. It was gratifying, thought French smugly, that his cavalry had had such a terrifying effect on the Boers. Their rapid flight also meant that they had abandoned their wagons, along with a substantial supply of food and ammunition. French was thankful for such gifts. He thought it was ironic that the Boers were providing him with better supplies than his own commander-in-chief. He knew the great value the Boers placed on their wagons, so leaving them behind would have been a considerable wrench; that was also rather pleasing.

French smiled. Colonel Hay would be away for some time checking on the progress of the supply wagons. He hoped that Hay would decide to remain with Kitchener or Roberts until he was ordered back to spy on him. Yes, things were generally most satisfactory. He turned to the men accompanying him.

"Captain Lawrence, can you take a patrol and make contact with General Kelly-Kenny? His 6th Division is to take over securing this river crossing. Entreat him to move his division with all alacrity. The longer we have to wait here, the more difficult the Boers are going to make our march to Kimberley. I understand that General Kitchener is with General Kelly-Kenny. You are also to express to him, in the strongest terms, my requirement for the infantry to reach this position at the earliest possible opportunity. Remind him of the Commander-in-Chief's instruction that this flanking movement is to be undertaken with the utmost speed, and inform him that the Boers are on to us and are already placing themselves between ourselves and Kimberley." French knew this to be somewhat economical with the truth, but now was not the time for concerning oneself with the facts. "And inform the General that the entire campaign is being compromised because we are unable to move off immediately. Advise General Kitchener that I hold him responsible for encouraging the commander of the 6th Division to get here as soon as possible, even if it means losing half his strength in doing so. Is that clear?"

"Yes sir."

Lawrence drew his horse away to carry out his orders. Turning to Haig, French asked, "Any intelligence about the Boer movements?"

"Only what we heard this morning from the Tigers, sir. The Boers do not appear to be establishing themselves north of us, so the route to Kimberley seems to be completely unencumbered. I am expecting an update imminently."

Haig smiled to himself, for over French's shoulder he had spied a troop of Tigers, including Lieutenant Roach, making its way towards them. French then heard the horsemen himself and on seeing who was approaching he turned his gaze back cocking an eyebrow at Haig.

"Impressive how timely the Tigers can be, sir," Haig grinned.

"Indeed." French gave him an up-and-down look, as though searching for something hidden about Haig's person.

The horsemen drew up in what French considered to be a rather over-casual manner. These Cape colonialists could do with a lot more discipline, he thought.

"Sir, Major Rimington has asked us to inform you of the latest Boer movements."

"Good, very timely."

Roach gave French an uncertain look and Haig grinned.

"Er, well, sir, there *are* Boers out there." French gave Roach a 'tell-me-something-new' look which made Roach feel even more uncomfortable. He fidgeted in his saddle, "As you would expect, sir."

"Yes, as I would expect. To the point please, lieutenant."

"Yes sir. The Boers are patrolling the area at all points of the compass."

"Including to the south, between us and the 6th Division?"

"Yes sir, including to our south. There are several patrols scattered across the veld, although each consists of only fifty or so men."

"How organised are these patrols? Are they attacking randomly or does there appear to be any co-ordination? Do we know who is leading them?"

"None of that is entirely clear, sir." In response to the stern look he received from French, he continued quickly. "We have gained from a captured Boer that the man in overall command is a General Christiaan de Wet."

"De Wet! By God! Not him again! What is this man? Some sort of a will-o'-the-wisp? He seems to have an ability to be everywhere at the same time."

"Indeed, sir. The Boer patrols are highly mobile and attack and skirmish whenever they get the opportunity and then simply melt away into the veld."

"Therefore, the answer would seem to be to not give them the opportunity, would it not?"

"Of course, sir. To a large extent we are succeeding in that."

"To a large extent? They have caused casualties?"

"A few, sir, but nothing we cannot deal with."

"Lieutenant, I have force-marched my cavalry half way across Africa in searing heat and without water and supplies, except that which we have captured ourselves from the enemy. My horses are in a perilous condition and my men are collapsing from fatigue. I am sure Field Marshal Roberts does not wish to have his forces further depleted by negligence on the part of the irregular troops."

Roach was at a loss on how to respond. He had passed the point of uncertainty and was seething with anger. He remained silent. Had he replied, he was likely to have been clapped in irons for insubordination and would only have reinforced this arrogant little officer's jaundiced view of the irregulars. He waited. French stared at him malignantly, but it was French who spoke first – he needed the information more than Roach felt obliged to report it.

"Anything else, lieutenant?" he asked impatiently.

"Yes sir, the enemy have not occupied the area between us and Kimberley."

"That *is* interesting news, lieutenant. And to our west?"

"We have not been able to probe much to the west, sir. The enemy is particularly numerous in that direction," Roach added defensively, "it being the direction of their main force. We will continue reconnoitring to the west, of course, as that is where a counter-offensive is most likely to come from."

"Make sure you do. I am particularly interested in what is happening to our west."

French stared across the veld towards where his foe was stationed. Before him was a picket line of sentries. He decided it was too close.

"Major, we need to push those sentries farther out, at least to the ridge beyond. Those damned Boers are a sneaky lot and I don't want them getting anywhere near my camp."

As Haig started to respond he was interrupted by a fusillade of rifle fire. He saw two of the sentries drop like sacks of fodder and the air around him hissed with the angry whine of bullets. Roach's horse reared up next to French and then fell, throwing Roach to the ground. But he was up instantly, snatching his rifle from its saddle holster and ordering his small group of men forward in a counter-attack. They wheeled their horses round and galloped towards the rifle fire with Roach in hot pursuit on foot. Almost before French had realised what was happening, Haig had grabbed his horse's bridle and galloped away out of range of the Mauser's bullets, hauling French's horse along behind him. A unit of mounted infantry, under the leadership of Colonel Ormelie Hannay, charged past them to repost the Boer attack.

"Haig!" shouted French as they slowed down, now out of danger. "This is intolerable. Get that blasted Rimington to pull his finger out and find out what is happening to our west. I want to know the movements of every damned Boer between here and Methuen's line and I want to know *now*! And get that damned picket line strengthened and pushed farther out."

Haig was off in an instant; it would be best to be out of the old man's way for a while.

French returned to his tent and ordered a mug of fresh Boer coffee. He sat in his camp chair and waited for Haig to report back, which he did in due course, with his own mug of coffee in hand. He shot a wry look at his commanding officer.

"The Tigers may have been timely, but their intelligence was rather wanting."

"Yes. Disappointing, as generally it is much better, but I suppose there is a lot going on out there, although that's no excuse. I shall give Rimington a piece of my mind when he reappears."

French visibly relaxed and, to Haig's surprise, laughed joyfully. "It's been ages since I've had bullets buzzing around my ears! Damn you, Haig, hardly had any time to enjoy the fun before you whipped me out of there!"

Haig joined in the merriment. "You're too important to be having that sort of fun, sir!"

"So they say. The Boers have the right attitude. Their commanders are allowed to get stuck into the nitty-gritty of a good battle, lucky devils."

Haig became serious. "Sir, that information about the Boers not putting themselves between us and Kimberley...."

"Yes, a very interesting bit of intelligence. I suppose it must be true. Even the Tigers couldn't get that wrong. If it is, it's very tempting – too tempting. How I would love to move forward and relieve Kimberley. I need to do it by tomorrow or Kitchener will take delight in my failure." Haig looked at him. "Oh, I made some vague comment to him about relieving the town by the fifteenth. The point is we should be doing it today, but the risks are too great. Until the damned infantry gets here we are stuck. We cannot leave this wretched place undefended. The Boers would be in like vultures and this time they would probably have sufficient numbers to split our forces and be a serious threat to our rear. They could slam the door shut, lock us up in Kimberley and cut off our supplies. No, we have to remain here. At least the horses will benefit from the rest and forage. It will make our objective more difficult, of course, for it will give the Boers time to occupy the territory between us and Kimberley, but at least it will make the job more exciting if they do. And next time I will make sure I am well away from your over-protective hand," he laughed. "Drink up, Major, we need to see what the Boers are up to."

French stood planted like a small English oak in the parched African grassland. With his field glasses clamped to his eyes, he stared northwards in the direction of his goal, the town of Kimberley. Before him was a valley, which ran in a northerly direction for two miles. Its entrance was about a mile wide. Its floor rose gently towards the head of the valley, which ended in a low ridge some eight hundred yards across. Behind the ridge, he was informed, there was a farm where water could be found. The valley sides consisted of cliff-faced koppies. The previous night their rocky faces had echoed with the ferocious roars of a leopard and the enraged barks of baboons as some life and death struggle had played itself out. But where the koppies had previously been reported as unoccupied, except by baboons and leopards, there were now distinct signs of human activity.

Through his field glasses French could make out the slouch hats and shabby forms of his foes. For all their unprofessional appearance and undisciplined manner, these Boers had an eye for a defensive position – there was no doubt about that. Their presence was going to make his march to Kimberley decidedly more difficult. To the west was the main Boer force; that door was shut. To the east, they could reach Kimberley via Paardeberg, but that would require a significant detour and would certainly mean that Kimberley could not be relieved by the following day. The Boers had placed themselves slap across his most obvious and direct route to Kimberley.

"So the Boers have taken advantage of the ponderous approach of our infantry." He turned to Haig, "Any update of the lack of progress of the 6th Division?"

"None, sir, other than General Kelly-Kenny's assurances that he is forcing the pace of his infantry as much as he dare, but they will not arrive before nightfall."

French looked out to the south where a grey smudge rose against the sky. It was still some way off.

"Am I to wait in this wretched place for the rest of the war?" he snapped. He strode to his horse and climbed on, wheeled it round impatiently and started back to his camp.

Sergeant Alfred Atkinson

Sergeant Alfred Atkinson could hardly breathe. He did not know the time; he did not care about time. All he knew was that it was dark, dark as pitch, and he was stumbling across an ash-blackened veld in a state of the utmost fatigue. His throat and lungs had been assaulted by a suffocating, fine grey dust all day and now the acrid ash also burned into them. His mind was tormented by a desire for pure, fresh country air, air such as that he remembered on the moorlands of Yorkshire, cool and moist... so moist! And where it rained. Damn, how he wished it would rain, a rain that would wash him clean of all the dust and all the ash that covered him and clung to him like an unwanted, foreign skin. It invaded his nose, his eyes, his ears, and his mouth. It spread under his clothes, like an insidious rash, and chafed his groin and his armpits. Men around him coughed and hacked as the dust dried their mouths and irritated their throats.

His fatigue was beyond belief; from the continuous, relentless marching. He was certain he had fallen asleep while he'd been walking, but had kept moving only through the monotonous rhythm that had taken over his legs, like the pumping pistons of a train. How long had he been marching? It was difficult to know. As far as he could remember, it was the 14th of February, but he could not be certain. Saint Valentine's Day! An image of Lucy appeared faintly in his mind and he clutched at it. Focusing on her face to make it grow in clarity, to make it more real. The cool Yorkshire breeze wafted a wisp of auburn hair across her smooth forehead. He could see and smell the heather behind her. He could even hear her laugh... could he? His ears tensed with the effort of listening. A violent crash of thunder broke across the sky and she was gone. The 14th of February? So he had been marching for four days. God in heaven, it felt longer than that. And where was that blasted river? It must be close. Despite his intense fatigue, Atkinson could still sense the press of the other men around him, all marching in the same exhausted manner. We cannot be expected to go on much farther. Surely, they cannot make us go any farther. How many miles already? Lord only knows.

Several flashes of lightning slashed across the distant sky. The entire host of men seemed to tense with anticipation, waiting for the cool, drenching rain, counting the seconds, one, two, three, four, for the portentous rumble, which seemed to shake the very ground as it rolled uselessly overhead. Four miles away, so no promise of rain yet. No splashing through puddles to cool his aching feet. Atkinson could not believe how hot his feet felt. Every drop of blood in his body must be down at his boiling feet. His soles throbbed with every step he took. His worn boots allowed sand in which chafed the raw skin of his burst blisters. More flashes of lightning cut the distant night sky.

Suddenly, Atkinson felt a crushing pain in his toes as he plummeted over a concrete-hard anthill. His howl of agony startled the men around him as though they had been woken from a deep sleep, and in the darkness they clumsily stamped on him and tumbled over him. What might have caused hoots of laughter under normal circumstances brought forth only cries of anguish and foul-mouthed tirades aimed at both the anthill and the fool who had caused the others to stumble and fall. Atkinson, normally a cheerful, easy-going fellow, lay on the ground sobbing in pain and self-pity. The bolt of his rifle mechanism pressed excruciatingly into his ribs, but the men on top of him were exhausted and were in no hurry to get off him.

His toes felt damp and sticky as blood oozed from his split foot and into his dilapidated boot. How he wished he was on one of the ambulance wagons he had seen trundling back towards Ramdam earlier that day, overflowing with those crippled by the march or toppled by heatstroke or dehydration. Why had he not stopped and claimed to be unable to carry on? Now he would simply be crushed to death by his own friends, who were beyond caring for anyone but themselves.

He understood their attitude as it was one he had experienced earlier in the day, when he had seen men crumple and collapse in mid-step in front of him, and it had been him who had been stumbling and cursing or simply walking around them, for he knew that if he stopped he would not have been able to start marching again. He had to keep his rhythm going: left, right, left, right. Even the dust storm, which had blown its stinging grains of grit into his face, did not cause him to falter. He had simply bowed his head against it, placed his hand on the shoulder of the man in front, closed his eyes, and prayed that he would not trip over an anthill of fall down an ant-bear hole. He had simply plodded on and on and on.

As Atkinson lay exhausted and hurting under the crush of his fellows, images flashed through his mind of the corpses of the dead horses that had lined the route of their march. There were so many carcasses that there were insufficient vultures in Africa to feast on them. The ugly scavengers had been a constant reminder of what might happen to the men should they fall out of line unnoticed. The disgusting birds squatted on the ground, their heads red with blood and their engorged bellies so distended they could hardly scuttle, let alone fly, away from the revolted soldiers who had some fun, chasing and slaughtering them. But there were so many and their ungainly flapping as they attempted to escape made them such unsatisfying prey that the men soon became bored. Besides, they needed what energy they had simply to march. Chasing vultures, they soon realised, while breaking the tedium of the march, was wasted effort.

And the flies! Every carcass crawled with them and, if approached, they rose as a buzzing black cloud and flew into the men's faces, settling around their eyes and mouths, sucking out whatever tiny amounts of moisture remained in their bodies. As a result, except when the occasional soldier walking in his sleep staggered too close, the putrid, stinking remains of the horses were given a wide berth.

That was during the day. In the pitch black of the night it was not uncommon for men to stumble into the bloated corpses. Atkinson had not done that, but now he thought that putting his foot through the rotten skin into the decomposing entrails of a dead horse would have been a less traumatic experience than lying here, as he was, crippled and the target of unconscious boots. The endless machine of marching men stumbled on around him, grumbling and cursing at the obstruction that made them break the rhythm of their stride.

Slowly, the men on top of him heaved themselves to their feet, moaning as they did so, and fell back in line to continue the pitiless trudge across the veld. But Atkinson remained on the ground; it was all he could do to pull his knees into his chest to protect himself from yet more trampling boots. The sense of lying still, of not moving, of not marching, was blissful. He could feel his mind drifting towards that warm, cosy sensation of pre-sleep. He felt his neck relax and his helmet gently take the pressure as his head slowly dropped to the ground. But in his stillness, Atkinson also became more aware of all the physical discomfort that racked his body. His feet throbbed at the end of his aching legs, his shoulders ached from the weight of his pack and every muscle screamed its desire for rest. And he could suddenly feel how hungry he was. So hungry that he could feel his stomach cramping from lack of food. It was as though his navel was touching his spine. Thirst burned up from his belly along his parched throat to the cracked dryness of his tongue and lips. But his mind continued to slowly drift away from these discomforts. His aching body relaxed, the river of men parted like water around a rock. The warm water tugged at his legs. He could feel himself floating downstream, the water of sleep soothing his aches and pains.

He vaguely became aware of someone calling. The voice was reassuringly familiar, sonorous. Alfie strained to hear. Then he felt his shoulder snag. The force of the warm current jolted his shoulder repeatedly against a rock. He became aware of a light intruding through his closed eyelids.

"Get him up!" someone instructed bluntly.

Atkinson snapped his eyes open and immediately closed them against the glare of a burning torch that was thrust towards his face. His shoulder was shaken again. He groaned and grudgingly opened his eyes. Flickering, shadowy faces etched on a black sky danced in front of his eyes.

"What's his regiment?" enquired an officer sternly.

"The Yorkshires, sir," came the reply.

The officer called above the men, "Two Yorkshires come and give this man a hand."

Two men broke rank and knelt beside Atkinson.

"Hey sergeant, get yourself up." It was Private Jonny Brown. "Come on fellow, up you get." Rough hands pulled Atkinson up from the dust and ash, and he turned to look at Brown as the private lifted him to his feet. The dancing light of the fire-brands made him look ghoulish.

"Hey Jonny, you've looked better," he quipped through his pain.

"Speak for yourself, sergeant. If your mother saw you now she'd have a high fit. You look like death warmed up."

Brown placed Atkinson's arm around his shoulder and handed his and Atkinson's rifles to Private Jimmy Carpenter, who, taking the weapons without a word, followed them as they started to move on.

"Jonny, you got any water about you?"

"A little. Here, help yourself. Only a little mind. Not sure when there'll be a chance for more."

Atkinson took a small, delicious mouthful of water.

"Much obliged, Jonny. Thanks."

"It's nothing, sergeant. You can buy me a pint in the George and Dragon next time we're home."

"That's a promise."

The pain in his toes was more tolerable now. The small touch of water on his lips had revived him and he was able to limp forward with Brown's support. Carpenter trudged silently behind them.

The time between the lightning and the rumbles of thunder had become shorter. The storm was close. The men could smell the rain in the air. They prayed for it to arrive, to clear the dust and ash from the air and wash it off their tired bodies. Atkinson raised his face to luxuriate in the fresh breeze that preceded the oncoming storm. He reached up to touch his face. His fingers ran over hard, bony features that he hardly recognised as his own. Even his mother would not recognise him and neither would his Lucy. He remembered how they used to smile and praise his good-looking, boyish features, but that was unlikely to happen now. He was only 26 years old, but he felt a hundred. He had suffered many hardships serving in the British army, but this trial of human endurance was the worst he had ever experienced. How his mother would berate the army for not feeding him properly. "Why, he's a mere shadow of himself!" she would exclaim. The memory of her voice brought a small smile to his dry, cracked lips, but did not remove the hunger that had returned to him.

At their last very brief halt many of the men had questioned why the army was starving them. It contradicted what they had expected from 'Bobs'. He was famous for the concern he showed towards his men. He had glowed with pride in what they had achieved by reaching the Riet River so quickly and wished them well on that morning that they prepared to march off into the veld. Atkinson recalled Roberts' jolly speech, even though it had been somewhat over-attentive towards the Highlanders. Those Scots were arrogant enough without being encouraged. But at least Bobs had allowed them all to rest and regain their strength and fill their stomachs. He had walked among the men while they ate and asked after them and about what news they had received from home. Yes, Bobs was the greatest officer the British army had, bar none. It was not he who had allowed the men to fall into their present pitiless state. The man who had done that was that scarecrow Kitchener.

K was the antithesis of kindly Bobs. He was tall and scrawny, with the look of a falcon about to fall upon its quarry, and he displayed the same lack of empathy for the men as a falcon did its prey. His *raison d'être* was to achieve his goal, and the sole purpose of the men was to allow him to do so, regardless of the cost to them. If this meant that supplies were left behind, K's view was so be it. And that buffoon General Kelly-Kenny did nothing. He was supposed to be in command, but it was obvious that the person calling the shots was K. Why was the General not protecting his men from the excessive demands of Kitchener?

Atkinson frowned to himself ironically. Here he was, complaining bitterly to himself, as he suspected every one of the thousands of men around him were doing, and yet they still marched on and would do so until it was literally impossible for them to do so anymore, and then they would simply collapse from the effort. The hairs on the back of his neck tingled from the sense of pride that ran through his veins. The British Tommy was irrepressible. He *would* do what was required of him for Queen and country. And he would do it in spite of men like Kitchener, not because of them. He would do it for the regiment and for men like Bobs. He would not let his commander down. The success of Bobs' plan rested with them. If they failed, then Bobs failed and the regiment failed and that would not do. So they would keep marching until their last breath. Atkinson felt his strength returning; he leant less heavily on Brown.

Another bolt of lightning zigzagged across the sky, changing night to day for an instant, and the monstrous clash of thunder that immediately followed made Atkinson leap out of his skin, which in turn made Brown jump with fright.

"Hey sergeant, calm down. How are you going to deal with them Boers if a bit of thunder gets you all worked up?"

With the deafening clap of thunder the rain came at last, huge drops that could be heard splatting onto the dusty ground. They fell slowly at first, raising a damp, dusty smell from the parched earth. All around Atkinson, the entire division of officers and men stopped. Whoops of delight went up and the men gratefully took off their helmets and looked up at the sky, stretching out their arms to welcome the cooling, cleansing, refreshing water from the heavens.

The drops stung Atkinson's sun-dried skin, but he happily stood with his face turned skywards and his mouth gaping to catch the drops as they fell faster and faster. In no time at all, the rain was coming down in a torrent, and it seemed as though he was standing under a waterfall. It was no longer possible to look up; as the cascade of water gave Atkinson the sense that he was drowning. But his mouth now felt moist and his face cooled. He dropped his bare head forward and the cold water rushed down his neck and back, washing away the dust and ash. Men around him laughed and hurrahed, and splashed their feet in the puddles that were already forming on the ground, the coolness on their aching feet was heavenly. But their elation was short-lived. All too soon the officers were barking orders above the din of the rain for the men to fall back in line and move on. Order was quickly restored, the lines reformed, helmets were replaced and once more the infantry were on the march.

However, once on the move it soon became apparent that the rain, so recently received with great joy, was as great a torment as the dehydrating conditions that had preceded it. The ground became treacherous with slippery mud and the men cursed as they skidded and slid at the slightest change in gradient. Already clumsy with fatigue and unbalanced by the weight of their packs, men slipped and fell about Atkinson as though they were on an ice-rink, often dragging down those marching next to them as they grabbed out frantically to stop themselves from falling. In the light thrown by the continuing flashes of lightning, Atkinson saw that several officers had taken the prudent step of dismounting, after being almost thrown by their horses as they, too, slid and slipped. Those men who had fallen were now plastered in a cold, clinging mud that had replaced their thick veneer of dust. Like the dust, the mud got into eyes, ears and mouths, and all around him Atkinson could hear men spluttering and spitting to clear their mouths of the distasteful stuff.

Atkinson shivered. The chill of the water that drenched him was now becoming uncomfortable. Dear god, he blasphemed to himself, if he was not being scorched by the sun and desiccated by the dust, he was being drowned by torrential rains. How he longed to be in the perfect, temperate climes of his beloved Yorkshire.

Atkinson and Brown clung to one another for support, but Carpenter, following close behind, had to reach out frequently to stop them from falling. Atkinson groaned each time it happened. The slipping and sliding was aggravating the pain in his foot.

Atkinson became aware of raised levels of shouting and cursing ahead of him. He listened hard to identify the cause. There was no shooting, so it was not the enemy. And then, just as someone yelled an order to stop, Atkinson, Brown and Carpenter found themselves slithering uncontrollably down a steep slope, ending up in a thrashing tangle of arms and legs at the bottom. A few men followed, but the main body of the division had lurched to a halt at the top of the bank.

After some initial cursing and flailing about, Brown suggested with mock politeness, "Excuse me, sergeant, but could you get your arse out of my face? Either I'm going to suffocate or people are going to start talking, and neither appeals to me!"

Carpenter was shaking in silent laugher as he pulled Atkinson off Brown. "Neither appeals to him, sergeant."

"Nor to me," laughed Atkinson, but his laughter was cut short by a shooting pain as he put his weight on his foot.

The rest of the division started to descend cautiously down the slope. Atkinson suggested that they got out of the away before they got bowled over by the sliding soldiers. They located their rifles and walked on. Within a few steps Atkinson was walking in water up to his ankles. He stepped aside to get out of the deepening puddle, but splashed into more water. As he walked the water rose higher up his leg and a current tugged at his trousers. He yelped with excitement.

"Bloody hell, Jonny, it's the river. It's the bloody Modder River!"

He threw himself forward against the increasing current of water as it rose up to the level of his waist and waded across. He had crossed the Modder River! He laughed and slapped Brown on the back.

"Jonny, my lad, we made it. We damned well made it."

A flash of lightning lit up the opposite riverbank and Atkinson saw a sallow tree in front of him and, further off, a loose collection of wagons. The tree was closer and he made for it, pulling Brown along. Carpenter followed. The ground under the tree was as soaked and muddy as everywhere else and the rain drove through the leaves as though they did not exist, but to Atkinson there was still the sense that the tree provided shelter. He sank to his knees and dropped to the ground. He was asleep before his head touched the muddy soil. It was two o'clock in the morning. He had been marching for sixteen hours.

Thursday 15 February 1900

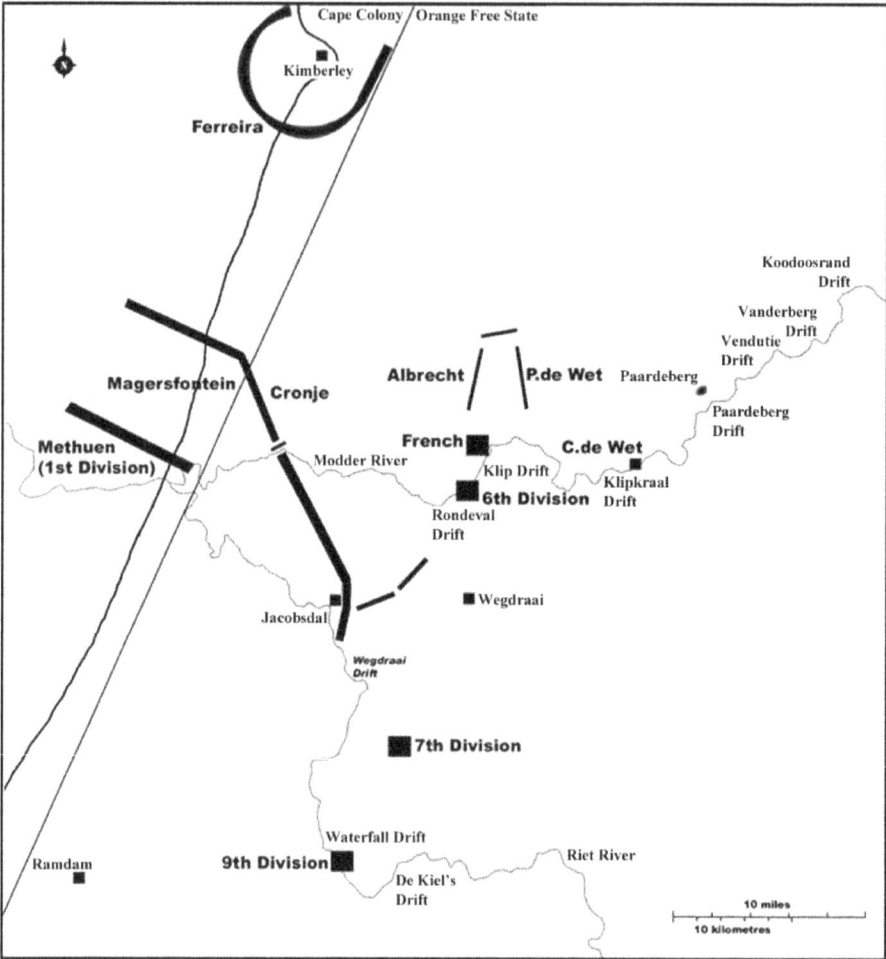

Map 6: Morning of 15 February 1900

Major Friedrich Wilhelm Richard Albrecht

Major Friedrich Wilhelm Richard Albrecht stood tall and erect in his smart Germanic Orange Free State Artillery uniform, his black pickelhaube helmet polished to a sparkle and the brass ball on top glinting in the early morning sun. He stood on the summit of a kopje on the southern end of the escarpment that formed the western wall of the wide valley that rose up from the veldt near the Modder River and ended in the plateau, beyond which was Kimberley. It was the gateway to the town.

Albrecht's kopje and its sister, about a mile to the east, were natural citadels that protected the entrance to the valley. Earlier that morning, when the valley floor was shrouded in mist, the two crags had looked like castles at a harbour entrance, but now that the mist had been burnt away by the hot, vivid sun, the stark dryness of the valley was obvious.

Albrecht scanned the line of kopjes and cliffs on the other side of the valley through his field glasses. Like the escarpment he occupied, it stretched off to the north for some two miles. The two walls of rock slowly converged so that at the head of the valley they were only eight hundred feet apart. At this point the cliffs fell away and the valley ended with a low, shallow ridge, which would not, in itself, present an obstacle to the cavalry, but then Albrecht was not convinced that the Afrikander forces were going to present much of an obstacle either. He studied the kopjes, but could not see anything, although he knew that the hills were occupied by the larger of the two commandos – four hundred men under Piet de Wet compared to the two hundred men and the two guns on his side of the valley. A further two hundred men occupied the ridge at the head of the valley. Just eight hundred men and two guns!

At the mouth of the valley the veldt opened out into an ocean of flat grassland, through which meandered the Modder River. The last few remnants of mist clung to its sparkling, brown surface. In one of the coils of the river, he could see the laager of wagons that had been abandoned by the Afrikanders the previous day when they had fled their positions at Klip Drift. But what really interested Albrecht was the increasing activity within the English camp.

He watched General French inspect his horsemen, and there seemed to be a very large number of them. Next to French was the fuller frame of another English general, Kelly-Kenny. Albrecht thought the tall, straight-backed man with Kelly-Kenny must be Kitchener. He had not seen this man before, but knew his reputation as an efficient operator. He supposedly had none of the bluster that was so often on show in the usually stuffy English generals.

It was obvious there were substantially more men in the English camp than had been there the evening before – Kelly-Kenny and Kitchener for a start. The cavalry guard outposts of yesterday had been replaced by infantry, and the artillery pieces were more numerous than the previous day. So, thought Albrecht, there were now three English generals on the Modder, and from what the Afrikander patrols had learned, two divisions, one of infantry and one of cavalry, totalling about ten thousand men. That was double what Cronjé had at Magersfontein and over ten times what he and Piet de Wet had at their disposal to stop the English getting to Kimberley. Interestingly, he had not seen the little Field Marshal, Roberts. This must mean that he was with the other regiments still making their way towards the Modder River, and when he did arrive he would bring even more infantry.

With only eight hundred men and two guns, the task of stopping the English was impossible. From their positions in the kopjes, the best that could be expected would be to delay the English for a few days. So the burghers had been ordered to scamper about the rocky outcrops to give the impression that there were more of them than was actually the case, but Albrecht could see little evidence of this happening on either side of the valley. Damned Afrikanders, he reflected, their down-fall would be their lack of discipline. Albrecht had higher expectations of the English and continued to watch to see if their disciplined lines would give a hint of their intentions.

What was clear was that the infantry was not preparing to move out. That was hardly surprising, thought Albrecht, since they had been in Ramdam only three days before. They would be incapable of any serious military manoeuvres, certainly for today, and hopefully for some time to come. So any potential action would come from the horse. Certainly, the absurd little figure of French on his oversized horse was much more active than either Kelly-Kenny or Kitchener. But there was no urgency yet. Albrecht could see a large number of cooking fires throughout the camp. He checked to make sure that he had not been duped and that the fires were as they seemed – for cooking breakfasts – and not as a decoy. Satisfied, he relieved his eyes of his glasses and strode back to his tent to commence his own breakfast, leaving Captain de Villiers to observe the enemy.

At 8:30 Albrecht returned to his station and asked de Villiers for a report. Breakfast seemed to be over and things were starting to move. The two of them studied the activity down in the English camp.

Below him was a magnificent sight: nearly five thousand horsemen were saddled up as though on parade. Three cavalry brigades and seven units of horse artillery were all facing north, towards their observers. They made a very fine impression, although, disappointingly for Albrecht, all were dressed in khaki rather than in their traditional regalia. To the left were Hussars, Lancers and the Heavy Household Cavalry. In the centre were Dragoons and to the right were more Lancers, their gay pennons, fluttering in the morning breeze, added some colour to the drab uniforms, the muddy river and the tawny veldt. Next to them were the less disciplined squads of irregular horse, their slouch hats contrasting with the domed helmets of the regular horse. The latter stood in disciplined stillness, only disrupted by the occasional shaking of a horse's head. Then, as if through some invisible force, the entire body of men and horses turned, as one, to face upstream and slowly moved off, in close order, towards the valley guarded by Albrecht and the Afrikander commando.

"Now there, Captain, is a highly disciplined army," enthused Albrecht.

"Yes sir," responded de Villiers, without much interest.

"Captain," retorted Albrecht impatiently, "if we do not learn discipline ourselves, we will make winning this war very difficult."

De Villiers did not respond and Albrecht focused on the English horse as they continued to march upstream following the line of the river. It was still possible that they would continue all the way to Paardeberg and then turn for Kimberley.

The English were obviously aware of the presence of the Afrikanders because they remained as close to the river as possible in order to stay out of range of their rifles and guns. However, the course of the river curved north-wards, so that the procession was forced to ride closer to the kopjes. It was too tempting a target for Albrecht's gunners and even though the English were at the extreme range of their guns, they opened fire. As usual, Albrecht was delighted with their accuracy, for the shells smashed into the lines of horsemen, sending showers of dirt and clouds of dust up into the air and throwing writhing horses and men to the ground.

The cavalry responded immediately and moved quickly into an extended, more open formation to present a more dispersed target. They quickened their pace to a gallop and raced along the course of the river, while units of horse artillery broke rank and prepared their guns to retaliate.

Albrecht's gunners continued to focus on the cavalry, but with only two guns at his disposal, the impact on the fast-moving horsemen was frustratingly small and Albrecht could see that their route along the river as it meandered to the east would eventually take them outside the range of the Afrikander guns.

De Villiers asked, "Shall I give the order to shell the English artillery, sir?"

"No," responded Albrecht. "My gunners will keep an eye on them. The trick is to wait."

Albrecht was confident that his regiment, unlike most of the Afrikander army, were disciplined enough to understand what to do. They knew they were not in any immediate danger and, as expected, the first English salvoes came up, over and beyond the Afrikander lines. Albrecht remembered the many months it had taken him, used to doing battle in European climates, to appreciate the peculiar visual effect of the exceptionally clear South African atmosphere. As before, the English had overestimated the range. This was a common weakness of the English artillery, and their riflemen, but, more importantly, it meant that they had placed their guns much closer to the Afrikander positions than they realised.

While the English were adjusting the aim of their guns, Albrecht's gunners did the same, but more quickly and more accurately, and the Orange Free State Artillery responded first. Before they could return fire, two batteries of English artillery were silenced. The second English barrage was not much better than their first and, as the OFS shells fell around them, they realised they had positioned themselves poorly and beat a hasty retreat – to a resounding cheer from the Afrikander gunners.

With the excitement of the short artillery exchange over, Albrecht returned to considering the horsemen. They had halted in extended order, beyond the range of his guns, in a position halfway between the two kopjes that marked the entrance to the valley. They had turned and now faced up the valley towards Kimberley. So they did know about this route to Kimberley. Now the question for Albrecht was what were they going to do? He assumed they would gallop towards one of the valley side escarpments, crossing the open veldt at speed, and then leap from their horses and take cover among the rocks and boulders that were liberally scattered at the bottom of the kopjes. Then they would slowly grind their way up towards the Afrikander positions. But which escarpment would they attack first? It was, he thought, going to be a long, hot and very bloody day.

There was a flash of morning sunlight on steel as Albrecht saw the officers raise their swords. "Here they come," he muttered to de Villiers.

A second later the front division of horses exploded in to action and hurled themselves up the valley. Those following the leading horsemen were almost immediately consumed in a huge pall of grey dust, to the extent that even the horses on the flanks of the stampede were hidden by it. But to Albrecht's surprise, instead of swinging to the left or to the right towards one or other of the escarpments, the dust cloud continued to roll straight up the valley. Albrecht dropped his field glasses to his chest in surprise.

"My God!" he exclaimed. "They're going for it! They are going to charge right through the valley!"

"They'll be in range of our rifles for the entire length of the charge!" De Villiers added with glee. "We will slaughter them!"

As the first division disappeared under its veil of dust, the Dragoons leapt forward with equal enthusiasm, also to disappear into the dust cloud. The remaining Hussars, Lancers and Household Cavalry were not long in bursting into life themselves, diving into the dust with a speed that suggested they were aggrieved at having to take up the rear position. They intended to make up for it by reaching the head of the valley before anyone else.

Albrecht watched, mesmerised. It was an awe-inspiring sight. Blast that dust, he scowled. To be able to see the full charge of five thousand cavalry from this vantage point would be an once-in-a-lifetime experience and he bitterly resented the infernal shroud of dust that obscured his view. Nevertheless, even to watch the dust storm as it rushed up the valley at the speed of a galloping horse was an incredible sight. Albrecht could feel the ground vibrate under his feet as the thundering of the thousands of hooves drummed across the dry landscape below and reverberated in his ears. It was a heart-stopping moment for any professional soldier. He watched the cloud as it dashed the two miles up the valley, barely slowing as it approached the ridge that cut across its path. The tidal wave of dust streamed over its crest and out of the valley.

Albrecht could see several individual dust trails steaming away from the English charge as burghers fled on their ponies. Having realised that they faced an unstoppable force, they were making haste while the going was good and he pitied those who had not been so cautious. The burghers had a particular fear of Lancers, from whom they had some very bitter experiences, not least at the Battle of Elandslaagte in Natal, where one Lancer was reported, rather tastelessly, as having said that the thrill of running down fleeing Boers was akin to, and as exhilarating as, a boar hunt. As a result, the burghers took great delight in dispatching Lancers whenever the opportunity arose, but today was not going to be one of those opportunities. The Lancers galloped straight through the Afrikander lines and in a wave of euphoria continued galloping, without any hint of halting, as though they were determined to charge all the way to Kimberley.

As the dust slowly settled, Albrecht looked to see what impact the Afrikanders had made on the enemy's thunderous charge, and was quietly pleased to see how few casualties were left on the veldt. He estimated that there were fewer than a hundred dead horses, their riders already walking back towards the river. As the Afrikanders had not been able to see where to shoot because of the dust, he suspected most of the deaths had nothing to do with the shells from his guns or the bullets from the burghers' rifles. No, he thought grimly, the deaths of the horses probably had more to do with the poor animals bursting their hearts in this last and glorious act of courage than anything the Afrikanders had done.

With the thunder and exhilaration of the cavalry charge over, Albrecht became aware of a distant boom of guns behind him. The English were obviously keen to keep us focused on Magersfontein, he pondered. This was a well organised campaign, but no less than might be expected from Lord Roberts of Kandahar. Here was a man with a different approach, a man who would adapt his strategy to the situation, who did not stick with the accepted ways of doing things. The question now was could General Cronjé adapt his ways to this new challenge?

Turning to Captain de Villiers he said, "Captain, the enemy is now definitely between us and Bloemfontein. The English seem very keen to relieve Kimberley, even at the expense of their horses, but some may turn back in order to capture my guns. That will not happen. I suspect their infantry will be too exhausted to be effective. Therefore, you will take the guns and hide them among these kopjes until the cavalry are far enough away for you to dash eastwards across the valley and on to Poplar Grove. After Magersfontein, that would be the next best defensive position for us to hold. Also, send riders to Kimberley and tell the commandants besieging the town to move their guns instantly. There is to be no hanging about. We do not want the guns to fall into the hands of the English. They are to take the guns to the north and then eastwards, and make sure the commandants understand that they need to have commandos protecting their retreat in order to slow the English cavalry down and prevent them seizing our guns. Dispatch a rider to General Cronjé to inform him that the English will have relieved Kimberley before the end of the day. Then send a message to General Piet de Wet asking him to meet me on this side of the valley. We need to report back to General Cronjé in person immediately."

"Yes sir."

De Villiers turned, barking orders at the burghers nearest to him to saddle up – one for Kimberley, one to Cronjé and one to de Wet. Then he strode away to save the guns. Albrecht watched him go. He suspected there were already burghers halfway to Kimberley or on their way to Cronjé eager to spread the news to their friends.

Albrecht

Albrecht turned back to look into the valley. So much for delaying the English for a few days! The Afrikander army had not delayed them for a single morning. There was now little evidence of what must have been one of the largest cavalry charges ever undertaken. All that remained were some remnant clouds of dust and the dark shapes of the fallen horses and their hapless riders walking in the wide expanse of the valley back to the river. Albrecht closed his eyes and stared at the back of his eyelids, visualising the procession of five thousand horsemen in perfect order, their stillness as they faced up the valley, the sudden leap into action of the horses and the man-made dust storm rushing up the valley. He stood very still and focused until he was satisfied that he had captured the scene in his mind's eye and secured it in his memory. Then he opened his eyes, gave the scene one final, appreciative look, turned and walked away, shaking his head in awe at the unbelievable event he had just witnessed.

General Pieter Arnoldus Cronjé

General Pieter Arnoldus Cronjé lent on the trek table, his head bowed, his knuckles digging into the rough, worn wooden surface. The late afternoon sun beat down on his shoulders. From under the brim of his slouch hat he watched the group of men approach him. They had come to attend the War Council he had called, although he believed that if he had not called it, someone else would have. Unusually, Cronjé had arrived at the War Council early. He normally waited for everyone to gather before he joined them – it had always been that way – but today he was early. He wondered if the other Council members would notice that he had arrived before them. He had miscalculated the English tactics and he was eating humble pie.

The men were led by General Koos de la Rey. The tall, full-bearded man was at Magersfontein on a brief visit on behalf of the supreme commander, General Joubert. With him was General Ferreira, who had commanded the siege of Kimberley and whose presence at the Council, rather than at Kimberley, where he was no longer needed since the relief of the town by the English, accentuated the point that he had made a mistake. Others included Piet de Wet, Major Albrecht and Commandant Pieter Kritzinger, a leader of the Cape rebels. Christiaan de Wet was absent again, but at least he was now keeping the leadership informed of his location and of English movements. And, Cronjé admitted to himself, it now seemed that Christiaan de Wet was in the right place, between the English and Bloemfontein, while the rest of Cronjé's forces seemed to be in the wrong place, with the English blocking their path.

The men joined Cronjé and stood silently, waiting. None looked him in the eye, and they avoided his gaze when he looked at each man in turn. Only de la Rey did not avert his eyes.

"Good afternoon, gentlemen," said Cronjé to open the meeting.

A few shrugged their shoulders in salutation and only Albrecht responded with a verbal greeting.

"Good afternoon, sir."

Cronjé smiled at the formal greeting. He wondered if the Major would ever get used to using the familiar 'Oom'. The day he did, he could consider himself a true Afrikander.

113

Cronjé broke the silence. "Gentlemen, let us pray. Neef Pieter," he said, looking at Kritzinger, "can you please lead the payer?"

"Yes, Oom Piet."

Kritzinger looked around the group and each man respectfully bowed his head.

"Lord, guide us in this, our time of need. We ask that you lay Your divine hand on our War Council. We ask for Your guidance and inspiration in our decisions and that You lead us to victory over Your enemies. We humbly ask this in Your name, Amen."

"Amen."

Albrecht noted that Cronjé kept his head bowed for a short time longer than the others, as if asking his Lord for personal guidance in the matters at hand. Eventually Cronjé lifted his head and looked at each man in turn.

"So, gentlemen, it seems that you were right and I was wrong."

"You could not know their plan, Oom Piet."

It was de Wet who had spoken and Albrecht was once again impressed by the respect that this old man, the Lion of Potchefstroom, held among the burghers. Even now, when his arrogance had led them to this pass, he still held their esteem.

"I thank you, Neef Piet, for your consoling words, but the truth of the matter is that the English have outflanked me. I have over-concerned myself with the threat to my front and closed my mind to the possibility that the English could risk the destruction of their forces in a seemingly impossible march across waterless veldt to threaten my rear. So we are where we are and we need to change the situation back to our advantage.

"I have called you to this Council in order to agree how we achieve this. The English have accomplished a bold and remarkable feat and have earned my respect, but we must not allow ourselves to fall into negative thoughts about our own abilities. We are now fighting on *our own* land, a land where, between us, we know every anthill. Our cause is righteous and we have God on our side. We may only be a small army, but with God's help we will defeat this arrogant empire, as we have done before. This is something we should never doubt."

Cronjé glared around the table, defying anyone to contradict him. None did, for most believed sincerely that what he had said was correct and the one who was not entirely convinced, de Wet, remained silent. Cronjé's eye finally fell on Albrecht.

"Major Albrecht and Neef Piet, can you please report on the position in which we find ourselves?"

The Council listened as Albrecht and then de Wet gave their reports. Albrecht's was factual, but stirring and impassioned in his description of the English cavalry charge. That of de Wet was more emotional, not only in his description of the size of the force they faced, but also in his pessimistic view of their own situation. When they had finished, Cronjé looked at the gathered men.

"In addition," he added, "The English have attacked Jacobsdal and we have had to withdraw from that town, so all our forces are now placed to the north of the Modder River. Are there any questions?"

"So we are trapped!" snapped Ferreira bitterly. "Your force has been stuck here at Magersfontein, apparently facing the enemy. I was keeping the English well contained in Kimberley. And they have slunk in behind us and cut off our route to Bloemfontein. Not only that, but with the commando on the north side of the Modder, we will have to cross it to get to Bloemfontein, most likely in the face of an enemy determined to prevent us from doing so." He glared at Cronjé, "I should not have wasted my time coming to this Council. I should have stayed with my guns when we broke off the siege of Kimberley."

"I understand your anger, Neef," Cronjé responded, "but let us not distract ourselves by over-analysing our *individual* situations. We need to focus on the next steps, not on what went before."

"If I may interject, General?" It was Albrecht who spoke. "I do not believe we are trapped. The English cavalry was so keen to relieve Kimberley they simply passed right through the area between Kimberley and the Modder River and have left it completely unguarded. Since then, they have seemed more interested in capturing our guns than in making sure the route to Bloemfontein was closed. And on the matter of the guns, I must congratulate you, General Ferreira. You did an excellent job preventing them from falling into the hands of the enemy. Even the arrogant English officers will be impressed with how you achieved that."

There was a general murmur of congratulation and Cronjé smiled benevolently on Ferreira.

"As for the infantry," Albrecht continued, "I believe they must be incapacitated with exhaustion. They have been on a forced march for days and the troops I saw at the Modder River this morning must have arrived there very late last night. And they have remained there. They have not attempted to secure the territory between the river and Kimberley, so they are not in a position to intercept us. Therefore, we could trek east between the English cavalry at Kimberley and the infantry on the Modder, and find a drift to cross the Modder beyond the one currently held by the English. In their exhausted state, they will not be able to chase us even if they discover us marching towards Bloemfontein. I see no great danger in attempting an escape between Kimberley and the Modder River, especially if we do so at night."

Cronjé looked around the group until his gaze fell on de Wet.

"Neef Piet, you were rather pessimistic earlier, do you agree with Major Albrecht?"

"No, Oom Piet, I do not. We have less than five thousand men and over four hundred and fifty wagons, and also women and children to take with us. It is crazy to think that we can trek across the veldt and sneak between the English cavalry and their infantry. It will be impossible to cover our tracks and the dust cloud we will create will be visible for miles. Regardless of how tired they are, the soldiers will be driven by their officers to chase us. They have numbers on their side; they will chase us even if it kills their men."

"But if it does kill them, that would be good, wouldn't it?" It was a weak attempt at humour by Kritzinger and no one laughed.

"That's why we have to do it tonight," Albrecht defended his suggestion. "If we travel at night, they will have less chance of realising that we have left. We'll have a head start."

"So we'll have a head start," retorted de Wet, "but we still have to cross the river. The English will know this and will make sure they occupy every drift along the Modder between here and its source. They can easily shut the door on us."

"That's why it is important that we leave tonight. Once we have passed the British at Klip Drift, we can cross the river at Klip Kraal Drift or at Paardeberg, or even at Koodoosrand Drift, if necessary. The English cannot hold all of the drifts and, with a head start, we should reach one of them before the English do."

The group fell silent, each contemplating Albrecht's proposal.

"Neef Piet?" asked Cronjé.

"Well, I don't know. There are a hell of a lot of English soldiers out there and my brother's information tells us that there are a hell of a lot more on the way. It will be very difficult to get past them and there *may* be enough of them to hold *all* the drifts."

"So we stay, while the English build up their numbers between us and Bloemfontein?" asked Ferreira, the irritation in his voice clear.

"Hell no, we can't do that! Of course we can't."

"So we have to leave?" asked Cronjé.

De Wet hesitated and then admitted with a shrug. "Yes. We have no choice. We have to leave."

"Gentlemen, is that the view of the Council?"

Everyone agreed, some verbally, some with a curt nod.

"So we have a decision. Now we must get ready to leave."

"General, if I could make one further point?" It was Albrecht.

"Of course, Major."

"I have no doubt you already understand that the key to our plan succeeding is speed."

"Indeed, Major, that goes without saying. We will make ready in a manner not to arouse the suspicion of the English as to our intentions, and move out as soon as it is dark."

The look on Albrecht's face made it clear he was not happy about some detail of the plan.

"There is something else, Major?"

Albrecht hesitated. He seemed to be mulling over a difficulty in his mind. He looked at Cronjé, took a deep breath and asked, "I assume you are including the wagons in your plans?"

The expression on Cronjé's face indicated the affirmative. Albrecht looked around the group of men.

"Of course that means that we need to travel at the speed of the wagons." Albrecht hesitated, feeling all eyes on him. "Might I suggest that in the interests of speed we… um… we leave the wagons behind?"

The countenance of every man present, including Cronjé, turned to one of shock. They stared at Albrecht as though Satan himself had suddenly appeared before them.

De la Rey slammed his fist on the table, flinching at the pain of his uncontrolled action.

"Have you gone crazy, man?" he stormed. "Do you expect our burgers to abandon their possessions and their families to the enemy?" He glared at Cronjé. "Oom, I need your shambok. This man may be on our side, but he deserves a thorough beating for suggesting such things."

"I did not mean we abandon the women and children," Albrecht placated. "Of course we must take them, but they can travel in Cape carts, which are faster." However, this compromise did not change the looks of disbelief to which he was being subjected. He continued feebly, "It was only a suggestion that I thought might help us with our situation, but I can see it is not a good idea."

"We take the wagons," said Cronjé grinning happily at the men around him.

Friday 16 February 1900

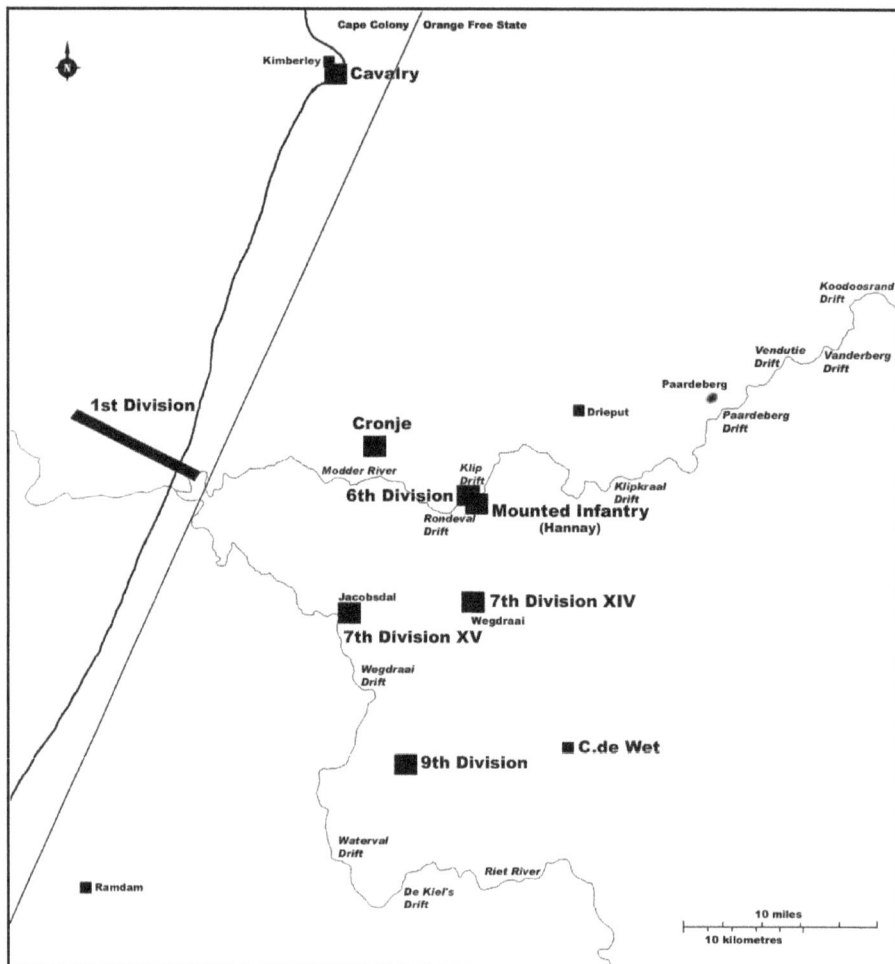

Map 7: Morning of 16 February 1900

Colonel Ormelie Campbell Hannay

Colonel Ormelie Campbell Hannay ran his experienced hand down the matted flank of his horse, feeling the protruding ribs ripple under his fingers.

"Well, old girl, you are not in as good a condition as when I first got you. No, not in a good state at all."

He reflected that even with two days of only light patrols and rest, the effect on the horses of the four days of marching had been devastating, especially with the reduced rations they were on.

"And now," he continued, half to his horse and half to himself, "there is the appalling news that a commando of Boers has snuck behind Roberts and captured two hundred of our wagons near Waterval Drift, with half our supplies, including all our forage. Sorry, old girl, but you are going to have to survive on the dry veld grass a while longer."

Men could cope, he mused. They could shoot their food on the veld and there was an abundance of game in the apparently barren landscape. He could not understand how on earth it survived. But their horses certainly were not able to flourish in the same way as the springbuck and other antelope. It was just as well that the antelope did survive, otherwise the men would be fairing as badly as the horses. Hannay patted his horse absent-mindedly. She hung her head as though resigned to the knowledge that her hunger was not going to be satisfied any time soon. Her discomfort was aggravated by the flies. Roused by the warming morning air, they were already swarming around her eyes and nostrils. It was just after eleven o'clock and the heat was mounting. It was going to be another sweltering day.

A movement caught Hannay's attention over his horse's back. Through the buzzing flies he saw a figure rising from a group of men sheltering under the shade of a stunted sallow. He was from one of the irregular units assembled from around the Empire, an Australian or perhaps a Canadian? Following the direction of the man's pointing finger, Hannay spied a small herd of goats making its way towards the muddy river. The light was clear and the air still – the heat had not yet reached the point where the landscape shimmered as though the earth was evaporating. Hannay watched as the soldier raised his rifle and carefully took aim. The rifle went off and to the great merriment and joshing of his comrades and a look of disgust from the rifleman the bullet struck the ground some distance beyond the goat. He was taking aim again when there was a very loud shout.

"Oi!"

The soldier lowered his rifle, looked around and snapped to attention. It was a regimental sergeant-major from the Welsh regiment, marching smartly towards the unfortunate man. His friends stopped laughing.

"How dare you?!" the sergeant-major yelled into the man's face.

"Sir."

"How dare you, soldier?"

"Sir. I thought they were only goats, sir."

"They are *only* goats, soldier. What are they?"

"Only goats, sir."

"So why are you wasting Her Majesty's valuable ammunition shooting goats."

No answer followed. The poor fellow stood as still as a statue.

"And you *did not* even hit it. You wasted Her Majesty's bullet without hitting anything. Are you incompetent?"

While the soldier was enduring the sergeant-major's withering attention, Hannay could see that his friends had turned away and were covering their faces in their slouch hats, their bodies shaking with silent laughter.

"Well, *are* you incompetent? Do I want soldiers who can't hit their targets in my army? Do we want our Dutch friends to know we have soldiers who cannot shoot?"

Still there was no answer.

"So, what happened soldier?"

"I shot too high, sir."

"You shot too high."

"Yes sir."

"Please explain to me," continued the booming voice, which had now attracted quite an audience, "why you shot too high."

"I set the sights wrong, sir."

"You set the sights wrong and you shot too high."

"Yes sir." Silence. "Er, because I overestimated the distance to the target, sir."

"Ah, so you *are* incompetent?"

"Yes sir."

"Corporal," the sergeant-major called out to no one in particular as a man ran up from the crowd that had gathered.

"Yes sir?"

"Please explain to this incompetent colonial why he finds himself in the embarrassing situation of setting his sights incorrectly."

"The reason, sir, is that the light conditions in Southern Africa are like none anywhere else in the world. The clarity of the air is such that it makes targets seem further away than they actually are. As a consequence, it is a failing of the average soldier, and most especially those from the colonies, that they tend to overestimate the distance to their targets. Unfortunately, sir, this does not appear to be a failing of the Boer, who has an unfailing eye for estimating distances. This explains why they are in the habit of being able to shoot the monocles from the eyes of our officers, sir."

"Thank you, corporal. Now take this colonial and please turn him into a rifleman. See to it that he becomes the army's most proficient estimator of distances by the end of the day."

Hannay could imagine that the corporal would be none too pleased at having been given that chore and would blame the unfortunate colonial for being the cause. He would take it out on him as a consequence. But the regimental sergeant-major had not finished.

"Anyone," he bellowed, "who can provide me with a fresh, tender and tasty hock of mutton for my evening meal will receive my personal week's ration of tobacco, but no wasting Her Majesty's ammunition."

The men required no further invitation. They were up in an instant and soon having a merry dance with the goats. Hannay, and an increasing number of men, watched with delight and encouraged the men noisily as they tried, with limited success, to capture the animals. A gaggle of Lancers, left behind by French as their horses could not carry them on the charge to Kimberley, were also watching. Hannay noticed two of them leap on to their horses and grasp their lances as they trotted into the arena.

"Oi, leave your damned thieving hands off my goats," the sergeant-major yelled after them. They laughed at him over their shoulders as they sped up, having spotted an opportune target. In short shrift, and with an extravagant flourish of the lance, the goat was skewered. This was followed by an equally extravagant flourish of language from the sergeant-major, who demanded that the infantry catch the rest of the animals before the thieving cavalry took them all.

One of the Lancers spied a particularly fine white beast attempting to make its escape. Galloping forward, he cut off its retreat and drove it towards the watching crowd with a whoop of excitement. The goat dashed wildly away from the pursuing horse and rider. It suddenly became aware of the wall of shouting humanity before it and, deciding that the single horse was a better bet, spun around in panic and charged back towards the galloping horse, which by now was virtually on top of it. Before either could take avoiding action, the goat was among the horse's hooves. The horse leapt into the air, all four feet leaving the ground, arching its back. The Lancer, who had not recovered from leaning forward in an attempt to impale the charging goat, threw aside his lance and grabbed any part of the horse that came to hand in a desperate attempt to hang on, but to no avail. He was flung clear of his saddle, landing in an ungainly fashion in a cloud of dust.

The cheer from the crowd, including those of his cavalry colleagues, was deafening. The sudden burst of noise stopped the goat in its tracks and it looked back at the chaos it has caused. As the Lancer recovered himself and started to sit up, the goat seemed to conclude that here was a target of similar size to itself, on which to take out its annoyance on having been chased and tormented. It lowered its head and rushed forward. The Lancer realised what was happening just in time to take avoiding action. He rolled away from the horns driving towards him, causing many cries of "Shame on you!" and "Stand up to it, it's only a *little* goat!"

Above all the noise of the crowd, the sergeant-major's voice boomed, "I want that beast alive! And I shall give a month's cigarette rations to the man who brings it to me."

The crowd ran forward and, with much joviality, the animal was eventually captured, but not before it had caused more than one soldier to land unceremoniously on his posterior. The sergeant-major was delighted.

"From now on," he announced in mock tribute to the animal when it was finally presented to him, "I shall call you 'Lance' and you will be our mascot. You felled a horseman so, I believe, you will bring us good luck against the Boer."

This was received with a great roar of agreement and much congratulatory attention to the terrified goat.

Hannay joined in the laughter. There was a day when he would have taken part in the fun, but now he had to behave like a senior officer – more's the pity. Anyway, he was too old to be chasing after goats. These last few days had been a very welcome break after the arse-breaking ride across the dusty, sun-bleached veld. As he ran his hand down the flank of his horse, which had taken the brunt of the forced march across the dust bowl, he was suddenly aware of someone calling his name. He looked up, but did not recognise the approaching horseman.

"Colonel Hannay!" The man was breathless; he had been riding hard. "Colonel, you are to assemble your men immediately and move out. The Boers have broken through."

What! The word did not break his lips. Outwardly, Hannay remained unperturbed by the news.

"Corporal, calm down, dismount, use the appropriate protocol and deliver the orders in a more seemly fashion."

The man dismounted and threw an untidy salute.

"Corporal, less haste, more speed."

"Yes sir." The corporal tried again, and this time his salute was more or less to Hannay's satisfaction.

"The message is?"

"From General Kelly-Kenny, sir. The Boers have broken through, sir. General Kitchener is livid."

"Kitchener?"

"Yes sir, he is beside himself, throwing orders around left and right, sir."

"So the order is from General Kitchener?"

"Yes sir. Er, no sir. Well, sir, General Kitchener gave the order, but it is from General Kelly-Kenny, I think, sir. He is the senior officer and was present when General Kitchener gave me the order."

"And why are you giving me the order, rather than one of General Kelly-Kenny's aides-de-camp?"

The corporal looked bemused and then answered, "I was passing the generals, sir, and General Kitchener hailed me over and gave me the order. Said I must get it to you immediately. The success of Lord Roberts' campaign depends on it, sir."

"Does it?"

"Yes sir."

"And so what *is* the situation, corporal?"

"Sir, General Methuen, who holds the Magersfontein front, decided to make a push on one of the flanks of the Boer trenches earlier this morning. His troops came under heavy and accurate fire and so progress towards the Boer lines was slow. However, they continued, under heavy fire, and managed to reach the trenches, only to find them deserted and about a hundred Boers galloping away."

"One hundred men? They were held off by one hundred men?" Hannay's usual composed exterior crumbled for a second.

"They thought there were more, sir," the corporal interjected quickly. "The enemy fire was sustained and very accurate, sir. We took a number of casualties. They had no idea that the Boers had abandoned the trenches. They must have done it with great care during the night."

"I see. So do we know where they are now?"

"We think that…."

"We think?" Hannay interrupted.

The corporal blinked. "Well, sir, we're not sure, but General Kitchener has ordered the Tigers to reconnoitre. So we will know for certain very soon, sir." The corporal added helpfully, "There is a cloud of dust to our north-east. It was believed to be General French's cavalry, but it might be Cronjé. That is where you are to go, sir, to pursue the Boers, if it is them, and to stop them from escaping, sir."

"So General Methuen allows the Boers to escape and we have to chase them across the veld and stop them. Does General Kitchener understand the poor condition of our horses?"

The corporal remained silent. Hannay recognised that he had been indiscreet in his criticism of his senior officers and changed tack.

"What other plans is General Kelly-Kenny putting in place to stop the Boers?"

"I hear, sir, that General Kitchener has divided his... er ...um," the corporal flustered, "um... General Kelly-Kenny's 6th Division into two and has ordered General Knox take the 13th Brigade of the division and continue north of the Modder River to support your efforts in stopping the Boers. The 18th Brigade, led by General Kelly-Kenny, or General Kitchener – it was not clear to me which one – is to cross back to the south of the river and quick-march upstream to capture the fords and prevent the Boers from crossing, thus cutting off their retreat to Bloemfontein. The 7th Division under General Tucker is to move up to Klip Drift and secure the ford so transport can to go on to Kimberley."

"That is quite a detailed understanding of the situation for one simply 'passing by the generals'." Hannay held the corporal's eye but the corporal did not respond and kept his expression neutral. Hannay smiled at the man and he relaxed.

"These orders, are they General Kitchener's or General Kelly-Kenny's?"

"They appear to be General Kitchener's, sir."

That was interesting, thought Hannay. Kelly-Kenny was the senior officer and yet Kitchener was making all the decisions and giving all the orders. So the rumours were true, Roberts did not trust Kelly-Kenny's abilities.

"And what of Lord Roberts, corporal? Where is he in all this?"

"It is understood that he is ill in bed sir, in Jacobsdal."

"Ill? Is it one of his recurring bouts of Indian Fever?"

"I believe so, sir."

Hannay gave the corporal an appraising look.

"Thank you, corporal. You ride well and have an ear for useful information. I would like you to accompany me. What's your name?"

"Corporal Charles Percy Hill, sir. Thank you, sir, but I am expected...."

"Don't worry about that, corporal," Hannay interjected. "I shall send someone to inform your commanding officer that I have requisitioned you." And, pointing to an officer beyond his horse, he added, "Now go to Captain Crosbie and pass the order on to him. We leave immediately."

The sun was high and burning as Hannay eventually crossed to the north bank of the river. He had been delayed by Kitchener, who had insisted on explaining to him directly the importance of his mission. To avoid the delay affecting the success of his task, Hannay had sent his mounted infantry out earlier in pursuit of the Boers. He had kept fifty men back and they were now splashing through the water behind him. He twisted in his saddle to survey them. They looked eager, up for the fight, but the horses were in a very sorry state. They were malnourished and looked exhausted. It was going to be a demanding day for them and Hannay doubted whether he was going to be able to make any real progress if a chase ensued. This was going to have to be a very measured pursuit. Some of the horses shied from climbing the banks out of the river bed and only did so with the persistence of their riders, and one stubbornly refused to move at all. Hannay gave orders for the rider to find a new horse and to follow after them. Once out of the shade of the riverside trees and onto the scorching veld, the horses plodded along causing small curls of dust to rise with each footfall. Once the trooper had caught up on his new horse, Hannay coaxed the horses into a reluctant trot. He could see various suspicious clouds of dust rising into the hot, cerulean sky and directed his troop towards the largest one.

Hannay and his men approached the abandoned wagon with more caution than they had the others. They had been riding for just over an hour and this was the sixth wagon they had come across. In essence, it looked like all the others, a single, isolated covered wagon, dazzling white and motionless in the middle of the furnace-hot veld. As they got closer, Hannay could see oxen lying in a collapsed state near the front of the wagon, some still tied in position along the length of the wagon's towing chain. Others had been released but, being too exhausted to follow the retreating Boer wagons, they had been left to wander the veld.

The cloud of dust in the distance still beckoned, but Hannay was not about to leave this wagon unchecked. Although, like the previous ones, it was unlikely that there was anyone in the wagon, Hannay's thirty years' military experience meant he was loath to ignore any equipment abandoned by the enemy. In addition, there were diff-erences about this wagon, not least the horse tethered on the far side of it, as if ready and waiting to provide an escape for any rifleman secreted within the wagon. The landscape was different here as well. There was a cluster of small koppies beyond the wagon on the otherwise flat veld, and this also made Hannay more circumspect. To avoid the wagon would mean moving closer to the koppies or making a long detour.

Hannay cast his eyes across the small hills, searching for movement, not that he expected to see any. The Boers' ability to take advantage of the defensive positions the hills provided meant they would make themselves invisible. He looked back at the wagon. The worst of two evils, he concluded, was to clear the wagon rather than move closer to the koppies, especially with the wagon remaining at his back. Hannay ordered half of his troop to halt. He and the rest of the men cautiously rode forward in very open order towards the wagon. They reached the point where they were within rifle range and, had a Boer been in the wagon, the chances of him letting off a shot, leaping on the horse and making off were diminishing. Hannay noticed Corporal Hill relax.

"Corporal, now is not the time to relax. Now is when we are in greatest danger."

As Hill turned to respond, the Mausers barked. The air was suddenly alive with the whine of bullets. Hill suddenly jerked away from Hannay and dropped from his horse. Hannay's mount collapsed under him. As it fell he snatched at the reins of Hill's horse, its eyes bulging with fear, and pulled it down with him. He forced it to lie flat so that his own dead horse provided at least some shelter from the tempest of bullets that ripped around them. Sandwiched between the two animals he glanced over at Hill, only to confirm what he already knew. Poor sod. Hannay bet that Hill's last thought would have been to wonder why he had allowed himself to be dragged along on this wild goose chase.

Hannay glanced around. Most of those who had advanced on the wagon had been able to turn and gallop out of the range of the Boer Mausers. Those who had not been able to do so had reacted instantly, dismounting, pulling their horses to the ground and taking up defensive positions behind them. It seemed that at least two of his men had taken bullets.

He scanned the veld for the source of his troop's discomfort, but the sound of the Boers' rifles echoed off the cliff faces of the koppies and Hannay could not determine where the shooting was coming from. He studied the koppies, but still could see no evidence of the enemy there. The modern, smokeless powder used in the Mausers' cartridges did not help as it gave no clue to the location of the barrels that were spitting out the bullets. Hannay kept low, peering cautiously around his dead horse. Bullets were plunging into the animal's flesh so frequently that the sound reminded him of popping corn. He stared through the shimmering landscape, trying to gauge where the bullets were coming from.

"There!" someone near him shouted. "There, in that line of shrubs. One thousand yards to the north-east."

Keeping a firm hold on Hill's horse, Hannay manoeuvred himself to get a better view. The fellow had to be mistaken. True, the scrubby vegetation he was pointing at did seem to form a more distinct line compared to that more generally scattered across the veld, but it was no taller than usual. There was no way the Boers could conceal themselves, let alone horses behind the scrub. Then he spotted a slouch hat poking around one of the bushes and below the hat he could make out the barrel of a Mauser.

"Bloody hell, I walked right into it. Bloody, bloody idiot," Hannay cursed himself. It was the horse. That bloody horse tied to that bloody wagon. And they were watching us all the time. Not from the koppies, but from some bloody donga. Hannay evaluated his situation quickly. They really would be wasting ammunition trying to hit any of the Boers in that cover. The ground was too open to rush them, either on horseback or on foot. They'd best get the hell out of here as quickly as possible. He rolled on to his back and, keeping a tight hold on the bridle of Hill's horse with his right hand, he cupped his left hand around his mouth.

"Men," he yelled at the top of his voice in order to be heard above the snapping of the Mausers and the shriek of the bullets. "We're in a bit of a fix. There's no way forward. On my move, mount as quickly as possible and get the devil out of here. You will rendezvous on me when we are out of range of the Mausers." Then he would redo this exercise in a more sensible fashion, he thought to himself.

He regarded the late corporal's horse as it lay beside him. Its flaring nostril blew flurries of dust around its face. It had been hit a few times, but the wounds did not look serious; none seemed to be haemorrhaging blood. Hannay was more concerned about whether it would be able to face the exertion of moving fast out of harm's way. He grabbed the bit hard and leapt up, pulling the horse up with him. As it rose, he swung into the saddle. It hesitated for a heart-stopping moment and then stood up. The Boer firing, which had lessened slightly, instantly returned to a crescendo as furious bullets whizzed about him. The terrified horse broke into a gallop and Hannay threw his eyes around the battlefield. While most followed suit, five stood up without their horses and were waving their hands wildly, calling out to their comrades. Hannay headed for the nearest man.

"I have you, Cartwright," he shouted. He pulled the horse round towards him. Cartwright crouched behind the corpse of his horse and waited. The air around Hannay churned with bullets, but he felt nothing punching into his flesh. As he closed on Cartwright, Hannay slowed the horse to a smooth canter, reached down and extended his arm. Cartwright linked forearms, the jolt almost pulled Hannay from the saddle, but Cartwright swung himself into position behind Hannay. Then, digging his heels into the horse's heaving flanks Hannay drove the animal into a gallop.

To his right, Hannay saw a rider and a trooper miss-time the rescue. The trooper bounced off the side of the horse, but recovered and sprinted after his rescuer. The rider swung his horse around and headed back. As they came together, the rider spun the horse around once more and lifted the passenger on board in one swift movement, and they were off, as though the devil himself was on their tail.

The Boers quickly understood the desire of the British to extract their stranded fellows from the field and they focused their fire on the horseless soldiers, forcing them to keep their heads down. Others concentrated on the rescuers as they drove their mounts towards their hapless friends. In two cases, the horses were shot from under their riders and they, too, had to take cover behind the stricken animals.

Hannay and his pillion galloped away from the line of spitting Mausers to join the men already safely out of range from the Boer riflemen. Hannay swung his horse around to assess the success of the hasty retreat. His men were returning fire, but their attempt to force the Boers to keep their heads down and stop shooting was having little effect. There were still five men stranded in the field of fire hiding behind their fallen mounts. A single horseman was still galloping across the battle zone. He headed towards one of the stranded men. As he approached, he lent forward and braced himself for the impact of swinging the trooper on board. The move was executed perfectly and a howl of support burst from the soldiers around Hannay. An instant later, however, the rider's head jolted sideways and his body went limp. He began to slip from the horse. His passenger immediately reached forward and snatched up the reins. Using one hand to control the horse, he wrapped his other arm around his wilting comrade. He drove the horse forward. Those watching screamed their encouragement.

Suddenly the horse plunged forward as its hoof sank into an animal burrow. The crack of snapping bone and its scream of pain were clearly audible above the noise of the battle. Hannay felt the bile rise in his throat at the horror of what the creature was experiencing. The riders were tossed through the air like rag dolls and landed in an explosion of dust. The firing from the Boer lines stopped, as though they were equally appalled by what they had just witnessed. The rescued soldier half rose and then collapsed. A stunned silence hung over the simmering veld. The injured horse writhed on its side in shocked silence, kicking up grey dust that settled on it like a ghostly shroud. Its broken leg stuck out at a sickening angle as it lifted its head and twisted its back in a vain effort to rise. It failed and collapsed back to the ground. It tried again and as it lifted its head a single crack from a Mauser shattered the silence. Hannay felt Cartwright jump in fright behind him. The horse's head crashed to the ground as if punched by an invisible fist. Dust billowed from around the head as though a down-stuffed pillow had been burst by the weight of its fall.

"Good God!" Cartwright muttered, "They are *bloody* fine shots."

Then, to everyone's amazement, the rescued soldier leapt up and pelted across the veld away from the Boers. The other four stranded men also took advantage of the silence of the Boer rifles and scrambled up. They bolted like rabbits, zigzagging across the veld. Even so, two never made it.

Hannay needed to regroup quickly. The last thing he needed now was to be caught in the open by a counter-attack by Lord knew how many Boers, whose horses were probably in better condition than his own and whose rifles had a greater range than his. He noticed an island of large rocks in the sea of parched grassland and directed his unit towards it.

Once among the rocks, Hannay spotted a dust trail in the distance. Concerned it might be Boer reinforcements he took out his field glasses and studied the approaching horsemen. He was soon able to confirm that it was the main body of his unit, which had left Klip Drift before him. They must have been attracted to the area by the sound of gunfire. He selected two soldiers whose horses were still in reasonable condition to intercept them and bring them in safely. Hannay made sure the wounded were as comfortable as possible. He looked across the veld to the casualties that dotted the grassland. He counted six motionless shapes lying under the scorching sun. He knew two were dead, but he could not be sure about the others. As soon as the fresh troops arrived, he would drive the Boers away and rescue the wounded and retrieve the bodies of the fallen.

But as Hannay looked over the battlefield, he could see the Boers were already in the process of evacuating their position. Horses with riders rose miraculously from the ground as they emerged from the dry donga they had occupied and cantered away – around one hundred of them, in his estimation. He scowled grimly as he recalled the words of the late Corporal Hill: "The enemy fire was sustained and very accurate, sir. A number of casualties were had." Yes, he had to agree. The Boers shot with a religious zeal.

Hannay watched as the Boers dispersed and moved towards and into the koppies. Soon they were nowhere to be seen. So this time they *were* in the koppies and, by God, they were going to be difficult to dislodge. As much as General Kitchener might wish it, with this calibre of rear guard to deal with, there was no possibility of catching or stopping the Boer wagons that day. It would have to be tomorrow, and even then it would take some doing.

With the Boers gone, Hannay ordered twenty men to return to the battlefield to care for the wounded. He then settled onto a rock, took out his pipe, lit it and puffed on it calmly as he watched the dusty approach of his reinforcements.

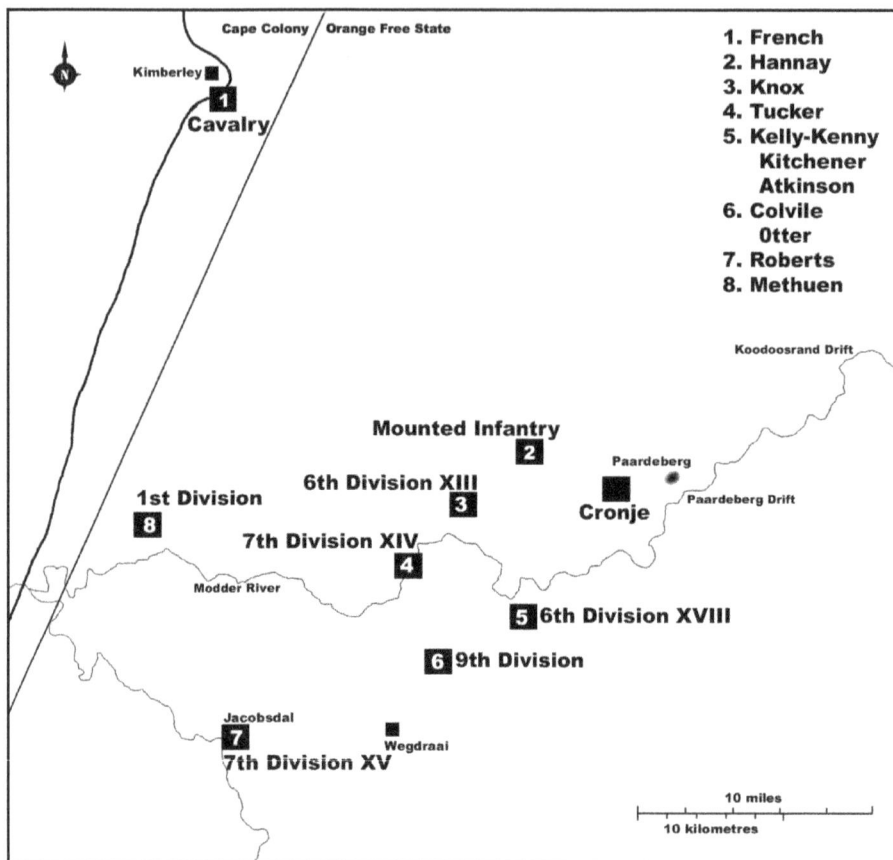

Map 8: Night of 16 – 17 February 1900

Saturday 17 February 1900

Lieutenant-General John Denton Pinkstone French

Lieutenant-General John Denton Pinkstone French sat comfortably on his horse. It was three o'clock in the morning, the moon was descending to the horizon and the clear night air was decidedly chilly. A shiver ran down his spine. He could not decide whether it was caused by the cold night air or the sight in front of him.

Before him in the cold, grey light of the moon, the dark figures that made up the remnants of his cavalry were gathering. It consisted of just one thousand two hundred men and horses. He realised it was the small number of cavalrymen that had formed up before him that had set his spine tingling. Of the four thousand men he had started with at Ramdam, only twelve hundred had horses fit enough to fulfil the order received from Kitchener late yesterday to cut off Cronjé's escape. It was going to be a tall order. He was going to have to be canny. If his twelve hundred were to stop an army of six thousand well-mounted Boers, he was going to have to be mobile and use the terrain to his advantage, harry the enemy, slip in fast and slip out fast. He would have to reveal small numbers of men, hide them and then reshow them to make the Boers think he still had his full complement of four thousand cavalry at his disposal. He would have to rely on his artillery. And their shooting would have to be accurate. Over the last few days he'd had them spending every spare minute practising range-finding. He would also have to be flexible in deploying his artillery: fire a few shots from one location and then move on to another. That would require a lot of work from the horses. He hoped they would be up for the challenge. He shivered again as he thought of the two thousand five hundred horses that had died or become incapacitated since they left Ramdam – an attrition rate of five hundred a day! That was twenty horses every hour for the last five days. It was a shocking testament to their march.

The riders had fared somewhat better. The people of Kimberley had treated them like heroes, offering them all manner of food, and Cecil Rhodes had laid on a fine banquet at a 'Heroes Reception'. The food had been plentiful and the wine had flowed. It had made French wonder why the relief of the town had been so urgent. Clearly,

Roberts had been under the impression that Kimberley had been about to fall. Rhodes had obviously been playing up the destitute conditions within the besieged town. Still, the news of Kimberley's relief would be well received in England and Roberts had personally sent a message of thanks to French and his cavalry. In light of the calamitous news coming from the Natal front, a good news story was definitely in order. Poor old Redvers Buller had been given yet another bloody nose. What was it they were calling him in the papers? 'Reverse Buller?' It was a cruel play on his name, yet French still allowed himself a mischievous chuckle at his friend's misfortune.

How fickle the public was: a hero one minute, an inconvenience the next. Indeed, in Kimberley, the initial euphoria towards his men on being freed from the clutches of the Boer did not last long, and the offerings of food had quickly dried up, leaving the men back on reduced army rations within a day or two. And they were *severely* reduced rations. French reflected ironically how it was that blasted 'minor commandant' de Wet who was the cause of the meagre rations to which his men were currently subjected. As well as making a nuisance of himself on the march between the Riet and Modder Rivers, he had managed to steal an entire convoy of wagons from under Roberts' nose. It was beyond French's comprehension how Roberts could have allowed de Wet and his gang of farmers to ambush and capture a supply train of two hundred wagons transporting two thousand rations of beef, biscuits and forage.

French re-ran in his mind the story he had heard about Roberts hearing of the loss of the wagons. He had asked the Head of the Army Service Department whether he could guarantee full rations for his men during the chase to prevent the Boers' escape.

"I cannot, sir," came the reply.

"Three-quarter rations?"

"No sir."

"Half, perhaps?"

"I cannot answer for it."

"Quarter rations?"

"Yes sir."

"Well," Roberts had replied, "I think the men will do it for me."

And thus the decision had been made to starve the troops for the love of their commander. Some of Kimberley's chattering class claimed that a lesser general would have shrunk from laying so terrible a burden on his men. French shook his head. His belief was that those claims simply ignored the initial carelessness with which the supplies were lost in the first place. There was no doubt that this war offered a real opportunity for a great commander-in-chief to shine. It was a pity, frowned French sourly, that the British army did not have such a commander in Southern Africa. He believed Roberts had been fortunate that the Boers had been caught out by the rapidity of his own cavalry advance. At Klip Drift, it had resulted in the enemy fleeing so quickly that they had abandoned their wagons, thereby providing ample supplies for the cavalry to replenish their own inadequate provisions. But French concluded that it did not excuse Roberts' loss of their own supplies, which had caused French to leave a trail of dead and dying horses in his wake.

A sudden cold wind played across the parade, bringing with it the sounds of Africa – a roar of lions and the cackle of hyenas. It made the horses restless and their nickering made French recollect himself. He rode forward to present his orders to his men.

"Gentlemen, while we have been driving the enemy from Kimberley, it appears that Cronjé's main force has been allowed to break through our lines and is now heading towards Bloemfontein." French stopped and waited.

"Sir?" came the awaited interjection.

"Yes, captain?"

"Was the 6th Division not supposed to secure the area and prevent the retreat of the Boers, sir?"

French left the question unanswered; he'd made his point.

"Let us not dwell on what should have been. We have been requested by General Kitchener to stop Cronjé crossing the Modder River. If they are allowed to cross the river, they are likely to set up another defensive position and that will require yet another expansive flanking movement, which," he added, looking at the depleted numbers in front of him, "we can ill afford. We are to ride along the Koodoosrand range towards the ford at Koodoosrand Drift. That is one of the last convenient crossing points for Cronjé. The infantry is marching in quick order to secure all the other fords between Klip Drift and Koodoosrand Drift. The aim is to prevent Cronjé crossing the river and then to capture him.

"It will be another long, hard march, and I have left our departure to the last feasible moment to allow our horses as much rest as possible, but no further delay can be endured. We have the benefit of a few hours of night before the sun rises and shrivels us like raisins, so let us make the most of it. No more talk; we move out."

He turned his horse and led the men into the darkness away from Kimberley. Major Haig was beside him. They rode at a gentle trot in silence for some minutes, French monitoring the uneven gait of his horse. Poor old fellow, he sympathised. French doubted that his horse would make it through the war, but if it could hold out long enough to allow him to stop Cronjé, then the war was likely to be significantly shortened. The old devil, Cronjé, was held in such high esteem as the saviour of the nation that the capture, or death, of the 'Tyrant of Potchefstroom' would have a very demoralising effect on the Boers' citizen army. And the Boers did not appear to have anyone who could fill his boots. French turned to Haig.

"What do you think, Douglas?" This was a personal conversation, man to man, a means of passing the hours in front of them in a more relaxed fashion. "About the importance of 'Oom Piet' to his fellow burghers? If he falls, do they all fall?"

"An appealing notion, General." Protocol did not allow Haig the same level of familiarity, but he felt comfortable substituting the usual 'Sir' for 'General'. "But I must say that I am unconvinced."

"You do not believe Cronjé is the key to our success?"

"I suspect he is an important part, but not the key."

"Oh? And what might *the* key be?"

"Cronjé certainly holds the key to Bloemfontein, there can be no doubt of that. Remove Cronjé and his force and the gates to the town are opened. Of course, the Boers will attempt to throw up any number of defensive positions in our way, but we have shown that we can out flank them. However, in order to repeat similar flanking movements, we would have to build up our strength in cavalry. The pace has been punishing, but you know that better than me. I suspect that, in future, as soon as we make a serious move to outflank the Boers, they will retreat. That is the Boers' weakness; they hate the back door being shut on them. Indeed, it surprised me that Cronjé stayed at Magers-fontein as long as he did. But then this is the first time we have done something this tremendous against them. They will learn and will not allow it to happen again. We will also have to learn and our lesson is that our forces must be much more mobile."

"Do you mean expanding the cavalry?"

Aware of French's low opinion of mounted infantry, especially the colonial riff-raff that Roberts had been recruiting, Haig responded cautiously.

"I do, General. We need to increase the number of cavalry in particular, but the problem is that our speed is hampered by the pace of the infantry. It would seem to me that support by a more mobile mounted infantry might be useful. For example, if the 6th Division had been able to get to Klip Drift more quickly, then we could have relieved Kimberley sooner, before the Boers had secured the ridges either side of the valley *en route* to the town. We could have taken a leisurely ride to Kimberley and saved the horses."

"True, but that was an extraordinary ride, by Jove." French laughed. "I may still have ordered the charge anyway you know, Douglas. The temptation for that gallop was too much to be sure that I would not do it again!"

He glanced across at Haig in the diminishing moonlight. Haig laughed nostalgically and French joined him.

"Yes, General, it was a stupendous ride, and I would not have missed it for the world." Haig chuckled with delight as he thought about it: the thunder of galloping hooves and the whooping men, the dust, the exhilaration of the horse toiling beneath him, rushing forward, and the sheer joy of galloping across the open countryside, with no hedge or barrier to slow the pace. "God, it must have been an impressive sight for the Boers looking down on us."

"I doubt any of them even appreciated the grandeur of it," responded French. "Those Boers may be able to shoot, and shoot damnably well, but they know nothing of the beauty and glory of battle or of the heritage of our regiments. Once we have defeated them, they will return to their farms as though the war never happened, except for the odd church service in honour of their dead. And the services themselves will have no pomp or style."

"It seems to me," countered Haig, "that they do not tend to commemorate their war dead, but rather pray to God in thanks for their victories, as though the men involved had little impact on the whole affair."

"It is a strange form of Christianity, almost zealot-like," agreed French.

"And *that* is the key to this war, General – and where our danger lies," added Haig, returning to the subject of why the defeat of Cronjé might not cause the downfall of the Republics.

French gave Haig a questioning look.

"What I mean is that it is *their* view that they are the chosen people and that the Lord has directed them to this land. The land is their God-given right and some of them, perhaps most of them, will defend that God-given right to the end, regardless of what happens to Cronjé."

"But once we have taken Bloemfontein and Johannesburg and Pretoria, what is left for them to fight for?"

"The Boers are not townsfolk, General, they are farmers. We may take their towns, but they will still hold their land. And they will use it to their advantage. Each farm can be used as a depot to supply a mobile army of small units that can cut our communications and the supply lines between the towns and cities. We will be shut up behind barricades in the towns, slowly starving to death, just like Kimberley, Ladysmith and Mafeking."

French pulled up his horse, bringing the whole troop to a halt, and considered Haig.

"It would appear you have been giving this some considerable thought, Major."

"Oh, not much sir," Haig laughed. "Indeed, very little, sir. I heard some of the Tigers having a heated discussion about it. But it does make a good story."

"No it does not," was the rather terse response. "In future, if you hear such absurd nonsense I suggest you put a stop to it. Those dammed colonialists will demoralise our men with such ludicrous talk."

With that, French swung his horse's head away and made off in a determined fashion. It was clear that he now wished to be left alone. What had started as a pleasant and friendly discussion had deteriorated into an irksome critique of British military strategy. Military history had taught and reiterated the importance of towns as strategic military targets, and tales that went against accepted military doctrine were unhelpful. Haig should have known better than to recount such stuff and nonsense.

Then French recalled that Haig had laughed at the absurdity of the notion. He conceded that Haig obviously placed as little merit in the idea as he did himself and he decided that he had been hard on Haig and that he would apologise when Haig deemed it safe to reacquaint himself with his General. French smiled. At least Haig understood the importance of the cavalry. He really should not have taken it out on his old friend, especially as, if it were not for Haig, he, General French, would most likely not be commanding the cavalry in Southern Africa. He thought it was ironic that he was fighting in the country that had bankrupted him. He had been a fool to become involved in speculating in that dubious South African gold mining company. It had not been one of his best investments. Indeed, it had threatened his career because an officer without means could not remain within the cavalry. French recalled how Haig had kindly offered to bail him out with a loan of £2,500 and then wryly remembered Haig's insistence on them agreeing a formal contract with interest. Crafty bugger! But he had saved French's bacon, and it was for that reason that he found himself in South Africa. The first thing he was going to do when he got to Johannesburg was to visit the offices of the broker and demand the return of his money.

French reined in his horse and settled in his saddle. While he waited for Haig to catch up, he studied the red glow of the western sky as an immense, deep scarlet sun started to creep over the horizon. It was going to be another boiling hot day.

Burgher Fredrick Abram Marais

Burgher Fredrick Abram Marais caught the youth, Johannes Petrus Coetzee, as he started to slide from his horse and shook him awake.

"Hey son, you need a bit more practice at riding and sleeping. That must be the tenth time I've had to stop you falling off your horse. You must be careful. I knew someone in a commando who fell off his horse and no one noticed. The next thing he knew he had a dozen English bayonets pointing at him."

"What happened to him?"

Marais did not answer. He was watching the immense, red sphere lift from the horizon. It was one of those spectacles that always held his attention. From the time he was a child, the huge, liquid, African sun rising from the earth had always mesmerised him. He watched it roll up from the rim of the earth, throwing shafts of red light through the scattered clouds and over the parched landscape and dancing through the dust billowing over the Afrikander caravan. He stared hard at the base as it rose into the heavens, watching the strange effect that made it look like some part of the sun was left behind below the horizon.

"Oom!"

Marais started. "Hm, sorry, what did you say?"

"What happened to your friend?"

"Oh, he managed to escape," Marais responded casually. "Just as well, because, like us, he was a Cape rebel so he would have been given some extra special treatment once the English had discovered that fact."

"Yes, that sickens me," spat Coetzee in youthful zeal. "The fact that the English treat us as traitors. I mean, can they really believe that we Cape Afrikanders feel any loyalty to their queen and country just because they took over our country? We do not even feel loyalty to Holland or France and that *is* our heritage, so why should we have any love for England?"

"Some Afrikanders do," Marais pointed out. He enjoyed engaging with this young man, who, although only 15 years old, had passion and a good brain. He was also, despite his age, an Afrikander of the old stock. In fact, it was surprising that his family was still in the

Cape and had not migrated with the others during the Great Trek – and this intrigued Marais.

After some thought, Coetzee spoke.

"Oom," he said, touching the brim of his slouch hat in apology for the fact that he was about to contradict the older man. "That is not love. That is convenience, laziness, even cowardice. Those English Boers have got too rich and fat. They have an easy life with nice jobs, given to them by the English government. They feel they have too much to lose. But in truth, they have already lost everything the Afrikander holds dear to his heart – his land and his independence. We have lost the Cape and Natal to the English, so we should fight for the South African Republics. That's what you think, isn't it, or you would not be here?"

"Of course."

As Coetzee was about to expand on his thoughts of the injustice of the English, he spied a particular wagon, its canvas canopy bathed in the red glow of the sun. Excusing himself, he rode off towards it. Marais had a suspicion that there was a girl involved. He grinned to himself and settled into the easy, rolling gait of his horse.

Around him a symphony of creaking and jingling rose from the wagons as they lumbered and jolted across the uneven veldt. Except for the occasional sneeze to remove the dust accumulating in their nostrils, the cattle were silent. Their heavily horned heads were low and their solid shoulders pushed against the bulk of the wagons they hauled behind them. Alongside walked the native drivers, in heavy coats against the cold and with rags wrapped around their faces to keep out the worst of the dust. Occasionally one would stir himself from his early morning lethargy to play his long, leather shambok over the backs of the cattle to encourage those animals he considered were not pulling their weight.

Marais looked up at the sun. It was losing its vivid red colour and was fast becoming an angry, burning orange. Roaming across the veldt were over four thousand horsemen, ghost-like figures swathed in an orange-tinted shroud of dust that, as he watched, turned into a fine yellow haze.

The coldness of the previous night was starting to abate. Ahead of him, a line of over one hundred wagons stretched into the distance and, behind him, a further two hundred extended as far as the eye could see into the morning shadows. Walking alongside the wagons were the women and children of the laager, brothers and sisters holding hands, with their free hands stuffed into their pockets against the residual cold. The mothers' long, dark, heavy overcoats, stained with months of rough living in the laager and in a war zone, brushed the dust into little sand-storms around their ankles, their wide bonnets hiding their pensive, dust-powdered faces.

To preserve the teams of oxen, only the very youngest and the infirm were allowed to travel in the wagons. Marais noted the silent acceptance with which even the young children trudged along, holding the hands of their mothers. It was said that even old Hester Cronjé was walking, setting an example for the others, against the pleas of her husband. She was, apparently, as stubborn as he was.

A horse drew up next to Marais. It was Coetzee. He had a huge grin across his face as he offered Marais some stormjager cakes.

"Thank you," said Marais, placing all but one in his pocket. As he ate, he asked, "How many wagons do you think we'll lose today?"

"Pardon, Oom?"

"How many wagons will we lose today? We had to abandon fifty at Magersfontein. We have left a trail of them in our wake and we left another eighty behind when we started up again last night. How many do you think we will lose today?"

"I don't know, Oom. The cattle are being driven hard, but if we can get to the river today and the cattle can be refreshed, then we might not lose too many more. I hope so anyway."

"I think we should have left all the wagons behind."

The youth laughed. "You townies!"

Marais joined in laughing to show he was not offended by the comment. Although Coetzee knew Marais to be a farmer, he had, for some reason, developed the view that Marais was a rather well-to-do, gentleman farmer, who spent little time on his farm and preferred to be in his local town doing deals.

"Us townies, hey?" he quipped.

"Yes, Oom. You no longer have that wanderlust. You know, the desire for new, open spaces, the need to move regularly to get away from all the other people – that spirit of adventure. It has gone."

"Yes. We are very dull, us 'townies'." Marais knew this would embarrass Coetzee and his remark had the desired effect.

"I'm sorry, Oom," he said quickly. "I did not mean you personally. Of course, you would not be here if *you* were like that."

"I'm joking, Neef Johannes. But tell me more about this spirit, this spirit of the Afrikander."

Coetzee studied Marais to make sure he was not being made to look a fool. "It's true, Oom," he continued earnestly. "Because of this wanderlust the Afrikander travels at a whim, but it also means that he takes everything with him. His whole house, all his family and everything he owns. A true Afrikander is unable to travel far from his farm without taking his wagon. It is part of him, part of his soul. Where most people would look for a hotel, the Afrikander will distain such ostentation for the comfort of his wagon. To leave his wagon behind when he travels any distance is like cutting off his arm. You have seen how unhappy the women become when they have to abandon their wagons. It is as if they have lost a child."

Marais gave Coetzee a sideways look. "But you did not bring your wagon. Are you also a townie?"

Coetzee returned Marais a look of horror. "Me, a townie! *No* way! Do I look soft in the head?" He hesitated. He really should be more careful with what he said, but Marais showed no signs of having taken offence. Indeed, unobserved by Coetzee, Marais was clenching his jaw to stop grinning and was trying to keep an impassive look to his features.

"I am a true Afrikander," Coetzee announced proudly, "Godfearing, independent and as honest as the day is long. And I will fight to the death for my right to independence and to worship my God and to protect my land."

"But, nevertheless, an Afrikander without a wagon," Marais pointed out mischievously.

Coetzee eyed him. He was not sure if his companion was treating him seriously. "I have a wagon," he said at last, firmly. "Back home, we have three wagons," he added pointedly, "I had to leave mine at home because it would have taken four times as long to get to the commando with a wagon than simply riding my horse. So I *had* to leave it behind."

"Very sensible. And that is precisely my point. We seem to be surrounded by the English army and yet we are travelling at a speed that allows tortoises to get out of our way. I'm not even convinced that we are trying to get away. If we are, then the wagons should be left behind, the women and children whisked off out of danger and we should be riding as though the devil was about to stick his fork up our jacksies."

The young man started at the mention of the dark angel. He gave Marais a disapproving look and slipped his hand into his coat to touch his Bible. Marais noticed the movement and continued quickly.

"Neef Johannes, don't you think we should be moving faster?"

"Oom Piet knows what he is doing. The General has beaten the English before and with God's guidance will do so again."

Marais felt the sharpness of the reply. Yes, this young lad was definitely an Afrikander of the old stock.

The two of them fell silent and Marais slipped once more into a reflective mood. Cronjé was going to need more than God's help to get out of this mess. Maybe, thought Marais, he was just a townie, because he did not feel the awe in which Cronjé was held. The strength of the feeling shown to the man by others was beyond him. Of course Cronjé was a hero of the War of Independence, but that was in 1881, when the English still wore red uniforms. It was also true that he had done well so far against the English – as a farmer general against a professional general. And, until recently, he had shown himself to be the superior tactician. But that did not change the fact that the Afrikander army had been following a policy of strategic retreat for the last couple of months, and now the English had a new general and were in the Orange Free State. If the Afrikanders did not change their strategy, they would soon find themselves defending the outskirts of Bloemfontein, and, Marais thought grimly, if they did not speed up, the English might even reach Bloemfontein before they did.

The fact that the English were very close on their tails was evidenced by the shooting they had heard the day before when they had halted the laager at Drieput Farm to rest the oxen. The shooting had been that of the rear guard, who had held a troop of mounted infantry at bay. There had been much talk about how the commando had fooled the English by hiding in a donga rather than in nearby kopjes as they would normally do. The English rode right into the ambush. But when English reinforcements arrived, the rear guard had sensibly retreated to a more secure location among the rocks of the kopjes. They were eventually driven off by an attack from further reinforcements of both mounted infantry and a division of regular infantry.

The infantry had simply marched up to the kopjes and initiated an attack without stopping for breath. The attack was said to have been astonishing to see. Marais asked himself a question that he thought must have crossed the minds of every man in the Afrikander convoy: how could they expect to defeat an army that has soldiers who act on orders, whatever the personal cost? There was no doubt they were extremely courageous men, these English. Nevertheless Marais noted with some satisfaction that the Afrikander rear guard had done its job. They had held the English off long enough for the oxen to be rested and re-inspanned to the wagons so that the laager could move off again. Except, of course, for those eighty wagons that had had to be abandoned because, even after resting, their teams of oxen were in such bad condition they could no longer drag the wagons from a standstill. It was terrible to watch the oxen straining against the inertia of the wagons, throwing their shoulders and chests against the unmoving weight, tossing their heads in frustration and distress, but without the strength to set the wheels turning. Many collapsed in their tethers, unable to get up again. He had seen grown men weep as they cut the animals loose and abandoned the wagons.

Yet even with the rear guard delaying them, the English remained on their tails, like hyenas after a wounded buck. And the English behind him were not the only concern for Marais. To the north, near Kimberley, was the main English cavalry and the Lord only knew what they were up to. Marais hoped they were still wasting their time chasing the guns around the countryside and that they had not yet turned their attention on the retreating Cronjé.

"Oom, look!"

Coetzee was twisting around in his saddle, first to his left and then to his right and back again, his finger jabbing towards the west. Scattered along the horizon drifted a series of grey dust clouds, like the smoke of bush fires. Marais counted four separate plumes.

"Hell's teeth!" he exclaimed. "So many!"

"So many what?" asked Coetzee dumbly.

"English," Marais replied, almost to himself.

"One could be de Wet," suggested Coetzee hopefully.

Marais stared through the developing heat haze. "It could be," he agreed, "but I doubt whether his small commando would make such big clouds of dust."

His attention, like many others in the commando, was focused on the left-most plume as it rose into the warming sky. He could make out the line of trees that ran along the top of the steep banks of the Modder River and the dust was rising from the veldt beyond the trees, to the south of the river. The facts struck him.

"They're not just chasing us, they are also racing us to the drifts! God in Heaven, we need to speed up or we are going to be caught like rats in a trap."

This time Coetzee did not concern himself with the blasphemous language of his companion. A new urgency developed within the Afrikander army. Shouts went up and men and their native drivers started to urge the oxen on with greater passion. They had to stay in front of the English, and they had to reach, and cross, the drifts at Paardeberg before they were seized by the English.

Lieutenant-Colonel William Dillon Otter

Lieutenant-Colonel William Dillon Otter, his adjutant, Captain John Herbert Cecil Ogilvy, and Captain Archibald Hayne sat upon their stationary mounts and watched the 9th Division stagger past them. They had been marching virtually non-stop since the previous day when new orders from General Kelly-Kenny had arrived, although some said they were from Kitchener. These were that the division was not to remain at Wegdraai, but was to follow the 6th Division on a march along the south bank of the Modder in pursuit of the Boers.

Otter was paying particular attention to his command, the Royal Canadian Regiment of Infantry. Turning to his companions, he asked in his provincial Ontario drawl, "Captain Ogilvy, what do you think of the performance of our regiment?"

Ogilvy scanned the Canadians. They looked as if they were about to collapse. Staggering like old men, they seemed incapable of taking another step, let alone carrying the forty pounds of kit on their backs. However, to say so was unlikely to go down well with his commander. Not because of any concern about the men's inability to cope, but because it might show the colonial Canadians in a poor light compared to the Imperial forces. He studied the other regiments filing past in front of them. The 9th Division was made up of regiments with considerable histories of battles fought and honours won. In the 3rd Brigade, there were the Argyll and Sutherlands, and three regiments of Highlanders led by General Hector Macdonald, a veteran of the First Boer War and known to his men as 'Fighting Mac'. It was said that during the Battle of Majuba Hill, after running out of bullets, he took the Boers on with his fists. He was also a personal friend of Lord Roberts, having campaigned with the Field Marshal in Afghanistan. The 19th Brigade contained another Highland regiment and two English regiments of note, the Oxfordshires and the Cornwalls. They were led by General Smith-Dorrien, a veteran of the Zulu War and one of the few British survivors of their defeat at Isandlwana. It was in this brigade that the colonial Canadian volunteers found themselves. Ogilvy thought it was unfair to compare the ragtag Canadians with the glorious heritage of the home regiments. However, he knew Otter would do just that, especially as the division's commander, General Colvile, on seeing the Canadians

151

for the first time, had expressed himself as being 'satisfied' with them – hardly a ringing endorsement in Otter's eyes. But as Ogilvy watched the regiments marching past, it was obvious to him that even the professional troops were struggling. It was little wonder for they had been on the move, and until recently jogging, for hours. The delay in Ogilvy's response caused disquiet in Otter.

"You're concerned about their performance?" he drawled.

"Indeed not, sir," Ogilvy replied, his Canadian tones being more clipped and, thought Otter with some envy, sounding more reminiscent of those of the British officers than his own accent. "In point of fact," continued Ogilvy, "I would suggest quite the opposite. I was noting our performance against those of the home troops. I believe we can be justly proud of our men. When one considers that they are a volunteer force, they are standing up to this challenge with considerable steadfastness. A few have nearly fallen out, but none have. That is no different from the home troops who, one might venture, should be performing to a much higher standard, being career soldiers."

Otter was mollified, but it was typical that Imperial officers were not around when the Canadians were performing well. Otter was aggrieved that his British commanding officer, General Colvile, had been only 'satisfied' with what he had seen of the Canadians when he had reviewed them earlier in the year. He felt disappointed that the General did not recognise the work that *he* had put into creating the well-drilled and disciplined regiment that the Canadians had become. But then Colvile was a professional, regular officer of the British Empire and one would expect him to have very high standards. More training was required, concluded Otter. The men needed even more drilling and soldiering to ensure his senior British officers did eventually notice the quality of his regiment. Rifle-manship, decided Otter, was an area where the entire British army was poor. So, he thought with a smile, the Canadians would become the best shots in the British army. And they had the Canadian shooting champion, Corporal McHarg, in the regiment. He would get him to train the men.

"Captain Hayne" he said, "Once we have arrived at Paardeberg Drift and the men have eaten, please ask Corporal McHarg to arrange musketry practice."

"Yes sir."

Otter watched Hayne as he wrote down the order. He took the

proffered slip of paper, signed it and returned it. Hayne tucked it into his dispatch bag. Content, Otter looked out across the expanse of veld that lay shimmering before him. Beyond the 9th Division he saw four plumes of dust rising above the dry African landscape. The furthest was the reason of all the current excitement, because its source was now known to be the retreating Cronjé. And the one between himself and the Boers was evidently caused by the 18th Brigade of the 6th Division, which was chasing the Boers along the south bank of the Modder in an attempt to prevent Cronjé crossing the river.

Otter became aware of an erratic skirl of bagpipes. Before him, the Gordon Highlanders limped along, a piper determinedly trying to expel enough breath from his exhausted lungs and into his instrument to inspire his mates with a stirring tune. The Highland Brigade commander, Major General Hector Macdonald, seeing the man's attempts, came trotting up with his entourage.

"Captain," Macdonald called to one of his staff, "Get that fine piper a flagon of water and a nip of whisky and have a cart brought while he drinks."

The group dismounted and stood around the piper while he refreshed his throat and rested his lungs. Once finished, the piper thanked the officers most kindly, but when offered the opportunity to be transported on the cart while he played his pipes, he courteously refused, saying that he could not do so while his fellow soldiers had to march. He pointed out that he had only taken some water and rested in order to be refreshed sufficiently to play the pipes and cheer the men up. So saying, he snapped to attention, saluted the officers, and thanked the General again for his kindness. He spun around, his kilt swirling around his thighs and took up the pipes' mouthpiece. Once the bag had inflated, he started to play *Highland Laddie*, at the same time picking up his pace to a respectable walk. It was a jaunty tune and Otter recalled the first time he had heard it. It was when the Canadians had first marched into the 9th Division's camp and the Highlanders had welcomed them by piping in the new arrivals. Then they had pitched the Canadians' tents for them and had made them a light dinner. The Gordon Highlanders had immediately become the favourites of the Canadians.

Otter watched as Macdonald remounted his steed and sat ramrod straight, holding his reins in one hand and resting the other on his hip, surveying his Highland regiments as they carried on past. Otter studied the man. It was wonderful to be associated with such a fine army and especially with regiments such as the glorious Highlanders. Their officers' sense of pride must have felt like a solar glow.

"Lord, to command a regiment of that quality must be a life-defining experience," Otter muttered to himself.

"Pardon, sir?" It was Ogilvy.

"Hmm? Oh, nothing Captain," Otter mumbled.

Although Ogilvy was indispensable, Otter felt that he did tend to invade his space and thoughts too much. Otter took his small notebook from his breast pocket and jotted down a few key words. The event would be retold in one of the many letters he would write once they were at camp.

Otter glanced up to watch the piper moving away and he noted that some of his own Canadians further up the line had fallen out and collapsed in disorderly heaps in the dust.

"Ogilvy, Hayne," he snapped, "Get those men up. How dare they behave in such a shameful manner, especially having just seen the correct manner in which soldiers should go about their business? Remind them that we are the rear guard. If they fall out, they will be left behind."

Hayne took out his notebook and started to write down the order.

"Captain, this is an occasion, one of very few, when a written order is *not* required," Otter chided. "Remind them also that if they should be left behind, the only people likely to help them to their feet will be a commando of Boers, and they are not likely to be very sympathetic to their complaints."

"Yes sir."

The two captains saluted their commanding officer, swung their horses around and hastened towards the group of incapacitated men, but not too quickly as they were aware of the need to preserve the health of their own, already drooping horses. Once out of earshot, Hayne spoke to Ogilvy.

"The old man is becoming more and more of a martinet."

"Oh that's not his problem," Ogilvy replied.

"It's not?"

"No."

"No?" prompted Hayne.

"No."

Hayne looked at Ogilvy. Smart arse, he thought. He really wants me to drag it out of him.

"John, stop being a smart arse. What are you driving at?"

"He's embarrassed."

"Embarrassed? What do you mean?"

Ogilvy remained silent. He was not going to incriminate himself by making disparaging comments about his senior officer. Hayne would have to work it out for himself. He had been around Lieutenant-Colonel Otter long enough to know how he ticked.

Hayne waited, but soon realised that Ogilvy was not going to enlighten him. Embarrassed? Thinking about it, Hayne realised that it did make sense. The steadfast display by the piper, followed by Canadians falling out of rank was bound to have been noticed by the Scots officers, and the Lieutenant-Colonel was bound to think that it would result in criticism of his command, a matter over which he fretted endlessly. Yes, Ogilvy was right. The old man had been embarrassed and it was likely to result in even more training to bring the Canadians 'up to scratch'.

The two captains reached the group of men to discover that they were completely motionless. At first, Hayne thought they were dead, but he and Ogilvy found that they were sound asleep. Two were soon roused, and with rough shoving and after considerable coaxing were sufficiently awake to re-join the ranks of marching men. The third was in a death-like sleep and no manner of shoving or prodding roused him. Eventually, Hayne resorted to wasting valuable water, throwing it in the man's face. This did the job. He became coherent enough to understand the dangers of being left behind and he allowed himself to be hauled up by two Scots privates who had come over to help. He was supported back into the ranks.

Otter watched as the men were cajoled and coaxed back into the ranks of the 9th Division. They had lost their place with the Canadians and were now marching with the Highland Brigade. It will do them good to mix with professional soldiers, Otter thought. He looked across at the cloud of dust. It seemed a little less distinct than before, as though it might be settling. Otter squinted at it. Had the Boers been stopped? Maybe the opportunity for the Canadians to prove themselves was drawing near.

General Pieter Arnoldus Cronjé

General Pieter Arnoldus Cronjé was delighted. He rode among the stationary wagons like a man who had just been informed that his terminal illness had been a misdiagnosis and he was in fact in perfect health. They had done it! They had got through the English lines and outpaced them. Now all they had to do was cross the river and everything would be fine again.

He continued down the line of wagons towards the river, where they had already started crossing the drift. He threw hearty comments to the men resting in the shade under the wagons, and stopped to talk to the women and children along the way, ruffling the hair of boys and patting the heads of girls. He halted often to partake, courteously, in the many cups of coffee he was offered. All along the length of the convoy of wagons native servants had established small camp fires, over which the coffee bubbled merrily. Even the cattle seemed enthused by the positive mood. They stood in their positions alongside the wagons' drawing chains, tossing their heads and stamping their feet impatiently. They seemed keen to move on towards the river, the stress and strains of the previous days' march apparently forgotten.

So, the next stop would be Poplar Grove. That would be the best location for the next defensive position and this time he would not allow the English to outflank him. He had learned a sobering lesson and would be much better prepared for the extravagant flanking movements that Roberts seemed prepared to risk.

This Roberts was certainly a different type of English general. The fact that he had discontinued the frontal attacks at Magersfontein suggested that he was not one of those generals who seemed to believe his soldiers were expendable – and there seem to be many English officers who did believe that. However, he still seemed happy to subject them to extraordinary discomfort and feats beyond the endurance of normal men. It was difficult to understand this English attitude, where officers could treat their men with distain and yet the soldiers seemed willing to go to the ends of the earth for them. It amazed him that they continued to follow orders. Even de Wet, with his liberal use of his leather shambok, had still suffered from burghers who refused to continue. It must be, he concluded, something to do with being 'professional' soldiers.

Well, postulated Cronjé, even with his professional army, Roberts' nonsensical death march had failed in its task. The English had not even been able to keep up with cattle-drawn wagons. Roberts had destroyed the effectiveness of his army and he would not be able to undertake a similar movement again. They would be much easier to deal with next time. And now all the Afrikander army needed to do was to ford the Modder River. Yes, Cronjé was in a very good mood.

As he approached the river, he moved away from the wagons lined up along the dirt track which sloped down towards the drift and rode along the edge of the high, steep bank. Below him the riverbank stepped down in a series of terraces to the wide, sandy bed, through which the muddy river flowed lazily. To his left and right, it meandered in wide, sweeping curves before kinking back in two sharp, dog-leg bends.

Downstream, a short distance from the river, set in the yellow veldt, was a small, insignificant kopje, and beyond that was the larger Paardeberg, its heights overlooking the drift of the same name. Cronjé studied the larger hill with a furrowed brow. No, he still could not see why it was called Horse Hill. It didn't look anything like a horse!

Paardeberg Drift was the main ford in the area. On its south bank nestled a small cluster of squat bungalows with corrugated tin roofs. Cronjé had trekked beyond the drift, because he thought the settlement would have restricted the movement of the large number of wagons that would have had to pass through it. And, although the Afrikander army was some distance in front of the English, Cronjé knew it was best to get his wagons over the Modder as quickly as possible. He had considered splitting them into two columns to speed up the crossing, but decided he would rather keep the burghers together under his control. There was no telling what some of them might have done if they felt he no longer had direct influence over them. They were just as likely to take off and return to their farms.

Cronjé looked from the dwellings at Paardeberg Drift, across the flat landscape to the line of four kopjes on the other side of the river, the Oskoppies. The largest and highest was nearest to him. Tucked below it he could make out the two stands of blue gum trees that marked the locations of Stinkfontein Farm and Osfontein Farm. As he looked at the large hill a shiver ran down his spine. All these hills would provide excellent positions for artillery should the English catch up with them. Cronjé deliberately shook and flexed his shoulders to rid himself of the thought. The English were miles away. He looked down at the Modder, where the first wagons were making good progress through the river. Cronjé called out to a burgher standing nearby who was also watching the activity.

"We have found an easy place to cross. It was a good choice, even though it meant trekking a bit further up the river."

"Yes, Oom Piet. It is one of the few places where we can ford the river with ease. But even here there are steep banks both upstream and downstream. The wagons will have to pass through in single file and I am worried that we will not have enough time for all to reach the other side before the English arrive."

"Don't worry. The English are nowhere near, and I have placed two commandos as rear guards, one on this side of the river, a few miles beyond Paardeberg, and the second on the south bank. That will slow the English down."

"That's good, Oom."

"So there is no need to worry."

"No, Oom, I suppose not, as long as the commandos can keep the English back long enough."

"They will," replied Cronjé with a hint of impatience. He changed the focus of the conversation. "I have also sent a commando and native labourers to Poplar Grove to establish our defensive position there, so that it will be ready when we arrive."

"Then we are fine. Just fine," concluded the man.

Cronjé continued to watch the activity below him. He looked at the sun. It was about midday. There was still ample time to get across the Modder. Satisfied, he turned his horse and trotted away from the river. It was time to return to his wagon for lunch.

The cattle had been outspanned and released to feed nearby. His wagon would be one of the last across the river and Hester had obviously decided that the cattle had been tethered to the wagon's tow-chain long enough and deserved some freedom. The canopy had been erected along the side of the wagon to form a lean-to tent. In its shade sat Hester, supervising their native servants, who were cooking a lunch of boiled mutton over a cow-dung fire. The smell of freshly brewed coffee wafted to him on the hot breeze. He called for a cup as he sat down next to his wife.

"Beautiful day," commented Hester.

"Yes, a beautiful day."

She took Cronjé's hand into her own. "This reminds me of the hunting parties we used to go on when we first got married, all those years ago. Do you remember?"

"Yes, what wonderful times we had. We will do it again when all this fuss with the English is over."

Looking around, Cronjé said. "I don't remember so many wagons in those days."

"Yes," laughed Hester, "there are so many more these days. They call it progress, you know. Civilisation is catching up with us."

Her final words were accompanied by a series of low thumps and half a dozen shells exploded overhead, spraying shrapnel across the Afrikander encampment.

Cronjé leapt up, throwing his mug to the ground.

"God in Heaven, how the hell did the English catch up with us?"

He looked downriver. There was no sign of the English anywhere, just distant dust clouds, but the shells kept coming. Then, one of the wagons exploded, blowing the cattle tethered to it to the ground. The animals at the front of the team scrambled up and, in panic, stampeded from the burning wagon, dragging injured and dead beasts behind them. In no time at all another two wagons were ablaze. Hell's teeth, thought Cronjé, how did the English suddenly learn to use artillery so accurately? He scanned the horizon and at last found the source of the bombardment. To the north! Puffs of smoke billowed from beyond a low ridge only one thousand yards away. How the devil had they got there? How had they got passed the rear guard? Then a group of about five hundred horsemen emerged over the ridge and cantered along its crest for a short distance before disappearing behind it again. Another group appeared, this time moving away from the artillery, apparently in some flanking movement. Then they, too, were gone.

"God in heaven," cursed Cronjé. It had to be French with his cavalry, and he had four thousand mounted men and nearly fifty guns. He was supposed to be in Kimberley!

"Aagh!" Cronjé groaned in a mixture of anger and anguish as the answer came to him. The enemy had not come from downriver; they had come from the north! They had not had to outmanoeuvre his rear guard; there was no rear guard to stop them. Idiot! How had he let that happen? Then, in a panic, Cronjé recognised the danger. They were too spread out! If French used his Lancers, they were done for. The burghers would disperse like leaves before a storm. They needed to concentrate their forces. They needed to set up a defensive position!

He turned and snapped at Hester, "Get into the wagon, Hester. Jim!" he called to his Zulu driver. "Inspan the cattle and move the wagon closer to the river." He looked about him and pointed. "Place it at the top of the bank near that group of trees. Get the other drivers to do the same and form a laager. Form a smaller laager for the women and children next to the main one."

He ran to his horse, leaping on to it like a man half his age, and galloped to the nearest burghers, who were running around in confusion as more shrapnel burst over the wagons.

"Gerrit! Dirk! Gabriel! Organise yourselves! I have instructed Jim to form a laager for the women and children by those trees. You must organise the rest of the wagons into a larger laager next to that. Get as many wagons up there as you can."

"Dirk, first, your son must ride to Poplar Grove and call back the commando and labourers. We will need to dig some trenches here instead. Then find as many of the War Council as you can, get others to help, and tell them to meet me by the same trees."

The three men ran off through the wagons. Complete pandemonium had descended. Men, women and children were running in all directions. Cronjé jumped from his horse to catch two terrified teenage girls who were running past. "Children," he said with gentle authority and loudly, in order to be heard above the shriek and crash of the bombardment. "We are building a laager for you and your mothers. See that group of trees? That's where it will be. I want you to gather every child and lady you see and tell them to let everyone else know. When you have done that, go to the laager yourselves and hide under the wagons. Start with those kids over there." He pointed to a group of confused children milling around in a state of bewilderment. The girls, forgetting their fear, sprinted off to carry out Oom Piet's orders.

"Hermanus," Cronjé yelled at a nearby burgher. The man rode over immediately. "Go and find the rear guard on this side of the river. We need them to fall back to support us here. And send someone to fetch back the rear guard on the south side of the river as well. Go!"

The man drove his heels into his horse's flanks and galloped off through the chaos of running women and their screaming children, riders, wagon drivers and panicking cattle. The noise was appalling. He paused only to pass the orders on to a second man, who swung into his saddle and sped off, splashing through the muddy river.

Shells continued to burst over the camp. Cronjé turned back to examine their source. To the left of the belching plumes of smoke he saw the small, insignificant kopje. His blood turned cold. In an instant he was on his horse and careering towards a group of mounted burghers who were galloping towards the newly forming laagers.

"Hey, Pieter!"

"Yes Oom?" Pieter called back, reining in his stocky horse as Cronjé came up to him. The others followed suit, pulling their horses up hard.

"Do you see that small kopje to the west, between us and the Paardeberg?" he hollered above the uproar.

Pieter shaded his eyes as he looked to the west.

"Yes Oom."

Cronjé lent towards him and shouted, "The English have missed its importance. If we can reach it, we will be able to shoot at them from there. Find as many men as you can and seize it. But be quick. I doubt it will take the English long to realise their mistake."

Pieter and his comrades were off in a cloud of dust. They bellowed at others to join them and they galloped towards the kopje. As they did so, they noticed a trail of dust rising from beyond the ridge and moving towards the same kopje. The English were racing them.

Cronjé spurred his horse into a canter and made for the quickly developing wagon laagers. He approached the distinctive stand of trees next to the laagers. The trees stood along the rim of the deep valley, the sides of which formed a series of natural sandy terraces of varying width that dropped steeply to the river some distance below. On one of these terraces, a few yards under the lip of the valley, and sheltered from the English artillery, Cronje found some of the War

Council already gathered, including Ferreira, Albrecht and Piet de Wet. Cronjé spoke as soon as he joined the Council.

"Gentlemen, the English have outwitted us. One day we will learn how to deal with them."

"If I may venture, General…" It was Albrecht who spoke.

"Yes Major?"

"…I would suggest that the lesson is speed."

Cronjé waited, as did the rest of the Council.

"General, we really have to leave the wagons behind and extricate ourselves immediately. The English will treat the women and children with dignity and kindness. We have nothing to fear in that respect. But there is a real danger that the commando will be caught in a trap. I have no doubt we can beat them, but if we do not leave now, they will be able to surround us. The kopjes around our position will make us vulnerable to artillery fire. Surrounded and under bombardment, it is very likely that they will force us to surrender."

As the final words came out of his mouth Albrecht knew he had lost the argument, for everyone in the Council looked at him in shock.

"Never!" Commandant Pieter Kritzinger, the Cape rebel, shot back. "We will *never* surrender!"

"You see, Major, you underestimate the courage and determination of the Afrikander. Now, enough of this nonsense. There are…"

"Excuse me, Oom?" It was Kritzinger who spoke.

"Yes, Neef, what is it?"

"While I disagree with the Major about us surrendering, I do agree that we should *not* stay here."

Cronjé was taken aback. "On what basis?" he asked with an edge to his voice.

"Oom, we already have the English attacking us from the north and their arrival was a complete surprise. At the moment, they are attacking only with guns and have not used their cavalry. We do not know how many horsemen are behind that ridge, but it is likely to be thousands – perhaps as many as there are of us." Kritzinger threw a pointed look at Albrecht. So much for Albrecht's claim that the English had ridden their horses into the ground. "We also know there are two divisions of infantry and two thousand mounted infantry after us. The rear guard will hold them up for a short while, but they will eventually be driven back by the sheer number of English. We must use what precious time they give us to escape because if we stay, when the English do get here we will be faced by twenty thousand enemy soldiers."

Even disguised behind his great beard, Albrecht had noted the twitch in Cronjé's features when Kritzinger had mentioned the rear guard. He asked, looking directly into those hard eyes, "The rear guard is still in place?"

Cronjé held Albrecht's scrutinising stare. "I have ordered them back to build up our numbers here."

There was a brief silence while the Council took in the implications of this. It was Piet de Wet who broke it.

"But Oom, even with the rear guard joining us, we are still only four thousand strong. What can we do against twenty thousand?"

Cronjé glared at de Wet and then at the other men of the Council in turn. He sensed there was a real danger of rebellion. He controlled his rising anger because shouting would not help if they were losing faith. A more subtle approach was required.

"Gentlemen, you worry too much," he started benignly. "We had the same odds at Majuba and back then we fought with old-fashioned, muzzle-loading rifles and attacked the English running up a hill. Today we have superior weapons to the English and we will build trenches to protect ourselves from their artillery, as we did at Magersfontein. We will send messages to our friends. Do not forget about General de la Rey and your brother." He gave Piet de Wet a proud smile. "They are out there," he swept his arm expansively to indicate the wide sweep of the South African landscape, "and they will come to our aid and drive the English away. General Joubert, our supreme general, will *not* abandon us. He will make sure we receive the reinforcements we need. Within two or three days our numbers will increase sufficiently to counter-attack and drive the English off our land and back to Cape Town. Surely, you do not want the English to advance any further into *our* land?"

The members of the Council felt ashamed. The General was right. It was their duty to stop the English, and maybe their situation would cause others to come and help them drive the hated English from their country. They remained silent.

"So enough," beamed Cronjé. "Let us consider how we defend our position. We will focus our defence around the wagon laagers here at

Wolveskraal Drift. We also have the numbers to allow us to defend some other drifts. The closest upriver is Vanderberg Drift and downstream Vendutie Drift. Both are on nice, tight bends in the river which, together with the steep river banks, will act as natural defences from which we can protect our flanks. That will give us a five-mile line to defend, with the laager in the middle. Paardeberg Drift is important, but I think it is too far for us to hold. Do you agree?"

There was a general nodding of heads.

"On the whole," Cronjé continued – he was on a roll and enjoying himself – "the steep and high-sided banks of the river, and the dongas that run into it, will provide our defensive positions, although a few improvements will be required here and there, especially on our flanks, where some additional trenches will be necessary.

"For the main defence around the wagons, we will dig a trench in a semi-circle from the river upstream of the laager, around the wagons and link it back to the river. I have recalled the commando and natives from Poplar Grove to help with this, but we will have to use the native drivers and herds-boys to help as well." Cronjé looked at de Wet. "I want you to arrange marking out the line of the trenches while there is still daylight. As soon as it is dark the English will stop their bombardment and we will start digging. Use all the natives at our disposal, even the domestic servants, and commandeer five hundred young burghers as well. In this soft soil," he stamped his heel into the dirt to emphasise his point, "that should be enough men to have the trenches dug by morning.

"Neef Kritzinger, you are to dispatch riders to let everyone in the Republics know we have secured this position, but that we need reinforcements to help us push the English back. Once you have done that, find the Irishman, Jack Lane. He must hide the ammunition wagons on one of these river terraces. Neef Ferreira, can you arrange to conceal the horses and cattle? If they can be herded into the lower terraces, the height and steep slopes of the river valley should hide them from the English guns. I think that is all. Are there any questions?" There were none. "Then thank you, gentlemen. We have work to do."

The audience was over.

Sergeant Alfred Atkinson

Sergeant Alfred Atkinson marched as close to the willow trees as he could. To his right, the dry veld stretched out to the horizon; to his left, the lush riverside vegetation, with its teaming birdlife and chattering vervet monkeys, was a startling contrast to the open veld. The low sun bathed the landscape in its golden rays. The long shadows of the sun-gilded trees cast dark violet swathes across the glowing haze of the grass. Through the tangle of the trees, vines and shrubby undergrowth Atkinson caught brief glimpses of the river. Its waters were animated and sparkling in the sun's fading rays, as though God has scattered a myriad of diamonds over the surface.

At least the thicker ground vegetation nearer the river meant there was less dust and the presence of the river made the air feel cooler. Of course with night drawing in, Atkinson knew that the cloudless sky foretold a return of bitterly cold temperatures.

The 6th Division had been marching for over thirty hours, since half past twelve the previous day, following the order for them to move quickly along the south bank of the Modder River and prevent the Boers from crossing it. They had left Klip Drift at a blistering pace – a jog that continued for mile upon mile. Kitchener had been determined that, having slipped through the net, the Boers were not going to escape, and the excitement of seeing the great cloud of dust, which rose from the Boer wagons, on the far bank ahead had kept the men going on and on.

The Boers had seemed to be just within their grasp and they had all been determined to make the best of the opportunity, but as the heat grew to that of a furnace it had simply become too much for the men, and even Kitchener had had to accept that without a rest they could have gone no further. He had allowed them a break of half an hour, during which most had immediately fallen asleep. Others, for whom hunger outweighed tiredness, had lit fires to make tea to help their parched throats swallow the impossibly dry biscuits. After what had seemed like a very short half hour, K had had them on the move again, but he had continued to let them pause every half an hour, if only for just a few minutes. Even in these short stops, men fell into deep sleeps from which it was difficult to wake them.

By dusk of the previous day it had become obvious that neither the mounted infantry nor the 13th Brigade, who were chasing the Boers to the north of the river, had managed to intercept them. To Atkinson, this was an astonishing fact.

How could lumbering cattle-drawn wagons out-pace mounted soldiers? He could understand why the Boers were out-pacing the infantry, for although Kitchener had urged the men on and on, the speed of their progress had inevitably slowed. It was only their professionalism and the sheer determination of every soldier in the division that kept them moving forwards. Kitchener had not allowed them to camp on the night of the 16th; instead, they had continued through the darkness. At least this meant they had been able to keep warm against the iciness of the night, thought Atkinson. After a short break at dawn, in which a further biscuit was devoured with the help of some tea, the slog had started again. It was to be another day of marching, marching, marching, another day of dust and flies and of soul-sapping heat.

As the morning had heated up, Atkinson had sought out the relative comfort of the riverside vegetation, away from the worst of the dust. He had fallen into the rhythm of his stride, and it had not been as bad today as on previous days, especially compared to the tramp from the Riet River to Klip Drift on the Modder. The reassuring presence of water nearby had also been a comfort, although it hardly looked like water. It was the colour of, and the taste of, mud – no wonder it was called the Modder River! Its taste had taken some getting used to, but he remembered the enthusiasm with which he had drunk it on that first morning at Klip Drift after the painful hike of the previous day and night.

However, the real reason for the march being less agonising was on Atkinson's feet. Having presented himself to the doctor as an invalid, he had been issued with a brand new pair of boots. He smiled gleefully to himself as he watched his new, but dusty, boots appearing and disappearing as he walked.

He could have become a wealthy man if he'd been persuaded to part with them. Money, cigarettes, war memorabilia could have been his. But none of these things had tempted him, for he, of all people, knew the value of a decent pair of boots. He had even procured a small brush and a tin of polish. He was not going to use a candle to polish his boots, as the others did. He was going to take extraordinary care of his new boots; they were a thing of beauty.

On the other hand, he had been sorely tempted by the offers of food rations. Ever since that devil de Wet had captured their supply wagons at Waterval Drift, the troops, and, Atkinson assumed, the officers, had been on quarter rations. Not to have full rations was a terrible thing under normal circumstances when at war, but to expect men to walk constantly for two days on quarter rations in this heat and dust was pushing them beyond endurance. Atkinson wondered how de Wet had been allowed to take the wagons. Kitchener was supposed to be in charge of the supply lines, and by all accounts he had made a hash of it. No wonder he was called 'K for Chaos'. If he was supposed to be in charge of getting food forward to the troops, one had to ask what he was doing so far forward himself, when the wagons were still a long way back and vulnerable to Boer attack.

It was inexcusable of K to have lost over two thousand rations of tinned beef. Atkinson started to regret the short-sightedness of his decision to keep his boots and not swap them for food. But his thoughts were conflicted, for if he had taken it, he would have been depriving his fellow sufferers of any food at all. At least this way he had comfortable feet and *some* food. But as he thought about it, he could feel the empty sensation in his own abdomen returning and the welling nausea, caused, he assumed, from his stomach not having anything to work on.

And yet he continued to march, as did all the other soldiers, and mostly without complaint. It was amazing what the men would do for 'Bobs', although Atkinson had to admit that having K around to ensure the orders were fulfilled did add an extra dimension and source of 'encouragement' to their marching. And since midday there had been another reason to lift the men's enthusiasm for the march: the continuous rumble of artillery fire.

The noise of the guns was still some way off, but the sound of the 12 pounder guns was unmistakable. The general buzz of news among the men was that General French and his cavalry had caught the Boers as they were attempting to cross the river. Kitchener was now even more determined that the enemy was not going to escape. A new excitement had been building among the men as the afternoon had progressed; the enemy was again within their grasp. They had marched almost continuously for a week to catch Cronjé, the objective of all their sweat and pain, and now the old devil was in sight and there was nothing that was going to stop the 6th Division from giving him and his commando a dose of their own medicine.

Atkinson grinned to himself. It was about time the Boers were taught who was in control. He hoped the officers had learned how to deal with them now, and would stop their ridiculous habit of making frontal attacks in full view of the Boers and their blistering fire-power. Atkinson was concerned that it was K who seemed to be in control, even though the old duffer Kelly-Kenny was the senior officer. At least Kelly-Kenny had some sense and a more thoughtful approach to war, although some considered that approach to be over-cautious. That was fine with Atkinson. Cautious generals usually caused less death among their men; unless, of course, they became hesitant and indecisive. But that generally had more to do with ineptitude and stupidity. Then disaster usually struck. Fortunately, thought Atkinson, Kelly-Kenny did not appear to be stupid or inept. As the oldest officer in Roberts' army, Atkinson decided it was Kelly-Kenny's experience that made his approach more considered. If he did have one fault, it was that he was too retiring when confronted with overbearing personalities, and K was certainly overbearing. Kitchener also seemed to carry some of Roberts' authority around with him, although the basis for this Atkinson could not fathom.

The dying sun threw its cloak of red over the dry grass and through the tangle of trees and undergrowth Atkinson caught glimpses of a now still and dark river. The daytime animals had fallen silent and those of the night had yet to stir. The men were exhausted and silent. The stillness was disturbed by the regular tramp of booted feet, the swish of canvas trousers through the veld grass, the creak of leather harnesses and jingle of metal on metal.

The sun fell towards the horizon, and the shadows of the trees became lost in the increasing darkness of the veld. Then the short African dusk came to an abrupt end and darkness enveloped Atkinson and his fellows.

Atkinson looked at the ground. He needed to watch where he was walking. The last thing he wanted to do was to trip over another bloody anthill.

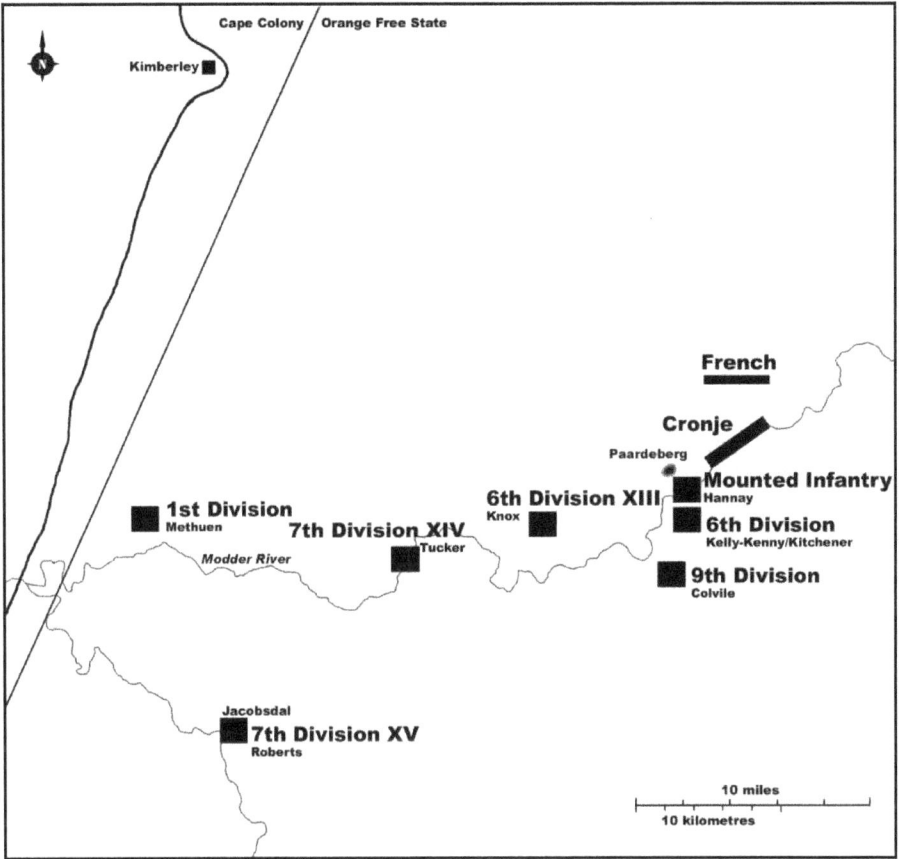

Map 9: Night of 17 – 18 February 1900

Sunday 18 February 1900
Bloody Sunday

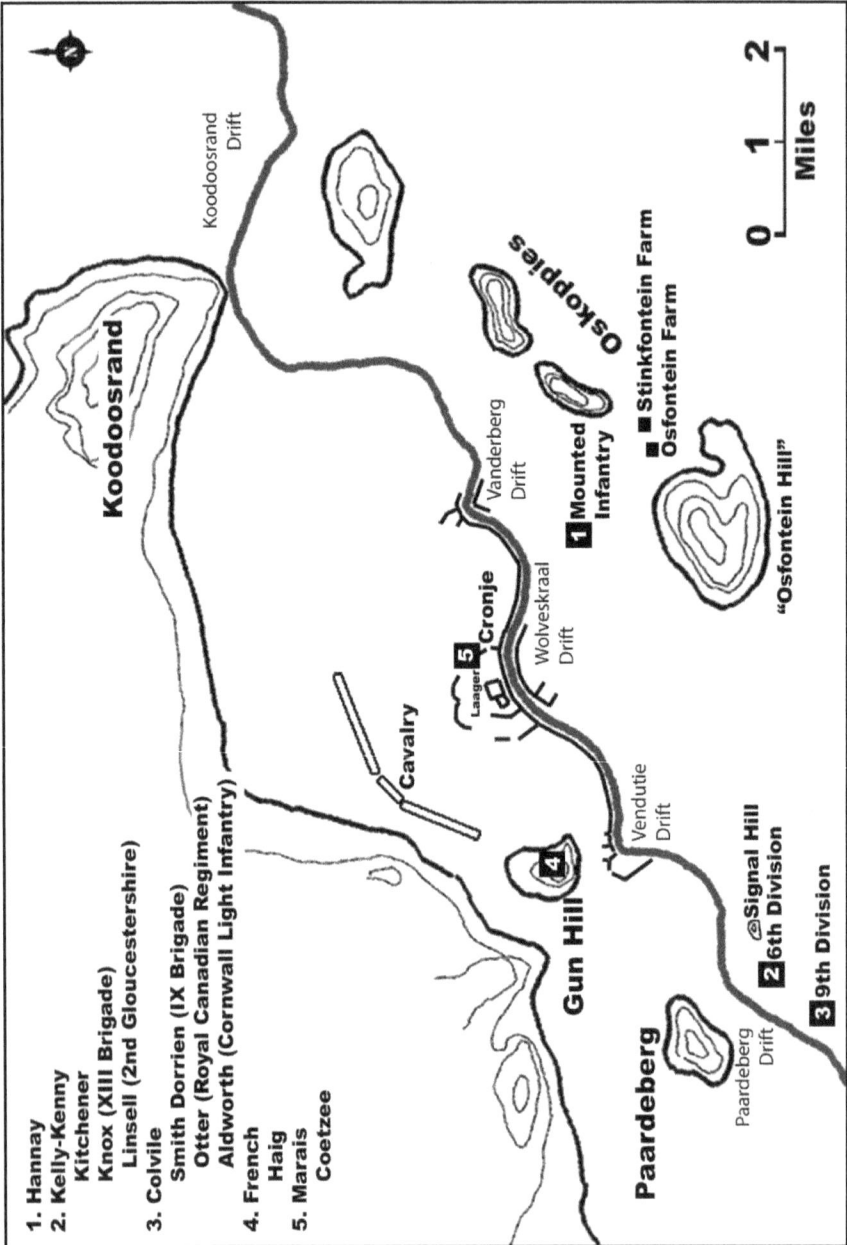

Map 10: 18 February, 6:00 am

Legend:

1. Hannay
2. Kelly-Kenny
   Kitchener
   Knox (XIII Brigade)
   Linsell (2nd Gloucestershire)
3. Colvile
   Smith Dorrien (IX Brigade)
   Otter (Royal Canadian Regiment)
   Aldworth (Cornwall Light Infantry)
4. French
   Haig
5. Marais
   Coetzee

Map labels:
- Koodoosrand
- Koodoosrand Drift
- Oskoppies
- Stinkfontein Farm
- Osfontein Farm
- "Osfontein Hill"
- 1 Mounted Infantry
- Vanderberg Drift
- Cronje
- 5 Laager
- Cavalry
- Wolveskraal Drift
- Vendutie Drift
- Gun Hill
- 4
- Signal Hill
- 2 6th Division
- 3 9th Division
- Paardeberg
- Paardeberg Drift

Scale: 0 1 2 Miles

Bloody Sunday, 6:00 am

Lieutenant-General Kelly-Kenny walked out on to the veranda of the bungalow that he had requisitioned as his headquarters. Actually, acquired rather than requisitioned, he thought, smiling to himself, as the owner had abandoned it before he'd had to formally requisition it. He had done well; it was the finest dwelling in the tiny settlement at Paardeberg Drift. Across the wide dusty trail that was an excuse for a main street he could make out Paardeberg Drift's second finest dwelling appearing out of the half-light of the emerging dawn. In that bungalow, Kelly-Kenny imagined Kitchener tramping up and down in his usual no-nonsense manner. Yes, concluded Kelly-Kenny, Kitchener may be acting above his rank, but he was not going to get his hands on this place. He stepped over to the balustrade surrounding the veranda, or 'steop' as the Boers called it, and lent against the handrail, adjusting his collar to keep out the bitterly cold dawn air.

His division had arrived in the early hours of the morning in the pitch dark and Kelly-Kenny was keen to get his first view of what was likely to be the battlefield, now that Cronjé's force had been caught. Beyond Kitchener's bungalow, a line of hills, the Oskoppies, was silhouetted against a blood-red sky. "Red sky in the morning, shepherds warning," he muttered to himself.

The immense, red orb of the African sun rose behind the hills and blooded the vapours of his breath. The low mist clinging to the dry veld turned into swirling lakes of blood. This was the veld that his men would probably have to advance across later that day to attack the Boer lines. Soon it would be stained with real blood, the blood of… "the Boers," he said emphatically. Speaking out loud to divert his thoughts from the direction they were heading, he focused again on the Oskoppies. He would call the largest one, that nearest to him, 'Osfontein Hill', after the farm that his intelligence officers informed him lay to the other side of it. The next hill would be 'Stinkfontein Hill', for a similar reason. A small hill lay between him and Osfontein Hill and he decided that it would be a convenient location for his heliograph. He would name it 'Signal Hill'. He had already marked these names on his map, such as it was. Kelly-Kenny reflected that one of the serious weaknesses of the British campaign in the war so far had been the lack of reliable maps. He had decided that if they were to do battle at this spot, one of the first things he would need to do would be to have all the strategically advantageous points mapped out. His thirty years' military experience had taught him the importance of knowing the lie of the land before engaging the enemy.

In the improving light, he could now see a dark, sinuous line of trees rising above the mist. They marked the course of the river as it wound its way through the veld in great, sweeping meanders. On the far side of the river, to the north-west, there were two prominent hills: Paardeberg itself was to his left and the other was north of him. The latter he had named 'Gun Hill' because soon after his arrival a dispatch rider from French had informed him that they had already placed artillery on it. French obviously believed a battle was going to ensue. That encouraged Kelly-Kenny, although he was not convinced that the Boers would still be encamped by the river. Why should they? They had seemed very determined to escape and he half expected them to have extracted themselves once more during the night. But French had seemed confident that he had managed to halt the Boers and prevent their escape.

Kelly-Kenny walked along the veranda, which encircled the bungalow, and studied the Paardeberg. It did not really look like a horse, he pondered; perhaps it did in full sunlight. He continued along the veranda to the back of the house and looked out across the garden, if one could call the scrappy, worn grass and a chicken run a garden. In the veld beyond he could see the approaching red-tinged dust cloud of Colvile with his 9th Division.

"Captain," he said to the man who had been following him at a discreet distance.

"Yes sir."

"General Colvile will be here soon. Give him my compliments for an extraordinary march and ask him to report to me immediately. And find out where Colonel Hannay has got to. He was ordered to cross back to this side of the river and join us here at Paardeberg, but he seems to have disappeared off the face of the earth."

"Yes sir."

The captain untethered his horse from the balustrade, swung into the saddle and galloped across the garden, sending the hens that had just emerged from their coop into a panic of flapping and clucking. Leaping the low wire fence that divided the garden from the African wilderness, he rode on into the swirling sea of blood-red mist. Kelly-Kenny watched the mist eddy across the veld after the horseman. His thoughts drifted back to the ominous events that were likely to take place later that day. With careful planning and a cautious approach success *would* be theirs. After all, he commanded the best army in the world and the enemy were nothing more than a bunch of farmers, although, he reminded himself, they were damned good shots. As he looked across the veld the mist seemed to turn an even deeper shade of red. He was not a suspicious man, but the portents were not good. Kelly-Kenny looked at his watch. It was just after six o'clock.

Lieutenant-General French stared into the Boer laager through his field glasses. He was pleased to be on Gun Hill. He admitted, to himself, that he had nearly lost the strategic position to the Boers. If he had not spotted the small commando charging towards it and reacted immediately by ordering a unit of his Lancers to capture it before the Boers, at *all* costs, it might well have been the enemy looking down on him from this point. It had been a close shave.

At the moment, however, the advantage of height meant little. A thick river mist hung over the enemy laager and the low angle of the early morning sun threw long dark shadows across the veld. He was not able to see into the enemy's position in sufficient detail.

"Damn it, Haig, can you see anything?"

"Only several wagons, sir. Do you think they're still there?"

"Damned if I know," replied French, straining every cell in his eyes in an attempt to see through the mist. "Blasted mist. Blasted climate. One absolutely broils to death during the day and absolutely freezes to death at night. Why on earth are we trying to capture these damned awful republics? And the people are no better; overly warm to their own kind and icy cold to outsiders. Not worth a tuppenny piece between them, if you ask me. And slippery as eels. They could still be there or they could be leading us a right song and dance, just as they did with Methuen at Magersfontein."

French stared down his field glasses again.

"See anything yet?"

"Nothing, sir."

Burgher Marais drew gently on his pipe, relaxing after the night-long effort of digging trenches. He sat on the cold, sandy step that ran along the bottom of the trench with his Mauser resting between his knees. He held his greatcoat tight to his throat to keep out the cold. The trench was roughly excavated and would need to be improved when they had more time. Its coarsely sculptured walls smelt of freshly turned earth. The aroma took Marais back to his farm in the Cape at ploughing time. If he closed his eyes and breathed in deeply, he could almost imagine sitting on the cool earth, with his back to a tree, the warming sun playing on his face, the melodic low of the cattle as they pulled the plough and turned the soil and the soft call of their driver urging them on. He could almost imagine it, but the weight of his rifle against his leg brought him back to reality, back to the brutality of war. He wondered how long the nostalgic scent would linger. He supposed the trenches at Magersfontein must have smelt the same when they were first dug, but all he could remember was the appalling stench of decay, body odour and excrement. Hopefully, the latrines would be better designed this time. And with a bit of luck, this time they would be able to use the river more frequently to bathe.

Although the night had been cold and the sandy ground easy to dig, the hard labour had continued all night. Now he had the desire to wash in the river, but daylight had caught up with them and that luxury would have to wait until tonight when he could bathe under the cover of darkness without the danger of being shot. It was not yet clear to him which parts of the deep ravine, through which the Modder flowed, would be visible to the English and which parts would be hidden.

Marais noted with satisfaction that the trench, although still requiring some refinement, already had some improvements over those excavated at Magersfontein, the formation of the sandy ledge on which he sat being one. It made waiting for the enemy a more comfortable experience compared to squatting in the bottom of the trench. It also meant that when it rained it would be possible to keep dry by perching on the ledge, out of the puddles that would inevitably collect in the floor of the trench. They had been lucky last night. There had been no rain, so digging, while hard work, had not been made more miserable by them being wet through as well. But the rain had not been far away. Some miles upstream there had been a tremendous series of storms throughout the night. The sky had been heavy with angry rumbles of thunder and the horizon had been rent by jagged streaks of lightning. It had been spectacular to watch. Marais wondered how long it would take for the storm waters to come flooding down to their stretch of the river.

He leant back against the cool, sandy side of the trench. Looking above him, he followed the line of the wall of sand as it curved over his head like a petrified wave. The opposite wall was similarly shaped and the two sides of the trench curved upwards towards each other, stopping short of meeting by about three feet. The earth wall then extended vertically for another foot or so and opened onto the veldt. From where he sat, Marais could not see the ridges of spoil that ran either side of the trench, giving the burghers additional protection when they looked out across the veldt. However, he could see the ribbon of blue sky running away from him in either direction until it was lost by the curve of the trench. All along the length of the trench there were sleeping men, many huddled together against the cold. At regular intervals men were standing with their heads peeking out of the narrow gap to keep an eye on the English.

Opposite him squatted the youth, Coetzee. His arms were folded around his knees in an effort to keep warm and his head drooped to one side as though he was dozing, so that his face was hidden by the brim of his hat. He remained still as a rock, but as soon as the gloomy trench grew light enough to read by, Coetzee took out his small Bible and paged through it meticulously until he found a passage that he wished to consider that morning. He removed his hat, placing it on a knee and settled against the wall in a more comfortable position. His lips started to move rhythmically. Marais watched him. Coetzee was completely absorbed by his Bible. He hunched over the book, his eyes hardly moving across the small pages. He probably knew the words by heart. Marais waited patiently for a pause in the rhythm of the whispered words.

"What are you reading, Neef?"

Without looking up from his book Coetzee replied, "The Psalms."

"Ah, the Psalms. Yes. My favourite is Psalm 23."

Coetzee scowled at him. The response was a sure sign of someone who did not consult the Bible as frequently as he should. Psalm 23 was the one everyone learnt as a child.

"Oom, on this day of the Lord, do you not wish to talk to Him?"

"I have, Neef, in my own way. I've asked him to protect us from the English guns and asked that our two will outshoot their forty."

"Do you have a Bible?"

"Of course." Marais reached into his greatcoat and withdrew his copy of the Book. It was not as well-thumbed as Coetzee's. "But I do not require it as some do. I consult it in quiet moments and get what inspiration I need when I have the time to truly focus on the words, but lately such moments have been few and far between."

"Yes, Oom, such moments are very few, so we must make the most of them." Coetzee returned to his reading.

Marais watched him as a father might watch a son. His own children were much younger than Coetzee, but he recognised the same determined streak in Coetzee that he had seen in his oldest son. He studied the soft, dark hair just starting to appear on Coetzee's jaw line and smiled when he recalled the mannish way in which the boy stroked it thoughtfully. Marais ran the back of his fingers over his own bristly chin and cheeks and absent-mindedly stroked his small moustache into place. He needed a shave. He had never been one to sport a 'traditional' Boer beard. Maybe that was why Coetzee considered him to be a 'townie'. Marais closed his eyes and rested his head against the wall of the trench. Above the softly spoken murmurs of the men around him he could hear the lowing of the oxen and the neighing of the horses that had been herded into the protection of the ravine and the melodious coo-coor-ruk calls of turtle doves in the trees beside the river. It was the sound of Africa. Then, from across the veldt came the sharp snap of Mausers.

Colonel Hannay was wondering where the rest of the British forces were. Indeed, he was wondering where the Boers were. He and his mounted infantry had been ordered, the previous day, to cross back to the south side of the river to intercept the retreating Boers. They had ridden well into the night, eventually halting in the pitch dark and settling down for a brief, cold sleep under a starless sky. Now, in the improving light and through the slowly dispersing mist, he could see to the north the dark line of trees that he thought should mark the course of the Modder River. To the east, black against the pale morning sky, was a range of hills. He was keeping a wary eye on them as they were likely to be hosting a Boer commando. To the south-west he could see a cloud of dust rising above the mist. He sent a unit of men to make contact. It was, he assumed, a British division.

Suddenly, from nowhere, bullets began to whizz around him like angry wasps. Damn it, not again, he scowled. Where the hell were they this time? He automatically swivelled around to the hills, but the noise of the Mausers was coming from the opposite direction, from the river. He rapidly examined the line of trees through his field glasses but could see no evidence of any Boers. Between his unit and the river lay open veld, offering no obvious cover for the enemy.

"Move away from the river!" he yelled.

His men did not need telling twice. They leapt onto their already saddled horses and bolted for the hills to their east. The firing died down. Thank the stars the Boers did not appear to be in the hills as well, thought Hannay. Calling to a nearby rider, he ordered him to find General Kelly-Kenny and inform him that they had made contact with the enemy.

General Kitchener and his aide, Major Hubert Hamilton, strode purposefully across the dusty road towards Kelly-Kenny's head-quarters. Dust puffed up around his recently polished boots and his misted breath trailed behind him. Kitchener noted that the bungalow in front of him was larger than his own.

Kelly-Kenny and Colvile watched their approach. Kelly-Kenny's face looked calm and passive but his jaw was tight and behind his back a forefinger tapped rhythmically in agitation. He had a plan and it was his plan that was to be put in place in today's battle. This arrogant administrator was not going to usurp his senior officer today.

"Good morning, sir." Kitchener saluted as he reached the dwelling.

"Good morning, General," Kelly-Kenny responded, with a more casual salute. Colvile snapped to attention and saluted as Kitchener came up the steps.

"At ease," said Kelly-Kenny.

From beyond Signal Hill came the sound of rifle fire. Kitchener turned and looked in that direction.

"Fine morning for a battle, sir," he observed.

"Fine morning but we will soon be wilting in the heat again."

"Indeed, sir. That is why we need to act immediately and decisively to clear the Boers out of their nest before it gets too hot."

"Attack? I have decided, General, that we are not to attack. Rather, we will invest the laager. We have sufficient men to close all possible escape routes and keep old Cronjé nice and tight. We have many more guns than he has, so we will keep him very well occupied. Using our superior fire power, we will destroy their morale to such an extent that they will creep out of their holes and surrender in no time at all. The message to the rest of the Boers will be clear. We have men and we have time on our side. Our victory is inevitable."

Kitchener stared at Kelly-Kenny as intently and unblinking as an Egyptian cobra.

"We have, as you say, sir, the men and the guns, but we do not have the time. If we should wait for their surrender by investment, we will lose the momentum we have gained from our march. The Boers will establish new barriers between us and Bloemfontein and they will send reinforcements to aid 'old Cronjé', as you call him. Do not forget that he is a hero of the Boer nations, probably their only hero. They will send their whole army to relieve him if they have to. We could end up being invested ourselves, attacked from both the laager in front and reinforcements from behind. No sir, that will not do. I agree that capturing Cronjé would be a devastating blow to the Republics, but if we do it *decisively*, rather than by sloth, the message will be very much stronger: 'Even Cronjé can be taken,' they will say. 'Even he who has held back the Empire to date can fall.' What hope would there be for the rest of the Boer farmers?"

Kitchener stopped, considered briefly and continued before Kelly-Kenny could interject.

"That's if they are still there, of course. They gave Methuen the slip the other day. A rapid attack is required, not least to inform us whether all the Boers are there or if we are once again being held here by a small number as a decoy. And if they have remained in their laager, an expeditious attack will convince them that they had better surrender quickly in the face of our superior forces."

"Thank you for your comment, General. I have spoken to General French, *the* senior officer on the field," he added pointedly, "and he informs me that the Boers had, by yesterday evening, already established a very close defensive position. If they have stayed, they will have prepared their defences even further during the night. The approaches to their laager are across the open veld. The situation is most reminiscent to that at Magersfontein."

"Except that we have many more men and superior leadership," interrupted Kitchener.

In most cases Kelly-Kenny would have taken the flattery to himself, but on this occasion he had the suspicion that the comment was not directed at him. Kelly-Kenny responded tersely.

"General, it is already decided." He stopped to emphasise the point and, as Kitchener took breath to argue, he continued. "As his cavalry is beyond any capability to force the issue, General French is to retire to the high ground of the Koodoosrand to prevent Boer reinforcements approaching from the north. *I* am to take command of the field on General French's orders. General Colvile's 9th Division is to secure the drift here at Paardeberg and my 6th Division is to continue along the south bank of the Modder and occupy the area between the river and the Oskoppies. The Gloucestershires are to occupy the larger, southern hill of the Oskoppies, which I have named 'Osfontein Hill'. When I discover the whereabouts of Hannay and his mounted infantry, I shall deploy him between the laager and Koodoosrand Drift to prevent an escape through that route. Artillery is to be placed on this side of Osfontein Hill and on Gun Hill – the small hill on the other side of the river – to strengthen the guns that have already been set up there by General French. Once all is in place, we will bombard the Boers into submission."

"Sir, I agree with the general deployment of our forces, but disagree that we sit back and allow the Boers to grow in strength around us. It is my contention that we attack forthwith." Kitchener noted the red-anger rising in Kelly-Kenny's face, so he played his trump card, "And our Commander-in-Chief endorses my view."

Kelly-Kenny glared at Kitchener. What, he wondered, did Roberts' puppy have up his sleeve?

"Indeed, General. What is the basis of your contention?"

"A dispatch I received this very morning, sir, from Field Marshal Roberts himself."

Kitchener produced, without any flourish or triumph, a note. He extended his hand in a simple motion as though the contents of the note had never been beyond dispute. Colvile took the paper, glanced at it, and held it out to Kelly-Kenny. Kelly-Kenny did not take it, his eyes drilling Kitchener, who stared back nonchalantly.

"Read it to us please, General Colvile."

Colvile cleared his throat. Then in a firm and clear voice, to ensure that all present heard the message clearly, he read: "To Lieutenant-General Kelly-Kenny, in matters regarding the deployment of troops in respect to the current situation at Paardeberg, you are to take any orders from General Kitchener as being my own." He looked up at Kelly-Kenny, "It is signed by Field Marshal Roberts."

Kelly-Kenny continued to glare at Kitchener. What was Roberts playing at? Both he and General French were more senior to Kitchener, and Kitchener's military experience extended to little more than surveying, logistics and quartermastery. When he had been in command in the Sudan at Omdurman, General French had had to save him from disaster. Yet Roberts favoured him.

Kelly-Kenny finally broke the silence that hung over the men. "General, the field is yours. I wish you good luck."

Kitchener gave the slightest nod and then, to both Kelly-Kenny and Colvile, he flung his orders.

General Kelly-Kenny's 6th Division would focus on the south bank of the Modder River. The Gloucestershires would occupy Osfontein Hill. The regiments of Oxfordshire, West Riding and Yorkshire would take up position between the Oskoppies and the river and strike at the Boer lines between their main laager and their upstream flank. The Essex and Welsh regiments would cross the river upstream of the Boers and attack their flank. General Colvile's 9th Division was to focus on the Boers' downstream flank. The Highland Brigade would launch their offensive from the south bank, while the Canadians, Shropshires and Gordons were to cross the river and assault the Boer positions along the northern bank of the river. The Cornwalls were to be held in reserve and would guard the baggage wagons in the meantime.

Artillery was to be deployed by the regiments as needed to support their offensives, with the exception of the 82nd Field Artillery, which was to be placed on Gun Hill, and another artillery unit, which was to be deployed near Osfontein Hill. The main focus of these two units of artillery would be the Boers' laager. The artillery was to open fire as soon as it was in place. General French was to secure the high ground of the Koodoosrand, as agreed, and if Colonel Hannay could be found, he was to be ordered to join the attack by the Essex and Welsh regiments on the north bank.

Kitchener looked around the circle of officers. He did not expect questions. The tactics were clear; they were to take up their positions and attack.

"Thank you, gentlemen. Should you need me, I shall be on Gun Hill." He turned and left, saying to his aide, Major Hamilton, "I think this will be a case of complete surrender. Come, Major, we shall be in the laager by ten-thirty."

Kelly-Kenny watched them depart. He muttered to himself, "On your head be it, sir, for I have witnesses to testify that you were in command of today's disaster for a disaster it most certainly will be."

Colonel Otter considered the note in his book again. He'd had to write the order down himself as it had arrived as a verbal message and, strangely, it came directly from Lord Kitchener and not from his divisional commander, General Colvile. The vagueness of the order concerned Otter a great deal. He was instructed to march his Royal Canadian Regiment across the river and attack the Boer flanks on the north bank at half-past nine. What Boer positions, he pondered anxiously. He had been informed of their general position but he hadn't even seen any Boers. Except for a smattering of rifle fire just after six o'clock, which he had recorded in his book, there was no evidence of the Boers anywhere.

Otter looked up from his notebook to the cold, brown, surging river. There had been no rain at Paardeberg, but the rain from the previous night's storm further upstream had already flooded the ford at Paardeberg Drift. It was not possible to 'march' his regiment across the river. Otter frowned as he watched his men, up to their armpits, struggle in the torrent of water, clinging for dear life to a rope that the Engineers had thrown across the river.

Otter observed that the men of the 82nd Field Battery were having an even more difficult time as they manhandled their unwieldy, twelve-pounder artillery pieces across. The horses could not be used as they would have been swept away. They had been loaded onto a flat-bottomed barge that was being hauled across the angry river with ropes. The barge had been hastily put in place by the Engineers when the condition of the river was discovered just before sunrise. Now it was in great demand for horses and senior officers and so the artillery crews had to drag their cumbersome guns across the unforgiving river. For much of the time the cannons were completely submerged in the heaving current. The men were repeatedly losing their footing and were in constant danger of being washed away, but some bright spark had thought of tying the men together with a rope, so that those who had been swept away could be hauled back, coughing and spluttering. It was all right for Kitchener, Otter frowned. He had been taken across in the barge.

Otter took out his watch; it was eight-fifteen. His anxiety grew. He would never be able to get his men across the river and in position for an attack in an hour's time. The vague orders and insufficient time to do what was needed left Otter feeling very unhappy. Even though the situation was not of their making, it could reflect badly on the Canadians.

Lieutenant-Colonel William Aldworth was also unhappy. He tugged at his moustache in agitation. What on earth was General Colvile thinking of, he glowered, leaving the Cornish Regiment in the rear to babysit the baggage. This was a job for some untried and minor regiment, not the Cornwalls, a regiment with a proud heritage whose honours included the battles of Gibraltar, Lucknow and Waterloo. Instead, the Canadians – irregulars from the colonies with no grand military heritage – had been chosen above the Cornwalls to sally off and have a go at the Boer. The Canadians were a jolly bunch, no doubt, but they were not *real* soldiers. They were no more than a bunch of teachers, bankers and clerks. What were the generals thinking, leaving heroic, regular and professional soldiers behind to do menial tasks while the colonials had all the fun? It was very unseemly. He recalled the lines of a poem by the late general, Sir Edward Bruce Hamley, about the Cornwall's regimental colours:

A moth-eaten rag on a worm-eaten pole,
It does not look likely to stir a man's Sole,
'Tis the deeds that were done 'neath the moth-eaten rag,
When the pole was a staff, and the rag was a flag.

But it did not make him feel any better.

Lieutenant Colonel Robert Frederick Lindsell, standing on the western brow of Osfontein Hill, had the veld and the Modder River laid out in front of him like a map. While the men of the Gloucestershire Regiment were establishing themselves on the hill around him, he studied the situation below. On the opposite side of the river, the Boer laager was clearly visible now that the morning mist had lifted. Around the laager there was an arc of what appeared to be freshly dug soil and extending from the laager to the left and right was the green vein of vegetation marking the course of the Modder River. The river itself was largely hidden in its deep, meandering ravine, although glimpses of its brown water were possible at the main crossing points. Spread out on either side of the river was the yellow, flat, dehydrated veld.

To the far right, well upstream of the laager and on his side of the river, Lindsell watched troops and horsemen moving down into the ravine to cross the river. These, he assumed, were the Essex and Welsh Regiments and Hannay's mounted infantry. On the opposite bank, those who had already negotiated the swollen waters streamed across the veld to take up their positions.

Closer to hand, on his side of the river and below Stinkfontein Hill, Lindsell could see the lines of soldiers from the regiments of Yorkshire, West Riding and Oxfordshire. They were already in position, standing as motionless as pins. Straight-backed colour sergeants strode up and down the lines, exhorting their men to do their best for the honour of their regiment and for Queen and country. Their shouts drifted up to Lindsell through the cool morning air.

Lindsell swept his gaze across the vast panorama, past the Boer laager and Gun Hill, to his left where the Highland Brigade was now standing ready, intense and silent, under the command of General 'Fighting Mac' Macdonald. Surely that was the General himself striding before the men, his arms gesticulating passionately and embracing the glory of the moment. Lindsell watched the General for a few minutes. Even from this distance the pride and passion of the Scottish regiments seemed to radiate from the man.

Looking beyond the Highlanders, towards the hill called Paarde-berg, Lindsell could see the Canadians, Gordons and Shropshires. Most had made it across the river, but they were not yet in place.

Of the enemy? Except for the wagons and the fresh earthworks of

185

the laager, Lindsell could see nothing. Other wagons lay abandoned between the laager and Gun Hill, the casualties of French's artillery the day before, but Lindsell was surprised that he could see hardly any cattle or horses. Some oxen were grazing contently on the dry grassland beyond the laager, but they would have been a small proportion of the herd required to pull the wagons. Lindsell took up his field glasses and scanned the line of vegetation, but saw nothing. No cattle, no horses and no Boers. The ravine must be deeper than it looked to be able to hide so many men and beasts.

Colonel Otter pulled himself out of the muddy water. Lord, that had been hard work. The torrent had almost swept him away twice. He recalled the conversation he had overheard between his brigade commander, Major-General Smith-Dorrien, and Major Hamilton, who had been passing on General Kitchener's orders to cross the Modder River. The Major-General, who had only just arrived at the scene, had asked where it was possible to cross, to which Hamilton has responded: "The river's in flood and Paardeberg Drift appears to be unfordable. However, Lord Kitchener, knowing your resourcefulness, feels sure you will get across somehow." Otter smiled as he remembered his commander's reply: that Hamilton's comment was more fitting of a courtier than a staff officer.

Otter took out his watch. Blast, they were late. It was already nine-thirty and they were not yet in position. He heard the sound of firing downriver. Damn, the battle had started without his regiment.

"Sergeant," he called. "Get the men up and out in quick order. We need to be in place before it's too late."

To encourage progress, he chivvied the men along himself.

Bloody Sunday, 10:00 am

Sergeant Atkinson looked to his right as the sound of firing started from that direction. So this was it. The battle had commenced. But where he stood there was no warning of the deadly mêlée he was about to enter. From the trees across the flat, grassy veld he could hear the plaintive calls of turtle doves. A cool breeze brushed his cheek, but Atkinson could already feel the warmth of the soaring sun on his back.

A small herd of waterbuck appeared from the vegetation near the river and stood silently watching the line of khaki humans. Suddenly Atkinson saw one of the antelope drop down as if struck by the hand of God. He started as an instant later a single shot rang out. The herd galloped away. The abrupt disturbance of the peace hit Atkinson like a bolt. In that line of trees were men whose sole intent was to kill him and as many of his friends as they could. He stared across the barren veld, trying to discern any movement in the trees. Nothing. The order to advance sounded and Atkinson stepped forward with the rest of the Yorkshire Regiment, walking at an even pace towards the trees.

Atkinson had never felt more alive. His nerve endings tingled and his stomach tensed in anticipation of the punch of a bullet. He tilted his head forward to present more of his helmet and less of his face towards the barrels that were pointing at him. He did not believe the helmet would save him from a direct hit – he had seen too many helmets with bullet holes driven through them – but it offered some mental comfort. He could hear the soft flop of hundreds of feet stepping onto the dusty ground. He glanced down at his boots, which had already lost their shine to the fine dust rising in swirls around his ankles. A springhaas leapt from its cover and bounded away from the advancing line of men. He thought he could hear a rhythmic rustle of the breeze through the trees next to the river, but it was probably the pulsating rush of blood in his ears.

He stared at the trees and tried to estimate their distance. He knew he was more than fifteen hundred yards from the river because that was the effective range of the Boers' Mausers and the range at which they would start shooting. And that would be soon. A chilling thought ran through Atkinson's mind – some Boers were pretty good shots at

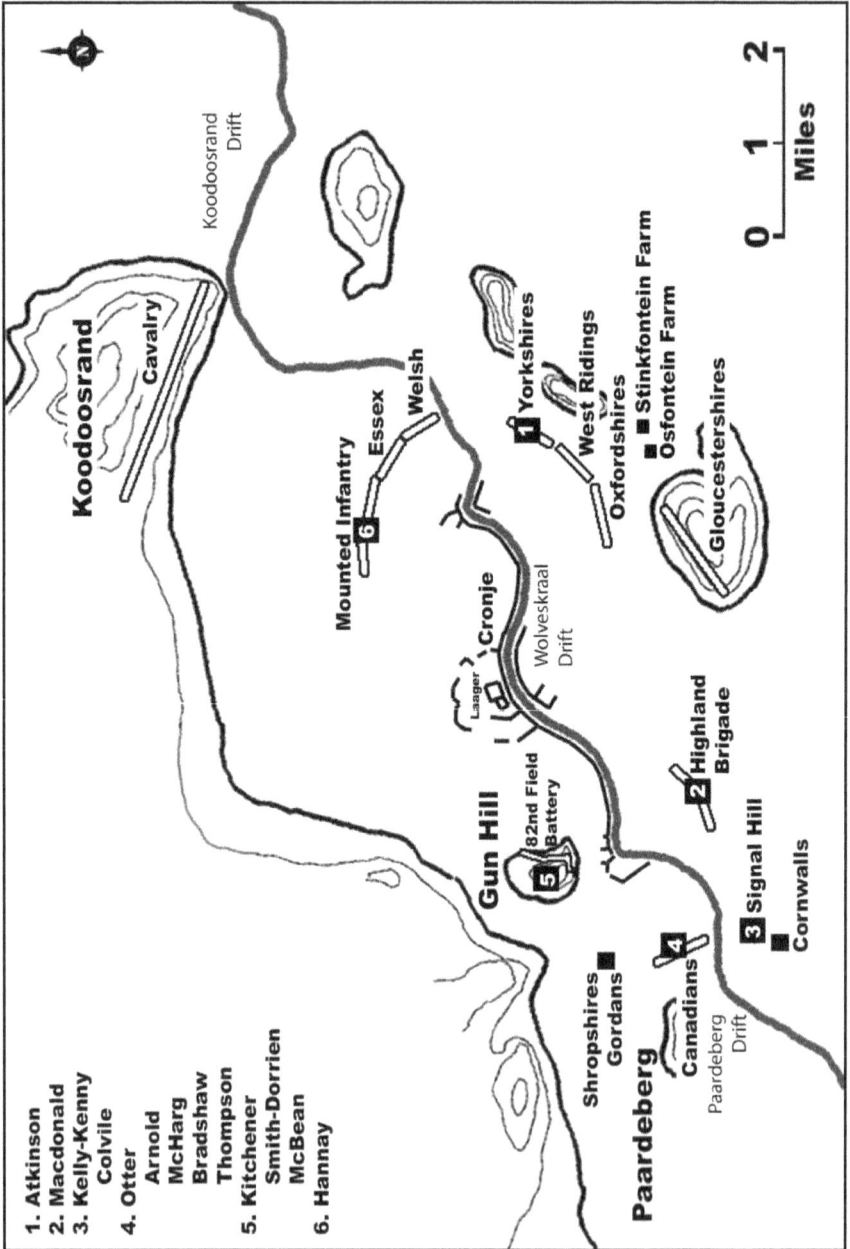

Map 11: 18 February, 10:00 am

188

two thousand yards. He stared at the ground ahead of him, trying to imagine the very spot at which he would cross the fifteen hundred yard line, and then scanned forward to where he estimated he would be twelve hundred yards from the enemy, the point at which his own Lee-Enfield rifle would become effective. That was the crucial distance. Those three hundred yards were the dead-man's zone, where to linger was to court death with no opportunity to respond. Atkinson's whole body tensed as he walked knowingly towards the killing ground.

Atkinson was snapped back from his thoughts by the first harsh crack of a hidden Mauser. Instinctively, he shouted the command to charge and leapt forward. The air, suddenly agitated by singing bullets, brushed his cheeks as he ran forward. The bullets plucking at his clothes gave him an extra urgency as he sprinted across the flat grassland. The noise was appalling: the screams and yells of the charging soldiers, the cries of those hit but, most of all, the cruel snapping of hundreds of unseen Mausers.

Some ran faster than himself, sprinting like cheetahs towards that magical line where they would be able to engage the Boers on more equitable terms, but they simply seemed to become a particular focus for the Boers and Atkinson saw each fall in turn. Some were stopped dead in their tracks or were flung back by the punch of the bullets, others kept on running briefly, carried by the momentum of their rush, and yet others pirouetted gracefully to the dust in a final dance of death as their lives were taken from them.

The open order of the initial charge was lost as the men instinctively started to bunch together under the onslaught of the enemy fire, seeking comfort in the closer company of their fellows. The man in front of Atkinson collapsed with a scream of pain as his leg was shot from under him. Atkinson leapt over him. As he landed, he raised his rifle to shoot. But shoot at what? He emptied his magazine in the direction of the trees in sheer frustration. He ran on. There was no point stopping to reload. There was nothing to shoot at. Run, run, that was the only choice. Get closer to the enemy so you can see them. That was the *only* option.

On either side of Atkinson the regiment drove forward through the pandemonium and crackle of battle, soldiers were crumpling and spilling into the dust in every direction, groaning and howling in anguish and screaming in pain. Then Atkinson sensed the change. The wall of bullets was taking its toll. Too many brave fellows had fallen. Too many could sense they were going to fall. The resolve of the men was being sapped by the enormity of the task ahead of them: a featureless plain, an unseen foe and a murderous blizzard of bullets. They started to throw themselves to the ground to avoid the ferocious tumult of the invisible projectiles. Atkinson spotted an anthill, made for it and dived behind it, staying as still as death while the hail of bullets he had attracted by his actions died down and moved to seek other, easier targets.

The air around him calmed down, and the furious noise from the Mausers seemed to reduce in intensity. Atkinson raised his head to assess the situation and immediately the anthill behind which he lay erupted into an explosion of dust. Bullets thumped through the top of his helmet, missing his head by fractions of an inch. Atkinson pressed himself further into the earth. Once his antagonists turned their focus elsewhere, he slowly rotated his head left and right, looking to the rear as far as he could, moving only those muscles that controlled his eyes. The sight was dismal. Scattered across the warming, arid veld khaki figures lay deathly still, intent on making themselves part of the earth. A number had managed to find anthills behind which they sheltered. Atkinson frowned at the irony. Those same anthills that had previously been the scourge of the marching men and which had personally caused him so much pain, and which he had cursed as the work of the devil, were now the most desired features of his and his comrades' immediate world. But many men lay on the ground unprotected by anything and the Boer marksmen were picking them off at will.

A little forward of his position Atkinson noticed a group of a dozen men in a particularly exposed location. The storm of bullets they were attracting kicked up a fine mist of dust around them. They shuffled around trying to reduce the size of the target they presented, but to the enemy marksmen this simply increased the challenge. The Boer's shooting became more leisurely, more measured and more accurate. The predicament of the British soldiers was untenable. Shouted tactics were hurriedly agreed. On a shout from one of them, those who could rose in unison and charged forward. Screaming in anger and to boost the bravery of their charge, they hurtled forward. Within thirty yards they had all fallen.

As he saw the last man fall, Atkinson dropped his face into the dust. God help us, he lamented, this was worse than Magersfontein.

Burgher Andries Hermanus Potgieter raised his head from the sights of his Mauser as he watched the last of the group of khaki soldiers fall into the dust. He adjusted the sights and then stroked the wooden stock of the weapon with his aged and sun-browned hand. In all his 61 years, this was the finest rifle he had ever possessed. The range and accuracy were astonishing. It was the best weapon a hunter could ask for and he had proved it earlier that morning by felling the waterbuck with a single shot, much to the annoyance of his commandant, who had yelled at him for shooting without orders. Idiot, Potgieter grinned to himself. Give an Afrikander a fine rifle and an antelope and the result was inevitable. No Afrikander could resist the temptation of the hunt; it was in their blood.

The main problem with the Mauser was the hardness of the bullets and their velocity, which meant that unless they hit a bone or a vital organ the bullets often passed right through their target without doing any real damage. It would be better to use softer bullets. The range would be less, but the stopping power much better. Potgieter felt that he would be more confident of stopping a charging lion with a soft bullet than with the ones he was using. So, with these bullets, a head shot was the best way to drop an antelope, or a man. That is what he had done with the waterbuck, but it was more difficult with a man. The trick with the smaller and more mobile target was to aim for the chest – there were lots of vital organs there, especially the heart.

Potgieter snuggled his elbows into the depressions he had sculpted in the rim of the steep-sided bank of the donga in which he stood. He dropped his eye to his sights again and panned across the dry veldt. From the low angle of his position, the yellow grass hid the prostrate khaki figures that he knew lay scattered across the grassland. No matter, he thought, some of them will be up soon to rush at them.

He looked to his right, down the row of bearded men in their slouch hats. Many had made footholds in the bank above the main terrace on which they stood. They were using these to raise themselves above the rim of the donga so they could take better shots at the English soldiers who were flattening themselves into the ground. Potgieter could see no reason to be impatient. They simply had to wait for the khakis to stand up and then they would make fine targets.

"Here they come!" someone bellowed to his left, and Potgieter immediately swung his barrel smoothly in that direction and dropped his right eye to his sights. Out of the corner of his left eye he saw a group of khaki figures dashing across the veldt. Keeping both eyes open, he swept the barrel to the left. As soon as a khaki figure appeared in front of his panning barrel he squeezed the trigger. There was no urgency in his action, just the matter-of-fact business learned from years of hunting. Potgieter saw the man falter as the bullet struck him low on the left side of his rib cage. He saw the small eruption of blood and dust as the bullet burst out of the man's right shoulder just below the neck. The man folded like a ragdoll. Potgieter did not see him hit the ground; he already had his second target in his sights.

General Hector Macdonald strode before the men of the Highland Brigade. Off to his left the sound of firing could be heard. It had been going on for about fifteen minutes. He looked at his men. At last he was satisfied with their formation – straight lines and in very open order. Those damned Boers were too handy with their Mausers for a closed order attack. He had turned his back on the river, daring any Boer to take a pot-shot at him. The brigade stood as still and straight as Scots pines, their kilts billowing gently in the warm breeze.

"Gentlemen," he called out loudly in his broad Highland accent, a voice that demanded attention. "Gentlemen, among those trees behind me are a very dismal folk. However, they do not appreciate their parlous state. Twice those same dismal people, crouching in their trenches below their slouch hats, have dishonoured us. We have lost many courageous friends to that bunch of farmers. Some of you may blush with humiliation of what has gone before. But do not feel humiliated. Think of those brave Scots who went before and whose lives were piteously cut down by the slouching Boers. Twice they have cut us down and, gentlemen, they will *not* do so again. We have received orders that will allow us to redeem our honour, orders from Lord Kitchener himself. Today we will avenge Magersfontein. Today we will avenge the deaths of our friends. Today we will have victory." Macdonald ended with a huge, roaring call, "What say you?"

"Victory!" came the thunderous response.

"What say you?" boomed Macdonald.

"Victory! Victory!" came the deafening roar in return.

Macdonald turned, raised his arm and, without shouting the order, leapt forward. There was no way he was going to be left behind in this fight. Instantly, the Scots charged after their 'Fighting Mac', there was no way he was going to be allowed to get to the Boers first.

General Colvile stood on Signal Hill, downstream of the Highlanders, and stared through his field glasses in complete shock. What on earth was going on? Who had given orders for his Brigade of Highlanders to engage the enemy? *He* most definitely had not. He looked on in frustration and horror as his brigade ran at the Boers. The shooting had not started yet, but his stomach churned at the thought of the consequences when it did. He looked on helplessly; there was nothing he could do to stop them.

Colonel Otter glanced distractedly at his watch, but did not actually notice the time. There was a tremendous amount of shooting and artillery fire going on, but in his immediate vicinity everything was at peace. If one could imagine that the distant rattle of rifle fire, barking of guns and explosions of shells was a thunderstorm, it was possible to believe that there was no battle raging at all.

Looking ahead, Otter studied the trees that hugged the course of the river. Between them and the Canadians lay an open, flat, grassy plain that sloped away gently towards the river. The river was closest to his right flank and then swept upstream in a wide arc across his front. The trees ended suddenly at a point opposite his left flank as the river turned in a sharp dog-leg bend away from him. In that entire stretch of river he could not see a single Boer. About a third of the way along from the dog-leg and some six hundred yards in front of him, a herd of springbuck grazed. The antelope had initially been startled by the noise of the guns, but had soon calmed down and settled back to grazing the parched grass. Even the wildlife seemed to be of the view that everything was quiet along this stretch of the river.

But Otter had his orders, and they were to muster at this point and attack the Boer positions. He lifted his field glasses to his eyes again and surveyed the trees quickly from left to right and then more slowly in the opposite direction. As the springbuck came into view he thought he saw something beyond them among the trees. He scanned back slightly and focused his glasses through the foliage. He loosened his grip on the glasses to stop them shaking and stared through the leaves. His eyes started to blur with the effort. There! A hat. A slouch hat. He whipped the glasses away to identify where in the trees he had seen the hat – about a third of the way along the river from the dog-leg. He took them up again, but the hat was gone. And although he continued to examine the trees in minute detail, no more hats were to be seen.

Otter took out his watch again. It was well after ten o'clock. He could not wait any longer. He had to assume that the main body of the enemy was in the vicinity of the hat. He strode to the front of the Royal Canadian Regiment and turned to face them.

"Men, we have been asked to undertake an important task. In front of us, among the trees, is the foe that we have been chasing for the last week. I am very proud of you. You have endured half-rations of dry biscuits and snatched gulps of foul and muddy water, and on this you have marched, virtually run, without complaint for days. Together we have suffered great hardship and pain. But now we have the old fox Cronjé well and truly holed up. Today, we can make the Royal Canadian Regiment a household name. Through our actions, we can make being a Canadian one of the proudest boasts a man can have. There are some Imperial regiments that have not been given the honour which has been bestowed on us. The great regiments of Cornwall and Gloucestershire are to our rear and it has fallen to us to drive the Boers from their trees and shrubs. I know you will not fail. I know you will honour the name of our great nation. God be with you and God save the Queen."

"God save the Queen," roared the men in return.

Captain Henry Mittleberger Arnold grinned at Otter from the regiment's right flank as Otter strode down the line towards him. "Well, I'll be damned," he muttered to himself. "Where did that come from? For someone who keeps to himself, the Old Man can sure do a good turn when the need arises."

194

As Otter reached Arnold, he returned the salute, at the same time saying, "Sound the charge, Captain."

Arnold turned to Bugler Douglas Williams. At 14 years of age, Williams was the youngest Canadian in the field. Arnold winked at the boy.

"Sound the charge, son."

With youthful enthusiasm, Williams dashed forward and leapt onto an anthill to give extra height to his diminutive five foot three inches and let out a blast to the right, then to the left and, for good measure, another to the front, towards the Boers. The men charged in a ragged open order that soon coalesced into clusters of sprinting men. Arnold snatched Williams off his exposed anthill as he sped past and Williams ran next to him still blowing on his bugle.

Otter watched them disapprovingly. When this was over, the men would need to practise a proper regimental attack. By God, they were not fighting the Native Americans in some dense woodland! This was the twentieth century and they were still behaving like roughneck colonialists.

General Macdonald was furious. The air was blue with invectives as he lay pinned behind an anthill like a lamb avoiding a hailstorm. He was on his back with the anthill supporting his head like a pillow. His foot burned. He looked down at it. The top of his boot had a neat hole drilled through it. He had not been able to examine the sole of his boot. Every movement to do so was met with a squall of angry bullets driving themselves into the anthill and dirt around him. But from the amount of blood dripping onto the soil he knew there was an untidy hole in his sole edged with his flesh, bone and blood. He felt a warmth creep over his foot as his blood seeped into his sock. He wiggled his toes experimentally and the pain that shot through his foot dissuaded him from doing it again.

Turning carefully, he looked out to monitor the progress of the brigade's advance, but there was no advance to monitor. In every direction lay wounded, dying or dead men, while the rest, trying to avoid those outcomes, pressed themselves into the earth. He dropped his head back onto the anthill and gritted his teeth in anger. This was not supposed to happen! It was insufferable that those damned farmers had laid the proud regiments of Scotland low yet again.

Macdonald had not cried since he was six years old when he defied a school bully and had suffered the consequences. On that day he had vowed never to cry again. But now, through sheer frustration, he found himself weeping like a shamed housemaid. The pain in his foot was as nothing compared to his all-consuming sense of outrage. He thought of the prostrated men around him and guessed it was probably about ten-thirty. Dear God, eight hours to sunset. Eight hours, during which they would be held down by the unending vigilance of the Boers. Eight hours, during which the slightest move to scratch an insect bite or which caused a metal buckle to glint in the sun would attract instant retribution. This was going to be worse than Magersfontein! He recalled the legs of the Highlanders after that day, the backs of their knees so sunburnt that the men could not bend their legs. It was only ten-thirty and already he could feel the sun's rays warming his face.

"Dear God help us," he pleaded.

But in the heavens the sun rose higher and glared down on the prone Highlanders. And those parts of their legs not protected by their kilts were already starting to glow a shade of dog-rose pink.

General Kitchener, with his field glasses clamped to his eyes, studied the veld from Gun Hill with increasing agitation. Everywhere the veld was peppered with prone khaki-clad figures. Occasionally, an individual or a small group would leap up and dash forward and Kitchener eagerly followed their progress. But they always either fell to the ground like rag dolls or threw themselves behind some small object or into some shallow hollow in the ground to take cover.

"I need more men," he muttered to himself. He took the glasses from his eyes and looked around.

"Lieutenant," he barked at the soldier nearest to him.

Lieutenant James Watermeyer stepped forward, snapped to attention and saluted.

"Sir?"

"Take the following orders to…." Kitchener hesitated. He had no idea of the name of the officer who was to receive the orders. "…To the commander of the Cornwall Light Infantry. *Not*," he emphasised, "General Colvile, but to the officer in charge of the Cornish. Is that clear?" Kitchener wanted a simple chain of command, not the complication of sending messages through senior commanding officers. Watermeyer nodded and Kitchener continued. "They are to leave the transport wagons and move to the left flank of the Highland Brigade to support their advance."

Kitchener was about to dismiss Watermeyer when he had a thought. He could use the Gloucestershire Regiment as well.

"Lieutenant, are the Gloucestershires still on Osfontein Hill?"

Watermeyer stared blankly for an instant. He had no idea.

"I believe so, sir."

"Good, once the Cornwalls have their orders continue to Osfontein Hill and instruct the Gloucestershires to move forward to support the Highland Brigade as well."

Watermeyer waited.

"Well, Lieutenant. Get on with it."

Watermeyer turned to go and as he did so Kitchener had another thought. He could not leave Osfontein Hill completely unoccupied. He called Watermeyer back.

"What is your unit?" he demanded.

"Kitchener's Horse, sir," Watermeyer responded proudly.

"Splendid. Instruct your commanding officer that you are to relieve them so that they can move forward."

"Relieve the Gloucestershires, sir?" asked the Lieutenant, with increasing anxiety that he was going to remember to whom to give what order. He would prefer to be given written orders.

"Yes, yes, the Gloucestershires."

Kitchener turned impatiently to continue his scrutiny of the veld.

Watermeyer, realised he would not receive any written orders. As he strode to his horse, he ran over the orders in his head.

Captain Arnold and Corporal William McHarg lay with a dozen other Canadians in a shallow depression in the otherwise flat veld. Along the rim of the hollow they could see only the crowns of the trees that hid the enemy, but they still pressed themselves to the ground, the bullets from the Mausers passing just inches above their heads. McHarg was reminded of a lizard he once watched squeezing itself into a flat rock to avoid being seen by a snake. He remembered grimly that the lizard had not escaped. Suddenly, the man next to Arnold cried out in pain and pushed himself up onto his knees in shock, screaming "I'm hit!"

"Get down!" McHarg roared, and then watched in horror as little explosions of dust erupted across the man's chest and abdomen. As the soldier crumpled, he tumbled forward and crashed on to the ground in front of Arnold and McHarg. He clenched his jaw against the pain and his eyes were wide with shock and panic and the knowledge that he was dying. Then, with a gentle exhale of breath that blew a little of the dusty veld towards heaven, he died. His body jolted as it was pumped with more bullets. McHarg saw the bullets exploding out of the khaki uniform as they passed through the dead man. One of the bullets hit the front of his own helmet with a dull thud, its momentum slowed by passing through the cadaver, and it dropped on to the ground in front of him. It lay in the dust, a small piece of smooth metal with a new veneer of shining red blood.

McHarg stared at it, mesmerised that such a small thing could cause so much destruction. But all around him turmoil had broken out. Men were shrieking in pain and fear, and everyone pressed themselves further down into the shallow hollow.

"What the hell is happening?" someone yelled. "How the hell are they doing that?"

"He's in a tree," shouted Private James Bradshaw. "The bastard has climbed into a tree and is shooting down on us."

Bradshaw took aim and emptied a magazine of bullets at his target. "Damn," he said in disgust as he swapped magazines, "I missed the bastard!"

"Where is he? Which tree?"

"How the hell do you expect me to describe it? He's in one of those damned trees in front of us. Just look will you."

Everyone stared at the trees, but the smokeless Mauser did not give its owner away.

"Can't see him. Can you?" shouted Arnold to McHarg above the cries of alarm and pain as bullets continued to play among the Canadians. McHarg shook his head. Arnold looked to his left. Bradshaw was about five men down the line of soldiers and shooting determinedly at the Boer.

"Private Bradshaw?" he hollered.

"Yes sir."

"I need McHarg to know where he is."

"McHarg, sir?"

"Yes."

"He's next to you, sir."

Arnold raised his head to look down the line of men at Bradshaw in complete bewilderment and instantly dropped it again as he felt a bullet snag the side of his helmet.

"You damned idiot, Bradshaw. I want McHarg to know which tree the Boer is in."

Despite their perilous situation, Arnold could not help noticing that several men were sniggering at the ludicrous farce that was developing on around them.

"Well, the man needs to make himself clear," Bradshaw muttered to himself, defensively.

"Bradshaw!" Arnold shouted.

"Yes sir."

"Who is lying to your right?"

"Private Lester, sir."

"Point out to Lester which tree the Boer is in and tell him to pass the message to his neighbour and so on 'til the information gets to me and McHarg. Is that clear?"

"Yes sir."

After a short delay, Bradshaw shouted back, "He's dead, sir."

"The Boer?"

"No sir, Lester."

Like some of the others, McHarg could feel his shoulders shaking as an uncontrollable laugh built up inside him. He struggled to stifle it and keep still because the last thing he wanted to do was attract the attention of the Boer marksman. At his right elbow he heard someone let out a snort of laughter which was quickly choked back.

"Sweet Jesus!" Arnold cursed. If it had been safe to raise his face to the heavens to ask for forbearance, he would have done so. "In the name of God, Bradshaw, show the nearest man to you, who *is* alive, which tree that damned Boer is in and then pass the information down the line to myself and McHarg."

Arnold could feel McHarg shaking with mirth next to him and he turned on him. "Corporal, this is not a laughing matter!"

"I know, sir. I'm sorry, sir."

Turning his face away from Arnold, he continued to try to control his shaking body. Arnold elbowed McHarg viciously in the ribs and the latter turned abruptly to see that he was pointing, indicating the location of the Boer marksman.

"I see him now, sir." That it was a difficult shot was clear from the fact that every man between Bradshaw and McHarg was firing his rifle and still the Boer remained in the tree. The tree was set well back in the riverside woodland and intervening leaves and branches made a clear shot impossible. McHarg crept forward, taking care to remain behind the protection of the dead Canadian's body. He rested his rifle on the corpse and estimated the range. He set the sights, tucked the butt into his shoulder and looked down the length of his rifle.

As he took aim he heard Private Richard Rowland Thompson wriggle closer to him on his right side.

Thompson whispered, "Oi Corporal, what you aiming at him for? I thought Bradshaw said he was dead." Thompson sniggered silently to himself.

McHarg pushed his face into the ground, clenching his jaw as hard as he could, but he could not stop a snort of laughter escaping, dust bellowing out from either side of his face.

"Corporal," Arnold spat at him, "If you do not control yourself, I shall have you court-marshalled and put before a firing squad."

"Yes sir."

McHarg put his tongue between his teeth and clamped down hard. He raised his rifle and took aim again. He blinked his eyes, controlled his breathing, released his tongue, which was hurting like blazes, and stared down the barrel. He breathed out and squeezed the trigger.

After a moment Arnold said, in exasperation, "You missed! He's still in the tree."

"Damn!" McHarg took aim again, squeezed the trigger and felt the recoil against his shoulder. He watched the trajectory of the bullet across the veld. The Boer remained in the tree.

"I definitely hit him. Damn, I definitely hit him that time."

"Well he's still in the damned tree and we are still being shot to pieces."

"Maybe it's his ghost," suggested Thompson.

"Private Bradshaw!" Arnold bawled.

"Yes sir."

"You started this blasted comedy show. Get back to command and request some artillery fire on that bloody Boer. And if the Boers don't shoot you in the arse while you're doing it, I'll do it for them later." To the rest of the men, he shouted, "The rest of you get out of here. While that Boer is in that tree this is *not* a good place to be." On his order, men dispersed in every direction to try to find a place where they would less exposed to the enemy. Not all were successful.

General Smith-Dorrien stood behind the artillery on Gun Hill watching the Canadian attack unfold. He turned to Lieutenant-Colonel McBean, commanding officer of the Gordons, "I must say I am very impressed with the Canadians."

"Yes sir. I am as well, although their method of advancing is somewhat unruly."

"Indeed, but let's not forget they are colonial volunteers. For all that, their courage cannot be doubted."

"Indeed not, sir."

Smith-Dorrien returned his field glasses to his eyes and studied the clusters of Canadians dashing forward a few paces and dropping back to the ground, some obviously as a result of being shot. Progress was painfully slow. Smith-Dorrien wondered whether he should send the Gordons and Shropshires in support, but was concerned that Kitchener may have had other plans for them. He looked at his watch. It was nearly twelve o'clock. What the hell does Kitchener want to do with my men, he pondered. He left Gun Hill hours ago without issuing any orders. Not that he had given any when he was on the hill. The last order – the only order – from that man was five hours ago and that had been to cross the river.

He studied the field of action again, scanning the trees lining the river for signs of the enemy, but could see very little of the Boers. What was more astonishing was the complete lack of gun smoke rising from the Boers' lines. He was getting no indication of the length of their lines or the number of men facing his own. There could be one hundred Boers down there or there could be thousands. How things had changed, he thought, since his first experience in Southern Africa against the Zulus.

Smith-Dorrien came to an uncertain conclusion. He did need to give the Canadians some support. The Shropshires and Gordons needed to advance. Smith-Dorrien removed his glasses from his eyes and looked at McBean.

"Colonel."

"Yes sir?"

No, he changed his mind. He should, he decided, wait to be sure that Kitchener did not have plans for his regiments. Instead, he smiled at McBean.

"Colonel, you are my witness to an oath that I shall not remove another whisker from my face until we have taken that damned laager."

McBean looked back at the General. It was a small sacrifice, however well intentioned. He returned the smile.

"Sir, I shall personally shave your beard off for you when we have captured the laager."

Lieutenant-General Colvile cursed under his breath. "Blast Kitchener. He is taking my staff and troops in no order and without any apparent system." Turning to Lieutenant-Colonel Aldworth, he asked, "So Colonel, could you explain the situation again?"

"Sir, earlier this morning we received orders, directly from *Lord Kitchener*...." Colvile noted the subtle emphasis on the name. "...for myself and the Cornwalls to break off our duties protecting the transport wagons and support the Highland Brigade in their attack on the Boers along the south bank of the Modder. As we were forming up to do so, we received another order, again from *Lord Kitchener*." There was that emphasis again. "This time we are instructed to cross the river and support the Canadians in their attack on the *north* side of the river."

Colvile remained silent, looking blankly at Aldworth. The latter continued uncertainly.

"I thought, sir, that you might not be fully aware of the situation and believed I should consult with you, as my commanding officer."

"I see. Thank you. However, Lord Kitchener is the overall commanding officer. You had best fulfil his orders."

Colvile had decided that he would not be taking the blame for this fiasco by countermanding orders. Aldworth hesitated.

"Yes Colonel?" Colvile asked.

"Sir, it's just that … ah … it's just that the men have not had lunch yet and, being on half-rations, they might do well to have something to eat before they advance?"

Colvile remained silent for a moment.

"Yes, let them have lunch. Then at least the poor devils will not have to attack on empty stomachs."

Sergeant Atkinson woke with a start. He immediately pushed his face against his anthill and pressed his body back into the earth, and lay as still as death. The oven-hot air around him still whistled with bullets. The heat pressed down on him like an iron, squeezing every ounce of moisture from his body. The brightness of the sun, reflecting from the shimmering ground, scalded his eyes. He narrowed them to thin slits.

A movement very close made him open them quickly. A lizard, resting in the shade of the anthill, studied Atkinson with interest, tilting its head this way and that. Atkinson studied it in return. A small, dull brown animal, usually it would not catch Atkinson's attention, but under the circumstances it became a thing of beauty. A Mauser bullet slammed into the anthill, showering dust over the lizard, and it scuttled away to a safer place.

Without the lizard to distract him, the desperate craving for a drink became Atkinson's main focus. He had no idea of the time and he was not about to try to reach for his watch, but he thought it must be well after midday. Or he hoped it was as he was not sure how much more lying out in the broiling sun he could endure. He was not the only one. Nearby a wounded man began whimpering for water. He was about a dozen yards from Atkinson and slumped in an uncomfortable position, but his stillness meant he was being ignored by the Boer marksmen. Atkinson stared through the flickering heat. He thought it might be Jonny Brown?

"Jonny, is that you?" he called.

There was no answer.

"Jonny. Is that you? It's Alfie. Is that you, Jonny?"

Again, there was no answer. But beyond the still figure, Atkinson saw the strange vision of a khaki-helmeted head floating above the ground on the bubbling heat haze. He thought it must be some unfortunate that had been decapitated during the battle, but then it disappeared and two more heads floated into view in a different location. The ground in front of them suddenly exploded into a vapour of dust and the heads were gone, only to reappear a second later, this time with shoulders and rifles. The apparitions fired a few shots and then dropped out of sight again as dust exploded around the spot where they had been.

Atkinson could not make head nor tail of it. Suddenly, he was aware of a commotion on his right side and before he could turn around someone leapt over his prone body and pelted in the direction of the floating heads. Atkinson watched, mesmerised. As the running man came close to the spot, four or five heads popped up with their rifles and, pointing towards the Boer lines, opened up a furious fire. The runner launched himself into the dancing air and a moment later disappeared into the bowels of the earth. The heads disappeared! Dear God, he was saved! Atkinson realised he had dived into a donga where others had already found safety. From where he lay, there was no evidence of its existence. He could not believe it.

A stir from the wounded man caught Atkinson's eye and his new position gave Atkinson a better view of him. It was Jonny.

"Jonny?" Atkinson shouted, "Keep still, I'll be over."

Looking beyond Brown, he reminded himself of where he had seen the heads. Then he tensed and prepared himself, leapt up and bolted towards Brown. Now that he was standing he could see the scar of the donga as it cut its way across the veld, snaking towards the river. Without stopping, Atkinson grabbed a fistful of Brown's uniform and dragged him across the veld and they tumbled into the donga. They fell in a tangle of arms and legs on top of those already there, Brown letting out a low groan of pain.

Atkinson laid Brown down in the bottom of the donga. The chest of his khaki uniform was stained with six blotches of blood. There were several bullet holes in his sleeves and trouser legs, each, strangely, with very small blood stains. Atkinson took up Brown's water bottle. It was empty. Taking a bottle offered by another soldier, he unscrewed the lid and let Brown draw from it long and hard.

"Thanks, Alfie," he croaked in a parched whisper. "You're a true Yorkshire knight. That was the finest drink of my life, a million times better than anything we ever drank at the George 'n' Dragon."

He winced in pain and looked at Atkinson for reassurance. The left side of his face was smeared with dirt and the right side was a painful-looking scarlet where the sun had burned itself into his skin.

"You'll be fine, old fellow," Atkinson replied unconvincingly. He smiled at Brown and patted his shoulder, and then downed what Brown had left of the warm water without stopping for breath.

"Where'd you find the water?" he asked as he handed back the empty bottle.

"At the river."

"There's a gap in the Boers' defences?" Atkinson asked incredulously.

"No!" replied the man, in a tone that suggested that that was the most ridiculous question he had ever heard. "If there was we would have sneaked through it and attacked their rear. But there is a bluff of land, and if you are extremely careful to stay behind it, you can get water from a pool near the river."

Atkinson looked at Brown and was reminded of his fellow Yorkshiremen still lying out on the veld. Lord, how many were suffering like Brown? He looked warily over the rim of the donga. There were dozens of them, all lying perfectly still, as if dead. Their motionless forms appearing to vibrate as the fiery air rippled around them. Despite appearances, Atkinson knew that many would be alive and in desperate need of help. He turned to the others in the donga.

"If you have water in your bottles, give them to me. If not, go down to the river and fill them."

Atkinson was given three bottles and two men cautiously made their way down the dry donga with four or five bottles each to fill from the muddy river.

Atkinson carefully started to raise his head above the rim of the donga, but this time, as soon as the top of his helmet broke cover the ground above him erupted with bullets. He ducked down quickly and took off his helmet, turning to the men around him.

"Move down the donga," he instructed them. "Place your helmets on sticks and raise them out of the donga to draw their fire."

He waited for them to get in position and as soon as the enemy started shooting at the decoys he scrambled out of the donga and raced towards the nearest man, throwing himself on to the ground next to him in a cloud of dust. Immediately, bullets started to whistle

205

past him. Atkinson remained as still as a corpse until the air around him quietened down. He turned slowly towards the man. Damn, too late! He had already passed to another world. With great stealth, Atkinson relieved the man of his water bottle. It was empty. Atkinson selected another prostrate shape and repeated the dash. The bullets seemed to fly around him with greater intent than before and Atkinson dived towards the man, who nearly leapt out of his skin when the unexpected visitor tumbled on to him. It was Band Sergeant William Hall and he cursed Atkinson liberally once he recognised him.

"Hey, Sergeant, how's your water supply?" Atkinson grinned.

"Thanks for asking," Hall replied sourly. "I finished it hours ago. I've been stuck behind this wretched bush the whole damned morning. Move a muscle and the bloody Boers shoot you to hell. And even if the bloody Boers leave you alone, the scorching sun sucks you dry. Christ," Hall looked at Atkinson though narrowed eyes, "I cannot remember the last time I had such an agonising headache! And it wasn't helped by the shock of you leaping on me! What the blazers are you doing scaring people witless like that?"

Atkinson held up a canister for Hall to see and a second later a bullet passed through it.

"Sweet Jesus!" Hall grabbed the canister and covered the two holes with his finger and thumb. "There's no need to advertise the fact you are acting the delivery man." He unscrewed the lid and drank deeply. "By God, that's the sweetest liquid I have ever had the pleasure of tasting!" He winked at Atkinson, "You're a life saver, Alfie. God bless you." Hall gave him a rough jab in the ribs with his elbow.

"There's a better way to save your life," Atkinson responded. "If you run in that direction," he said pointing, "you will find a gully that will offer you more protection than this scrubby little bush."

Hall looked across the veld and then at Atkinson dubiously.

"Believe me, Bill, it's there. Now, on my signal, you go in *that* direction and I will go," he looked around for his next target, "over there. Ready, steady, go!"

The two men darted off like rabbits from a trap.

Atkinson sprinted towards the next prostrate man. The Boers were getting the measure of him now and he could feel the Mauser bullets plucking at his clothes. He landed next to Private Bruce with a thump and lay still for what seemed like hours before the bullets stopped whizzing around them. Bruce was in a bad way. He was lying on his back, barely conscious. His face burnt crimson and his mouth and lips parched and cracked dry. He had wounds to his neck, chest, stomach and thigh, and great smears of blood discoloured his uniform.

Atkinson cautiously lifted one of his remaining bottles, but it was empty – the water had trickled out through a bullet hole. He took the last one and carefully dribbled water on to Bruce's dry lips. They parted. Atkinson gently poured a little water into his desperate mouth.

"God bless you!" came a scarcely audible whisper.

But this time the shooting did not die down for long and Atkinson realised that his presence was endangering Bruce, drawing more fire to the already badly wounded man. He decided to leave the water bottle with Bruce and move on. Atkinson whispered to Bruce that he would see him later and then scrambled up and made for the donga as quickly as he could with bullets chasing him like angry wasps. As he lunged for the rim of the ravine he felt a punch to his arm that flung him off balance and threw him down the steep side of the donga. Immediately, the others were around him, roughly handling him to make sure he was OK. The bullet had gone straight through the fleshy part of his upper arm and left remarkably tidy entry and exit wounds. In no time he was bandaged up and being congratulated on his heroic work. Atkinson thanked them and then asked for the filled canisters.

"What! You're not thinking of going out there again?"

"Of course. There are men dying from thirst out there. It's the least I can do. I was paid the same kindness once and it had a miraculous effect on my morale."

The men looked at each other guiltily. They did not have the same compassion. Were they cowards? They could not look Atkinson in the eye as the five water canisters were passed to him.

"It's a bit warm and muddy, but it will have to do."

Atkinson smiled at the man handing him the canisters, "I'll tell them it's Bovril," he quipped.

"More like Boervril," someone responded, but the pun felt lame.

Atkinson found his helmet and put it on. "No need to take unnecessary chances," he grinned, and then he was over the top once more and sprinting towards another soldier. The men left behind cheered and shouted and kept up a hot fire towards the unseen Boer riflemen. Each time Atkinson successfully reached someone those in the donga let loose a huge roar in celebration.

But not everyone was cheerful. "The Boers are getting the line of Alfie," remarked an anguished Sergeant Tate. "They've clipped him a few times."

The shouts and cheers grew more strained as everyone started to realise that Atkinson's luck was running out. They cheered with relief as he dropped at a fifth man and even more loudly as he rose and sprinted back towards the protection of the donga.

Suddenly, Atkinson's head lurched to the side, his helmet was flung from his head, his torso folded and he dropped, falling hard on his side. The cheering died instantly. Atkinson did not move.

"Hell's teeth, they've got him! The bastards have killed him!"

Angst rushed through the men as they stared at the crumpled form lying in the dust. Then Atkinson rolled over.

"He's not dead," shouted Tate. "He's not dead!"

"I want two volunteers," hollered Colour Sergeant Hughes. "There's no way we are leaving him out there."

Everyone pushed forward, eager to be involved in the rescue of their regiment's newest hero. Hughes selected four men to accompany him – Sergeant Tate and Privates Diplock, Kenny and Dibble. He chose four because he knew he was going to need extra men to cover the inevitable losses.

"We go out in very open order, fast, *very* fast. We grab him and we get back. Simple." He looked each soldier in the eye. Simple.

The five men scrambled out of the donga and sprinted towards the still form of Atkinson. Immediately the air became ferocious with Mauser bullets. Diplock was the first to succumb. Even before he reached Atkinson, he was thrown over by the force of the bullets that penetrated his body. Hughes, Tate, Kenny and Dibble made it to Atkinson's side. Each grabbed a limb and lifted him. As they turned for the safety of the donga, Tate was thrown backward by a hail of bullets. He collapsed to the ground, lifeless. The remaining three toiled across the veld with their cumbersome load. Kenny and Dibble held an arm each and Hughes followed with a leg in each hand. The roars of encouragement from the donga almost drowned out the spiteful snapping of the Mausers and the vicious whine of the bullets. Twenty yards to go…. Fifteen. Atkinson's weight suddenly increased for Kenny and Dibble. Without stopping for a second, they looked back to see Hughes' body lying sprawled in the dust. They staggered on, tumbling over the edge of the donga, just as three others scrambled past them in the opposite direction to gather in the corpse of their Colour Sergeant.

Atkinson was unconscious but still breathing. The bullet that had knocked off his helmet had gone through it and into the side of Atkinson's head, leaving a cruel, jagged and bloody hole to which remnants of his helmet clung. Dibble carefully moved Atkinson's head to look for the exit wound, but there wasn't one – the bullet was embedded in his brain. Atkinson was gently laid next to the body of his late friend, Jonathan Brown. His wounds were tended to and bandaged to the best of their ability. He needed the ministrations of qualified medical staff, but that would have to wait until the evening; only then would it be possible to remove him to the field hospital at Paardeberg Drift.

Dibble and the others nearly jumped out of their skins as a tremendous clap of thunder exploded in the sky, drowning out even the sounds of war. Turning Dibble saw an ominous bank of menacingly black clouds rolling over the Oskoppies. The heat was still stifling, but there was a subtle change in the atmosphere and within minutes, the scene had changed from one of desiccating heat to a downpour of drumming rain. The sense of relief was immediate. Dibble lifted his face to the stabbing raindrops. The flat, barren veld disappeared behind a screen of rain and the noise of thunder and of the water driving into the ground was deafening. In no time, the previously dry donga was a torrent. Dibble and the others had to drag their wounded and dead comrades from the floor of the ravine up the banks to stop them from being washed away. Men moved about like eccentric ghouls in the flashing lightning and great peals of thunder shook the earth. Then, as quickly as the rain had come, it was gone and the sun returned to bake the soaked landscape. The shimmering heat haze was replaced by a slow-rising steam.

The silence was profound. The soldiers and gunners had not recovered from the sudden ending of the storm and they all seemed awestruck in wonderment at the silence. Then, from Gun Hill, came the familiar crack of an artillery piece and all hell broke loose again.

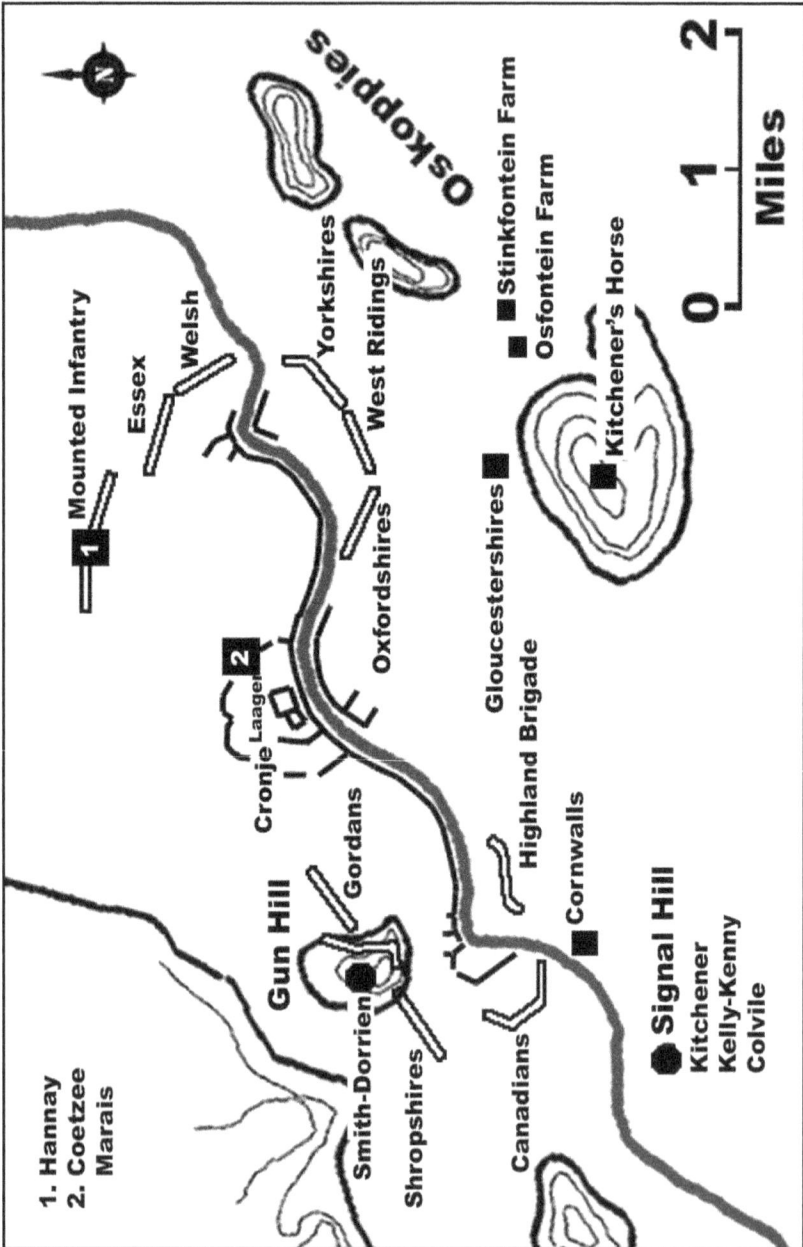

Map 12: 18 February, 2:00 pm

Bloody Sunday, 2:00 pm

Colonel Hannay stared at the sergeant in disbelief.

"I assume you have misreported the order," he said.

The sergeant stood stiffly to attention, steam rising from his rain-soaked uniform. "No sir. That was precisely what Lord Kitchener said. He had me repeat it to him, sir."

"A verbal order? Do you expect me to be so reckless on the basis of a verbal order?"

"I could not possibly say, sir. We are not receiving written orders, sir. The General sends only verbal messages."

"From Kitchener? Was General Kelly-Kenny present?"

"Yes sir, and General Colvile. Lord Kitchener has joined them on Signal Hill."

"And General Kelly-Kenny did not countermand the order."

"No sir."

"Repeat the order, so I can make sure I've not misheard it."

"Sir, you are to storm the Boer laager, enter it and disrupt the enemy in order that the infantry can regain the initiative and complete their advance on the Boer positions."

"Does the General understand the consequences of his order? Does he realise that not a single man will get into that laager. And even if we do, we will be faced with the fury of four thousand Mausers. Our disruption will be like that of a fly on the backside of a buffalo. It is a suicide mission. Everyone will die." Hannay glared at the sergeant, "I shall await a *written* order from General *Kelly-Kenny* on this matter."

The sergeant went to speak, but held his tongue.

"There is more?" asked Hannay.

The man hesitated. "Yes sir. Lord Kitchener said that if you felt unable to lead the attack I was to inform you that he could ask General French to do so."

Before he could stop himself, Hannay stepped forward and raised his hand to strike the sergeant. Only at the last instant did he hold back from smashing his palm across the man's face. The force of his furious blow would have sent the sergeant sprawling to the ground. He stood poised with his hand raised high above his head. The sounds of the battle raging about them were lost to Hannay. All he could hear was the rush of blood in his ears. He felt his face burn. The sergeant remained motionless, but Hannay noticed that he had clenched his jaw in anticipation of the strike. The lower lid on his left eye twitched under the tension in his jaw muscles. With a supreme effort of willpower, Hannay lowered his hand and the sergeant's face relaxed. Hannay leaned forward so that their two faces were only inches apart.

"The man is a mindless warmonger," he snarled, "and if he persists in this reckless endeavour not a man will be left standing."

Hannay turned to his adjutant. "Prepare some coffee and make it strong. We'll need it for our return." To a captain nearby he ordered, "I want fifty volunteers. None of them are to have wives or children."

He strode furiously to his horse and mounted. The sergeant had not moved. Hannay glared at him, but left him standing to attention. Something had to be the focus of his anger and for now it was the sergeant. He leant forward and stroked the auburn neck of his horse. He felt some of the anger drain from him, but the tension remained. He hoped he would be able to hide his feelings of foreboding from the young men who were being gathered by the captain. He removed his helmet and wiped the sweat from his forehead with his sleeve. He ran his hand through his grey hair before replacing his helmet.

He studied the horsemen forming up in front of him. My god, they looked young, he thought. But that was to be expected; he had ordered that they should have no wives or children. So, at the most they would be in their twenties. Less than half his age! They would leave no legacy to mark their existence – no children to show they had lived. For a moment, Hannay thought of changing his order and taking older men, those with families, so that these young men could experience more of life. But no, he knew he had made the right decision. His heart went out to the mothers and fathers whom he had decided would lose their sons this day. He hoped they would understand and be proud of the sacrifice their sons were about to make. At least there would be no grieving wives and children.

A horse pulled up alongside Hannay.

"The men are ready, sir," said the captain as he saluted.

"Thank you, Captain." He looked at the man next to him. Hannay knew he was married with two young daughters.

"Captain, I wish you to take this to my adjutant and ask him to make sure it is delivered." Hannay withdrew from his breast pocket the letter he had written to his wife, a letter prepared in advance of action, but one he hoped he would never have to send. He had always anticipated it being found and sent after his death; he never expected to hand it over personally. He slowly stroked his thumb over the name and address he had written on the envelope. Then he sat up straight in his saddle and handed the letter to the officer.

"Thank you, Captain. That will be all."

As the captain wheeled his horse around to hunt out Hannay's adjutant, Hannay looked briefly at the men in front of him. When he spoke, it was in a clear, strong voice.

"We are to attack the Boer laager. You are to divide into two units." With a cutting motion of his arm he indicated where the division was to be. "Those of you to the right are to wait here until required," he commanded. "You are not to take action until ordered to do so. Those to the left are to come with me. You will *not* advance until you hear my specific order. *Not* until you hear a specific order, is that understood? Thank you and God's speed."

He turned his horse and trotted up the ridge that hid them from the Boers. On reaching the crest he stared down the shallow slope across the open veld. A thin mist rose from the grassland as the last remnants of moisture from the storm were wrung from the soil by the relentless sun. Just under a mile away was the Boer laager, enclosed in its protective arc of trenches. To his left, the veld was littered with the prone khaki figures of the Essex and Welsh infantry, and the occasional shot rang out across the grassland as a Boer took a pot-shot at a soldier who had foolishly exposed some part of his body to the rifleman. Ahead of him, the veld was clear of bodies. There were no major obstructions; a few animal burrows and anthills, but no ravines or gullies, no walls or parapets. Under normal circumstances, a horse could simply walk over the low trench defences. By any standards, it should be a simple charge. But Hannay knew this war was different from any he had been involved in. He knew his enemy was the most devastating and effective he had ever faced. He was already within range of the more proficient of the Boer marksmen and he was just two hundred and fifty yards from the invisible spot that was the gateway to hell on earth. It would take him twenty seconds to reach that point, maybe twenty-five from a standing start and then a further two minutes before he reached the enemies' lines. He stared down the gentle slope at the scar that had been cut through the veld by the Boers. He knew the chances of the charge succeeding were nil.

Suddenly, he thrust his heels into the flanks of his horse, which lurched forward into a gallop. It took a few seconds for those behind him to realise that Hannay had initiated the attack without giving any order for them to follow. But their surprise was soon overcome. Ignoring his instruction to wait for the order, the band of twenty-five riders howled a charge and drove their horses forward. They thundered after their leader.

Johannes Coetzee spotted the lone horseman start galloping towards them, followed at some distance by a further group of cavalry. He nudged Marais, "Look Oom, what do you think he's up to?"

The perplexed Boers watched as Hannay sped towards them.

"They must be coming to spy on our defences. I bet he'll turn away at the last moment and report what he has seen."

But the horsemen simply came on.

"I don't care what he is up to," spat out Coetzee. He raised his rifle, aimed and fired. The snap of his Mauser was quickly followed by others.

Hannay, although largely protected by the head and shoulders of his horse, felt the snag of bullets as they passed through the flesh of his upper arms. Then he felt his horse falter and a few strides later its soul left it, driven out by the impact of the multitude of bullets that drilled into its flesh. As the horse collapsed under him, Hannay was thrown forward like a rag doll, landing, tumbling and sliding in a mix of water vapour and dust. Before the dust had settled he was up and sprinting at the Boers, screaming at them in rage. He managed to gain fifteen yards before the weight of their bullets dragged him down.

As he fell towards the ground, time seemed to slow, seconds turned into minutes. His senses were filled with the thunderous beat of galloping horses. On the ground, he could feel the earth vibrating to the crash of their hooves. He managed to lift himself up onto his elbow. He looked back. Beyond the still form of his horse, a small band of horsemen stormed across the veld. The water vapour rolled aside as they charged through it. They leaned over their horses like jockeys at the Derby, driving their mounts onwards. In their free hands, their weapons of war were raised in defiance of their foe. Their mouths were open wide as they screamed the charge and hurled abuse at the enemy. But Hannay could not hear their words above the thud of the hooves. The noise beat to the rhythm of his blood coursing through his body. He could hear its pulsating rush in his ears. He felt his heart swell with pride at the courage of his young soldiers. A second later that same heart exploded as a bullet smashed through it.

Hannay crumpled to the ground, his eyes open, but unseeing. He did not see the horses hurtle past him, leaving in their wake a trail of writhing, screaming horses and spilt and sprawling riders. He did not see his small band of brave soldiers decimated by the sheet of Boer bullets. He did not see, as the last man fell, the riders he had ordered to remain behind burst over the crest of the ridge. They screamed in defiance at the Boers and at the needless sacrifice of their commander and their friends. They charged towards their enemy intent on avenging their deaths. And they fell like apple blossom in a hailstorm. None made it as far as Hannay.

Coetzee looked up from his Mauser incredulously. "Sweet Jesus," he blasphemed. "The crazy bastards! Why did they do that?"

General Kitchener, on Signal Hill, surveyed the carnage of horses and men across the river through his field glasses. "The *damned* fool. Did he really expect to do it all by himself?"

Kelly-Kenny dropped his own glasses to his chest and glared at the back of Kitchener's head. "The fool is much closer to hand," he muttered. Taking off his helmet, he turned and strode down the slope to his horse, followed by Colvile. They would have nothing more to do with this madman's battle. Kitchener did not notice their departure. His mind was full of the next part of his battle plan.

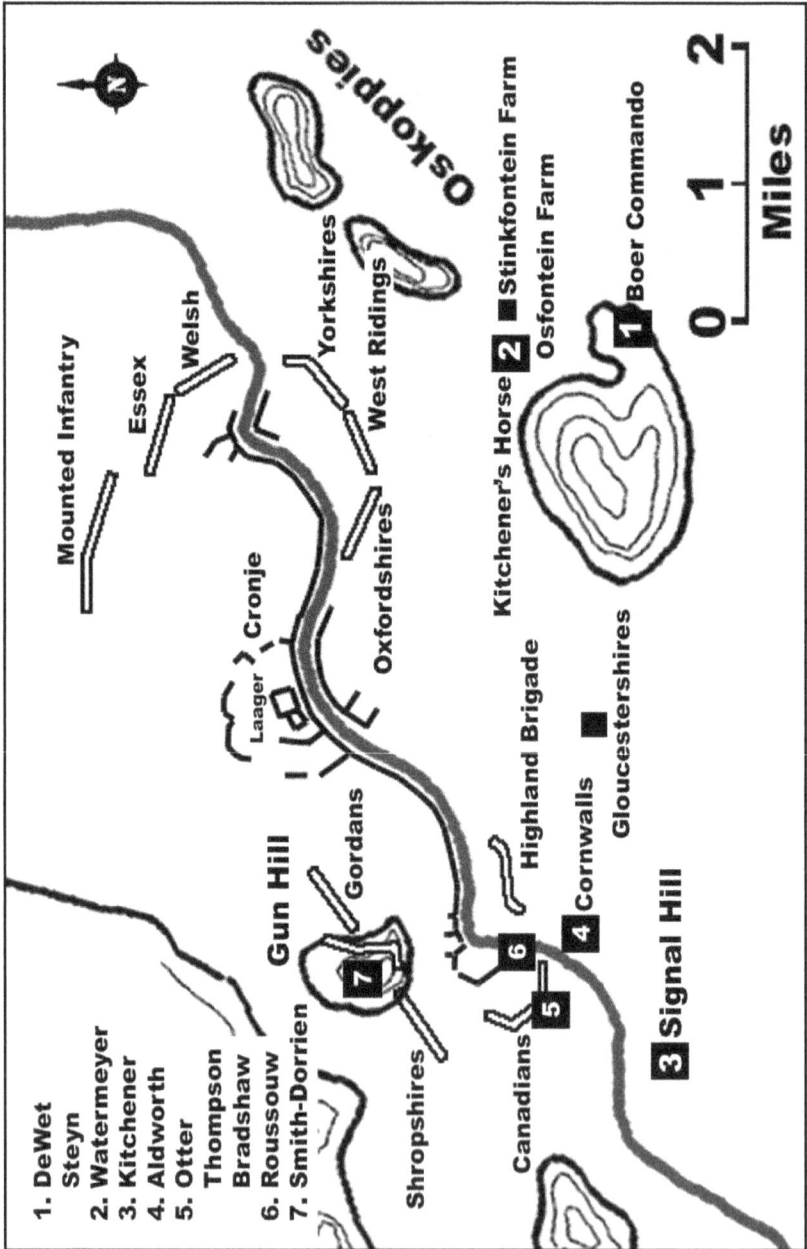

Map 13: 18 February, 4:00 pm

Bloody Sunday, 4:00 pm

General de Wet took out his watch. It was nearly four o'clock. Three hours of daylight left, he thought. There was still plenty of time to secure a strategic position on the battlefield, and de Wet knew just the one he would have. Indeed, he was already standing on its lower slopes. He had been somewhat surprised that he and his commando had managed to reach the base of the southern and largest kopje of the Oskoppies chain without any challenge at all. But then he had already learnt the strategic value of using small, highly mobile commandos in this war. The English did not seem to have a military answer to the tactics he was developing of fast, short, sharp, mounted attacks.

He stood with his officers behind a tumble of rocks in the extending afternoon shadow of the kopje. Studying Osfontein Farm through his field glasses, he counted about fifty soldiers and their horses milling around the farm buildings. Beyond the farm, a mirage shimmered over the veldt from which the smaller kopjes of the Oskoppies range rose like dark islands. To his left, looking like discarded flotsam, de Wet could see the myriad forms of prone English soldiers and beyond them, like some giant serpent swimming through a silver ocean was the glaucous ribbon of vegetation that marked the course of the Modder River.

The air rang with the cacophony of war, the rattle of rifle-fire, the deep thump of canon and the crash of exploding shells. The explosions were concentrated over the wrecked laager. The shells burst in erratic, spiked clouds or threw great palls of dust from the ground. A sulphurous vapour hung over the laager and from its midst a dark, polluting plume of smoke rose into the vast African sky.

De Wet looked back down the shoulder of the kopje on which he stood. At its base was his commando of three hundred mounted burghers. It would have been fewer, but for the recent addition of Commandant Steyn's commando. He turned to his officers.

"Gentlemen, Captain Theron's scouts have informed us that there are virtually no English on the kopje and the only force in the vicinity is the troop of about fifty mounted infantry at Osfontein Farm. I do not understand why the English have ignored this kopje. Its strategic importance is obvious. So we are going to take it for ourselves. Once in our hands, it will give us control of a substantial part of the battlefield and we will be able to offer General Cronjé an escape route. Of course we will need to convince him of the need to abandon what is left of the wagons. He will also have to leave the women and children to the mercy of the English, but they are an honourable people – in that matter at least. Does anyone have any further thoughts on this approach?"

A general shaking of heads indicated there were none, but Steyn asked, "How are you going to convince Oom Piet to abandon the wagons when he had refused to do so thus far?"

"I shall send Captain Theron. General Cronjé has a great respect for him. If anyone can convince the General, he will be able to do it."

But de Wet knew it would be a difficult task to convince the stubborn old man – even for Dannie Theron.

"General, how do you propose to deploy our forces?" asked Steyn.

"I shall take a hundred burghers to secure this kopje and you, commandant, will take the rest and capture Osfontein Farm. It is open veldt between us and the farm, but the rain has helped us; you will be able to approach without creating too much dust. The enemy also seem very relaxed. They will not be expecting you and I doubt they are being vigilant. If you move quickly, you should be on top of them before they realise what's happening."

Steyn grinned. He was looking forward to giving the English a good hiding. He walked down the slope to gather his men.

Lieutenant James Vipan Maitland Watermeyer, of the Kitchener's Horse, patted the neck of his mare as she drank deeply from the water he offered her, water he had just drawn from the well at Osfontein Farm. He smiled at the appreciation his horse showed for the drink and he cooed and fussed over her. He was even more pleased that he had not been one of the men ordered to remain on the summit of the koppie. The heat up there had been unbearable. There was no shade worth speaking of and the sun beat down on the rock and arid soil with unremitting spite.

They had been sent up to relieve the Gloucestershires during the hottest part of the day and their water had run out quickly. Even a sudden rainstorm had offered only a temporary respite. The koppie had simply soaked up the rain water or channelled it down its slopes, leaving nothing with which the men could quench their thirsts. Men and horses had started to collapse from heat exhaustion. In the end, the commander of the troop felt he had no choice but to send them down to Osfontein Farm to allow them to cool off and replenish their water supplies. He had discussed the matter with his officers, including Watermeyer, and they had concluded that in their current state the men would not have been able to stave off an attack from the enemy if it had come. They'd agreed that there did not seem any immediate likelihood of Cronjé attempting to capture the koppie – the Boer leader was completely surrounded by British forces – so the commander and a few soldiers had remained on the koppie, poor devils, while Watermeyer had led the rest down to Osfontein Farm.

Watermeyer looked casually towards the line of trees that marked the route of the river and from where the sounds of battle rattled and rumbled. Other than the pale yellow vapour hanging over part of the river, there was little to see. There were no great sweeping manoeuvres of large columns of soldiers of the type he had read about in military histories of the British army. This battle consisted of dispersed clusters of men sprawled out across a huge battlefield without any apparent co-ordinated effort. Even within the individual sub-battles, there seemed to be very little going on. Having just descended from a hell-hole himself, Watermeyer had great sympathy for those lying prostrate across the scorched landscape. He had only been able to endure a few hours on top of the koppie. Some of those men, exposed to both the burning sun and the terrifyingly accurate shooting of the enemy, had been out there for six hours! God it was hot! He removed his hat and, taking the pail of water from the horse, splashed the cold liquid over his face and around the back of his neck. He fluttered the front of his shirt to relieve its clammy hold on his body. He stared back at the motionless forms that littered the veld.

In his enthusiasm to volunteer, Watermeyer had given no thought to what the war was about, except at a superficial level when discussing the 'facts' with his mates over a beer. But now, seeing and hearing the realities of war at first hand, he realised that he did not understand why the British government was so keen to acquire this barren landscape. There did not seem to be anything of any merit in this country. It was swelteringly hot, dusty and desolate, and at night it was freezing cold. Why would anyone, except those on the margins of society, wish to live here? He wondered if any of his comrades in the Kitchener's Horse thought the same. He looked around the farmyard. Several men stood along a low stone wall watching the battle. However, the majority showed no interest in proceedings and were taking advantage of the lull in their involvement in it by dozing in the shade of the ubiquitous blue gum trees that grew around the farm outbuildings. Others were scrabbling through the recently abandoned farm house to see what treasures it held.

Gradually, Watermeyer became aware of a change in the rhythm of the battle. There was a new sound with a new tempo encroaching on his senses. It sounded like galloping horses! But there were no horses in the direction of the river. He spun round to look in the opposite direction, ducking under his horse's head to get a better view. His skin crawled and the nape of his neck tingled. Oh shit!

Not five hundred yards away he saw dozens of Boers at full gallop heading in his direction. The horses' thrashing hooves pounded in his ears. The riders were silent, intense and glaring at him, their reins were already hooked in their elbows, and their rifles were already being raised to their shoulders. They would be on him in seconds!

"Boers!" he bellowed.

In one fluid movement Watermeyer leapt on to his horse, unshouldered his carbine and emptied the magazine of its bullets in the general direction of the rapidly approaching enemy. This act brought an instant reply from the Boers, a tempest of rifle fire. A bullet smashed into Watermeyer's shoulder, nearly pitching him from his horse. He went to snatch the reins, but winced in agony. He seized the reins with his other hand, whirled his horse around, plunged his heels into her flanks and drove her towards the stone wall.

The soldiers previously standing in front of it were gone and he could see them on the other side now, trying to organise themselves to repel the attack. As his horse leapt over the wall, Watermeyer looked down on those sheltering behind it. Some had already thrown their carbines down in disgust. They had been caught napping and they knew that the only outcome now would be an undignified and humiliating surrender.

Watermeyer galloped on until he believed he was out of range of the Mausers. Only then did he draw his horse to a halt. He turned back to see what was happening. The farm had been overrun by the enemy. Galloping towards him was a single horseman, with half a dozen others in hot pursuit. Watermeyer waited for the lone rider and, as he came closer, he turned his horse and galloped off. He was joined very quickly by the other rider and, together, they raced towards the safety of Paardeberg Drift.

General de Wet was in high spirits. He was in possession of the kopje that commanded the southern theatre of the battlefield and he would *not* give it up quite as easily as the English had! However, the sight before him severely tempered his good mood. He had been aware that the English force was large, but he had not been prepared for what he saw. He did not know how many soldiers were attacking Cronjé, but it was much more than he had expected. It would, he had already realised, be impossible to push the English back – not even if he had the entire armies of both Republics at his disposal. The best approach, he concluded, would be a tactical withdrawal to regroup to fight another day.

De Wet studied the battlefield. English cannons seemed to be firing from all directions and were concentrating their attack on the laager, but the main battery was on a small hill on the other side of the river. Much closer, on the veldt between his kopje and Paardeberg Drift, was a battery comprising four cannons. They would be within range of his Mausers, his 37 mm Maxim-Nordenfelt 'Pom-Pom' and his only artillery piece, a Krupp cannon. Once his Pom-Pom and cannon were in place, his initial attack would target that battery.

While the English cannon fire focused on the laager at the centre of Cronjé's lines, their infantry were attacking Cronjé's flanks upstream and downstream. In these parts of the battlefield, the veldt was peppered with khaki forms. It was clear that the English attack had stalled. The Afrikanders were keeping them at bay. De Wet smiled. It seemed that the English had learnt nothing about the firepower of a massed Boer defence. He discarded any empathy he felt for the individual soldiers; if their officers would not learn, the burghers would continue to take advantage of their stupidity! Nevertheless, even if half of the English were killed, they would still outnumber the Boers. Cronjé had no choice. He would have to evacuate his position. And de Wet believed it was possible.

In targeting Cronjé's flanks, the English had left the veldt between

221

Cronjé's laager and de Wet's position on the kopje empty of troops. A charge by mounted men through this corridor was possible, especially with covering fire from de Wet's commando on the kopje. They could, smiled de Wet, repeat what General French had done the other day. Once through the corridor, Cronjé could continue on to Poplar Grove, where he would be able to hold the enemy and with careful planning avoid being out-flanked, surrounded and besieged. He would have to abandon the wagons of course. Unfortunately, the women and children would also have to be left behind to the care of the English. But it was the only way. He had made his decision. De Wet summoned his heliographer and gave him instructions to send a message to Cronjé to be ready to abandon his position.

De Wet then watched as his artillery was dragged along by his men. The Pom-Pom could hardly be called a cannon − it was more like a very large gun − but, together with the Krupp, it was all he had. De Wet was also concerned about his lack of ammunition. He did not have many shells and would not be able to sustain a long artillery battle, so he would need to be very selective in how he deployed them. He indicated to the burghers where to position the artillery pieces. Then he placed two lines of riflemen in front of the guns and pointed out their target. He gave the order for a concentrated attack on the English battery.

The surprise was complete and devastating. Before the English field battery could turn and redirect their fire at this new and ruinous foe, one gunnery team had been completely overwhelmed. The gun stood unmanned, its barrel pointing forlornly towards the azure sky. The remaining gun teams endeavoured to turn their cannon on their pitiless enemy, but they also suffered horrific casualties. The hail of fire and loss of men made their firing sporadic and inaccurate. A second and then a third gun fell silent. De Wet watched in admiration as a lone gunner took on the entire firing activities of the final gun − unloading and loading, returning to the firing position and, as if on parade, standing to attention to fire, and then repeating the process.

"If you stop firing, you idiot, we will also," de Wet muttered to himself, but the lone gunner gave no quarter until, at last, he too crumpled onto his gun, succumbing to the sheer weight of bullets aimed at him.

"God in Heaven, I would like to know that man's name," said de Wet in awe. But his name was to be lost to history.

General Kitchener stamped about on the summit of Signal Hill in abject fury. He stopped in front of the man standing to attention and glared down at him. "How the hell did it happen?" he demanded.

"It appears, sir, that a large commando of Boers surprised the Kitchener's Horse while they were watering their horses at Osfontein Farm and they were subsequently also able to take the hill."

"Damned colonial irregulars!" Kitchener fumed. "They were to secure the hill, not fool around playing at farmers! Who do we have who can retrieve the situation?"

"I believe, sir, that the nearest regiment is the Gloucestershires."

"Good. They are to halt whatever they are doing and drive those blasted Boers off *my* hill."

A bemused look passed over the man's face. Had the Gloucestershires not just been taken off that hill? But he did not risk articulating his thoughts. The inconsistencies in Kitchener's approach were obviously not recognised by himself.

The order was passed on to the Gloucestershire Regiment that they were to about-turn, retrace their steps and take *Kitchener's* Hill back from the Boers.

General Smith-Dorrien watched from Gun Hill as the Gloucestershire Regiment turned about and marched back to the hill from which he had seen them depart earlier in the day. *What* the hell was Kitchener up to? He had thought the Gloucestershires were being sent to support the Highland Brigade's attack on the Boers. That would also have helped relieve the pressure on his Canadians. He shifted his gaze to his side of the river to watch the Canadians below Gun Hill, where they were still engaged in the struggle against the Boer flank. There appeared to be little change in proceedings. Maybe some of the khaki dots on the veld were a little closer to the enemy, but in general their situation was just as precarious as it had been most of the day – they were still pinned to the ground like insects in a display cabinet. So, not only had the Highland Brigade been deprived of reinforcements to push through their offensive, but his Canadians has also been let down by the flip-flopping decisions of his commander. Smith-Dorrien felt that now there was no reason for any further delay. He would have to commit the Gordons and Shropshires. He sent the order for them to advance.

Burgher Johannes Roussouw stared absently across the shimmering veldt. In the distance, the dark mount of Paardeberg was silhouetted against the late afternoon sky. To its left were the squat bungalows at Paardeberg Drift, their iron rooftops radiating heat back into the oppressive atmosphere. From the houses, Roussouw traced the brown line of the river as it cut across the landscape until it was lost behind the shoulder of veldt that ran up to the donga he occupied.

He had never before seen the veldt so devoid of life. There were usually some animals wandering quietly across it, but now there was nothing. The Khakis were also keeping their heads down; they had stopped leaping up suddenly and rushing forward.

Roussouw had been standing in the same position for so long that his feet had started to go numb. He stamped them rhythmically on the narrow step he had scraped into the side of the donga to bring some life into them. His firing station was one of the last positions in the donga before it opened into the main ravine. On his left, the Modder flowed sluggishly, as though it was too hot even for the river to move with any energy.

The Khaki's attack had stalled. They had gone to ground and not one of them had moved for over an hour. It was frustrating!

Roussouw had been amazed to learn that the Khakis in his part of the battlefield were Canadians. "What the hell has this war got to do with Canadians?" he had asked a fellow burgher. The answer had been a shrug and the response, what the hell had it got to do with Australians and New Zealanders?

He laid down his Mauser and reached into a deep pocket to retrieve a piece of biltong. As he did so, he saw a movement out of the corner of his eye. He looked along the loop of the river and on the opposite bank he noticed the entrance of another donga. From this angle, only the upper slopes of the donga were visible, but emerging from it were the heads and shoulders of men – men dressed in khaki! As the soldiers moved cautiously out of the donga and down into the main ravine, they were lost from view, but more were following – a lot more. He nudged the old Boer next to him.

"Hey, pa. Look." He jabbed a finger towards the English.

The old man raised his grey, bushy eyebrows in surprise. His pale sapphire eyes sparkled in the afternoon sunlight. Roussouw picked up a few pebbles and lobbed them at other Afrikanders down the line, putting his finger to his lips when they looked across at him and pointing at the enemy soldiers. He selected four middle-aged and experienced burghers as well as his aged father. He knew them well and had hunted with them many times. They could shoot the piggy eyes of a rhino at five hundred yards. A youth looked at him appealingly, but Roussouw shook his head and gave him a severe stare to make sure he understood that he was not invited. The youth scowled back, but knew not to disobey.

Roussouw whispered and signalled his plan to crawl across the shoulder of veldt to the rim of the main ravine to have a better look. The hunters nodded their understanding. Skilfully using what little cover the long grass and low scrub offered to conceal their advance, they crept out of the donga and slithered across the sandy ground.

A few feet from the edge of the ravine, they removed their hats before sliding the last short distance, and peeked over the rim down towards the river and the enemy. They watched the increasing number of khaki figures emerging from the donga. The morning's flood waters had passed through and the river level had dropped, so the English had had to cross a strip of wet sand before they reached the river. But they were not stopping to drink. They were crossing.

Roussouw could sense the tension in the Khakis; he had seen antelope behaving in the same way as they approached waterholes. That stealthy, wary stepping which, even though they were completely in the open, they hoped might make them invisible to predators lurking in the undergrowth. He had once been in that position himself when following a wounded buffalo through some thorn scrubland. He remembered the way the skin on his back had rippled and tightened when he sensed that the buffalo had stopped running and was waiting for him in the dense vegetation, watchful and tensed to attack.

Several of the English soldiers were in the river up to their waists, holding their rifles high and pushing against the current. Others must have already crossed, but the sweep of the river prevented Roussouw from seeing their landing point on his side of the river.

"Hey pa, this reminds me of the time we went hunting eland on the

Vaal River. The scene is almost identical."

The old Burgher smiled wistfully as he remembered. That day had also been hot. The hunt had been unsuccessful and they were about to give up. Jan must have been no more than 11 or 12 years old. It had been Jan who had heard the clicking hooves of the eland. They had dismounted their horses quietly and crawled to the top of the river bank. And there, below them, were the noble animals, six khaki beauties making their way warily to the river. They had managed to drop three and watched the rest dash back into the bush.

Roussouw nudged his father.

"Hey pa, have one of these."

He held up a bullet. The grey-haired man studied it, taking in the carefully cross-cut bullet head. He looked questioningly at his son.

"Jan, we are not supposed to use those. They will ruin the barrels."

"Pa, I have three. You can have one and I will use the other two. One round will not ruin your precious rifle. Our ammunition is too hard; it goes right though the English. We should use softer bullets which have more stopping power. I have saved these and now seems as good a time as any to use them. Do you want one?"

The old man shrugged and took it. He removed the standard round from the breach of his Mauser and replaced it with the dum-dum. Roussouw did the same. He took up the rifle and aimed the barrel.

"Choose a Khaki!" he said quietly to his men. "Mine is the one just coming out of the donga."

Roussouw aimed at the soldier's temple. He decided he did not like the Khaki. He was too relaxed. He obviously believed the Afrikanders were not a threat and he was in no danger. Well, thought Roussouw, *he* would pay the price for the English invasion of his country. He squeezed the trigger. The dum-dum exploded in the infantryman's head. The contents of his skull erupted onto the man standing on the slope behind him. The man leapt back and dropped his rifle in shock. He looked down at his blood-splattered shirt in disbelief. Roussouw hardly had to move his aim. Before the khaki realised where the blood had come from he was dead.

Seven men died in less than five seconds. Pandemonium descended. Those not already in the river scrambled back to the safety of the donga and fired wildly in the direction from which they thought the shots had come. Those in the river pushed forward as quickly as they could. The Boers turned on them. Roussouw targeted the one nearest the point where he would disappear from view. Before he could pull the trigger that soldier had disappeared, but the next man pushing through the water was not so lucky.

Lieutenant-Colonel Aldworth was feeling belligerent. It was late, after five o'clock, and he and the Cornwalls had only just completed their crossing of the river. Although he had asked that his troops be given the opportunity for lunch, he had not expected the repast to take as long as it had. Then he had wasted time searching for the ford upriver from Paardeberg Drift that he had been instructed to use.

The ford was supposed to be closer to the Canadians' position on the other side of the river and its use would have saved time by allowing him to join the Canadians more quickly. He had marched his regiment upriver only to find there was no ford. Too much time had already been wasted, so rather than delay further, he had ordered his regiment to cross the river at the first suitable place.

Fortunately, the donga they had discovered gave easy access into the main ravine and the flood earlier in the day had receded, but the river still ran deep, up to a man's waist, and once his troops had dropped down into the ravine and started wading across, they had discovered that their elected fording point was within range of Boer marksmen. But it was already late in the afternoon and there was no time to lose. So he had urged the men on, deploying covering fire to protect those crossing the river.

Some soldiers of the Highland Brigade, realising what was happening, had also provided supporting fire, but the enemy had made the crossing very difficult and there had been too many casualties. And those blasted Canadian colonials, who were to be the beneficiaries of his reinforcements, had offered no support by engaging the Boers. He sought out the Canadian commander to inform him of his arrival and to give him a piece of his mind.

Lieutenant-Colonel Otter was surprised by the sudden appearance of the irascible young officer and his company of Cornishmen. Although of the same rank as Otter, the brash Englishman was over ten years his junior and Otter was peeved and insulted to be informed that he had been sent to finish the business with the Boers. He insinuated that the Canadians had failed to achieve their goal through tardiness, a lack of experience, a lack of courage and a lack of leadership. Otter glared at the narrow-faced officer and responded curtly to the peremptory demands for information on the dispositions of the Canadians and the Boers.

"Lieutenant," Otter responded, "my men have been stuck out there the entire day, fighting with fortitude and resolve under the broiling sun. They have suffered great losses but have not lost heart. They remain determined to win the day."

"In that case, *Lieutenant*, with our help they shall do just that."

"Indeed? I have seen no more than ten Boers all day. Advancing towards an invisible enemy has had no success thus far. So what *is* your plan?"

Aldworth looked Otter up and down. His jaw tensed and the tips of his handlebar moustache twitched with indignation.

"Sir, it is obvious that this situation can only be won with British pluck and proper leadership. Soldiers require to be led from the front. If we cannot see the damned enemy, we shall damned well have to get close enough to do so. When we achieve that, we will cause great consternation among our farming foe and they shall run like a flock of sheep. It is a known fact that the Boer flees the moment he can see the whites of his enemies' eyes. So I propose to finish this business and to do so with fixed bayonets."

Otter stared back at Aldworth in complete astonishment.

"That would be sheer lunacy!"

"You'll be staying behind, then, I assume?"

Otter flushed with anger. He saw a maniacal sparkle in Aldworth's eye. He said nothing. For a moment he was uncertain what to do. This idiot was dangerous, he thought. He was a danger to himself, to his men and to anybody involved with him. Otter stood his ground. He would stay behind and so would his troops. He was not going to become involved in this officer's stupidity. He would not allow the companies he had held back in reserve to join the attack.

Aldworth turned to one of his captains and snapped an order at him for his company to fix bayonets and to rush the Boer lines. The men did so and stampeded forward, yelling a death howl so bloodcurdling that a prickle ran down Otter's spine. As soon as the first company were off, Aldworth repeated the order and the next company rushed forward. Both attacks were met with furious fire from the Boers and soon both companies had joined their Canadian comrades, flattening themselves into the sand and dust of the veld.

Aldworth was undeterred. The error in the attack, he surmised, was its weakness in numbers. The solution, he concluded, was a concentrated attack with as many troops as possible rushing the Boers simultaneously. That would dilute their firepower over a wider front. In sufficient strength, some soldiers would get through and turn the enemy's line. In a raised voice, full of determination and pride, Aldworth addressed the remaining company commanders of the Cornwall Regiment.

"Companies G and H are to fix bayonets and await my order. We will attack *en masse*. We shall overwhelm the enemy by sheer weight of numbers."

Within earshot of the command stood the Canadian captains of Otter's own G and H companies, which he was holding in reserve. Assuming that this newly arrived and dynamic English officer was addressing them, they ordered their companies to fix bayonets. Aldworth, hearing the clatter of Canadian bayonets being fixed, glanced around. He turned to Otter with a withering look.

"It seems that you have been holding your men back against their will," he grinned maliciously. "Watch closely, sir, for you are about to observe the true meaning of leadership and British pluck!"

Otter considered ordering his companies to stand down, but he was not sure they would listen. They were all staring intently at Aldworth, hanging on his every word. Then Aldworth addressed them all.

"Men, let us make the name of the Cornwalls ring throughout the world!" To the Canadians, he bellowed, "My friends, I shall give five pounds to the first man to reach the enemy trenches. Bugler, sound the charge."

Before the bugler had finished, Aldworth, seized with a wild excitement and bloodlust, charged, closely followed by his adjutant and the Cornish and Canadian regiments.

Those already out in the field and lying as flat as possible were heartened by the sudden appearance of large numbers of khaki troops dashing past them. They were also caught up in the frenzy of the attack and leapt up to join their fellows. Private John Todd of the Royal Canadian Regiment roared "Come on, boys, this beats Manila hands down!" But Todd's shouts of encouragement were abruptly silenced as a bullet burst through his throat. The death of Todd was quickly followed by that of Aldworth.

Otter watched in horror as more and more soldiers tumbled to the ground. Some simply collapsed and lay deathly still, others writhed in the dust in agony, and many dived to the ground to evade the blistering frenzy of bullets. Otter's ears rang with the snapping of the enemies' Mausers. It was impossible to pick out the sound of individual rifles; their cracks mingled into a continuous and deadly din. It was as though the Boers had a new and horrific weapon that could fill the air with death. Otter's whole frame trembled with anger at the wanton loss of life. Before him, the attack faltered and stopped, and again no one on the veld moved.

Private Richard Rowland Thompson of the Royal Canadian Regiment lay still as stone. He had made it to within one hundred and fifty yards of the Boer lines, but it was impossible to get any closer. The air was alive with bullets. Suddenly, five soldiers burst past him in a desperate charge. They did not get far. Thompson recognised one of the men, writhing and screaming in pain, as Private James Bradshaw. Thompson dashed forward a dozen feet and dived down next to him.

"For Christ's sake Jim, shut up and keep still!"

Bradshaw clenched his jaw. "Arghh!" he groaned. "It hurts like a bastard!"

"Where?"

"My knee! My bloody knee!"

Bradshaw let out a scream as another stab of pain coursed through his leg. He twisted and clutched at his shattered knee, but his movement only resulted in further bullets smashing into him. He screamed again. Thompson grabbed his uniform and held him still.

"Keep still, you bloody idiot!"

Desperate to stay still, Bradshaw gritted his teeth and let out a stifled animal-like whine. Thompson partially hidden from the Boers by Bradshaw's body, wriggled nearer to his friend so their faces would be closer and encouraged him to remain quiet. Then Thompson noticed dark red, slug-like pulses of blood oozing from a wound on Bradshaw's throat. Thompson's heart nearly stopped and he clamped his fingers over the wound.

"Jim, forget your bloody leg! You've been hit in the throat. It looks like your jugular has been nicked. Now calm down and *keep* still! We're just going to lie here until we get rescued. Okay?"

"Am I going to die?" Bradshaw asked. His eyes wide with fear.

"Not if you stay calm."

Christ, thought Thompson, how the hell were they going to get out of this fix? It would be impossible for Jim to move with his shattered knee. And when it became dark, he would not be able to carry Jim as well as keep pressure on his wounded neck. His only hope was to be rescued by stretcher-bearers and that was unlikely. Never-the-less, he raised his head to see if there were any nearby that he could call to and his helmet was ripped off his head by a Mauser bullet. Shit! Thompson ducked down and held onto his friend's throat for dear life. He surreptitiously looked around him. In every direction lay Canadians and Cornishmen, hundreds of them. And even though he heard the recall being sounded, they remained where they were, unable to move for fear of attracting a Boer marksman's bullet.

Lieutenant-Colonel Otter stared out across the veld and its litter of khaki uniforms. He removed his helmet and wiped the sweat from his brow with a handkerchief. He glanced at his watch. It was a quarter to six. Even this late in the day the heat was stifling. At least, he thought grimly, the men would only have to endure a further hour or so out in the open veld before darkness rescued them.

General Smith-Dorrien had seen the Canadians being joined by another regiment and had wondered who they were and who had ordered them to join his division. He had then watched in astonishment and horror as they made their suicidal charge against the Boer positions. He was livid. There had been no orders all day and then one, given without his knowledge, had called for *his* men to throw themselves at the enemy in an utterly foolhardy attack. It was incomprehensible! This could not continue! They had to change tactics. They could not afford to waste men like that. He lowered his field glasses and yelled at the nearest officer to find out what the bloody hell was going on and who was giving the orders. Smith-Dorrien felt a sudden desperate need to sit down. He sat heavily onto a rock and rested his head in his hands. The slaughter was too much.

231

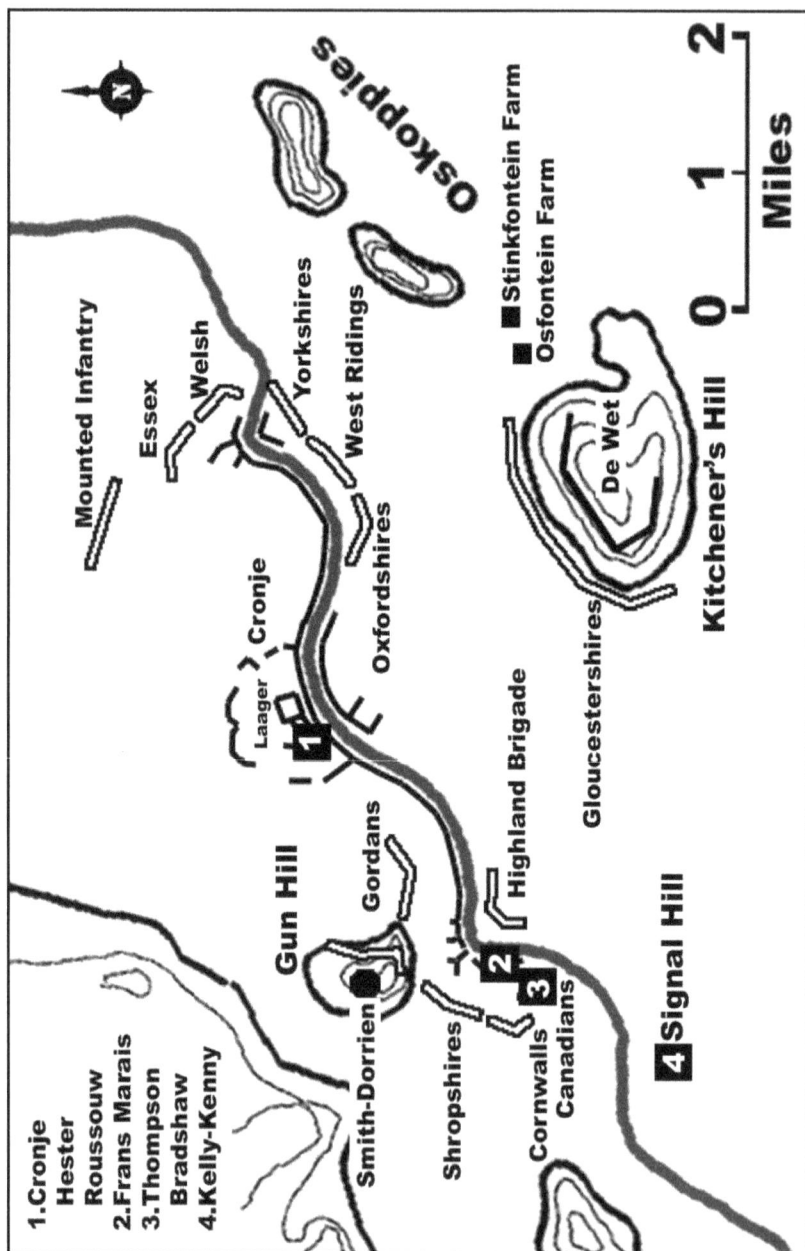

Map 14: 18 February, 6:00 pm

Bloody Sunday, 6:00 pm

General Cronjé scrambled out of his trench and looked around. It was a scene of complete devastation. Virtually every wagon in the laager had been destroyed, either by shells ripping them apart and scattering their contents far and wide or by the resulting fires, which still burned and from which a tower of black smoke rose above the acrid yellow blanket of lyddite fumes. Soon there would be nothing left except black ash and twisted steel. The laager had offered no protection for the women and children, who had been forced to abandon the wagons and had joined the men sheltering in the dongas and trenches.

Now that the English had destroyed the wagons, they had turned to using mainly lyddite shells. The shells fell around him randomly, but none close enough for Cronjé to feel threatened. In fact, Cronjé had a disdainful disrespect for this English weapon. Although the exploding shells left an unpleasant yellow cloud hanging over the area, their noise was far worse than their effect. During the bombardment at Magersfontein, Cronjé had seen a shell burst above a herd of grazing oxen and, although some had been knocked over by the blast, none had been killed and only a couple had been wounded. He wondered why the English used such ineffective ordnance.

Hester called to him and he turned and grasped the extended arm of his small wife and gently pulled her from the trench. It was their daily ritual to watch the African sun set. They had been doing so for years and a few stray bombs were not going to put them off. They had not at Magersfontein and they would not now.

But Hester held her hands to her face in distress at the sight of the devastated wagons. The destruction of the possessions and livelihoods of her family and friends was complete. Since the original plan had been to stay with the wagons in a defensive laager, little had initially been removed from them. When the wagons had been abandoned people had hurriedly gathered armfuls of possessions to take with them. But the wagons had still contained many valued pieces of furniture and chests full of personal possessions. These now lay shattered and strewn across the veldt. It was a difficult thing for a woman to bear, to see her home destroyed in this way. Cronjé placed

233

a comforting arm around her small, quivering frame, drawing her into the protective mountain of his body.

"Do not despair, my love. They are but material goods. We still have each other and the Lord will provide for us, as He has done in the past."

"I know Piet, but why have they done this? This did not happen at Magersfontein. And what of those folk without the means to buy new things? It is them I feel sorry for."

"The Lord will look after them as well as He will after us," Cronjé said, embracing her more tightly. "Now, let's watch the sun as it sets and give thanks to God for preserving us on this day, His day of rest."

In the chaos of the falling shells he led his wife to a fallen trunk of a shattered tree and guided her to sit on it. He sat next to her and together they faced the golden orb as it descended slowly towards the horizon. He tenderly took one of her hands and, cradling it between his own, smiled at her. The sound of the Mausers had died down, except for the occasional shot at an impatient Englishman who had tried to extricate himself from the battlefield before he was protected by the darkness of the approaching night. The shelling, having built up in the hour before sunset, now also subsided and silence descended over the veldt. Normally at this time of day, as the temperature cooled, animals would be enjoying a last flourish of activity before they bedded down. Birds should have been singing and darting among the trees and monkeys should have been frolicking in the branches. But there was nothing to be heard. The silence was unnatural, unnerving. It was as though the wildlife was too self-conscious to make a sound. It seemed that any noise would be an unfitting celebration of the destruction that had been wrought. The trees, with their shattered trunks and splintered boughs, stood stark and jagged against the darkening sky, as though ripped apart by angry gods.

The sun had turned crimson and Cronjé and his wife basked in its red glow. Great shafts of red radiated through distant clouds. But the silence unsettled Hester and she clung to her husband. Slowly, she realised that the silence was not absolute. Slowly, she became aware of a sound, but she did not recognise it.

"God in heaven, there must be hundreds of them out there," murmured Cronjé.

And then she knew what the sound was. It was the soft moans and whimpers of wounded and dying men. Too exhausted to cry out, their anguish diminished to moaning and weeping. It reminded Hester of the sound friends made at funerals, not the frenzied howling of the children or mothers of the deceased, but the soft, private weeping of those on the margins of the tragedy. But the sound grew stronger and louder as men started to realise that with the coming darkness those of their comrades who could leave would soon be doing so. Then they would be left to their own horrors and agonies, undiscovered, helpless and uncomforted to die alone in a dry, savage and dark place, miles from their loved ones. So they started to wail and call and scream to attract the attention of someone, anyone, who might come to them and carry them back to the security of the camp. The howls and moans and shrieks built into a crescendo. Cronjé felt his skin crawl.

Hester placed her free hand on those of her husband. "Piet," she whispered, "Can we go back to the trench? We cannot pretend. We are not at home. We are not alone. There is too much suffering out there for us to ignore."

Cronjé looked down into her face. The catch in his throat prevented him from speaking. He wished she was not here. He wished she was many miles away, safe and sound on their farm. He thought of asking her to leave the next morning. He would negotiate the safe passage of the women and children away from of the battle. But although her face was crumpled in sadness, the steely glare remained in her eyes and he knew she would not countenance such an idea. He nodded and they stood up and walked back to their trench. The dying sun threw its cloak of blood-red hues over the veldt around them.

As they reached the trench Hester said, "Piet, I must help our own wounded. Thanks be to God we do not seem to have as many as the English, but we have enough. You should come as well." At his dubious look, she continued. "I know you have many priorities, such as inspecting and checking the damage to our defences and checking the supplies of ammunition, but for them to see their leader will give them great comfort."

It was not his natural state, giving kind words and consolation. He would rather be inspecting the defences, but what Hester said was true.

"Of course, you are right my dear. The other matters can wait."

They made their way along a trench and down the steep ravine to a large terrace that was hidden from the view of the English. The trees here had not been bombarded and during the day had provided shade for Cronjé's wounded heroes. As he and Hester approached the terrace they could hear the cries and moans of their own brave burghers. Listening to the sounds of his wounded Cronje was grateful that his army had suffered less than one hundred casualties.

He stood and watched the girls and women moving among the men, doing what little they could to relieve the suffering of the wounded. Damn those German doctors. He should not have allowed them to stay behind at the hospital in Jacobsdal. He should have forced them to come with the laager. But not only was he short of doctors, he also lacked medical supplies. He cursed the short-sightedness of his burghers. When they had abandoned the wagons they had not thought to prioritise the medical equipment, but had focused on saving what personal possessions they could. Now they were suffering the consequences. There was not much that could be done to dress the burghers' wounds and alleviate their pain.

The best thing the burghers could do in future was to stay out of trouble. That meant keeping themselves well hidden. The main threat was from bullets. There were very few injuries caused by the shelling as their trenches and dongas kept them well protected from the bombardment. It was fortunate that the Afrikanders were experienced hunters who were well versed in using cover to the best advantage. Also, once the enemy had fallen to the ground, most of them had had the sense to keep their heads down rather than to continue shooting. So, generally the Afrikanders were not exposed to too much danger.

Some of the enemy, however, had made a real nuisance of themselves during the battle. The Canadians attacking his downriver flank seemed to be pretty good shots. Cronjé gave a little grunt of respect; they would also be hunters and would therefore know how to shoot. Their success had also been helped by some over-enthusiastic burghers. There was, for example, the fool, Piet van der Merve, who had climbed a tree to get a better shot at the Canadians and, because he was worried about falling out of it, had strapped himself to a branch with his cartridge belt. Of course he had been seen and the Canadians had shot at him. He had been hit, but had been unable to free himself. Stuck in the tree, he had become a frequent target for the enemy. When his lifeless body was eventually cut down, he had 365 bullet wounds – one for every day of the year!

Cronjé started to move among the wounded offering self-conscious words of comfort. As he did so, he was enthusiastically hailed by a burgher with a bandaged hip. It was Johannes Roussouw.

"Oom Piet, we did well again, huh?" he called out to Cronjé.

Cronjé strode towards him. Here was someone to have a conversation with, someone who would focus on what had gone well, rather than dwelling on his individual hardship and pain.

"Yes, Neef, you did very well. *You all* did very well. I am very, very proud of you. Of you all," he said loudly and clearly, in order to broadcast it widely to the distressed men around him.

Cronjé squatted next to Roussouw, but Roussouw called out to a girl walking past.

"Hey, young lady, find Oom Piet a stool. Do you know who this is? It is the 'Lion of Potchefstroom'. Do not leave him squatting like a monkey. Hurry, girl, hurry."

A stool was procured and graciously accepted by Cronjé. He noted Roussouw's father lying on the other side of him, apparently asleep.

"Is your father all right?"

"Huh?" Roussouw looked at his father and nodded. "He's fine, just tired. He's not as young as he likes to think he is. He had to drag me here by himself. We were doing really well against the English, you know. Keeping them back, stopping them from crossing the river. But then they spotted us. They got themselves into a good position on top of the opposite bank and started shooting at us. There must have been hundreds of them. It was like hell itself. Only three of us got back to the donga. And I did only because pa dragged me out of danger."

"How do you feel?"

"Me? I'm fine. I took a bullet to the hip. It hurts like buggery and I shall probably have a limp, but I'm fine. I will have a great story to tell the grandchildren. So, Oom Piet," Roussouw changed the subject, "how did we do? When will we drive the Khakis off? When will we drive the English and Canadian bastards from our country?"

Cronjé considered his response.

"Not yet," he replied, and continued quickly as Roussouw's face fell in disappointment, "I mean not by *ourselves*. There are too many khakis. That does *not* make me afraid, but we do not yet have sufficient burghers to force the issue here."

"Aaagh, Oom Piet! You should not doubt the courage of our burghers. Each one of us is worth ten of them. Numbers do not matter. And anyway, they do not use their superior numbers to their advantage. The Khaki officers simply throw their men at our bullets as though there is no tomorrow. We few burghers are an equal match to any English army. Don't you think?"

"I do agree with you, neef. Yes, the burghers are extremely brave and their shooting is far better than the Khakis and much feared by them. But the Khakis are like ants, and I fear that yet more may arrive. For all the bravery of our burghers, to send our army out to attack them would be reckless. No, we need to wait until our reinforcements arrive. See, de Wet has already secured a strategic kopje on the other side of the river. When the other commandos arrive tomorrow, or the next day, we will surround the English, just like they surround us at the moment. The new commandos will shoot from the outside and we will shoot from the inside and the English will not know what to do. They will simply lie down on the ground again and this time we will advance towards them. They will have no choice but to surrender and then we will drive them out of our Republics."

Roussouw lay back on his blanket and smiled up at Cronjé.

"You see, Oom Piet, I knew you would have a plan. As soon as I am able to get up I shall be back in that donga. I cannot wait for us to beat the Khakis again."

Cronjé laid his hand on Roussouw's shoulder.

"Yes, neef, I do have a plan and I look forward to you joining me soon, very soon."

He rose and left Roussouw and the other wounded to the ministrations of the women.

But left to his own thoughts Cronjé knew he had a problem. The bravery of his burghers did not counter-balance the fact that the numbers did not add up. He had four thousand burghers and they were facing tens of thousands of trained English soldiers. His forces were spread sparsely along the river banks and if the English threw their full strength at his centre, he would not be able to hold them back. His flanks would be separated and defeat would be inevitable. And surely the English generals would use different tactics after their failures so far. If he was to hold the English back while he waited for reinforcements, he was going to have to reposition his defences. He needed to pull in both flanks by about a mile. He was confident he could defend a three-mile stretch of the river until the reinforcements arrived. It would mean abandoning the dongas and the good defensive positions they currently held, but that could not be helped. He went through his options again in his mind, but could not think of any viable alternative. He decided that he would leave his burghers in their present positions until just before dawn. The English had a nasty habit of attacking during the night and he did not want them launching an attack at the same time that his men were withdrawing. He sought out two field coronets and instructed them to pass his orders on to the commandants at Vanderberg and Vendutie Drifts.

Lieutenant-General Kelly-Kenny watched Smith-Dorrien and his aides ride off into the night back to Gun Hill on the northern bank of the Modder. He had heard angry words pass among the group of officers as they left Kitchener's headquarters, and quite rightly so. They had all been summoned to Kitchener's bungalow and were expecting to be given a report of the day and orders for the next morning, but the generals soon discovered that they had been called in to give *their* accounts of their day's actions. Then they had been summarily dismissed. Kelly-Kenny had overheard Smith-Dorrien mumble to his adjutant, "That blasted prima donna. If all he wanted was a report, he could have sent one of his minions to receive it, instead of wasting our time."

Kelly-Kenny sympathised with the comment. It was bad form of Kitchener to have the generals running around at his beck and call. That was what his aides-de-camp were for.

"Sir."

Kelly-Kenny turned to the man who approached him.

"Yes corporal?"

"I have your horse sir."

"Hmm. I think I shall walk, thank you. You go on ahead and arrange for someone to prepare me a night cap."

"Sir?" the corporal responded in a 'do-you-think-that-is-prudent?' kind of 'sir'.

Kelly-Kenny raised a questioning eyebrow.

"I shall be fine, thank you, corporal. I think I can look after myself."

"I did not mean to be impertinent, sir. It's just that there are lions and other dangerous animals out there, not to mention Boers."

"Thank you for your concern, corporal. I shall see you back at the camp within the hour. But to reassure you, I shall take my horse with me in case I need him."

"Very good sir."

Kelly-Kenny took the reins of his horse and led it away into the darkness. As he did so, he glanced at the bungalow across the road. Was it just this morning that he had lent on its balustrade? How long ago that seemed. He stopped and looked across at the building. A warm glow of lamplight shone from the windows. The shadows of the medicos tending to the wounded moved across the squares of light. They had a long night ahead of them. On the veranda he could just make out the shapes of men lying restlessly, moaning in their discomfort, also attended by the hospital orderlies, their ghostly white coats covered in dark stains.

The wounded had started to pour in after about eleven o'clock and he had insisted on handing over his bungalow to their greater need. He had had his kit transferred to the British army camp outside the small settlement of Paardeberg Drift. With nightfall, the need to accommodate the ever growing number of casualties returning from the battlefield had become overwhelming. Most of the other bungalows in the small village had been commandeered, but even this was not sufficient and men were also being laid in the open in the gardens behind the dwellings.

The number of casualties had not been confirmed yet, but it was apparent that there was likely to be well over a one thousand men killed and wounded. It was an appalling result and with nothing to show for it. If it was true, it was a terrible indictment of Kitchener's command. It would be the worst casualty list of the war, even worse than the defeats of Buller and Methuen.

Kelly-Kenny stood quietly in the stillness of the cold night air, his horse tossing its head at the fearful smell of blood. He listened to the agonised whimpering and groaning of the wounded. He tried to imagine the scene inside the house and immediately felt sick at heart. He found it increasingly difficult to bear the sights and sounds of military hospitals, especially as he had moved up the ranks, because their occupants were the consequence of the decisions he made.

At least Kitchener would take most of the responsibility of the day's appalling casualty rates – he would make sure of that. But Kelly-Kenny felt that he could not abdicate all responsibility. He had to accept his role in what had happened. He threw another brief look at the sad building and then turned away and led his horse out of the hamlet and into the dark veld.

As he walked, Kelly-Kenny tried to sort out his own thoughts. They seemed to be in the same chaotic turmoil as the hospital he had just passed. Could he have done anything to reduce the wanton loss of life? What *should* he have done? Had he allowed his chagrin at losing command to Kitchener cloud his judgement? Should he have challenged Kitchener's decisions? What about the ignominy of losing Kitchener's Hill to the Boers? Should he have countermanded Kitchener's order to remove the Gloucestershires from the highest point overlooking the battlefield? That had been a ridiculous decision. And now they had lost the strategic high-ground to the enemy. Kitchener had lost both the Kitchener's Horse and Kitchener's Hill. Kelly-Kenny allowed himself an ironic smile.

The rumour was that the Boer general now in charge of Kitchener's Hill was de Wet. Who was this man? A few days ago nobody had heard of him, but now his name was on everyone's lips. He was said to have seized Roberts' supply wagons, captured a unit of over fifty mounted infantry in addition to those of the Kitchener's horse. And now he was at Paardeberg and in possession of the most strategic position on the battlefield.

The Gloucestershire Regiment had not managed to dislodge him by nightfall and so he was lording it over them from his eagle's nest. This de Wet needed to be treated with a bit of respect. Yet more soldiers would be lost trying to retake the hill, but retake it they must, because Kitchener, by allowing de Wet to seize it in the first place, had given Cronjé a possible corridor through which to escape. The area between the river and the hill could not be defended, not with de Wet looking down on them. Kelly-Kenny grunted to himself in disgust. After the huge effort that had been undertaken to come within an ace of capturing Cronjé, now he had an opportunity to escape.

Kitchener had had the manpower at his disposal to secure the hill, but had squandered it.

Kelly-Kenny's thoughts drifted to his commanding officer, Lord Roberts. He also bore responsibility for the unnecessary suffering of the men. For one thing, allowing the loss of the wagons to de Wet meant there was a lack of medical supplies. In addition, there was a gross shortage of ambulances. The unfortunates who had been evacuated to the hospital in Jacobsdal would have endured a journey in diabolical conditions, being transferred there in ox wagons. The poor devils would have their bones shaken from their broken bodies by being transported in those ponderous contraptions.

Kelly-Kenny's thoughts were brought to a sudden halt by his horse throwing its head and yanking back his arm. He stopped. It was dark as pitch and quiet as a grave. Then he heard a rustle of vegetation. He stared into the inky blackness, but could see nothing. He removed his pistol from its holster. He knew it was a futile act. If there was a lion in the shadows the puny gun would be useless. His horse became skittish. He stepped back to it and stood against its shoulder. He put an arm under and around its throat and muttered calming words. However, the calming words simply increased the sense of tension. He felt his scalp crawl as though a thousand spiders had just scurried through his hair. His back suddenly seemed very exposed and he instinctively turned to look into the blackness behind him. There was definitely something out there. Beyond the small sphere of his visual world something was moving. Something that was monstrous, sinister and unnerving.

He had heard of lions taking down buffalo. But despite the futility of it, he mounted his horse. At least the additional height gave him some small sense of security. He made to move the horse forward but, with a spine-chilling realisation, he found he had no idea which way to go. Acrid, nauseous panic rose in his throat, but he supressed it instantly. He snapped his logical and tactical brain into play. He pushed the earlier source of the anxiety to the back of his mind so he could concentrate on the new and more immediate threat of being lost. He had heard stories of men being lost for days in the bush and who had perished just yards from wagon trails. To deal with this situation he required a clear and undistracted mind.

Standing up in his stirrups he scanned the darkness around him. It was hard to believe that within five miles of him there were over twenty thousand men. There was virtually no evidence of them. Not one camp fire could be seen. But Kelly-Kenny exhaled a sigh of relief, for there was *one* small indication of human presence in the oppressive blackness. Behind him, he could discern a faint orange glow against the dark sky. Kelly-Kenny reasoned that he must have walked over and down the back of one of those innumerable folds in the veld. It was difficult to gauge the distance, but the ridge line of the fold must only be a few hundred yards away. And beyond it, the glow must be that of the burning wagons of the Boer laager.

Turning his horse, with some urgency, he rode quickly in the direction of the reassuring glow. Although he knew it was likely to originate from the burning remains of the Boer laager, it was the only indication of humanity in the vast sea of blackness that surrounded him. As he rode hastily up the slope, the warm orange glow grew in intensity and size. He crested the ridge and the flames of the laager appeared out of the darkness some distance away. To his delight, closer to hand he saw the myriad little camp fires that marked the British encampment outside Paardeberg Drift. Never in all his forty years of service had he seen such a wondrous sight! He stayed his horse so that he could gaze at the fires and savour the view.

He was surprised at how far he must have walked into the bush, and he was shaken at how easily he could have been truly lost. If it had not been for that glow in the sky, he could very easily have walked in the wrong direction. He grinned at the irony that it had been a 'signal' from his enemy that had saved him. But now, in front of him, there was the friendly glow of all those little fires in the vast expanse of black. He could faintly hear the skirl of a bagpiped lament and the sonorous rendition of familiar songs drifting up to him on the breeze, songs of friends reunited after the trauma of battle. He could also hear the snappy, shouted orders of non-commissioned officers. He felt a catch in his throat. He knew this was to be his last campaign. The army was his life, and the men down there his family. How he loved them!

His horse stamped impatiently and gave a skittish whiny. Kelly-Kenny briefly glanced back into the darkness with its unfamiliar creatures and unnerving sounds. Then he urged his horse on, back towards his familiar world and to safety.

Burgher Frans Johannes Marais was nervous, and his young finger twitched over his trigger. He recalled the time at Magersfontein when the English had almost got to their trenches in the dark of night. That time the enemy had stumbled into the tangle of wires and tin cans that Cronjé had ordered to be laid out in front of the trenches. The noise had warned the commando that the English were trying to sneak up on them and they had laid a spray of bullets into their foe and stopped them in their tracks. Marais remembered that night. There had been a deep silence. The men had been talking in low whispers. The atmosphere had been tense. Everyone had felt that something was about to happen.

It was the same tonight. If anything, the silence was greater. There was no whispering. Everyone was listening. The cacophony of shouting and the cries and moans of the English wounded had died down. Marais strained his ears for the slightest sound. There were no wires or tin cans out there tonight. There had been no time to lay them out. He was listening for a whispered command from an enemy officer or the tumble of a kicked rock – anything that might suggest the stealthy approach of the enemy.

This was the part of war Marais hated most. Actually, he had decided that he hated war, full stop! How different he felt now compared to the beginning of the war. He recalled the bemused look on his parents' faces as he'd walked back to them after pouring the sand into President Kruger's hand, and his father's grave words that evening over dinner about the need to defend their land from the Uitlander invaders, and how his mother had wept and prayed. He remembered his initial excitement about the war, how he and his friends had talked excitedly about joining the commando and fighting for the 'Lion of Potchefstroom'. Oom Piet would show the English how to fight and in no time they would be driven back to Cape Town and forced to surrender. He remembered how he and his friends had run around pretending to shoot the girls, who had had to play the part of the English enemy because none of boys would do so. He remembered his shock and disappointment when his mother said he could not join General Cronjé's army and how he had begged his father to be allowed to go with him. And how his father had overruled his mother, saying that their country needed every able fighter it could find – and anyway, he had fought alongside his own father at Frans' age. He remembered the pride with which he had sat on his horse and wheeled it away from his home and his tearful mother, and galloped with his father and his elder brother to town to join the commando.

The excitement of war had worn off quickly and now he hated the English. Not only because they had invaded his country, but because their war had caused him to be in many situations where he had never been so terrified in all his life. Even the time he'd been charged by a wounded lion had not been as frightening as he now felt. He was not a coward, or at least he hoped he was not, and he had no fear of being shot. He had already seen many men shot and he thought he could bear that. What really petrified him was an enemy soldier suddenly appearing out of the dark and stabbing him with a bayonet. He felt his abdominal muscles tense involuntarily at the thought of the steel blade entering the soft tissue of his stomach. He gagged at the idea of it. How he wished he was farther back and not in the front line. Or even better, that he could be back at his father's farm away from this terrifying situation. But the General had ordered them to wait here until just before dawn and then they could withdraw. The General obviously expected a surprise attack.

He took his nervous finger off the trigger and touched the three clips of bullets he had laid out next to his rifle. He ran his finger along the length of the smooth, cold metal and moved the three clips a little closer to make sure they were within in easy reach for rapid reloading. They were normally stored in the bandolier strapped across his chest, but he wanted to be sure he was able to pour bullet after bullet into the enemy. His Mauser held only five bullets, but with the additional clips to hand he hoped that he had enough to hold the English back, at least temporarily.

Marais wondered how his brother was feeling. He was further along the donga. Was he also scared? They had often spoken about how terrible the war was and how they wished they were back at the farm, tending the cattle or hunting. He thought of his mother. He remembered the tears streaming unchecked down her beautiful face as she said goodbye and the harsh look she gave her husband for allowing him to go to war. How he missed her. How he hoped he would see her again. He wondered how she was doing on the farm without his father, himself and his brother. He hoped his four younger brothers were helping out. He wondered if his mother would have liked to have had daughters. He thought she would. He smiled. He would also have liked to have sisters. There was a time when the thought that having sisters would have been unbearable – horrible bossy things – but now it would be wonderful to have some sisters, especially older ones. They would bring a homely feel to the farm. Although his mother tried to do so, it was very hard with a house full of men. When he married, he would like lots of daughters, and sons as well of course. He would take them hunting and fishing. His thoughts of marriage brought a vision of Maria to mind. His beautiful Maria. When he returned home, he would seek permission to court her.

A sudden yell right in front of him, immediately followed by several rifle shots, made Marais jump out of his skin. He snapped up his Mauser and emptied its bullets into the dark veldt. A shouted order to cease fire followed quickly. Marais stared into the silent darkness. His ears tingled with the effort of trying to hear the approaching enemy.

Private Richard Rowland Thompson swore vehemently as he flung himself back to the ground as the bullets whistled over his head. He grabbed Bradshaw, who had started from his fitful doze, and pushed him to the ground.

"Stay down! It's all right! Stay down!"

Thompson sought out Bradshaw's throat and reapplied pressure to the wound.

"What the hell was that all about?" rasped Bradshaw.

"Shh," hissed Thompson. "I just about shat myself. That's all."

Then he laughed. It was a silent, shoulder-shaking laugh. Not because there was anything funny to laugh at; it was simply an uncontrolled reaction to their situation, a mechanism for releasing the tension that had been building for the last seven hours. Seven hours of holding the wound closed. Seven hours of laying still. Seven hours of shouting and calling to attract the stretcher-bearers, to the point of exhaustion. And then there was the hunger. He had raided his emergency rations. It was against regulations, but he and Bradshaw had not eaten for… how long? He could not remember. So it seemed all right to eat the rations. And now the darkness was all-consuming and crawling with wild and dangerous beasts.

"What's so bloody funny?" whispered Bradshaw harshly.

"We nearly got eaten by some bloody animal."

"What!"

"Shh! I was just thinking about whether we would *ever* get away from here when I felt a tug on my boot. Thank God, I thought, help at last. Someone has found us. As I turned, I heard a snarl. Christ knows what it was, but it was big and ferocious and hungry. Well, my guts nearly emptied into my pants. I shouted and whipped up my rifle, and let off what rounds I had left. Big mistake! The bloody Boers opened fire! Christ! I don't know how I wasn't hit, but I think they shot whatever it was that grabbed my foot."

"Has it gone?"

"I don't know."

"Christ, Dick, if they only wounded it, it could be even more dangerous than before – hungry and *bloody* angry!"

Thompson twisted his head to stare into the ink-black night. He unclipped his bayonet from his rifle and grasped the handle tightly in his fist, his body tense and ready to strike out with the blade. Christ, he wished he had not used his last bullets shooting at whatever it was that had tugged at his foot. He turned onto his side and pulled his knees up, drawing his legs into the safety of his body. He had never felt so vulnerable. Shit! Where the hell were those stretcher-bearers?

"Hey? Where are you?" someone called in a deep whisper.

Thompson looked up. Had he heard the whisper or imagined it?

"Is there anyone there?" he whispered loudly.

"Yes!" came the response. "Keep whispering, so we can find you."

"Over here, you bastards! What took you so bloody long? Be careful, the Boers are especially trigger happy tonight. Over here!"

A low, crouching shape loomed before him. Thompson held his bayonet ready.

"Reveal yourself before I shoot the hell out of you," he lied.

"Canadians. It's OK, we're Canadians. We've come to get you. We've got a stretcher."

"Thank Christ! Help me with Jim. He has a wound to the throat and will bleed to death if we're not careful. He also has a smashed knee. Tell you what, I'll keep the pressure on his neck wound while you put him on the stretcher."

There was a thump, which was followed by a surprised voice. "Shit man, what's that I just fell over!" And then a startled, "Hell's teeth, it's some kind of animal!"

"Be quiet, you idiot!" Thompson said in a snarled whisper. "I don't know what it is and I don't bloody care. Just get Jim on that damned stretcher and let's get the hell out of here!"

Field Marshal Roberts fell back on the piled-up pillows of his bed in the Jacobsdal hospital. Sweat broke out on his brow but he did not think it had anything to do with his fever.

"My God, it sounds like a massacre! Less than half the Royal Canadian Regiment accounted for. That's more than one thousand three hundred men in that regiment alone!"

"It is still early days, sir. They will turn up."

Roberts heaved himself up again and glared at the officer who had just delivered Kitchener's dispatch.

"What is your name, Major?"

"Hamilton, sir. Major Hamilton."

"Are you questioning me, Major Hamilton?"

The man stiffened into a smarter attention.

"No sir. My sincere apologises for my impertinence, sir."

Roberts turned away and paid the man no further heed, but he thought Kitchener kept the most disagreeable company. He lay back on his pillows and rubbed his temples. Nearly one thousand five hundred soldiers unaccounted for in a single regiment and the news was equally bad from the Highland Brigade, the Cornwalls, the Gloucestershires... the list went on and on. Probably over five thousand men! At least! Not all would be killed or wounded – his experience told him that – but he had never had so many missing after a single battle. He had never *heard* of so many missing after a battle!

He forced his fevered mind to focus on the figures. Methuen's casualties were less than nine hundred at Magersfontein, nine hundred and fifty if one included the missing. What about Buller? How many did he lose at Spion Kop? Somewhere between one thousand and one thousand five hundred men, but that included prisoners and the action took place over *two* days. It would seem that Kitchener had presided over a disaster of at least equal proportions to Spion Kop. That would make it the worst catastrophe of the war so far. This was appalling. The ballyhoo Spion Kop caused in the British papers was very detrimental to the war effort, with people and parliamentarians calling for the wholesale withdrawal of troops from South Africa. The idiot! The absolute idiot! Roberts looked down at the dispatch and read it again.

We did not succeed in getting into the enemy's convoy today, although we drove the Boers back a considerable distance along the riverbanks. The troops are maintaining their positions and I hope that tomorrow we shall be able to do something more definite.

"At least we had *some* success today, Major. It is good to see that we drove the enemy back a good distance. In that case, we must be virtually in their laager."

Hamilton looked uncomfortable. He had a desire to protect his mentor, Kitchener, but he could not be expected to lie to his commander-in-chief. He remained silent.

Roberts sat up and glared at him. "Major, how far did we push the Boer back?"

"I'm not sure we did, sir."

"General Kitchener states quite clearly that he did. Is this communiqué untrue?"

"It may not fully reflect my understanding of the situation, sir."

Roberts did not push any further. He disliked the man, but was impressed by his loyalty to his superior officer. He would expect the same from his own subordinates. But it was clear that Kitchener had mishandled the whole affair.

"Major!" Roberts snapped at Hamilton.

"Yes sir."

"You are to return to General Kitchener at once. You are to inform him that he is to do nothing further. He is to wait until I have inspected the situation at Paardeberg Drift myself. Nothing, do you hear? He is to do nothing at all. I shall be there tomorrow and he is to *await* my further orders. Is that clear?"

"Yes sir." Hamilton saluted smartly and retired, relieved to be out of the firing line but dreading having to deliver the message to Kitchener.

Roberts rested his head back on the pillows and closed his eyes. This damned fever, he thought, in frustration. It was his *bête noir*, the only blight from his long, illustrious career in India. It returned frequently and drained him of his physical and mental strength. And now, of all times, he wished it was not so, and that he could find a cure. That fool Kitchener was supposed to keep the cautious dolt Kelly-Kenny on the ball, not make a complete pig's ear of everything. Good God, did he have to do everything himself?

"Singh," Roberts called out.

"Yes, sir," responded Singh as he entered Roberts' private ward.

"Singh, I need to go to Paardeberg Drift tomorrow. However, this damned fever has knocked me for six. I require more rest before I leave. What is the time now?"

"It is just after midnight, sir."

There was nothing he could do before daybreak. "Wake me up at three o'clock. I wish to be on the road by four."

"Yes sir."

Roberts settled back into his bed, but it was some time before his concerned and feverish mind let him settle into sleep.

Monday 19 February 1900

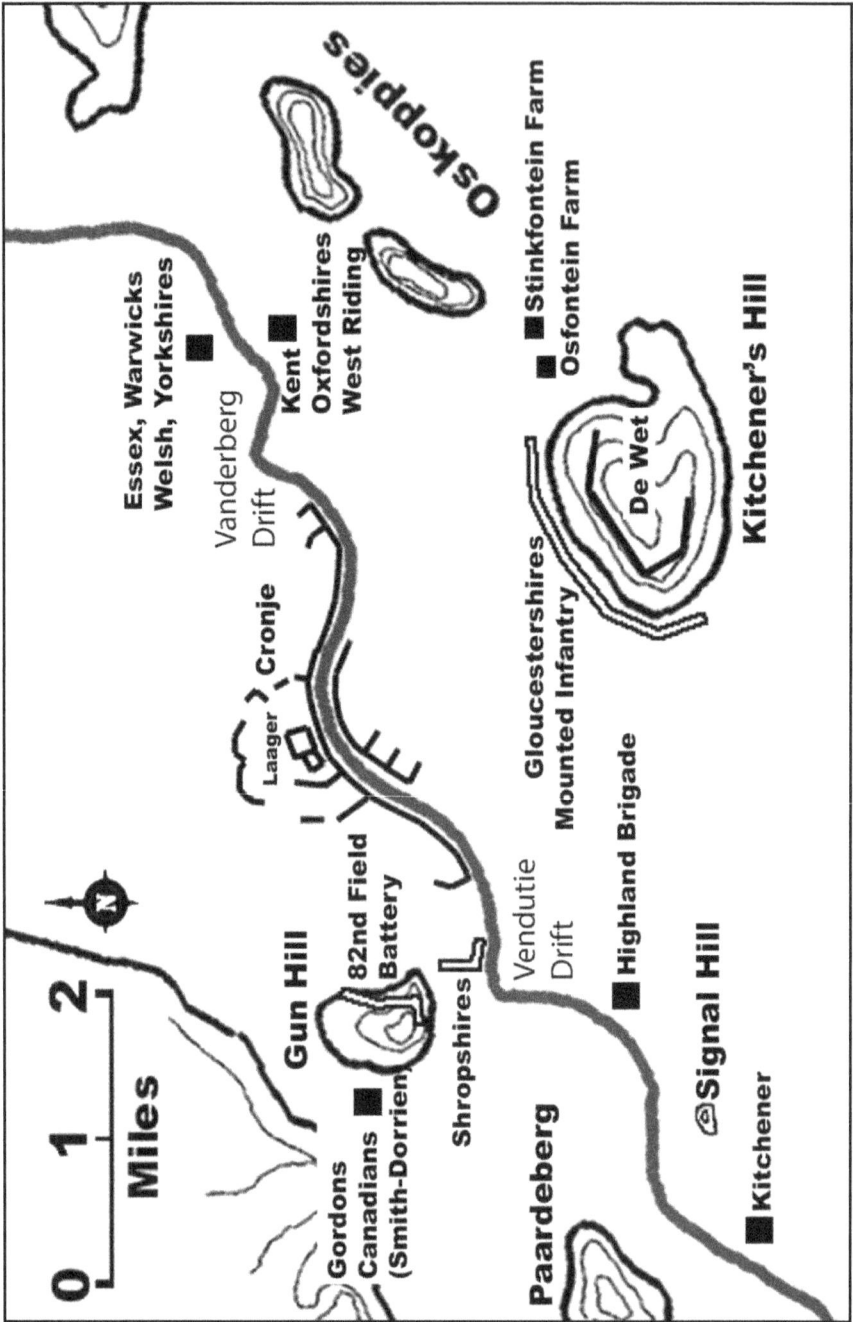

Map 15: Morning of 19 February 1900

Major General Horatio Herbert Kitchener

Major-General Horatio Herbert Kitchener was unsettled. He grasped the balustrade of the veranda that encircled his bungalow. With his weight on his arms, he leant forward and stared intently at the brooding bulk of Kitchener's Hill. Behind the hill, the first light of dawn was brightening the sky. As he breathed, the cold air caught the back of his throat. His mind mulled over the request he had just received from Cronjé.

On the face of it, it was a simple petition for a twenty-four-hour cease-fire to allow time to bury the dead and tend the wounded, although he thought Cronjé's appeal for British doctors to treat the Boer wounded was a bit rich. But it was not the request from Cronjé that had unsettled Kitchener. It was the fact that Roberts had been explicit in his orders that Kitchener was to do *nothing* until Roberts himself was at Paardeberg. Did this include responding to petitions for a truce? Or was the aim of the order to prevent Kitchener from taking decisive action against the enemy? Could he therefore take the initiative on this matter of the cease-fire?

To his left Kitchener could see a thin twist of smoke scarring the morning sky as it spiralled lazily from the charred remains of the Boer laager. Had Cronjé suffered such great losses that he now needed to seek a truce? That *would* be good news. The bombardment had obviously served its purpose and the swingeing attacks by his superior forces must have caused a great number of casualties and will have sapped the morale of the farmer-soldiers. It was obvious that yesterday's tactics had worked and should be followed through as quickly as possible. But that was not to be. Kitchener thumped his fist on the balustrade.

"Blast Roberts," he cursed to himself. "He had better get here quickly or the advantageous situation I have created will be lost."

Kitchener returned to his more immediate problem. He wondered if agreeing to an armistice would have an added demoralising impact on the Boers. If he gave them the opportunity to bury large numbers of their family and friends that must have a dispiriting effect on them. After all, he thought, they are only civilians and would be more affected by the burying of their friends than his stoic, professional soldiers would. But he came back to the question as to whether he had the authority to agree to the armistice? The Boers would take advantage of the lull in hostilities to improve their defences. Kitchener had a begrudging respect for the ingenuity with which the Boers had used the terrain and trenches. As an enemy, they were extremely elusive and difficult targets. No, he concluded, they should not be allowed time to improve their defences. Having said that, until Roberts arrived, he could do nothing to stop them doing so. But that was Roberts' doing, and not his own.

A sparkle of reflected sunlight flashed from the summit of Kitchener's Hill and he studied the hill again with antipathy. Those damned Boers were still there and the Gloucestershires had failed to dislodge them. One thing he had done was to order the late Colonel Hannay's mounted infantry to cross the river and support the Gloucestershire Regiment at the base of the hill. Surely, Roberts could not deem that as ignoring his orders? The fact that the commando of Boers had made an appearance late yesterday only confirmed Kitchener's concern about the larger number of reinforcements that the Boers would send to relieve Cronjé. His decision was made.

Turning to the man standing to attention behind him, he ordered, "Tell General Cronjé I am not in a position to offer him an armistice."

As the man began to turn, Kitchener held up an authoritative finger, stopping him in his tracks. Kitchener thought for a moment and then added, "Tell Cronjé also that should he surrender unconditionally, his wounded will be given the fullest attention by our doctors."

With an imperial flick of a wrist, this time the man *was* dismissed.

General Pieter Arnoldus Cronjé

General Pieter Arnoldus Cronjé stood above a trench. The air was cold and he turned his face up to the warming glow of the morning sun, pulling intermittently at a piece of biltong with his strong teeth. The biltong was too soft and rather bland. Around him the encampment was an ants' nest of activity and it would continue in this fashion as long as the English bombardment held off. In fact, he was surprised that the English had not already started their barrage of cannon fire. Yesterday the shelling had continued well into the evening and he had expected it to begin again with the very first rays of the sun on this new day. But there was nothing. The veldt was its normal, serene self. He smiled. This was the best part of the day. He had always enjoyed these cold, fresh mornings, the air showing on his breath and the slight breeze fluttering it away, and the antelope, wildebeest and other wildlife feeding peacefully before the heat of the day drove them to the shelter of the trees and shrubs. It was glorious! Why would anyone want to live anywhere else in the world? He raised his arms into a full-chested stretch and breathed in the cool air. He grimaced at the faint acrid burn of lyddite and smoke that remained from the previous day and at the depressing sight of the wreckage of the laager.

Cronjé had to admit that there was little holding them back now. They could abandon the laager and make a run for it. De Wet had secured the strategic Oskoppies and had given the English a good hiding. De Wet's position provided them with the cover they needed for a tactical retreat. He looked across to the hill from which a heliograph had been flashing continually from the moment the sun had risen. It winked at him, inviting him to dash for the hill and to freedom to fight another day.

De Wet seemed very keen for Cronjé to run and, for a brief while, he was tempted. But although he had no wagons left, he still had women and children to worry about. And then there was the lack of horses. The poor animals had suffered severely in the initial bombardment. The English had deliberately targeted them. It was inhuman for a so-called civilised people to behave as they had done. The result was that there were not enough horses for the burghers, let alone for the women and children, and he was not going to abandon them to the enemy. So, in truth, there was no option to leave. And why should they? With de Wet dominating a strategic part of the battlefield and other commandos arriving soon, it would not be long before there were enough Afrikanders to drive the English back and out of the Orange Free State. In addition, they still had enough ammunition to repeat many times over the achievements of yesterday. So there was *no need* to rush away.

A burgher called out to Cronjé, and he turned to face an approaching group of riders. The leader dismounted and Cronjé smiled and grasped his hand.

"Good morning, Neef Pieter. How are you this beautiful morning?"

"I am well Oom Piet, thank you."

"Good, good. Did you have time for your prayers yet?"

"No Oom. I shall say them as soon as I have finished here."

"Good. So what did that skelm Kitchener have to say to my request? I see their guns are silent, so I assume he was happy to agree to a truce."

"No Oom, he did not."

"No!" A look of surprise crossed Cronjé's face. "Why?"

"They gave no reason. They kept me waiting for a long time and then simply said 'No'."

"And the doctors? Are they to provide us with doctors?"

"Only if we surrender."

"Never!" Cronjé burst out in anger. "We will *never* surrender."

"What now, then, Oom?"

"I have another message for you to take back to that fool. Tell him that, as he is so unmerciful in refusing a truce, he leaves me little choice. He can do as he pleases."

"Yes Oom, but what about my prayers?"

Cronjé glared at the man from under hooded eyebrows, "Say them while you ride to deliver your message!"

General Christiaan Rudolf de Wet

General Christiaan Rudolf de Wet stared through his field glasses at the hive of activity in the laager below him. Dropping his glasses to his chest he turned to look at his heliographers. They were still at work. They had been winking at Cronjé as soon as the sun had allowed. The message was simple. "I have opened up an escape route. I have fresh horses. Gather all your able men and join us on the kopje." He had been repeating the message for nearly two hours, but while there was plenty going on in the laager, none of it suggested that Cronjé was listening. Indeed, all the evidence indicated the opposite: that Cronjé had no intention of leaving and every intention of staying where he was. The stubborn old fool.

De Wet took up his glasses again to study the English encampment that had been established near the little settlement at Paardeberg Drift. The white tents were planted as regularly as the rose bushes in front of Bloemfontein town hall, but where yesterday there had been rank upon rank of wagons, now there were none. They must be away fetching more supplies, de Wet surmised. The English obviously planned to stay. The convoy of wagons might offer another opportunity to capture more English supplies. But surely Roberts would not be so foolish as to leave his wagons unprotected again. Much as he might be tempted to send some men after the wagons, de Wet knew his had none to spare.

De Wet was intrigued at the general lack of activity among the enemy troops. Although he could see many soldiers, they were mainly restricted to their encampments. And the guns had remained silent all morning. There seemed to be a phoney air of anticipation, as though something should be happening, but nothing was expected. Even the infantry that skulked around the base of his hill showed little signs of movement. It was all too quiet.

De Wet adjusted his slouch hat. He needed to remain vigilant. He walked over to the nearest stone rampart that the burghers had thrown up during the night. Standing on the stone wall, he surveyed his own situation. His force consisted of only three hundred burghers. He had had to bring his troops up from Osfontein Farm when the English had counter-attacked. The farm could have been easily surrounded and the risk of losing men in defending it was too great. On the kopje, his commando was well hidden and this, together with their superior rifles and marksmen, gave him the advantage. But his lack of field pieces remained his greatest weakness. He hoped that the supplies of ammunition he had requested from Bloemfontein would arrive soon.

De Wet turned back to look at what was left of the laager and noticed the dust trail of a troop of at least one thousand mounted infantry trotting towards his kopje. He had seen them crossing the river earlier in the morning and now it was clear that they were to join the infantry already tucked in among the rocks at the foot of the kopje. De Wet watched the approaching horsemen with rising concern. Once they had joined their comrades there would be over one thousand five hundred English soldiers ready to attack his position. But more worryingly, the regiment he had faced yesterday afternoon were foot soldiers, who had attacked with the speed of a tortoise. It had been easy to gauge what they were planning to do and to put counter-measures in place. But a mounted unit was a different pot of coffee. The infantry had tried a frontal attack yesterday. Today he anticipated a flanking movement. He would need to move his gun and Pom-Pom to protect his flanks.

De Wet turned to give his orders to his captains. As he did so, he saw activity in the vicinity of the laager. Lifting his field glasses, he watched as a double line of English horse approached the laager. It was obviously not an attack. It had a certain feel of pomp and circumstance about it, as if the English were on parade. Lancers were sitting ram-rod straight on their horses, their lances held upright with their little banners fluttering joyfully in the warming morning breeze. Most interesting of all was the horseman at the front of the parade, for his lance bore a large white flag.

General Pieter Arnoldus Cronjé

General Pieter Arnoldus Cronjé stood legs apart with his feet planted firmly on the soil of his homeland, his hands clasped behind his back. Together with six other burghers he studied the lone English horseman as he approached under the protection of a white flag. He felt a flash of pride. His hard-lined response to the English general had had the desired effect. While he had not expected another visit, the white flag fluttering enthusiastically above the rider, showed they had seen sense in agreeing to a truce. Behind the horseman his small escort of Lancers waited uneasily, with their gaudy little banners flapping from the tops of their lances.

The Lancer stopped in front of Cronjé and his group of men and examined their faces. They were the most dishevelled bunch of soldiers he had ever seen. They looked like a collection of tramps. They stood silently in filthy greatcoats and scuffed, muddy boots. Their dishevelled beards hid their faces, but their eyes bore into him from under the brims of their hats. Each one held a Mauser that seemed to twitch with murderous intent. The Lancer looked around. There was no one else visible, yet his skin crawled as he imagined the many rifle barrels that would be pointing at him from other Boers hidden in their trenches. His perturbed state of mind was not helped by the fact that as he had encouraged his horse forward, his comrades had reminded him that in this war the white flag had not always been a guarantee against being shot. Shifting tensely in his saddle, he squared his shoulders in defiance of the rifles and the taciturn glowers of this intimidating group. Their silence was starting to annoy him. Why had this rabble been sent to parley with him? Was this even the proper reception committee? He picked out one of the bearded faces at random and, in an authoritative tone, directed his comments at him.

"I am instructed to speak to your leader, Pieter Cronjé. Can you fetch him?"

Behind the beard, the burgher whom he had addressed showed complete incomprehension, but a bear of a man with a similar large beard standing beside him erupted in anger.

"You arrogant little bastard," he called out in Dutch.

This time it was the horseman's turn to show incomprehension.

The Boer repeated his insult, this time in English so heavily accented that the Lancer simply sat in his saddle and shook his head. The Boer spoke more slowly, articulating each unfamiliar word with care.

"Listen, Khaki. First of all, you wish to speak to *General* Cronjé and, secondly, who the hell do you think you are to demand that the General attends to you?"

The Lancer threw a glance over his shoulder to gather some confidence from the distant presence of his colleagues, who now seemed rather too far behind him. This defiant reception was not what he had been expecting. He squared his shoulders once more and sat taller in his saddle.

"In that case, can you inform the *General* that we are here to accept his surrender and to escort him and his senior officers to Lord Kitchener?"

The Boer's beard parted as his jaw fell open and he let out a bark of incredulity. He stared at the Lancer, his jaw moving soundlessly. Other than his initial surprised vocalisation, the Boer was stunned into silence. The only sound to be heard was of creaking leather as the Lancer fidgeted in his saddle. The other Boers craned their necks to see if their spokesman was all right. Suddenly, he let out an enormous laugh that rose from his belly and erupted from his barrel chest like thunder. He gripped his sides with his shovel-like hands as if he were in pain. Everyone stared at him and looked at each other quizzically. Eventually regaining his composure, the Boer turned to Cronjé.

"Oom Piet, this idiot has come to accept your surrender."

He burst out laughing again. It took a few seconds for the message to sink in. When it did, a chorus of laughter burst from the burghers. The horseman twisted in his saddle to look at his colleagues, who seemed even farther away. When he turned back he noticed that there was one bearded Boer who was not laughing. Cronjé stepped forward.

"What is the meaning of this stupidity?" he demanded, his normally grey eyes almost black with anger.

The Lancer stared at Cronjé. It was obvious he did not understand.

"Frans," Cronjé shouted above the laughing, "ask this fool what he is talking about."

The huge Boer, Frans van Zyl, stepped forward and repeated the question in English.

The horseman looked at the Boer. He decided it was time to be more civil. He looked at Cronjé, who was obviously the Boer in charge, and addressed his response to him.

"Sir, it is our understanding that the Boers have agreed to an unconditional surrender."

"On what basis do you make that assumption?" demanded van Zyl without Cronjé's prompting.

The Lancer delved into his saddle bag and retrieved a piece of paper. He scrutinised it. It was the English interpretation of Cronjé's response earlier that day. He was now not entirely convinced it was an accurate translation. He read it out loud:

"To Lord Kitchener, commander of the armies of the British Empire, from General Cronjé, commandant of the Transvaal Republic commando. Since you are so uncharitable as to refuse me a truce, you leave me little choice but to do as you please."

"I think you will find you have missed the word 'invading' out of the sentence. 'Commander of the *invading* armies of the English Empire'," van Zyl retorted. He turned to Cronjé and translated what the Lancer had read.

Cronjé exploded. Shaking his fist at the horseman, he yelled, "I shall never surrender alive. Let Kitchener bombard us as he pleases." He swung on his heel and stomped off. The huge Boer grinned at the horseman, shrugged his broad shoulders, then turned and followed Cronjé. The rest of the Boers did likewise, laughing and slapping each other on their backs. The Lancer had not understood a word Cronjé has said, but the message was clear. He turned his horse and as he did so his shoulders drooped. At the top of his lance the white flag hung dejectedly.

Field Marshal Frederick Sleigh Roberts

Field Marshal Frederick Sleigh Roberts sat staring at the map on the table in front of him. He shook his head to try to clear the remnants of fever that was befuddling his mind. He lifted his eyes and looked beyond the poles of the open-sided tent that served as his headquarters until his wagon arrived from Jacobsdal. Outside, the morning coolness had burnt away and the neat rows of white, conical tents were already dancing in the developing heat haze. The canvas roof of the tent flapped lazily. Soon it too would be stilled by the brutal sun.

A gentle cough brought Roberts' attention back to the map and then to the faces of the men who sat around the table with him – the cautious, but experienced Kelly-Kenny, Colvile and, as he now recognised, the impetuous and careless Kitchener. The heroic French was some way off to the north, keeping the Boer reinforcements away. Smith-Dorrien was somewhere near Gun Hill on the opposite side of the river. Roberts had asked that he be found and summoned to join them.

"Thank you, gentlemen, that briefing was most useful. General Kelly-Kenny and I shall now make a tour of the positions we have discussed." He took out his watch. "We shall meet back here in …?" he looked at Kelly-Kenny.

"We should be finished in two hours, sir."

"In two hours then. Will someone arrange for our horses to be brought for us? Thank you."

As the men left, Roberts turned to Kelly-Kenny.

"General, let's start on Signal Hill. That should give us a good overview of the situation. We'll walk there and discuss my plans as we go."

They ducked out of the tent and started, in silence, up the slope of the hill, their entourage following at a respectful distance with their horses. Roberts remained silent for some time. Kelly-Kenny followed suit. When Roberts eventually spoke, his first comment took Kelly-Kenny by surprise.

"We seem to be in a bit of a pickle." His tone seemed dejected.

Kelly-Kenny glanced at Roberts briefly, but immediately faced forwards again, seemingly to concentrate on his ascent of the hill –

the route was marred with jagged rocks, anthills and low, thorny shrubs. Before he commented, he thought it best to allow his commanding officer to elaborate.

"Sir?"

Roberts halted as he coughed loudly into a handkerchief and then wiped his brow. "This damned fever," he explained, "it makes me breathless." As he started to walk again he continued, "I noted Kitchener's demand for a continued frontal attack." He looked at Kelly-Kenny. "He was quite damning of yours, and Colvile's, proposal to sit it out and bomb the Boers out of their trenches. Indeed, he was rather discourteous."

Kelly-Kenny frowned, but did not take up the invitation to comment. He maintained his apparent focus on his ascent and waited for Roberts to continue.

"I am not minded to follow Kitchener's suggestion. It did not work at Magersfontein. It did not work yesterday. It would be reckless to repeat that action. Although it seems that the Boers have fallen back overnight, I believe that had little to do with our approach yesterday and more to do with an expeditious strengthening of their positions."

Kelly-Kenny nodded in agreement but maintained a grim countenance. He was encouraged by Roberts' comments. It appeared that Roberts agreed with his own thoughts on the matter. He was about to respond and encourage this line of thought when Roberts interjected.

"Ah, we are here."

Standing together on the summit of Signal Hill, they saw the battlefield laid out before them. Kelly-Kenny waited a few minutes while Roberts regained his breath. A light sweat had broken out on his brow. When he had recovered, Roberts gave him a small nod and Kelly-Kenny gestured to one of the men who had followed them. He came forward unfurling the map and held it open for the two officers.

"We are here," Kelly-Kenny pointed at the map. "And that is Kitchener's Hill," he indicated the contours on the map and then pointed to the hill itself.

"It is very disappointing that the Boers hold it," Roberts said.

"Indeed it is, sir. As we discussed earlier, de Wet has a small commando of, we believe, five hundred men and a couple of guns, but he is well established and the Boers are able to make good use of any shelter, as you know. As you can now see, from there, he and Cronjé are able to dominate the battlefield between the river and the hill."

"What of this man de Wet?" Roberts asked, as a thought grew in his mind. "He's not the same man who captured our supply wagons and the fifty-strong troop of mounted infantry?"

"It's difficult to say, sir. The Boers have large families, and three generations from one family can be fighting in the same battle. We are aware of at least one other de Wet associated with Cronjé, but it seems likely that the de Wet on the hill is the same person who took the wagons."

"If he is the same man, he is becoming something of a thorn in our side. It is because of him that we do not have enough provisions to sustain our men properly." Roberts fell silent and Kelly-Kenny waited. Roberts' next statement was unexpected.

"Are you aware, General, that yesterday we probably suffered the worst casualties of the war to date?"

It sounded like an accusation. Kelly-Kenny turned to face his superior. Roberts had given Kitchener command of the battle. He now knew that had been a disastrous decision. Was Roberts trying to deflect responsibility for the previous day's disaster on to him? Kelly-Kenny's eyes narrowed. He would defend his position robustly if required, but, he thought, it was best to start cautiously. His response was expressed to forestall the accusation.

"Yes sir, it was an appalling tragedy. I walked past the main field hospital last night and it was overflowing with casualties. It is in the bungalow I had vacated earlier when the extent of the casualties became apparent. I might ask that you suggest that General Kitchener does the same, sir," he added pointedly. That brought Kitchener into focus as the perpetrator of the tragedy. Before Roberts could comment, Kelly-Kenny went on.

"The sound of suffering coming from the hospital was appalling, so much so that I was unable to enter."

That sounded callous, he thought, so he added quickly, "But, I doubt if my presence would have alleviated the poor souls' suffering. Rather, I thought it might simply reinforce the recklessness of their commander... General Kitchener," he inserted hastily, to avoid any supposition that he was accusing Roberts. "...Of the General sending them against an enemy that was so obviously dug into a strong, defensive position."

Roberts looked directly into Kelly-Kenny's eyes. The accusation was noted but not yet accepted. Kelly-Kenny's stomach tightened. He might have overdone it. The name had rolled from his lips easily and carelessly in what might appear to Roberts as a coarse attempt to blacken Kitchener's name. Roberts may not realise the injection of Kitchener's name was to remove any apparent accusation from himself. The accusation hung between the men like the blood-dripping sword of Damocles, either to be sheathed or turned back on Kelly-Kenny. He held Roberts' gaze. He had no status within Roberts' circle and perhaps his views had weakened his standing further, but he had expressed his views and he would stand or fall by his words.

"Indeed," said Roberts and, turning away from Kelly-Kenny, he added, "one must be very careful of the men's sensibilities."

The sword slid silently into its scabbard. Despite the excessive midday heat, Kelly-Kenny felt a cold chill run down his spine. That was the closest he had come in his career of becoming embroiled in high-level military politics and it had been an exceedingly uncomfortable experience. He was not a natural at it and he was too old to learn. He determined never to do it again.

"The wounded?" Roberts asked, "How are they?"

"It is a poor situation, sir. The medical supplies were in the wagons taken by de Wet. As a result, and despite the efforts of the medical staff, the men are suffering greatly. We are also desperately short of ambulance carts. We have to transport the wounded to Jacobsdal in ox wagons. The discomfort must be extreme."

Roberts fell silent again. That damned provisions convoy. That damned de Wet. He had seen an opportunity and taken it. Roberts frowned sourly. He knew the fault lay entirely at his own feet. Because of his tactical error, the men were now suffering, the same men who, on his arrival that morning, had broken into spontaneous and enthusiastic cheers. Roberts smiled grimly to himself. He knew that the word going about the camp was that now 'Bobs' has arrived nothing further would go wrong. Well, he had served them poorly thus far. Roberts churned the facts over and over for a little while longer. Kelly-Kenny waited patiently. Then Roberts turned to him.

"General, I see no alternative but for us to withdraw and fall back on Klip Kraal Drift. Once we have our convoys and medical provisions in better shape we shall reinitiate our drive towards Bloemfontein. I would like you to identify a number of positions along the route to Klip Kraal Drift and secure them to protect our rear as we consolidate our forces."

Kelly-Kenny felt as though he had been hit over the head with a rifle butt. It took him some moments to regain control of his tongue and even then he was only able to utter, "Sir?"

Roberts studied Kelly-Kenny's stupefied expression. The man had obviously not been expecting a decision along the lines he had just outlined. It was apparent further explanation was required.

"General, the facts are these. The enemy control a key part of the field and are unlikely to give it up without a significant loss to our forces. We have seen what they can do when they are in well-established defensive positions. Our provisions are insufficient to keep our men up to strength and our medical provisions are appallingly short. The combination of the effectiveness of the enemy fire and our own poor provisions give me no confidence that a continued offensive on their positions will succeed. The British public will not countenance further losses of the level we suffered yesterday."

Kelly-Kenny remained silent for a moment and then saw the weakness in Roberts' arguments.

"Sir, I agree. You are right in all respects, except... if I may suggest one."

Roberts inclined his head at Kelly-Kenny's hesitation.

"Yes, General, please express your view. The British army has never engaged an enemy of this sort before. This is a new type of war, a modern war. I value your advice. What alternative do you have to our withdrawing?"

"Thank you for your confidence, sir. While it is true that the British public would react badly to further losses on the scale of yesterday, the British press are just as likely to look poorly on a withdrawal from a position where, it can be argued, we hold the upper hand. And I do believe we have the upper hand. With careful tactics we can push our advantage towards a final solution. While I would, of course, follow any order you give with fortitude and discretion, I should add that some of your more hot-headed senior officers may not be so discreet with their views."

This time Roberts smiled at the more subtle accusation.

"So your advice is to sit tight and bombard the Boers into submission?"

"Yes sir. I am of the view that they could be pounded into submission without risking additional casualties to our forces." Kelly-Kenny hesitated and then continued. "There are two other factors that favour this approach. First, as you know, the 7th Division follows in your tracks to this place and that will substantially strengthen our forces and allow us to tighten the circle around the Boers. Our ultimate goal must be the surrender and capture of Cronjé, as his capture will have a significant demoralising effect on the Boers."

"And de Wet? What of him and his hold on Kitchener's Hill?"

"He must, of course, be displaced as a matter of urgency. His occupation of the hill is the weak card in our hand. We must rid ourselves of him."

"And your second factor?"

"You will not be aware of this yet, but the entire convoy of wagons was dispatched this morning to collect more provisions. If we withdraw from Paardeberg, we will have no wagons to transport our stores. We would be in a worse situation at Klip Kraal Drift regarding the supplies than here, and we would have to abandon our wounded."

Roberts grunted at that. He had not been aware of the lack of wagons. "Thank you for your council, General. You have put your case well. I see no opportunity to withdraw at this point, but it may still be the more expeditious course for us to take in due course. I shall ponder further on the matter. In the meantime, arrange for the bombardment to recommence. We have given the Boer too much peace already today. Let us remind them that we are still here."

Burgher Fredrick Abram Marais

Burgher Fredrick Abram Marais sat on the step that had been formed at the base of the wall of the trench. He leant back onto the cool wall of sand that curved over his head. Through the gap that ran the length of the trench Marais could see a band of blue sky. The sun was at its zenith. It shone boldly into the trench, throwing a river of light along the floor of the trench, driving out the cold shadows of earlier in the day. But the temperature in the trench remained cool and comfortable.

The Burghers had taken the opportunity, during the morning, while the English guns were quiet, to improve the structure of their defences and also to clean them out. After only one day they had lost their fresh smell, but their reworking had restored that pleasant aroma of freshly turned soil. When the bombardment had restarted, the burghers had retreated into the trenches, away from danger. A few men stood on flat rocks or boxes of ammunition and peered out of the trenches, watchful for any attack from the English infantry. But most of them, like Marais, sat along the sand bench, chatting quietly or drinking coffee or dozing.

Now that there were many men in the trench, there was a change in the air. Out in the open it had not been noticeable, but in the confined space of the trenches the odour of unwashed humanity was starting to invade the senses, a smell simultaneously sweet and acerbic. Marais was aware of his own smell, and it was not pleasant! He decided that he would have a bathe in the river tonight.

A few minutes previously he had stood on a rock and looked out over the veldt, as much for the fresh air as to watch for an attack, but it had been like sticking his head into an oven. And, while there were a huge number of shells exploding all around, he had seen no English soldiers. So he had retreated back into the coolness. The regular shower of stones and soil falling around him was a constant reminder of the ferocity of the English bombardment. Dust, with the sun shining through it, hung like a curtain down the length of the trench.

Marais retrieved his Bible from a pocket. It was ironic that when all was quiet he had been too busy to read his Book, but now that all hell was being let loose by the English guns he had time for 'quiet' contemplation. After Coetzee's rebuke, he had decided to look at the

Psalms again. He rubbed the palms of his hands on his trousers to remove the dirt that still clung to them from his earlier labours. It was a pointless act for his trousers were as ingrained with dirt as his hands. He opened his Bible and turned the pages. His eyes fell on the words of Psalm 55: *I would hurry to my place of shelter, far from the tempest and storm.* Perfect. As he prepared to read, he was interrupted by Coetzee throwing himself on to the sand bench next to him.

"Ha! I see you have found some quiet time for your Bible, Oom," Coetzee laughed ironically.

Marais smiled. It seemed that making time for 'quiet contemplation' was going to be a challenge. He noted that a young woman had also sat down beside Coetzee. She, like himself and Coetzee, wore a slouch hat, had a bandolier slung across her chest and she rested a Mauser against her skirted leg. Marais lent forward to look around Coetzee and smiled at her. She returned a bold smile, her long, dark hair falling in front of her face as she also leant forward. She tucked it behind her ear. Marais noted that her hand was clean, as were her clothes – except for the ubiquitous veneer of dust. The contrast between the girl and the scruffiness of the men was striking.

"Are you going to introduce me to your new friend?" he asked.

"Huh? Oh yes, of course. Oom, this is Alletta Bezuidenhout. Lettie, this is Oom Fredrick. He is a Cape rebel, like me," Coetzee added proudly.

"Hello, Alletta."

"Hello, Oom Fredrick."

"I see you are appropriately equipped for the situation."

"Yes," interjected Coetzee. "Her father was wounded, so Lettie took up his rifle and has joined her brothers in the trenches. She says she wants to avenge her father."

"Very commendable," smiled Marais. "I see you have borrowed you father's slouch hat as well. Very fetching. Have you had any luck in avenging your father?"

Alletta answered quickly, before Coetzee could do so on her behalf.

"No, not yet." Then, more slowly, "The English are being more cautious today, sending over shells and keeping their soldiers safely out of firing range."

"Yes, it is damned frustrating," said Coetzee.

Marais cleared his throat and threw a critical look at Coetzee for the youth's inappropriate language in front of the young lady.

Coetzee smirked. "Oom, you do not have to worry. Just now Lettie was abusing the English with language that made even me blush!"

He laughed at his joke and Alletta looked away, but she did not turn sufficiently to hide the red glow of her cheek.

"The English are throwing hundreds of shells at us," Coetzee continued. "What a waste of ammunition! It has virtually no effect when we are in our trenches, unless a shell actually drops right into a trench, of course. Then it is pretty horrendous. I saw one poor guy whose stomach was completely…"

This time Marais's clearing of his throat did stop Coetzee before his description became too graphic.

"But that does not happen very often," he added quickly, "and most of the shells cause no casualties at all. It is amazing how many shells are coming over. How long will they be able to keep it up? Surely they must run out soon."

Marais shrugged, "I don't know. The English Empire is the largest that has ever existed. They say the sun never sets on the lands owned by the English. Their resources are probably limitless."

"So why do they want our Republics as well?" enquired Alletta.

"Who knows?" replied Marais. "Cetchwayo, the king of the Zulu nation, is supposed to have asked the same question when the English invaded Zululand in '79. I suppose when you own so much, you might also desire that little bit you don't have. The true reasons are likely to be very complex and already forgotten. *Now*, though, the main reason the English will have for wanting to win the war is that they won't want to lose face with their European adversaries. The English would be the laughing stock of Europe if they are beaten by two tiny countries run by farmers."

Alletta stared at the ground, biting her lip. When she spoke her words were edged with emotion. "So they will not stop until they take our land?"

Marais shrugged his shoulders and remained silent, but Coetzee was quick to respond.

"And what of us? What of us Cape rebels? Does that mean we have no future? Will we be hunted down like animals?"

"For all their faults, the English are a just people," Marais answered. "At least we will have the opportunity to put our case to a court of law. We may get away with our lives."

"A court of law? Oom, do you know any Cape Afrikanders who have been accused of treason by the English and found innocent and not hanged?"

When Marais did not answer, Coetzee persisted, glowering at him, "Do you?"

"No."

"A just people, my arse! For us Cape Afrikanders there are now two choices: die by hanging or die fighting. I know which one I will choose! Come, Lettie, let us get back to defending our country!"

Taking her hand, he led her away. Marais looked after them briefly and then returned to his Bible.

Captain Daniël Johannes Stephanus Theron

Captain Daniël Johannes Stephanus Theron approached General de Wet, announcing his arrival by calling out, "Oom Christiaan."

De Wet lowered his field glasses and turned away from his scrutiny of the Gloucestershires and mounted infantry's slow ascent of the kopje. A huge smile appeared on his previously stern face as he recognised Theron.

"Neef Dannie, you made it! Of course you did. A few English soldiers could not stop the famous Dannie Theron."

Theron flushed. "Thank you, Oom, but it is you who is giving the English a very rough time. I simply observe what they are up to."

De Wet laughed. "Ha, but you are very sneaky about how you do it. I heard that you once sat around the camp fire with English soldiers and talked to them about their plans. Now that takes balls."

"Aagh, it was not so difficult. It is not difficult to pretend to be one of the colony guides and many of the young English soldiers, if a little naïve, are no different from you or me. They are just people trying to make the best of a bad situation."

De Wet eyed him and scowled. "Indeed? It is a shame they are doing it in our country."

Then he smiled. It felt good. He smiled so little these days.

"Come, let's get some coffee. There is one good thing about the English – their wagons are always full of the most excellent coffee," he laughed.

The two men, each with a mug of freshly brewed coffee, sat down on two large flat rocks, facing each other. For a while they sat in silence, enjoying a moment of relative calm, sipping their coffee and ignoring the distant rumble of the English guns and the crash of exploding shells, and the occasional snap of a Mauser whenever an English infantryman was foolish enough to show himself.

Theron studied the man in front of him: he was 45 years old and already resting on his square shoulders was the weight of saving the greatest Afrikander general from the clutches of the largest army in the world. De Wet sat in a stiff, straight-backed fashion, like an officer from a bygone time, but it was already obvious to Theron that he had a very modern military brain. Watching his stern features, his forehead furrowed in thought, Theron could almost see his mind working through the different options and scenarios, developing tactics and planning contingencies. Theron shifted into a more comfortable position on the hard rock and his movement broke de Wet's concentration.

De Wet looked across at him and smiled thinly. "Lots to think about these days," he said. "So Dannie," Theron noted the familiar tone in which he was often indulged by senior officers, being, as he was, a 'hero' of the Afrikander Republics. "The English did not give you any trouble while you were ascending this kopje?"

"No, Oom. We had a look around before we came up to see what they are up to. They are focusing on your flanks but have kept a reserve force at the base of the kopje at your centre. Have they attacked the centre at all today?"

"No. As you say, the focus today has been on both my flanks. Yesterday they went for the centre."

"You will know, of course, Oom, that they have you covered on three sides. The eastern slopes are still open, but that route could be very quickly closed."

"Yes, we're in a precarious position. I have lookouts monitoring that side of the kopje and at the first sign of the English closing that gate we will be off. The last thing we need is for the English to encircle us as well. The problem is that the English *will* eventually get around to it, and then not only will we lose the advantage of the high ground, but we will no longer be able to help Cronjé. When you arrived, I was watching yet another division of English infantry on its way to join the battle. Soon there will be more soldiers here than Roberts will know what to do with. He is not a fool. He will realise the strategic value of this kopje and he will take it back. There is nothing I can do to stop him. Even with the hundred men who came with you, I still have only four hundred burghers to defend this kopje. I would be like that kid who stuck his finger in the dyke."

"Hans Brinker?"

"Yes, that's the fellow. But it is a bad example," continued de Wet grimly, "because he managed to stem the tide. I do not believe I will be so lucky. There is no one coming to our aid."

De Wet fell quiet, his forehead tensed in thought. After a few moments Theron asked, "How long does General Cronjé have?"

"Tomorrow, maybe the next day, but by Thursday I think we will have been driven from this kopje. After that, it will be very difficult for the General and everyone with him. If they do not leave…"

De Wet left the consequences unsaid. They were obvious to both men. They remained silent, the crash of shells now intruding more ominously on their thoughts. Then De Wet turned to Theron.

"Dannie, I need you to go to General Cronjé and explain the situation to him. You need to convince him to leave."

"I will go, of course. And I will try my best, but it may not be enough."

De Wet looked Theron in the eye. "Dannie, Cronjé needs to evacuate his commando. I hesitate to ask you to do this because there is a real danger that you may be caught and that would be a significant loss not only to our cause, but also to me personally. Yet I believe only you can convince him."

Theron held de Wet's penetrating stare. "Thank you, Christiaan. I shall be especially careful on this mission, both for the cause and for our friendship." He smiled broadly and de Wet smiled back at the slim-featured man.

"I cannot give you a written message lest it fall into the hands of the English." De Wet was grim faced. "So the message is a verbal one. Do all you can to make the General see how precarious his position is and that if he wishes to continue to fight the English, he and his commando have to leave their laager. We still have a corridor through which they can escape, and we will keep it open for them when they break out, but they have to come soon. Tell him we have sufficient horses with us, even if they have to double up to escape. We also have more horses at Poplar Grove, so every burgher will have a fresh mount."

Theron looked at de Wet, and de Wet held his gaze. They both knew that was not strictly true.

"We just need to get them out," de Wet continued. "We can sort out the details later. Dannie, General Cronjé needs to understand that *our* fate depends upon him escaping with all of his men. He needs to know that should he fall into the hands of the enemy, it would be the death-blow to *all* our hopes. You *have* to urge him to abandon the laager and everything in it. He must fight his way out by night. We are here to protect him from pursuit by the English, but we cannot hold this position for much longer." All signs of the earlier smile had disappeared from de Wet's features.

"I shall do it, Oom."

"Thank you, Dannie. May God help you to succeed."

The two comrades stood up and shook hands. De Wet placed his free hand on Theron's shoulder. "God be with you."

Theron turned and walked towards the eastern slope of the kopje. A few yards from de Wet, he stopped and turned back. He liked the man and wished to give him a final gesture of friendship before he left. But de Wet already had his field glasses clamped to his eyes once more. The landscape had taken on the golden glow of the sinking sun. He was studying the large dust cloud beyond Paardeberg Drift that was drifting across the gilded veldt. It signified the arrival of yet more English troops and guns.

Theron hurried on. Cronjé had one last chance of escaping, and convincing the obstinate, old general of that now rested on *his* shoulders.

General Horace Lockwood Smith-Dorrien

General Horace Lockwood Smith-Dorrien dismounted his dusty horse and walked towards the tent that served as Roberts' temporary headquarters. Three of the sides had been secured against the on-coming night chill. A brazier had been lit and next to it Smith-Dorrien could see the diminutive Roberts, his small stature exaggerated by the taller figures of the other officers already present: Kitchener, Kelly-Kenny and Colvile. Smith-Dorrien noted that Lieutenant-General Charles Tucker was also present. He must have ridden ahead of his approaching 7th Division. Smith-Dorrien had observed, as he made his way towards Roberts' tent, the tell-tale dust cloud, stained red by the dying sun, which had signalled the arrival of Tucker's division.

Entering the tent, Smith-Dorrien stopped and saluted the Field Marshal, "Good evening, Lord Roberts."

"Ah, good evening, General," responded Roberts.

Roberts wasted no time.

"Gentlemen, now that we are all present, let us proceed. It is apparent that we have a great opportunity to impose a crushing moral defeat on the Boers. The question is how best to achieve it. There are currently two schools of thought: a continuation of the progressive approach, as proposed by Lord Kitchener."

Kitchener's unblinking, cobra-like stare fell upon Smith-Dorrien. The others looked at him grimly. Smith-Dorrien thought he detected the slightest sideways shake of Kelly-Kenny's grey-haired head.

"Or," Roberts continued, "to lay siege to the laager and bombard the enemy until they submit to an unconditional surrender."

Kitchener remained unmoved, except for a narrowing of his eyes, but the other generals leaned forward minutely. It was not entirely clear where Roberts stood on the matter, but if he favoured the former, surely he would have ordered a full attack that day. Word was already spreading around the camp that he had consulted closely with Kelly-Kenny on the matter and his view – of a more cautious approach – was well known.

"You wish me to decide, sir?" asked Smith-Dorrien.

"No, General, that is my responsibility. But I do wish to take your counsel. Your division, being to the north of the Modder, is best placed to take the offensive, should we wish to do so. So the question is do you believe you can carry the laager with a full-frontal attack, using the manpower at your disposal?"

Although he knew the answer to the question immediately, Smith-Dorrien did not respond directly. There was a third way, to which he had already given some thought.

"Sir, to repeat the action of yesterday would be…" Should he use the word 'fool-hardy', which is what he believed? He looked at Kitchener and held his cold stare. He continued, "…entirely inappropriate. We took considerable losses and to subject our brave men to such tactics again would be imprudent." Turning to Roberts, "If I may impose my own deliberations on the matter, sir, I would suggest that we maintain the blockade of the Boer positions and continue the intense bombardment, being careful, of course, to avoid the areas occupied by the women and children, and while…"

"Pardon? Wait!" Roberts interrupted, aghast. "General, did you say women and children?"

"Yes sir. I did."

"What women and children?"

"The Boers have their families with them, sir."

Roberts stared at Smith-Dorrien, incredulous. "You knew this?" He turned his gaze on each of the men in turn, directing the question to them all.

"Yes sir," said Colvile, "And we have taken every precaution to ensure no harm came to them."

"You have taken every precaution? How?"

This time Kelly-Kenny responded. "When the Boers established their laager, they arranged their wagons in two areas – a large ring of wagons with a smaller one adjacent to it. It was apparent that the latter was for the women and children, but the wagons were quickly abandoned by the Boers. We assume, …um… we believe, the women and children have been allocated some of the central trenches between the river and the location of their original laager."

"You are sure of this?"

Kelly-Kenny hesitated. "As sure as we can be, sir, given that the Boers are generally very difficult to see at the best of times. We are vigilant for the women and children and try not to shell the stretches of trench where we believe them to be."

Roberts was speechless for a few moments. "Have you offered them safe conduct away from the battlefield?"

All eyes turned to Kitchener, followed by those of Roberts. Kitchener remained silent.

"Captain!" Roberts called out.

An officer entered the tent, stood to attention and saluted. "Sir?"

"I am countermanding my previous order to bombard the Boer positions first thing tomorrow morning. The bombardment is to be delayed. At first light tomorrow, you are to go to General Cronjé and offer him our guarantee of safe conduct for all the women and children out of their laager and away from the battle zone."

"Yes sir." The officer saluted again and departed.

Roberts lent on the map table, staring at the map to get his thoughts back in order. "Continue, General," he said without looking up.

Smith-Dorrien cleared his throat.

"Once the women and children are safely away, we should resume the intense bombardment of the Boer position. At the same time, we will roll up their downstream flank. To facilitate this, I suggest that the regiments currently engaging the Boers *upstream* should continue to do so. Their assault should be vigorous enough to keep the Boers busy on that flank, but measured. The intention is *not* to push forward, but for the Boers to maintain their current positions. We do not want them to fall back. This will ensure that the enemy's lines remain extended along that stretch of the river. Consequently, the Boers will need greater numbers to defend that flank, leaving fewer men to counter our main attack, which will be against their downstream flank. For this, I propose the use of my Division to push the Boers back towards their laager. I would use the Gordons, Shropshires and Canadians for this purpose."

Kitchener audibly sniffed at the mention of the irregular colonials for such a critical role. After all, it was the irregulars that had lost him Kitchener's Hill. Smith-Dorrien turned his eyes on him, daring him to comment, but Kitchener remained silent.

"I would include the Canadians because they are as courageous as any of our regular troops, and they have a knack for self-preservation. I have observed how they use the terrain to steal towards the enemy. It is something we could all learn. Direct, frontal attacks do not work against an enemy with the firepower of the Boers. The men are simply marching to their annihilation. It is something we should already have learnt from this war.

"The Canadians have proved their worth and I believe they will be able to advance with the stealth required to achieve the goal without undue losses, especially if this is done under cover of night. As we advance, we will capture the trenches and earthworks of the Boers. These will need to be adapted for our own purpose, so my plan would require support from the engineers."

Smith-Dorrien stopped, but his demeanour demanded silence, as he considered if he had missed anything. No, he had not.

"That should do it. In a few days we will have their surrender," he concluded and looked at Roberts for his commendation.

Smith-Dorrien's suggestion was met with reflective silence. Roberts did not respond immediately, but continued to stare at the map on the table.

"Hmmm," he said eventually. "Yes, I agree. That should do it."

"Sir, if I may?" Kitchener said.

"Yes General?"

"Sir, we must not forget the Boers in this."

"I was under the impression they are receiving our full attention."

"I mean those outside the laager, sir."

"Would that include those currently occupying Kitchener's Hill?"

The pointed remark was mumbled so it was difficult to discern who had said it, but it was clear enough for everyone to hear. Kitchener glared at each man in turn. They returned bland stares. Only Kelly-Kenny appeared to have a twinkle in his eye. Kitchener looked at Roberts, for his support, but he was disappointed.

"Sir," he continued. "There remains a serious risk that the Boers will send reinforcements to relieve Cronjé. We already have one making a nuisance of himself."

This brought forth a cough from one of the assembled officers, which Kitchener ignored.

"I agree, General," Roberts said quickly. Things were becoming a little puerile and there were more pressing matters at hand than generals wishing to score points. "So we must make sure we have everything in place to keep Cronjé in and keep the other Boers away. De Wet will be the first priority. He will be knocked off his pedestal, and we will get back your hill."

The final comment had not been intended as a dig, but in the context of previous discussion, some would construe it as such. So Roberts continued smartly, "Gentlemen, I concur with the tactics proposed by General Smith-Dorrien. I believe them to be well thought out. Good work, sir." Smith-Dorrien nodded his thanks.

"So, we are to hold our present positions on the Boers' upstream flank, engaging only to keep them busy. On their downstream flank the Gordons, Shropshires and Canadians, supported by the engineers, will make a stealthy advance. The Gloucestershires and mounted infantry will continue to focus on removing de Wet from Kitchener's Hill. That Boer general is as slippery as an eel, so I want some of General French's cavalry to support them. Our main aim must be to prevent de Wet and his commando from escaping. General Colvile, please arrange the delivery of my orders to General French, but I would wait until tomorrow before sending out a dispatch rider. Lord only knows exactly where General French is at the moment and we know how easy it is to get lost at night in Africa."

The men laughed at the little joke aimed at Kelly-Kenny.

"General French is to provide two formations of cavalry," Roberts continued, "one under Brigadier General Gordon and the other under Brigadier General Broadwood. Their objective is to support the infantry in capturing de Wet. Finally, General Tucker, I am delighted that you have joined us. Once your 7th Division have had some rest and something to eat, please have them ready for action. For the time being, though, I shall hold them in reserve."

Roberts looked around the circle of men. They all seemed to understand his battle orders.

"Now, it has become apparent that our supply lines leave much to be desired. If we are to succeed, miles from the railway, the supply of equipment, medicines and food has to be faultless. General Kitchener, you and I spent a month after our arrival dealing with this matter, and," he added to avoid doubt, "we made significant improvements. But the Boer attack on our wagons has exposed a weakness. I wish you to take charge of this problem. You are to return to the railway depot tomorrow and ensure we receive the supplies we need."

Kitchener remained motionless, but his jaw clenched perceptively. Was this a genuine concern that required the resources of such a senior office or was it a ruse to remove him from the front?

"General, you do understand?" Roberts asked irritably.

"Yes sir. The supply of ammunition and provisions is key to your success here."

"Indeed. It is an issue of considerable urgency, especially with regard to food, clean water and medical supplies." Roberts looked around at his officers and smiled. "So it is decided. Thank you, gentleman, and good luck."

The generals snapped to attention, saluted and began to depart. Kitchener was irritated that the amateur Boer army was being treated with such caution. It indicated a level of respect towards the enemy that was undeserved and, one might say, a lack of conviction among the British command. As they left the tent Kitchener attached himself to Smith-Dorrien.

"General?" he said sharply, to catch Smith-Dorrien's attention.

Smith-Dorrien slowed and turned to Kitchener, tilting his head and cocking an eyebrow.

"General, I am aware that you have given your plan of defeating the Boer considerable thought and I congratulate you on its merit. I have no doubt you appreciate the importance of securing a quick surrender. If we remain immobile around these Boers too long, we will suffer the humiliation of a war of attrition. There is still the risk of Boer reinforcements arriving. And if you were to be expeditious in your attack on the Boers, you would be applauded by the great British public. You would be a made-man," he concluded, trying to appeal to the other officer's vanity.

Smith-Dorrien pursed his lips and furrowed his brow in an expression of exaggerated contemplation of Kitchener's remarks and then answered, "You have heard my plan and I shall only do otherwise if so ordered by *Lord Roberts*." He looked into those cold blue eyes and added, "General, you should now play your part in our success, by doing as *you* are ordered and making sure we have the provisions and ammunition we need to achieve the resolution of the plan."

Kitchener did not respond, so Smith-Dorrien concluded the conversation. "Good evening to you, General." He lengthened his stride, leaving a glowering Kitchener trailing behind.

Tuesday 20 February 1900

Captain Daniël Johannes Stephanus Theron

Captain Daniël Johannes Stephanus Theron, shadowed by the two burghers who had challenged him as he crept towards the Afrikander lines, strolled purposefully along the trench. The sun had been up for an hour and the English guns were still silent. They had continued until the last moment of dusk the day before and he had expected them to recommence with first light this morning. But all was pleasantly quiet. He could even hear bird song seeping into the trench. The low sun had not yet penetrated into the depths of the trenches and he made his way through the cold shadows. Then, through the gloom he saw the man he had been sent to meet.

Even in the dimness of the trench, the contrast between the general he had left the evening before and the one he was now approaching was dramatic. Where de Wet was 'New Testament', slim with a well-groomed uniform and a neatly trimmed goatee beard that framed youthful, reflective features, Cronjé was expansive, dishevelled and brash, enveloped in his greatcoat, his wide-brimmed hat darkening his glowering features, which were hidden behind an untidy, dark, full-faced beard. He was definitely 'Old Testament'. Nevertheless, the general smiled broadly when he recognised Theron.

"Dannie! My goodness, what a delight! What on earth are you doing here? Have you come to inform me that my reinforcements are on the way?"

"Good morning, Oom Piet. I have come from General de Wet."

"Ah, yes General de Wet. His heliographer has been winking at me continuously since Sunday, asking me to come and join him on the kopje. It does look rather a small kopje for so many of us."

"No, Oom, General de Wet wishes you to leave this place and fall back on Poplar Grove. There we can establish another Magersfontein and keep the English out of Bloemfontein."

"But Roberts got around Magersfontein. That is why we are here, is it not?"

"Yes, Oom, you're right about that, but this time we will be ready. General de Wet believes if we establish a strong defensive position at Poplar Grove, with your Transvaalers holding the centre and your flanks protected by mobile commandos to stop the English encircling you, you will be able to hold out against them. We will then send other commandos around to their rear and disrupt their supplies. They will not be able to endure such a campaign and will see the futility of their situation and will have to retreat to the Cape. Once there, we can harry them into suing for peace, as we did after Majuba."

"Majuba! That seems like a lifetime away these days. But Dannie, what is all this talk of leaving? Look, you can walk around the trenches as though you're on a Sunday stroll. The English are having no material effect on us. If we can secure a supply of food, water, ammunition for the rifles and more canons, yes, we definitely need more canons…. I only had two to start with and we lost the second one late yesterday evening. The English have an incredible number, but all they do is blow soil and dust around. If they carry on like this, soon all the soil we dug out of the trenches will be back inside them." Cronjé laughed and Theron smiled in return.

"The point is we already have the English tied down. But we need reinforcements! And we need them soon. I have been calling in my agony 'Come and relieve me', but there has been no response. What other instruction do I need to give for people to hear and understand what they need to do?"

As he finished speaking, a burgher came striding towards them.

"Oom Piet, there is another group of English riding towards us under a white flag," he said.

 Cronjé was unimpressed.

"Go and find Frans van Zyl to speak with them and see what they want this time," he said dismissively. "I have more important matters to deal with here." As the burgher turned to go, Cronjé called to him. "Wait, Neef!" and to Theron he continued with a smile, "I assume, Dannie, that you have not come to us on a social visit and that I should call a War Council to discuss some matter of importance?" In response to Theron's nodded agreement, Cronjé said to the burgher, "First, find Major Albrecht, Pieter Kritzinger and the others and request that they join me and Captain Theron for a War Council at the usual place. Once you've done that find Frans and take him to the English." To Theron he continued, "While we await an answer, let's go and sit in the sun and wait for the others. Have you been given any coffee this morning? No? Then we shall get some on the way."

Cronjé and Theron sat on little tripod trek stools, the morning sun warming their backs. Sitting in a circle with them were five other officers, including Heinrich du Toit, Pieter de Wet, Albrecht and the Cape rebel leader, Pieter Kritzinger. They constituted the hastily convened War Council, which had gathered on their usual terrace on the upper slopes of the ravine behind the laager, but the formalities had not yet started and the men sipped their coffee and chatted among themselves. Theron was at the centre of the discussion, which focused on the war effort outside their present battle. Below them, cattle and horses were being cautiously herded out of a series of large dongas down to the river for watering. The neighing and lowing mixed with the sonorous tone of the men's conversation. In contrast to the trees along the rim of the ravine, most of those within the valley had survived the onslaught of the English bombardment and in the morning sun they looked verdant and teemed with bird life.

"Now Dannie," Cronjé said by way of starting the formal business of the Council, "explain to us exactly how General de Wet plans to whisk four thousand men and one hundred and fifty women and children, and our causalities, through the English lines. Is he some sort of angel?"

"No, Oom, he is just a man, like you and me and our friends." His hand swept in an arc around the circle of burghers. "He is simply trying to do his best for his country and fellow citizens. He is of the belief that you and your commando would rather not be surrounded by the English army where you might be slowly strangled of your power to defend yourselves."

"You need not fear us surrendering, Dannie, as we have already explained to the English that we will never surrender while there is one breath within us." There was a brash pride in Cronjé's statement.

"But Oom, do you expect all our brave burghers to die *here*?"

"Dannie, you of all people understand that once the English took up arms against us, it is our individual promise to the Republic to fight, with a gun in one hand, our Bibles in the other and under the guiding hand of our Lord, to the death if necessary, to protect our rights to liberty and self-government."

He cast a paternal smile at Theron. Theron nodded in agreement.

"Oom, neither I nor General de Wet doubt the courage of our friends. Nor do we doubt their determination to drive the English from our land. We all know that God will deliver us from this evil, but God also helps those who help themselves." Theron hesitated. He looked Cronjé in the eye, trying not to be over-assertive but rather to show genuine concern. He continued in a softer tone. "Oom, may I enquire how we are helping our cause by trapping ourselves along this stretch of river. Are you not running out of food and water? The conditions must be very difficult for the women and children and the wounded. Would it not be best to make a break for it and fight another day in another place?"

Cronjé sat back on his stool and let out a deep sigh. He scanned the faces of the silent burghers around him and lifted his gaze over their heads to the land that he loved so much, the land he had already won back from the English once before, which he had defended against the Zulus and Xhosas and other native tribes. When he spoke there was a gruffness to his voice and a far-off look in his eye.

"Dannie," he paused to steady his voice. "Dannie, my friend, you are young and agile and have new ideas for fighting new wars. I am an old fool." There was much respectful disagreement among the listening burghers, but he raised a hand to hush them. "I have fought the English before and now I find myself fighting them again. This time they have set foot in our beloved Republics; this piece of land is already no longer free. What am I to do? Fall back yet again, and let them have more of our land? I have fallen back three times already, but then I was on their land and I was not giving them anything. Now it is different. This time if I fall back, I give them something that is ours, something that is part of all of us, something that is part of me."

The silence that followed was profound. The men all stared at the ground, at *their* land. They absorbed each pebble and grain of sand. Someone cleared his throat and looked up at Theron. It was du Toit.

"Neef Dannie, I understand General de Wet's concern, but the Khakis are like locusts. We have fallen back three times and still they come, and each time in greater numbers than the last. If we keep falling back, we will eventually be in Bloemfontein and then we will have a plague at the very gates of our city." The circle of men nodded emphatically. "Neef," du Toit continued, "does General de Wet really wish that we fall back even closer to his capital? He is a good Free Stater. Surely he would wish us to keep the English away from his city. He must see that where we are now is better than any other place between here and Bloemfontein?"

Theron did not respond. It was Cronjé who broke the silence.

"You are right, Dannie, when you say our God helps those who help themselves. He helped us find our Promised Land and *we* helped Him by protecting it from those who would take it from us. How many times have we done so?" Cronjé paused as though counting the many battles in his head. "Too many," he answered his own question. "So it cannot be right to retreat and offer up more of our land to the enemy. The English would have our land and we have to stop them in their tracks. That is our contribution and may God help us do so."

"I understand," replied Theron.

There was nothing more to be said. As if to emphasis Cronjé's melancholic mood, a shadow fell over him. The officers looked up as the frame of van Zyl loomed over Cronjé.

"Ah, Neef Frans, come and join us."

The circle opened and he sat on the earth in the space created.

"So tell us, what does the little general want? Has he agreed to an unconditional surrender?"

Van Zyl joined in the laughter and when it had subsided, answered, "No Oom, but he is being chivalrous."

"Oh?"

"Yes Oom. The English officer said that Field Marshal Roberts has just heard that there are women and children in the laager and he apologises for any distress that the bombardment has caused them."

"Well, that's very gracious of him. Tell him 'thank you' and suggest to him that if he stops bombing us entirely that would be very obliging of him, and I am sure our wives and children will visit him, to thank him, when he is our prisoner." More laughter followed.

Van Zyl smiled. "I shall tell him, Oom. But the main message was an offer of safe passage for our women and children so that they can be removed from our laager. 'Away from danger,' the officer said."

"Tell him, no!" snapped Cronje. He scowled. "Not only does the little bastard want our land, but now he also wants to take our women and children. Thank you, Neef Frans, there is nothing else to add. Just tell them no, but take your time in letting the messengers know; it is very pleasant sitting out here and I expect they will start today's bombardment as soon as they hear our response. Oh, and on your way can you ask someone to bring us more coffee? Mine has gone cold."

Burgher Johannes Petrus Coetzee

Burgher Johannes Petrus Coetzee dismounted the pony and ran an expert hand down its right rear leg. Marais, leading his own horse, watched as Coetzee skilfully assessed the animal's hindquarters.

"How is it?"

"Hmm, not so good," muttered Coetzee.

Marais looked on as the inspection continued. Things had moved quickly for him and Johannes since Dannie Theron had arrived. There had been a consensus within the War Council that the army would stay and await the reinforcements. However, Pieter Kritzinger had serious reservations, especially in respect of his small band of Cape rebels. He had not expressed them during the morning's Council, because he had not wished to cause a schism and he understood that the Transvaalers had to decide their own destiny, but he'd discussed the matter afterwards with his officers and Theron. His conclusion was that there was a real risk that Cronjé's force might be captured by the English. God forbid, but if it happened it would be very bad news for the Cape rebels. Theron had not been able to guarantee that reinforcements were on the way. Indeed, he had intimated that they were unlikely to arrive. Kritzinger had decided that the risk of capture was too great and that his commando stood a better chance of fighting another day if they made a dash for the kopje occupied by de Wet and joined up with him.

When word had got around the laager that the Cape rebels were leaving, a number of other burghers, mainly from the Free State, also resolved that they would be better off with de Wet. This included Piet de Wet. It had been agreed that he would lead about one hundred men out of the laager. These burghers were gathered in the depths of the ravine exercising their horses along the sandbanks to loosen their muscles after days of inactivity.

Although the ravine was deep and steep-sided, the midday sun blasted into its depths and the leaden air seemed to push down onto the burghers and their horses. Marais and Coetzee had finished working their horses and had moved into the shade of the sallow trees that hugged the slopes.

In the distance, the war went on. An hour after the rebuttal of the English offer of safe conduct for the women and children, which Hester Cronjé had heard about with delight, the bombardment had restarted. But down by the river, with the noise muffled by the steep banks and thick vegetation, it sounded part of a different world. In this more peaceful place there were even vervet monkeys scampering about the trees, excited by all the activity going on below them.

Marais had been lucky. He still had his own horse and it was still in reasonable condition. Coetzee's had been killed by shrapnel on the first day the laager came under fire. Like a number of burghers who wished to depart and who had lost their horses, he had faced the problem of acquiring a mount fit enough for the race to de Wet's hill. They had to beg and buy animals from those who were to remain, but were loath to give up their horses. They had already lost most of their possessions and their rifles and horses were the last things of value they owned. More importantly, giving up their horses meant giving up any hope of escaping themselves. Through hard bargaining, large offers of money and bullying, sufficient animals had been procured, but many were in poor condition. Coetzee scowled to himself. His was probably one of the worst.

Coetzee glanced across at Marais' mount enviously as it rested after its brief canter along the sandy riverbed. Although in better health than most, even Marais' horse had lost a lot of weight and he'd had to make an additional buckle hole in the straps to ensure the saddle sat securely on its back. Marais saw the envious glance and considered offering Coetzee his horse, but he came to the conclusion that Coetzee's lame pony would do better with a smaller, lighter rider. As it was, it had been decided that the slowest horses would ride at the front of the commando as it galloped towards de Wet. They would set the pace so that no one would be left behind. And Coetzee's lame pony would be riding at the front. Marais reckoned that if they swapped horses, and he rode on the lame horse, he would slow the pace to an unacceptable level.

"Good afternoon, Oom Fredrick."

"Hm, oh, good afternoon, Lettie. How are you?"

The girl threw him a delightful smile. How she reminded him of his eldest daughter.

"Very well thank you. I have come to say goodbye to you and Johan," she said with forced cheerfulness. Marais noted the unhappy edge to her voice.

Coetzee stood up from his inspection of the horse.

"Hello."

"Hello, Johan. Is everything ready?"

"Yes, except I have the lamest horse you can imagine. I doubt I'll get above a trot on the poor beast. I'll have to push it hard. We might make it to the kopje, but I don't think it'll survive. Hopefully, General de Wet does have extra horses for us."

"Climb on him and let's have a look."

Coetzee mounted and walked the horse around Alletta while she expertly assessed its gait.

"You are right. That horse will destroy itself galloping to the kopje. It is doubtful you will even make it. Wait!" she said, and turning on her heel she headed off in the direction from which she had come. Both men were bemused by her unexpected departure.

"Lovely girl," commented Marais. "She knows her mind."

"Yes, one day I would like to marry someone like her." Actually, he'd like to marry *her*, he thought.

"But you're not staying with her?"

"Oom Fredrick, I would love to, but you said it yourself, it is too chancy for us to stay. If we're caught here, there is only one outcome for us rebels. I may end up having a few more days with Lettie if I stayed, but I would rather spend my whole life with her, and the only chance of that happening is if I get away from here. When we have beaten the Khakis and the war is over, I shall come and find her. And if she will have me, we will be married."

"It is a shame she cannot come with us."

Coetzee remained silent. It was pointless discussing the matter further. Both men knew that would never happen. He could not expect Lettie to leave her family, especially under the present circumstances. The two of them had never even discussed the possibility. They both knew the answer. Coetzee half-heartedly inspected his frail horse, his mind now mulling over more important matters.

"Here she comes," said Marais.

Coetzee looked up. A puzzled expression crossed his face. Alletta was leading a large horse. Like the others, it was undernourished and its coat matted and dull, but compared to many it was an outstanding specimen. She stopped in front of Coetzee and with a determined look in her brown eyes announced, "This was my father's horse." Coetzee thought that was a strange statement because he knew that her father was still alive. "And now," the girl continued, "he is yours."

Coetzee was dumbstruck. He had never owned a horse of this quality. He stared at her.

"Here, take him" she insisted, holding the reins out to him.

"But your father …?"

"I told him. He is satisfied. It is better that one of our heroes has him and not some English dandy, don't you think?"

"Lettie, I don't know what to say."

"Don't say anything. Take it before my father changes his mind."

Coetzee took the reins. He wished he could hug her. He would give anything to be able to embrace her, but their conversation had already attracted attention and he could see that many were following it with more interest than he liked. To embrace her would bring shame on her and ruin her reputation. He looked sorrowfully at her.

"Lettie, I shall never forget this. You are the… the most wonderful girl I have ever met. I wish I had the words to describe how I feel for you, but I do not." His voice faded into a throat-catching whisper and a self-conscious silence hung between them. Then Coetzee reached into his coat pocket and took out his Bible.

"I have the perfect words," he declared, "from David himself, that killer of giants."

Taking her hand, he laid the Book in it and placed his other hand on top. Looking deeply into her eyes, he said, "Though I walk through the valley of death, I fear no evil for you are with me."

Coetzee threw a glance at Marais. The older man had kindly turned away to reduce his embarrassment, but Marais was thinking that although the sentiment was beautiful, he would make sure to tease Coetzee for quoting the very Psalm which the youth had chided him over when he'd confessed it was his favourite. Coetzee focused on the girl. She did not move a muscle.

"Lettie, I want you to take my Bible. When the war is over I shall come to you to take it back."

Alletta nodded dumbly. Then, with her free hand, she reached into the pocket of her dress and took out her own small Bible.

"Johan, you must take mine in return or you will have nothing to inspire you in the dark days ahead. When we are together again you can return it to me."

"Thank you Lettie, I will take it, but it will be my memories of you that will inspire me. The memory of your smile and your hair and…."

A cough from Marais brought Coetzee up short.

"Sorry to interrupt you two love birds, but we need to get ready. We will be leaving very soon."

Alletta blushed deeply, while Coetzee frowned at Marais. But he was right. Alletta helped him transfer his rifle, spare ammunition, bedding and other personal belongings to his new horse. Barely had they finished when the order was given to move out. Coetzee led his horse towards the river, with Alletta at his side. They walked in pensive silence. Alletta hitched her skirt up slightly as they crossed an area of wet sand and when his hand gently brushed hers it sent a tingling sensation through his stomach. With the next sweep of his hand he stopped it so that it rested against hers. She looked at him and gave him a tearful, tight-lipped smile. He felt the lump in his throat expand and returned a brief smile.

At the edge of the river, they waited for the other riders to take their horses across. Now that Coetzee had a better mount he would ride near the rear of the commando.

"Goodbye, Lettie. God be with you." He was staring at the ground, his eyes shaded by the rim of his hat.

"Goodbye, Johan. God go with you."

She looked around to see if anyone was watching. Everyone seemed to be focussing on the men already in the river. She ducked under his hat and planted a soft kiss on his youthful cheek. Coetzee raised his eyes to hers. Her brimming tears sparkled in the sunlight.

"I shall see you again one day, Johan, and I will look forward to that day with all my heart." She looked at him wistfully. Then she smiled. "Now you must *go*." She stepped back to emphasise her point. He blew her a kiss and walked forward into the river.

Coetzee kept looking back while he swam with his horse across the river, and as he mounted, and again, twisting in his saddle, as he rode across the sandy riverbank towards the donga that split the sandy cliff. At the entrance to the donga he stopped, turned the horse and stood up in his stirrups, waving his slouch hat high above his head as a last salute to her. Alletta responded from the opposite bank, jumping up and down and waving her arms. Coetzee replaced his hat, took one last deep look at the beautiful young girl, turned and drove his horse into the donga to catch up with the burghers ahead of him.

All along the slopes of the donga bearded men stood in their greatcoats and slouch hats. Some simply watched the riders go by, others called out messages of good luck, and a few stepped forward to give letters for loved ones to the departing riders.

At the head of the donga the riders gathered in a wide hollow to organise themselves. Marais was somewhere in the middle; Coetzee at the rear. Then the riflemen lining the donga let rip with a torrent of Mauser fire and the riders broke out of the donga in a tight group. De Wet dominated this part of the battlefield, so there were fewer enemy soldiers to ride through. Nevertheless, there were good numbers of Khakis between them and their goal. But the sudden appearance of the riders took them by surprise and the deadly fire laid down by the Afrikander marksmen forced them to keep their heads down.

The compact nature of the group of riders gave the Boer riflemen the maximum sweep of fire at the enemy without endangering their comrades, but Coetzee still lay low over his saddle. He had been sceptical of keeping the commando close together, but now he could see the reason for doing so, and another reason also became apparent. The English artillery had also been taken by surprise. There was a short delay before shells started whistling overhead, and in their haste to react to the fleeing Afrikanders, they had over-estimated the range. The shells exploded beyond the galloping riders. As the English missed their targets, Coetzee laughed loudly, whooping with excitement: not only was God on their side, but it seemed the very land itself was playing its part in confounding the invaders.

Coetzee looked ahead. Over the heads of the riders, partly obscured by the dust kicked up by the horses, he could see the largest of the Oskoppies quivering in the hot afternoon air. To the left of the kopje was their target, the stand of blue gum trees that marked Osfontein Farm. The trees danced in the shimmering heat haze. Coetzee could sense a feeling of elation building up within the riders. They knew General de Wet was waiting for them. In just a few more minutes they would reach the farm and win their freedom from the English. They had succeeded.

Lieutenant James Vipan Maitland Watermeyer

Lieutenant James Vipan Maitland Watermeyer stood on the outskirts of Osfontein Farm, studying the slopes of Kitchener's Hill. He held his field glasses in his free right hand; the other was secured to his chest with a sling that kept his wounded shoulder immobile. That was the deal he had struck with the doctor at the hospital in Jacobsdal, a Dr Conan Doyle. The deal had allowed him to escape from the wretched hospital. It had quickly become apparent to Watermeyer that he was more likely to die if he stayed in the hospital than if he returned to the field. It was not the doctors' fault. It was simply that they did not have enough medical supplies to treat the large number of casualties who had been delivered from the battlefield. God, he could not imagine how the medical staff endured the cries of pain and the stench. And the flies! He had never seen so many flies in one place in his life. He had been unable to bear it and had made his escape at the earliest opportunity. His respect for Dr Conan Doyle and the other staff had grown immensely in the short time he'd had to suffer the nightmare.

To his great distress, Watermeyer had not been able to return to the actual fighting. Instead, he was reduced to doing his bit as a dispatch rider, and while it was an important task, he was frustrated at missing out on the fun. Still, it was better than sitting around doing nothing.

Watermeyer dropped his field glasses to his chest. His injured shoulder ached, an irritating reminder of his last visit to Osfontein Farm. A chill ran down his spine as he remembered how the Boer commando had seemed to appear out of the very land itself. There was nothing left of the Kitchener's Horse except himself and one other; the rest had been taken prisoner. He had to admit that those Boers knew how to use the terrain and their horses to maximum effect. He grinned respectfully.

As he looked at the slopes, he absent-mindedly patted the neck of his horse. Now that he relied on her to do his job, he made sure she was always at his side. As before, there was little evidence of the enemy on Kitchener's Hill; just the noise of their Mausers and the 'pom-pom' of their Maxim-Nordenfelt. Of the Imperial forces, he could see many khaki figures darting from rock to rock and crawling through the vegetation as they made slow progress up the hill. At least they had also learned to make the most of the terrain and had stopped presenting themselves as easy targets to the damned Boer sharpshooters. He wondered how the Boers endured the heat. It would have been like an oven on the top of the hill. They had been up there for two days now and not once had they come down for water. They must have evolved to suit this God-forsaken country. That chap Darwin should have done a study on them.

Then, above the sound of the battle to retake the hill, a new sound encroached on his senses. His scalp crawled uncomfortably. He looked to his left, in the direction from where the Boers had come last time, but all appeared to be calm. The few mounted infantrymen who had been sent forward to secure the farm before the main body of the British army arrived were dozing under trees and in the shade of farm buildings. Their horses were resting under the blue gum trees that surrounded the farm house, grazing nonchalantly on their oats. The noise was becoming clearer and it sounded like galloping horses.

Watermeyer felt a terrible sense of *déjà vu*. He snapped his glasses up to his eyes and swept the area east of the farm anxiously. There was nobody there, but he had broken out in a cold sweat, and he could feel a cold trickle running down his side. Then one or two of the horses suddenly looked up in the direction of the river. He ducked under the neck of his own horse and followed their gaze. Watermeyer smiled at his over-reaction. The previous Boer attack had obviously made him more jumpy than he realised. Through the heat haze approached a shimmering body of horsemen. They were not charging, but coming at a rapid canter. It was the expected reinforcements to help secure Osfontein Farm.

He raised his hat and waved it in salutation, but the riders did not respond. Why should they? As he watched them, he thought that he would have a word with the senior officer about the best way to deploy his men, not just to hold the farm, but to prevent the Boers from escaping from Kitchener's Hill. Watermeyer was concerned about the possibility of this happening for, as far as he was aware, the British attack was focused on only three sides of the hill. It was his view that some of the reinforcements should be placed on the fourth slope to close the Boers' escape route. It seemed an obvious oversight and he could not understand why it had not already been done. As he turned to mount his horse, a few shots rang out and bullets whistled across the farmyard. Watermeyer jumped in shock. The sound was unmistakably that of a Mauser!

Tense and alert to danger, he urgently scanned the landscape around him. He swiftly sought the source of the shooting. But the only troops visible were those already heading his way. Surely not! He whipped up his field glasses as the compact group of riders started to spread out, forming an extended line. The manoeuvre was provocative rather than friendly. He stared in horror as the riders emerging from behind their comrades swung their rifles from their shoulders. Through the haze and dust the riders became more discernible; the slouch hats, the stocky ponies, the bearded faces and their dishevelled appearance. Alarm rose inside him as he saw the horses spurred into a full gallop. The Boers tore towards the farm, firing as they came.

"Sweet Jesus, Boers," he swore to himself.

Leaping on to his horse, he screamed at the top of his voice "Boers!"

Hampered by his injury, he was unable to control his skittish horse, which had absorbed his sense of urgency, as well as keep an eye on the enemy and also unshoulder his carbine. He tried for a few seconds but it was useless. The enemy were virtually upon them. The British troops had been taken completely by surprise and were rushing around in chaos. Men were running for their horses and snatching up their rifles. Even though the enemy were riding at full gallop, their shooting was appallingly accurate. Several men and horses fell under the onslaught.

Shit, thought Watermeyer. He was furious. He could not believe he was in the same position as two days ago. Indeed, this time it was worse because the Boers were between him and the larger part of the British army. How the hell were they able to attack the farm from the direction of the river? It was unbelievable. The British generals should all be taken out and shot.

Again, his options were limited: be killed, captured or try to escape! This was no time for heroics. He snatched at the reins with his good arm and plunged his heels into his horse's flanks. He drove the animal into a gallop towards Kitchener's Hill. There was no opportunity to stop and look back this time because he knew that in escaping the Boers who were attacking Osfontein Farm he was galloping into the range of the Boers on the hill. He had to keep going until he reached the shelter of the rocks and shrubs on the lower slopes of the hill. But he did twist around in his saddle to see if any of his comrades had managed to escape. He saw various dust trails dashing way from the farm, some following him. But others had not been fast enough and they were already being rounded up by the jubilant Boers. Watermeyer decided to concentrate on reaching his own destination. Even if he lived for a thousand years, he did not wish to visit, see or even hear mention of that blasted farm again.

Wednesday 21 February 1900

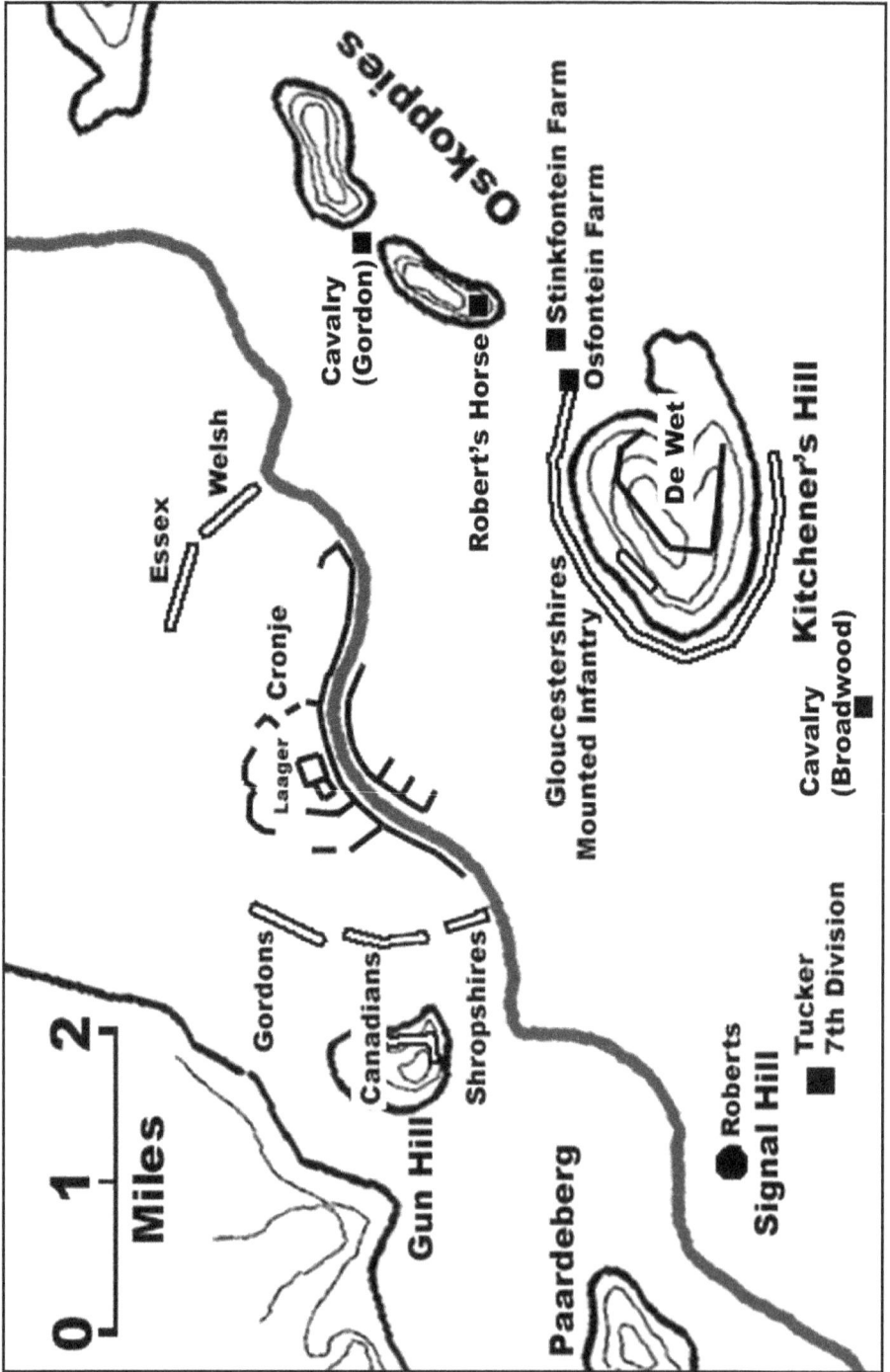

Map 16: Morning of 21 February 1900

Burgher Fredrick Abram Marais

Burgher Fredrick Abram Marais was wet and cold and his muscles were stiff from lying for hours on the hard, rocky summit of Kitchener's Hill. Nevertheless, his head dipped and bobbed as he drifted between dozing and waking. Marais started awake for the umpteenth time and stared through the inky blackness. Somewhere in that darkness were the English troops who had occupied the western rim of the kopje the previous evening. As a result of the success of the English attack, he and the others who had escaped from the laager yesterday afternoon had been called up from the relative comfort of Osfontein Farm to help reinforce the Boers' position on the kopje.

The discomfort of the burghers had been exacerbated by a dramatic storm that had burst over their heads during the night. The clouds had been so low that it had felt as though the thunder was actually inside Marais' head. The flashes of lightning that had lit up the landscape had revealed the pathetic shapes of men huddled under what inadequate protection they could muster. Marais had brought a ground-sheet from the laager, but in its perished state it had soon been torn asunder by the stormy winds and had offered little cover from the driving rain.

General de Wet was determined that the English would not take another inch of the kopje. He had brought every burgher at his disposal onto the kopje and had carefully placed them to counter any attempt by the English to drive them from it. The General's orders had been clear. No man was to move from the position he had been allocated and to abandon his post was to invite a good thrashing with the General's shambok. He had a reputation for using it to whip undisciplined burghers into shape and no one doubted the determination with which he would use it under the present circumstances. So, while Marais had heard much grumbling from those around him, no one had abandoned his post.

He was relieved to see the first lightening of the sky. Soon the sun would be up and he would get some relief from the cold which had penetrated to his very bones. With the improving light an eddying mist rose from the rain-soaked plateau of the kopje. An officer made

303

his way stealthily along the line of burghers, shaking them to make sure they were awake and whispering for them to be alert as movement had been heard from the English positions. Marais stretched his arms and legs to loosen his stiffened muscles. He shivered as the movement brought his limbs into contact with different parts of his cold, soaked clothes.

During the tense, uncomfortable night there had been no talking among the men and now Marais looked at the man lying next to him. He did not recognise him.

"Hey," he whispered in greeting, stiffly reaching out with his hand, "Marais, Fredrick Marais, from Langkloof in the Cape."

"Morning, Fredrick. Field Coronet Speller, from Wepener in the Free State," his neighbour whispered in return, taking Marais' hand. He added sourly, "Not that it's free anymore."

"What happened yesterday? It looked like things were going well from where we were at the farm."

"They were until just before nightfall. Then the English made a concentrated attack on our centre. Unfortunately, most of our soldiers and our more experienced officers were looking after our flanks, making sure we did not become surrounded, so we were unable to hold off the attack when it came. That is going to be our biggest problem from now on, the huge superiority in numbers the English have over us. We are too few to be everywhere that the English show up. So the burghers had to fall back to this ridge. At least we still have the advantage of looking down on them. If we are lucky, we may be able to repeat the victory we had at Spion Kop. What a great victory that was! God was with us that day."

"If the English have learnt anything about us, they will know never to get themselves into a similar situation again."

"Then let us hope they do not learn, hey? And judging by the way they attacked you last Sunday, they do not learn very quickly."

"No, they do not seem to," Marais agreed.

"It amazes me how they have come to own so much of the world when they use such primitive military tactics."

"That is because they have not had to fight a modern army in the other places they have invaded. They have only had to face savages with spears and leather shields."

"Well, this time they have bitten off more than they can chew. They had better learn quickly or their defeat, and a defeat it will be, is going to be very costly."

The two men fell silent. They watched for any signs of movement from the enemy positions, staring into the cold, swirling mist that was now tinged with red hues from the first rays of the sun that would soon rise behind them. It was Marais who broke the silence.

"I hear one of our officers surrendered."

"Huh?"

"General Spruit? I hear he surrendered to the English."

"Who told you that!" The harsh whispered response was a demand rather than a question.

"No one in particular. It seemed to be the talk of the burghers when we arrived last night."

"Rumours and lies!" Speller spat out.

"Oh?"

"You shouldn't listen to what those idiots from the Johannesburg Commando say."

"I'm not sure it was them who said it."

"I bet it was. Those town burghers have no respect of us Boers."

"So, he did not surrender?"

"Of course not. He would never do such a thing."

"He is still with us on the kopje, then?"

"No."

Marais could sense Speller was growing irritated, but he was intrigued and so he persisted with his questioning.

"He is not with us? Did he go home?"

Speller looked at Marais as though he had just materialised spontaneously out of thin air.

"Man, you really are dumb! I thought you Cape guys were supposed to be smart! Why would he go home?"

Marais shrugged his shoulders. He decided not to carry on. The conversation was going nowhere and Speller did not seem to want to talk about it. He took up his Mauser and stared down the barrel again. After a short silence, Speller whispered acerbically, "It was that idiot Meyer's fault."

"Meyer?" Marais repeated, trying not to show too much interest.

"He was the field coronet in charge of defending the centre of our lines, but the pressure got too great and, just as night fell, he had to fall back to where we are now. I have no quarrel with him for falling back; sometimes that is the right thing to do. But he did not inform General Spruit, and the General, hearing cheering from the position Meyer had just abandoned, assumed it was his own men. He walked over to see what was going on. Of course the next thing we hear is 'Hands up, Boer' and the General was captured. There was even greater cheering when the English realised they had caught themselves a general. Boy, did they make a big song and dance about it?" Speller finished sourly.

"That was bad luck, hey?"

Speller did not reply. He glared at the mist that hid the English from him. Suddenly, he raised his finger to his lips and cocked his head to listen intently. Marais followed suit. Through the red mist and faint dawn light, muffled noises of movement could be heard and then a half-whispered command to 'Fall in'. The two men checked their rifles were cocked and ready and dipped their heads down to their rifle sights. On either side of them the action was repeated down the line of waiting burghers. The dull clatter of rifle mechanisms was followed by a silence that pressed down on them as though the mist was made of lead.

The entire commando seemed to be holding its breath. Everyone was straining to hear the faintest sound from the enemy facing them. Marais stared down the barrel of his rifle until the landscape started to jump about in front of his eyes. He looked up briefly, blinking his eyes to relax them. The mist was thinning now and the rising sun was bringing more light onto the hilltop. Suddenly, Speller leapt up.

"The bloody cowards!" he yelled. "The bloody cowards! They have abandoned the hill!"

"Get down, you fool," someone shouted. "Do you want to get yourself killed!"

But Speller strode forward across the brightening landscape with the confidence of someone about to enter a boxing match he knew he could not lose. He reached the edge of the kopje's summit and glared down its slopes. Lifting his rifle, he started to shoot at the retreating English soldiers. He wounded two before they became more cautious about using the rocks and vegetation to cover their retreat. The entire edge of the summit was soon lined with Mausers snapping angrily at the now rapidly withdrawing English. Speller was one of the last to cease fire and lower his rifle. Marais was standing next to him.

"It seems they did learn from Spion Kop after all."

"Worst luck," grumbled Speller.

He raised his rifle and took one last shot at a straggler. The soldier leapt in fright as the bullet smacked into a rock next to him and he dashed forward to join his mates. The burghers jeered at him and then started to cheer as it sunk in that they had won back their kopje.

"Now it is our turn to cheer, hey?" Marais smiled at Speller.

Speller looked at him. "Yes," he replied. "Now it is our turn." And he leant over the crest of the kopje, raised his rifle above his head and snarled at the retreating figures below.

Marais looked across at the remnants of the laager on the far side of the river. If only Cronjé would make his move, then they could leave this hill. It would be a disaster if, having escaped from one besieged position he was to end up in another. And General de Wet's situation was precarious. There was only one slope still open as an escape route. With the number of English soldiers increasing by the hour, it was not a good position to be in.

General Christiaan Rudolf de Wet

General Christiaan Rudolf de Wet looked grimly in the direction of the cheering. While he had been led to believe the English had been driven off the kopje, in the early morning light he could not ascertain the cause of the hullabaloo, and the last time there had been such a commotion he had lost a very capable general. Of course he still needed to know what was going on so he dispatched Field Coronet Meyer and some men to see what all the noise was about. As he did so he noticed Captain Theron approaching.

"Hello Dannie," he greeted Theron cheerfully.

"Good morning, Oom," came a weary reply.

"Come, it sounds like you need some strong coffee."

"Yes, that would be good."

The men walked together towards a small fire over which hung a steaming coffee pot. Soon they were cradling mugs of piping hot coffee to warm their hands. As they sat down, Field Coronet Meyer returned to give his report.

"Yes, Neef Meyer?" de Wet enquired.

"Oom, the English *have* abandoned the position they took last night and it has been re-occupied by Field Coronet Speller."

"Very good," de Wet said. "And our ammunition? How much do we have left?"

"We have plenty of bullets, Oom, but only a few shells for the Krupp and only five belts for the Pom-Pom."

"Hmmm, that's not good. Tell the gunners to hold their fire until they are sure of hitting their targets. Once their ammunition is exhausted they are to withdraw and fall back to Poplar Grove. Also, make sure everyone has their horses ready. We may all need to make a very quick exit."

"Yes, Oom." Meyer strode off to pass on the orders.

"So, Dannie, how is General Cronjé? When is he planning to escape from his laager? The burghers who came out yesterday said he was not going to, but I assume you were able to convince him otherwise."

Theron stared into his coffee and took a cautious sip of the boiling liquid.

"No, Oom, I did not manage to convince him."

"The stubborn old fool," de Wet said sharply. "Does he not understand his situation? Even if the entire armies of the two Republics were here, we would not be able to defeat the English – not from these positions. He needs to evacuate and we need to fall back to Poplar Grove. Once there, we can set up a proper defence of the Republic and make sure Roberts doesn't try any more of his fancy tricks. Does Cronjé not understand?"

Theron avoided the question. "General Cronjé is determined not to give up another inch of land to the English. He has decided that the river is where he is going to make his stand to stop the invasion."

"Let us hope it is not his last stand, hey, as happened to another famous general not so long ago."

Theron looked at de Wet. He hoped the outcome for Cronjé would be different from that for General Custer. "The burghers are with him on this also. They are adamant that the English are not allowed to advance any farther."

"But most of them are Transvaalers. Surely, it is for us Free Staters to decide how best to defend our country. If we get it wrong here in the Free State, then they will really have something to worry about because the next stop will be the Transvaal!"

The two men fell silent. It was no use developing that line of argument further. It was a dead end. It was Theron who eventually broke the silence.

"As well as their concerns about losing more territory, the burghers do not want not leave their wives and children to the English. Even if they had wished to leave, many did not believe that we had enough horses with us to allow them all to ride away. Many of their horses and draught animals have been killed. Those who escaped yesterday were given some of the best horses that were left and even they were a sorry bunch of animals."

"What about the burghers who escaped yesterday? Do they not care that the English might take more of our country?" De Wet had already spoken about this to his brother but he was keen to hear Theron's view as well.

"They care more, Oom. They are mainly Cape rebels, so they are very determined that the English lose this war. If the English are victorious, then their futures are perilous. No, their decision to leave the laager was a pragmatic one. Even if the rebels believed the General would win, it cannot be a certainty, so it was better for them to escape, just in case."

De Wet nodded slowly. The logic of the argument was undeniable.

"And I have more use for them here than General Cronjé does. I need every last one of them to defend this kopje. It is the most strategic position on the battlefield and the English are desperate to take it back. See, they are sending even more troops to do so."

The two men watched the block of dark khaki uniforms that was approaching from the direction of the river. They could also make out another dust cloud heading in their direction, this time from Paardeberg Drift itself. Closer inspection revealed it to be mounted cavalry. That was not good. At that precise moment the first English shell exploded on the summit of the kopje.

"Here we go again," de Wet said. "Dannie, go and find yourself something to eat while I take care of this situation." Then, more to himself than to Theron, he added, "If we are driven off this kopje, we shall regroup on the kopje on the other side of Stinkfontein Farm."

Brigadier General Robert George Broadwood

Brigadier General Robert George Broadwood trotted, in the late morning sunshine, with his cavalry towards Kitchener's Hill. At last, he thought, an opportunity to be involved in the fun again. Since the exuberant charge up the valley towards Kimberley, the war had turned out to be something of a disappointment for the cavalry and for the last two days he and the rest of French's Division had been shunted off on some sideshow, chasing after the non-existent reinforcements that were supposed to be relieving Cronjé. Had it not been the cavalry that had brought Cronjé to book? It was insufferable that the infantry had been allowed to take the glory of battle when the cavalry rightfully deserved that reward. He had heard all the arguments about the horses being exhausted and that there was the threat of mounted Boer reinforcements arriving to support the besieged Cronjé, but he had remained unconvinced.

There had been no hint of any reinforcements coming from the direction of the Koodoosrand Hills, where French's Division had spent their time patrolling. Indeed, when the Boers had arrived, it had been a triflingly small commando and they had simply strolled past the infantry and disowned them of the most strategic hill of the battlefield. This whole affair at Paardeberg could have been concluded in short order if the cavalry had been allowed to charge *en masse* over the Boer trenches and into their midst. Such an action would have resulted in a quick surrender and the slaughter of Bloody Sunday would have been averted. The tactics that had been used on that day had been a surprise to General French. The General had blamed Kitchener, which did not surprise Broadwood, as he sensed some ill-feeling between the two men.

Broadwood shrugged his shoulders. What did he care for the infighting between the prima donnas of the senior ranks? As long as their wrangling did not place his men in unnecessary danger and he was allowed to get on with his job. And at last he had been given orders that would allow him to do so. But Broadwood ground his teeth in annoyance over the fact that the order had taken so long to arrive from Field Marshal Roberts. It had apparently been issued on Monday night but had not been delivered to General French until

Tuesday evening. French had been hopping mad at the delay. He had discussed the order with Broadwood and Brigadier General J.R.P. Gordon. In essence, it was to prevent the escape of General de Wet from Kitchener's Hill and the tactics agreed between them were to ensnare de Wet in a pincer movement.

Gordon and his Lancers had forded the Modder at Koodoosrand Drift and had hidden themselves in the smaller hills of the Oskoppies. Broadwood had taken a sweeping loop around the north of the battlefield and had crossed the Modder at Paardeberg Drift. The looping march had meant a further frustrating delay, but he was now approaching Kitchener's Hill. Ultimately, he was to place himself across de Wet's escape route, but care was required because, as he knew only too well, the Boers did not like their escape routes being closed. As soon as de Wet realised that he was in danger of encirclement, he would be off. The manoeuvre would need to be subtle. Broadwood continued to make it look as though he was going to reinforce the main infantry units attacking the hill. At the last moment he would swing around the hill and close the trap. If de Wet did manage to fall back before Broadwood was in place, the plan was for Broadwood to corral him towards Gordon's force hidden in the Oskoppies. And then they would have him.

General Christiaan Rudolf de Wet

General Christiaan Rudolf de Wet scanned his field glasses across the landscape; the farms in the distance were now heavily occupied by English troops. They had been quick to retake Osfontein Farm, this time in large numbers, after de Wet had ordered the Cape rebels to abandon it and help defend the kopje.

"They do learn eventually," he grunted to himself.

Should he need to abandon the main Oskoppie, he would now have to give the farms a wide berth so as not to warn the English of his intention to occupy the next kopje in the range. He was sure the English would race him for it.

He looked back towards the cavalry. He could see that it was moving to support the attack on his left flank. Shells were coming in thick and fast now and de Wet dropped down between some rocks for extra cover. Doing so meant that his view of the left flank was obscured by the intervening terrain. He watched the English at Osfontein Farm as they fell in and started to march forward. He presumed they would reinforce the attack on his right flank.

Above the storm of exploding shells, he heard his name being called. He stood up so the person could see him.

"Over here!"

Meyer came over and jumped down beside him, making the most of the safety provided by the rocks.

"Oom, we have run out of ammunition for the Krupp and the Maxim and have had to withdraw the guns. The pressure on our flanks is now pretty bad."

Another burgher suddenly dropped down beside them and Meyer nearly jumped out of his skin. He cursed the burgher vehemently, but the man ignored him. It was one of the lookouts de Wet had posted to watch for any encircling movements by the English that would threaten their escape route. There was urgency in his voice.

"Oom, the cavalry that came in from Paardeberg Drift has not joined the main attack on our flank but is sneaking around to our rear. If we remain here a minute longer, General, we shall be surrounded."

De Wet noted the formal use of his rank and the strain in the man's voice. He threw a quick glance at the other kopje through his field glasses.

"OK, let's go. Meyer, spread the word on this side of the kopje that everyone is to evacuate, and," he pointed at the burgher, "you tell everyone on the other flank it is time to leave. I shall meet you at the horses. Be quick. We have no time to lose."

Shouting orders as he went, de Wet made his way to the horses and started to organise the withdrawal. "Come, come," he urgently chastised those who did not seem to sense the need to hurry. A youth ran towards de Wet.

"Oom, do you know where Fredrick Marais is?"

"Who?"

"Fredrick Marais," Coetzee repeated. "He is a Cape rebel, one of the men who escaped from the laager yesterday."

"Ah, some were sent to support Field Coronet Speller. He may be there. Speller is in the centre. I have sent Field Coronet Meyer to tell him to fall back. He should be with us soon. In fact, there's Meyer now. Have a word with him."

De Wet pointed out Meyer who was slithering down the steep incline of the depression in which the horses were corralled. Several burghers hurried down the slope after Meyer, but Coetzee did not recognise any of them. He dashed across to Meyer.

"Where is Fredrick Marais?" he yelled above the clamour of shouts and shells and the commotion of the retreat.

"Who?"

Coetzee hesitated. Damn, he could not remember the name of the officer de Wet had mentioned. "Scheller?" he blurted. "Where is Field Coronet Scheller?"

"Scheller? Ah, you mean Speller! I don't know?"

"I thought General de Wet told you to tell him to retreat?"

"No, not me. I was told to warn the right flank. Someone else was sent to the left flank."

"But they are in the centre, not on the flanks."

Meyer looked at him blankly and then shrugged his shoulders. "Then they must still be there."

"We have to go back and tell them to evacuate."

"Are you mad?" Meyer swept his arms around to indicate the tumult around them. "When they leave, I am leaving," he shouted to make sure Coetzee had heard. "Anyway, Speller is no fool. He will surrender when the Khakis get too close, so there is no need to worry about him."

Coetzee threw Meyer a disgusted look and then rapidly scanned the jostling crowd of faces around him. Eventually, he located de Wet, who was already mounted and ready to head out. He hurled himself towards him, grabbing his horse's bridle to calm it as he caught de Wet's attention.

"Oom," he yelled, "Field Coronet Speller has not been told of the retreat."

"What?" de Wet bellowed in disbelief.

Coetzee misunderstood the reaction and started to repeat himself.

"I heard you, Neef," de Wet interrupted loudly. "Then you had better go and tell them. Where is your rifle?"

"With my horse."

De Wet gave the youth a disapproving look and then lifted his own rifle from its saddle holster and handed it to him. "I want it back when you return," he ordered.

"Yes sir."

Coetzee took the rifle and hurtled through the disordered commando, pushing and shoving his way through the horses, unseating at least one rider in the process. He scampered up the steep-sided depression and into an inferno of exploding shells, smoke and lyddite fumes, which choked and smothered him, but at least they hid him from the enemy. Suddenly, he broke out into bright sunshine and in front of him were fifteen men being hard-pressed by an advancing English force.

"Retreat! Retreat!" Coetzee yelled as loud as he could with his fume-filled lungs. But the burghers remained where they were. Coetzee ducked low and dashed forward, throwing himself against the crude stone wall that was the Boer's main defence.

"We are retreating," he screamed at the man next to him.

"Really. And how do you suppose we do that with the damned Khakis ready to stick their bayonets up our arses the minute we turn around? You are too late, son. We'll be surrendering once we've killed a few more of the bastards."

Coetzee looked desperately along the column of men and spotted Marais farther down the line. Thank the Lord, he thought. Crouching low behind the wall, he raced towards Marais as bullets whizzed over his head and ricocheted off the stones beside him.

"Oom, Oom!"

Marais looked around in surprise. "Johan? What the hell are you doing here?"

"We are retreating. You must come."

"What? And get myself shot in the back? I don't think so."

"But they will hang you!"

"And now they will hang you also."

The burgher next to them lowered his rifle.

"I hate to interrupt," he snarled sarcastically, "but either leave or stay. If you stay, stop talking and shoot as many English bastards as possible before we have to surrender. But if you want my opinion, friend, as you are a Cape rebel, I would take this boy's advice and get the hell out of here." He glanced over the wall. "I would say you have five minutes before we surrender." The burgher turned away to resume his shooting.

Before Marais could think, Coetzee had grabbed his sleeve and pulled him bodily away from the wall. And then they were running, running for their lives, back into the cover of the yellow-green fumes. Coetzee dragged Marais along with youthful anxiety. They reached the rim of the hollow where the sudden change in the gradient caught Marais by surprise. He tumbled head first down the slope, ending up in a heap at the feet of the Meyer's horse. Coetzee was right behind him. As he dashed past, Coetzee grabbed Marais' shirt again, ripping it as he pulled him up and towards their tethered horses. As they scrambled into their saddles, de Wet rode up to them. He caught the rifle that Coetzee tossed to him and gave Coetzee an enquiring look.

"The Khakis have captured them," Coetzee shouted, "We need to ride and bloody quickly."

They spurred the mounts into a gallop across the hollow and into the mouth of the shallow valley that ran down the side of the kopje, down which the commando was already swarming.

The men poured out of the valley at the foot of the kopje, but immediately slowed at the sight before them. Their route had brought them onto the veldt just one thousand yards from the regiment of khakis marching from Osfontein Farm to join the attack on Kitchener's Hill. Both sides were taken aback by the sudden appearance of their enemy, but it was the more disciplined English soldiers who reacted first. In unison, they fell to one knee and opened fire. The Boers, caught in the open, milled about in panic. The whistle of deadly bullets was intermingled with shouts and screams of anger, confusion and pain rising from the Afrikanders.

De Wet fought his way through the tightly packed horses towards the front of the commando. The confusion was close to panic as horses and men pushed and shoved to evade the hot metal bullets that were biting into their flesh. De Wet saw several burghers thrown from their mounts as their horses reared in terror and a number of burghers simply dropped to the ground, fatally hit. De Wet dragged his horse's head hard right and spurred her on, yelling for his men to follow. In seconds, the Khakis were left behind, their last shots fired in frustration at their rapidly retiring enemy. Galloping across the veldt, throwing up a cloud of dust in their wake, the commando rode in a wide arc around the enemy-held Osfontein Farm.

De Wet took care to avoid Stinkfontein Farm, even though it looked deserted. He guided his commando towards the bulk of the Oskoppie that towered beyond the farm. De Wet knew the kopje was long and narrow in shape. His could see the southern rounded snout of the kopje and the curve of its slopes sweeping off to the right. The snout was closest so this was where he would attempt his ascent. As he approached the kopje he studied the slopes to gauge the best route for getting his mounted commando to the top as quickly as possible. Selecting a promising-looking route, he spurred his horse towards it. As he got within a thousand yards of the kopje, the sound of Lee-Enfields suddenly burst from its lower slopes. The air whined with bullets as though he had disturbed a swarm of invisible hornets.

"The English have already taken the kopje," he yelled back to the uneasy throng of men behind him. "Fall back!"

Blast! De Wet thought quickly about what was the next best thing to do. He considered whether to take the next kopje or to attack the English on this one? As his men wheeled their horses to the right and started to gallop away, de Wet decided to attempt to take the northern end of the kopje. From there he could attack the English from their

317

rear and drive them off it. The commando, however, had assumed that de Wet's order was to withdraw from the battlefield. He was now towards the rear of his commando and he drove his horse along the left flank of it bellowing at them to slow down. Half way along the body of galloping riders he decided he could wait no longer. Screaming, "This way! This way!" at the top of his voice he veered off to his left in an arc towards the northern end of the kopje. Those near him followed suit, as did a few in front of him. But those leading the way had no idea what was happening behind them and carried on riding ignorant of the change in direction

De Wet slowed to a canter and stood up in his saddle as he rode, waving his hat and yelling as he went. The men with him did likewise. Slowly the riders who had rode on realised what was happening and started to turn their horses, but it was a disorganised affair and the commando was well strung out before the last rider swung his horse around. Keeping to a steady canter to allow his commando to regroup, de Wet rode parallel to the kopje, looking for another convenient route up its slopes.

Then he noticed a cloud of dust rising from behind the far shoulder of the kopje. He realised immediately that it was not dust caused by infantry. It was moving too fast. It could only be another unit of mounted infantry. Why were they there? It could not be to occupy the kopje as they could have done that from the far side. Maybe they were being sent to secure the third kopje? It was possible. Whatever their objective, their presence made it an imperative that the burghers climbed the kopje as quickly as possible. He spurred his horse on, moved closer to the kopje and scoured its slopes for an obvious and rapid route up. He still kept an eye on the dust cloud to see if it stopped. That would indicate that the enemy intended to ascend the kopje too. But it kept rolling forward.

Suddenly, the source of the dust cloud broke from behind the kopje and charged across the veldt straight towards de Wet and his commando. The kopje was not the target after all. The target was de Wet himself!

Cursing fervently, de Wet wheeled his horse hard to the right and drove her away from the kopje and the charging horsemen. The men followed his lead, some peeling off at intervals to shoot at the English and discourage them from continuing the chase. Shells started to whistle over the heads of the commando, raising columns of dust. With the commando riding directly from the kopje and the English charging at them from its northern tip, the enemy was approaching them at a tangent. De Wet watched them over his left shoulder and noted that an increasing number of the English horsemen were falling back. Their horses were in poor condition, thought de Wet, and unable to maintain the pace of the charge. He was confident he could outrun the English, but to make sure he veered his commando to the right so that he was riding directly away from them. Then the burgher next to him pointed ahead and to the right.

"More English!" he shouted.

De Wet stared at this second cloud of dust as it streamed across the veldt. It was still some distance off, but it was following a trajectory that cut across his current course. Right, thought de Wet, there could be no more messing about. He turned his horse a quarter left and galloped as hard as he could from the battlefield and towards Poplar Grove. For the time being, Cronjé would have to fend for himself.

Thursday 22 February 1900

Doctor Arthur Ignatius Conan Doyle

Doctor Arthur Ignatius Conan Doyle had overslept and now walked briskly down the dirt road towards Jacobsdal Hospital. The previous night the senior military surgeon had eventually ordered him to leave the building. It had been well after midnight. He had trudged back to his hotel like a sleepwalker, physically exhausted. Yet the horrors of what he had seen at the hospital had continued to play on his mind; the ghastly images had burned themselves into his subconscious and he knew they would haunt him for the rest of his life. On reaching his room he had collapsed onto his mattress with only a derisory attempt at changing for bed. Except for a soporific awareness of an almighty thunderstorm sometime during the night, he had slept like a baby.

He had woken late and with a start, feeling groggy and thick-headed, as though he had been asleep for only ten minutes, he had dragged himself from the comfort of his cot. But now washed, refreshed and furbished with a delicious breakfast of bacon, eggs and sausages, he walked smartly towards the hospital.

The low building squatted under its roof of green-painted corrugated iron, its white walls visible through the parade of scaly-barked blue gum trees that lined the road. The windows, which had been closed during the night against the cold, were now thrown open to allow the stench of death, decay and filth to escape, but also in anticipation of the heat that would soon turn the building into an oven. To distract himself from the distressing scenes that would greet him on his arrival at the hospital, he took a particular interest in observing the small things that were happening around him.

It was a glorious morning. The smell of eucalyptus hung heavily in the air and turtledoves called from the gum trees. Their "coo-coor-ruk" calls were rhythmical and beguiling. The cooing echoed in his mind, slowly forming a chorus line to a song. He shook his head to clear the sound and to think of something else, but the repeated refrain "How're your soldiers? How're your soldiers?" kept playing on his mind. He stared down the wet dirt road and remembered being stirred by the thunderous storm during the night. The air felt washed and fresh, and dust free, but a fine mud stuck to his boots, like a dirty orthopaedic cast. He noted the thin veil of vapour rising from the dirt as it evaporated in the mid-morning heat and watched it swirl around his ankles.

The white sun was well up in the sky and Conan Doyle adjusted his cap to shade his eyes. The temperature seemed to be increasing by the minute and he was regretting his decision to don his heavy coat, but he consoled himself with the thought that he would need it later. It would be another long day at the hospital and he would not leave until well into the night. The walk back to his hotel would be cold.

As he approached the hospital he noticed a large group of men lounging on the adjacent grassless square. The men were sullen and silent. Steam rose from their scruffy, tattered clothes. They had obviously spent the night in the open. Blue gums had been planted in the square and many of the men reclined in their shade, slouch hats covering their faces. Walking among them or standing on the perimeter of the shambolic group were khaki-clad guards. Their rifles held limply in their arms or across their chests. Conan Doyle spied a small, tidy sergeant engaged in conversation with a young, lanky corporal. They were standing in the shade of a large blue gum. He walked across to them and they broke off their tête-à-tête as he approached. The sergeant watched him with a stern face and the youthful corporal's features broke into a friendly, toothy grin.

"Where did you find these raggedy fellows?" Conan Doyle enquired of the sergeant.

"Those over there," the sergeant pointed vaguely at a collection of shabby figures a short distance away, "were captured by the Shropshire Regiment yesterday evening. As our guns fell silent, some of the Shropshires took advantage of the fact that the Boers probably thought we were going home for the night. They were close to the Boer positions and burst out of their donga, stormed across veld and leapt into the Boers' trench."

"Took the beggars completely by surprise," the corporal interjected with a chuckle. "They gave up without firing a shot."

"Those," the sergeant indicated the fifteen men closest to them, "were taken by the Gloucestershires when they recaptured Kitchener's Hill. The Boers gave the Gloucestershires a rough time. Many of the poor devils have ended up in there," he inclined his head sharply towards the hospital, "but as soon as the Gloucestershires got close, the Boers simply threw down their rifles and surrendered."

The corporal took up the narrative sourly. "They do that you know. Shoot the blazes out of us, but as soon as we get within bayonetting distance, they throw down their rifles and put their hands up. Bloody cowards, if you ask me, begging your pardon, sir." He gave the tall gentleman in front of him a sideways glance.

"I appreciate your frustration, corporal," returned Conan Doyle, to ease the man's embarrassment. "It is true. The Boers certainly seem to have a well-developed sense of self-preservation."

"That they do, sir."

Conan Doyle cast his eye over the subdued, shabby group of men who, despite the increasing heat, were huddled inside their greatcoats. Their faces were largely hidden under wide-brimmed slouch hats. The contrast between the dishevelled appearance of the Boers and their smart uniformed guards was striking.

"Let's not forget," Conan Doyle continued, "the word 'boer' means 'farmer'. They are not professional soldiers like yourselves. Nevertheless, it astonishes me how many of your comrades have ended up in our hospital because of these farmers." He looked at the low, white building across the square. Heat radiated off its roof, causing the air above it to dance wildly.

The sergeant glared at the riff-raff in front of him and grunted non-committedly.

"Are you a doctor in there, sir?" he said instead.

"I am, and inside that building is the evidence to support my case. There are hundreds of men inside, wounded and dying. And let me tell you that each one has an average of five bullet wounds. Nice clean wounds, mind, but five to a man."

"Five?" exclaimed the corporal.

"On average, yes, and one poor fellow had nearly twenty."

"Twenty?" the corporal asked in disbelief. "How can a fellow survive twenty bullet wounds?"

"Unfortunately he didn't, but others with not many fewer have survived. The wounds are very clean, you see. The small-bore, high-velocity rounds of the Mauser go straight through the body, leaving quite tidy entry and exit points. So as long as they miss bone or vital organs...."

Conan Doyle's voice faded away. The two soldiers had stopped listening. Something of more immediate interest had caught their attention. They were looking in the direction of the hospital, from which several pairs of orderlies were emerging through a side door. Each pair carried a stretcher which bore a body, wrapped like an Egyptian mummy in a sheet so soiled it was more brown than white in colour. They walked in a brisk, business-like procession along the side of the hospital, turning at the corner to pass out of sight around the back of the building. Before long they reappeared, their stretchers now empty and went back inside the hospital to repeat the process. Conan Doyle grimaced at the thought of the shallow graves, hollowed out of the dirt, into which the bodies would be delivered with minimal ceremony.

"Making room for more poor sods," the sergeant muttered, almost to himself.

"Poor devils," Conan Doyle responded.

"Seems the Boers got them in the end," the sergeant said venomously, his neat moustache bristling as he pursed his lips.

"Perhaps," replied Conan Doyle, "but it is more likely that they died from enteric fever."

"The 'modders'?" asked the young corporal.

Conan Doyle smiled at the British soldiers' propensity to find a nickname for everything that caused them discomfort.

"Yes," he replied. "It's reaching epidemic proportions among our soldiers."

"The idiots," said the little sergeant bitterly. "They were told not to drink the water. Especially those camped downstream from the Boers. The Modder River was brown and muddy beforehand..."

"Did you know 'modder' is Dutch for 'muddy'?" the tall, thin youth enquired of Conan Doyle.

Before he could answer, the sergeant intervened impatiently, "Of course he does, you dolt! He's a doctor!" Then he continued as though the corporal had not interrupted. "...And now it's also infested with the fetid corpses of horses and cattle *and* the occasional Boer. It is said," he carried on indignantly, "that the Boers threw their dead animals into the river deliberately to poison the water. Short of shooting the men, it was impossible to prevent them from drinking the filthy stuff."

"Dead horse soup. That's what we call it." The gangly corporal informed Conan Doyle gravely.

The sergeant scowled up at him. "They were so desperately thirsty by the end of the day's fighting, there was no stopping them."

"Looking at those sheets, it must be disgusting in there," said the corporal, tilting his head towards the hospital.

Conan Doyle nodded grimly.

"It is disgusting!" said the sergeant. "I had to go in there yesterday, myself. I shan't be doing that again, I can tell you. The place is overflowing with men. They are lying on the floor between the beds, under the beds, anywhere there is space. Doctors, nurses and orderlies have to step over the men and carefully pick their way between the bodies. And the stench! It is unbelievable! I've never smelt anything like it in my life – and I grew up on a pig farm."

"Did you?" the corporal asked in surprise. "I never knew that!"

The sergeant ignored him. "The smell was appalling, even though, as you know, sir," he gave Conan Doyle a look of the informed, "the hospital staff have erected latrines at the ends of the wards, for those who can stagger that far, in a vain attempt to reduce the men's embarrassment at fouling their own beds. It has not helped much, as the majority of patients cannot even leave their beds. It's the poor beggars in the hospital who have to deal with all those shitty sheets and blankets I feel sorry for," said the sergeant in a tone of disgust. "You'll not catch me changing bedclothes after someone's sprayed the contents of his arse all over them."

"It sounds horrible!" said the corporal. "Is it true?" he asked Conan Doyle earnestly.

"Of course it's true," the sergeant answered. "I saw it with my own eyes, and I'll tell you something else. That's not the worst of it. The place is swarming with flies, a haze of buzzing flies. Great plagues of them are crawling over the men and their food as soon as it is brought to them, buzzing around their eyes and noses and crawling into their mouths whenever they try to eat or drink."

"The poor bastards!" The corporal looked a Conan Doyle. "Is there nothing the medical staff can do to help?"

Conan Doyle frowned and held his palms up despairingly. "There is little we can do in the circumstances," he replied miserably. "I fear there is the real danger that more will die from enteric fever than from being shot in this war. It is the vilest, filthiest and most dangerous form of disease to have polluted the hospital so far. What a contrast the hospital is now compared to when I first visited it with Field Marshal Roberts on the day we took Jacobsdal."

He stopped reflectively. Was that only seven days ago?

"Lord Roberts had been informed, on entering the town, that there were British prisoners in the hospital. He made his way there at once and I accompanied him as part of the medical team. I was astonished at the quality of the facilities in the hospital. For a small town in the middle of nowhere, Jacobsdal had a hospital that would be the envy of many cities in England. The nurses were mainly local Boer girls, of course, but the doctors were all German. The wards were shipshape, the place was immaculately clean and the uniforms of the medical staff were starched and with edges of Germanic precision. We walked through the wards in a hushed silence, past beds containing bearded men." Conan Doyle allowed himself a chuckle. "The look of surprise on their faces at seeing British officers marching through their hospital was a sight to behold. At last we arrived in the ward with the British patients. There were thirty-seven of them. The men informed Roberts of the great kindness that had been shown towards them since their capture. One or two even commented, surreptitiously, that they would not have been cared for this well had they been treated in a British military hospital. The contrast between then and now is like the difference between heaven and hell.

"The hospital and its staff were overwhelmed by the arrival of hundreds of wounded and dying men on Monday, after the first day of engagement at Paardeberg. The situation has not been helped by the fact that the Boer nurses abandoned us, but at least they took their Boer patients with them. And then men started to arrive with enteric fever. It is now a foul-smelling, gut-wrenching place, with men laying on every inch of floor space available."

Conan Doyle looked at the two men in turn. "You can be proud of your comrades. Throughout the tragedy unfolding in the hospital my admiration for and pride in the British soldier has grown beyond measure. It is an astonishing and mightily impressive thing, the stoicism with which the British soldiers accept their discomfort and the appalling conditions they have to endure."

"There's nothing that can match the courage and fortitude of the professional British soldier," muttered the sergeant, his chest pushing forward in pride. The corporal nodded in silent agreement.

Their reflective moment was broken by a sudden exclamation from one of the Boers nearby.

"God in Heaven, it is him!"

Conan Doyle and his two companions swung around to find a Boer was coming towards them holding an open book in one hand and stabbing at the open page with an excited finger.

"Hey, you! Sit down immediately!" the small sergeant shouted. The corporal unshouldered his rifle and anxiously thrust his bayonet in the direction of the approaching Boer. The other guards followed suit and stood ready to quell any disorder among their prisoners. The Boer stopped and held his hands high. He shook the book as though waving a small flag. The pages fluttered like bunting.

"Sergeant, I would like to speak to that man," he said, pointing at Conan Doyle. "I have something to ask him."

"You sit down right now, unless you want a bayonet up your arse," he shouted back.

"Sir," the Boer addressed Conan Doyle in passable English, "I believe you will find this book of interest." He held the open pages towards Conan Doyle and pointed at the portrait of the author on the inside page. "You are Arthur Conan Doyle, are you not?"

Conan Doyle was astonished and could only reply, dumbly, "Yes."

"Will you sit down!" yelled the sergeant.

"Sergeant, I only want to speak to Mr Conan Doyle."

"Who?"

"Arthur Conan Doyle, one of your most famous writers."

"What? Who? You mean 'Sherlock Holmes' Conan Doyle?" The sergeant turned to Conan Doyle and stared at him. "Are you Arthur Conan Doyle?"

"Yes, sergeant."

"The author of 'Sherlock Holmes'?"

"Yes, I am. Now I think you should let that man through."

But the sergeant turned to the other guards. "Hey boys, this here," he shouted, pointing towards Conan Doyle, "is Arthur Conan Doyle. You know, the bloke who wrote 'Sherlock Holmes'." He gesticulated for them to come over.

While the sergeant's back was turned, Conan Doyle stepped forward and beckoned the Boer to approach. He walked over, smiling, and took Conan Doyle's hand, shaking it vigorously, to the astonishment of the rest of his comrades.

"Oi, clear off!" asserted the small sergeant, grabbing his prisoner to shove him away.

"Hold on a minute, sergeant. The fact that there is a war on does not mean we have to forget our manners. This gentleman has something he wishes to ask me and I would like to do him the courtesy of allowing him to do so."

Addressing the Boer he asked, "You speak English?"

"Yes." And in response to Conan Doyle's raised eyebrow, he continued, "It's not that uncommon, even among us country burghers. Some of us have even been educated in your English universities, although it must be said we generally prefer the Dutch or German institutions. My name is Speller. It is a pleasure to meet you, Mr Conan Doyle."

"The pleasure is mine, Mr Speller."

"If I could impose on you, I wonder if you might sign this book for me." Speller offered the book to Conan Doyle and he took it. Holding it in front of him, a look of delight came to Conan Doyle's face. It was a copy of *The Exploits of Brigadier Gerard*.

"If I may say so, Mr Conan Doyle, the stories in that book are just the thing to take one's mind off the tedium and the horror of war. I have read the stories several times over."

"Thank you, Mr Speller. You are very kind. Of course, I shall sign it for you." Conan Doyle started to hunt his pockets for a pencil, without success. "Sergeant, do you have a pencil?"

"Not on me, sir."

"I have one somewhere," ventured the corporal and he set about searching his pockets.

Conan Doyle looked at Speller, "I hope you and your friends are being well cared for, Mr Speller."

"Yes, very well indeed, thank you. To tell you the truth, many of us are happy to be out of the war. Our main wish is to get back to our farms and businesses."

"Aha," said the corporal, and he presented Conan Doyle with an inch-long stump of pencil.

"Thank you, corporal," said Conan Doyle, taking it. He held the book in his left hand so that it lay open across his palm and wrist, and wrote a short dedication and signed his name. As he handed the book back, a thought struck Speller.

"Mr Conan Doyle," he asked, "would it be possible to give us a reading of one of the stories in the book."

Conan Doyle raised his eyebrows and threw a look at the hospital. He should really be in there already. What the hell, he thought. The surreal nature of the situation appealed to him and it would make for an excellent after-dinner tale.

"Why of course," he smiled. "What a splendid idea. It will be a new experience for me. I have given many readings in the past, but mainly at more gentrified gatherings, especially in America." He hesitated and then added quickly, "Of course I refer to the surroundings and not the audience." He cleared his throat uncomfortably.

Speller grinned. "I suspect it is true for the audience as well. Come, let us find a suitable seat for you so we can start."

A water barrel was appropriated and, once settled, Conan Doyle opened the book and read down the contents list. He looked up at the ranks of rugged, deeply tanned, bearded faces before him. "Would you like any story in particular?" he asked Speller.

"May I suggest *How Brigadier Gerard Won his Medal?*" responded Speller.

"A good choice."

Conan Doyle thumbed to the appropriate page. He scanned the first few lines, looked at his audience briefly and began in his warm, Edinburgh accent. "*The Duke of Tarentum, or Macdonald, as his old comrades prefer to call him, was, as I could perceive, in the vilest of tempers. His grim, Scotch face was like one of those grotesque doorknockers...*"

Friday 23 February 1900

Lieutenant-Colonel William Dillon Otter

Lieutenant-Colonel William Dillon Otter sat beneath a willow tree, his back against its rough trunk. He was positioned a little way up the northern slope of the Modder's steep-sided valley. Below him, the brown waters flowed lethargically, breaking into separate channels around exposed sand banks. The contrast between the river today and that which he had had to cross six days before amazed him. At their deepest, the channels were just three feet deep, but for the most part the river was even shallower. If one could still call it a river, thought Otter, grimacing. It was more like an open sewer of the worst kind. The low flow of water and the various sand banks had caused the dead oxen and horses drifting down from the Boer laager to become stranded. Over the days, more and more rotting corpses had collected until there was now rank upon rank of putrefying animal flesh lying across the width of the river. Otter estimated that there were up to two hundred corpses washed together in a chaotic mass of legs, bloated bodies and heads twisted at impossible angles. Otter had also noted the occasional human body.

The smell was stomach-turning. He clamped a perfumed hand-kerchief over his nose and mouth as he watched his men working in the river below. The swarm of flies that whined around him was maddening, but they were as nothing compared to the black blizzard of them that rose around his Canadians labouring in the river.

Otter had enormous sympathy for them. Although he had been ordered to clear the river of the wall of riven flesh that was polluting the water and spreading disease, he had requested volunteers for the task rather than issuing an order. To the considerable merit of the men, they had agreed to do it, not with any enthusiasm, it had to be said, but rather with a stoicism of knowing that an unpleasant job of work had to be done. Regardless of the individual discomfort, they all realised there was a greater good in removing the source of the all-pervading stench.

Otter had originally stood beside the river in support of his men, but the sight of their poles piercing the putrid flesh, the punctures releasing streams of maggots and oozing, rancid slime, caused Otter to gag once too often. This and the intolerable stench had eventually

335

forced him to retreat from the river and into the shade of the willow tree. His guilt was lessened by the fact that he was pestered by flies, although not as much at this distance from the river as he had been when beside it.

Otter watched the men distractedly. Their faces were wrapped in cloth against the evil smell as they clambered over the bloated corpses. They had removed their boots as well as their trousers because the first soldier who had stepped onto a corrupt carcase had discovered that the fetid flesh would not support the weight of a man. His boot had plunged through the hide and filled with a disgusting mess of blood, slime and maggots. At least bare feet and legs could be more easily cleansed of the mush that clung to their skin.

The men had also learned that there was a technique required to pole the rotten hulks downriver. Simply thrusting the pole into the animal invariably meant that it pushed straight through the corpse and into the sand below. So, with two men to an ox, the poles were directed to pass through the carcass and to rest on its spine. The animal could then be levered and heaved to slither through the shallows into the deeper water to be swept away by the current, probably to catch on some other sand bank further downstream. But that, Otter concluded, would be someone else's problem.

Otter tilted his head back and rested it on the rough bark of the willow. Six days ago it was they who were downstream. In those six days they had performed incredibly well. They had shown extra-ordinary courage and had withstood suffering with steadfast fortitude. And now they took on the most repugnant of tasks without complaint. He was proud of them. He wondered if their performance had been noticed by the British officers. He thought it had, but he would write a commendation to General Smith-Dorrien to make sure.

He closed his eyes and tried to ignore the tickle of flies crawling over his face and hands. Actually, what surprised Otter in particular was not that the Canadians had done so well, but rather that they'd done it despite the abysmal conditions they had had to endure in the course of the battle. It appeared that the stiff-lipped officers of the greatest army in the world were happy to subject its lower ranks to a life of squalor and discomfort – to a level, indeed, that would embarrass the most poverty-stricken Canadian. At least, Otter conceded, there was now sufficient food for the men. They were no longer on the starvation rations they'd had to tolerate for the first four days after leaving Ramdam.

However, the continued lack of water wagons was very concerning, especially because those who returned from the exertions of battle each evening were mad with thirst. The river was no longer a safe source of drinking water. Initially, it had been difficult to convince the men of the dangers of bathing in the river and drinking from it. Earlier in the week he had had to place guards all along the riverbanks to stop anyone from going near the liquid filth. But now they could actually see and smell the foul flesh polluting the river, it was no longer necessary to set guards.

There was a rumour going around that the Boers were deliberately dumping their dead animals into the river to pollute it. It could have been true, of course, but Otter thought they had probably done so from necessity. Having seen the disgusting mess in the river for himself, he concluded that if he was a Boer trapped in the laager with an increasing number of dead animals piling up, then he would also use the river to get rid of the stinking corpses. They could not allow them to contaminate the laager – that much was obvious.

Of course water was not the only necessity in short supply. Since leaving Ramdam his troops had been in the field for two weeks. Was it only two weeks? It seemed much longer. In those two weeks they had marched for miles and been exposed to the blistering heat of the sun and the bitter cold of the night. They had endured clinging dust and swamp-making rain, and they'd suffered the ravages of war. As a result, their uniforms were in tatters. But no new uniforms had been issued and therefore the men had no change of clothes. They were wearing rags worse than those of a Canadian trapper who'd been lost in the wilderness for months. In addition, the lack of opportunity to wash or shave gave his men a rough, unkempt appearance. Indeed, were it not for their rags being khaki in colour, they would be indistinguishable from the rough-necked Boers they were fighting.

But the worst of it were the lice. He had managed to remain uninfected for some time after the men had started to scratch like monkeys, but he now also bore the indignity of playing host to the irritating bugs. Of course he had had to put up with these abhorrent little critters in previous campaigns, but never to the same extent as he did now. His body and head were alive with them. It was as if he could physically feel them crawling across his scalp. He ruffled his hair vigorously in a vain attempt to dislodge them.

Otter's reflections were suddenly disturbed by the sound of gunfire. He looked up to where the summit of Kitchener's Hill rose above the rim of the river valley and stood out darkly against the ranks of clouds that hung ominously in the sky. The sound of musketry seemed to be coming from the direction of the hill.

"Kitchener's Hill!" Otter said to himself. The irony of it! For while Field Marshal Roberts had sent Kitchener away from the front, this reminder of the man loomed over them all. Otter hoped that Kitchener would do a better job in charge of logistics and supplies than he had done when in command on Bloody Sunday.

He stared at the stark shape of Kitchener's Hill and listened to the crack and rattle of gunfire that echoed from its rocky slopes. The noise of that battle overlaid the low rumble of cannons and the crash of the British bombardment of the laager. Otter reflected on the strange nature of the war. All around him there were men pitted against each other in a deadly game of life and death, killing or being killed. Yet here he sat leaning against a tree looking serenely and calmly across a river as if he were on a picnic. Even the task being undertaken in the river had taken on a light-hearted tenor. The men seemed to be enjoying it in some macabre way, challenging each other to races while pushing the carcasses along the sandbanks or running across the bloated bodies while trying not to break the fragile skin and plunge their feet into the vile mire beneath.

But Otter knew this tranquillity would not last. He had already received his orders for the afternoon. After lunch they were to return to the forward positions. But at least the next attacks would be more managed affairs. His Canadian irregulars had shown the rest of the army, Otter thought proudly, that the most efficient method of attack was to dash forward over short distances after the artillery had blasted the heart and soul out of the Boers. The Boers had seemed less able to resist quick, sharp attacks, especially if the little cover that was available was used effectively to sneak up on them.

As a consequence of these new tactics, his regiment had lost fewer men since Bloody Sunday and had gained more territory. Yes, Otter concluded, it was a much better approach. And, except for an occasional British officer who tried to interfere to speed things up, he had been left more or less to his own devices. He had made steady advances of two or three hundred yards each evening; sneaking forward during the night, digging shallow trenches in the sandy soil before the sun rose the next morning. This last tactic seemed to cause the Boers considerable consternation. Otter grinned to himself. It must indeed have been rather disconcerting for them to wake up to find their enemy some hundreds of yards closer than they had been the evening before. He thought the increasing closeness of the Canadians to the main Boer positions must be having a terrible effect on their morale. On the other hand, Otter noted with an inner pride, the morale of the Canadians was very high. He watched his men as a father would his sons. A paternal smile crept across his face.

The increasing fierceness of the fighting taking place in the direction of Kitchener's Hill drew his attention again. The Boers seemed to be very keen to take back the hill. Beyond it, Otter noticed that the clouds were thicker and darker, and the occasional distant rumble of thunder added to the cacophony of war. He studied the clouds for a while. The storm seemed to be heading their way. So yet another drenching was on its way, he concluded. He hoped there would be enough water in those clouds to wash the remaining corpses farther downriver. He absentmindedly waved his hand at the flies crawling over his face and scratched at a particularly irritating louse as he watched the approaching storm.

General Christiaan Rudolf de Wet

General Christiaan Rudolf de Wet was fuming. The angry crashes of thunder and the jagged barbs of lightning emulated his mood. The usual sense of the vastness of the veldt was lost behind the dark sheets of rain that pelted him and the intermittent bursts of hail that pummelled his back. The torrential weather obscured the late afternoon sun and turned day into virtual night. It also hid from his view the rest of the commando as it slowly plodded its way back towards Poplar Grove. None of his officers had ventured close enough to come into his sight, let alone to talk to him, not since he had bitten the heads off those officers who had tried to chew over their failures with him. Now they were all giving him a wide berth to avoid further lashings from his acid tongue.

This was his second retreat to Poplar Grove and his disillusionment and frustration bore down on him as much as the rain. His hunched attitude in the saddle was as much an indication of his rage as a protective pose against the bitter weather. The downpour had started just after he had ordered his commando to disengage with the enemy. It felt as though God was mocking him.

The plan to recapture the Osfontein kopjes had obviously been too ambitious, he smouldered. Yet better disciplined troops with a bit of mettle and professionalism would have achieved the simple goals. It was precisely the sort of plan required against a sophisticated enemy such as the English. His commandants had all known what to do. They had discussed it in great detail for two days, since they had first met at Poplar Grove, and they had gone over it again yesterday evening before they started moving into position. Guts – that was what had been missing and the will to follow things through.

It was obvious now that the burghers had not been in good heart even before they had begun the assault on the kopjes. The situation with General Cronjé was having a very bad effect on the morale of the men, and he was not even defeated yet. De Wet did not wish to imagine what would happen if Cronjé should be captured by the English. It would be a disaster. Not only would the Republics lose one-tenth of their army, but the defeat of the Lion of Potchefstroom would have a calamitous effect on the burghers. It would cause many to drift back to their farms and the eventual loss of men would be even more damaging than those lost with Cronjé. That was why it had been so important for their offensive against the English to succeed.

As far as de Wet was concerned, the day had been a double failure. He had not achieved his objective of recapturing the main Oskoppie, nor that next to Stinkfontein Farm, and he now had to accept that it was not possible to secure an escape route for Cronjé. But, secondly, Cronjé had done nothing to help him. The old fool must have known that the Afrikander army would counter-attack, and yet not a single shot had come from the laager in support of his offensive. Not being able to use the heliograph to inform Cronjé of his plan had made a co-ordinated attack more difficult.

"Damned weather!" de Wet snarled, thumping the pommel of his saddle in anger.

It had been the first continuously cloudy day for weeks, making the heliograph useless. De Wet tilted his head slightly to look to the heavens and the pool of water on the wide brim of his hat cascaded over his shoulders. He was beginning to wonder whose side the Good Lord was on.

But even without the heliograph, Cronjé would have heard the distinctive Mauser-fire as soon as the assault on the Oskoppies had begun. He should have realised that something was afoot. It had been Cronjé's chance to escape. If he had done so quickly, they could have abandoned the attack on the English and the entire Afrikander army could now be marching to Poplar Grove to regroup. De Wet smiled ironically. Under those circumstances he would have welcomed the storm that he was currently cursing. The English would not have been able to find them in this weather and he, Cronjé and their army would have got away.

But Cronjé had not joined the attack. However, the fault was not all the General's. That imbecile, General Philip Botha, had dilly-dallied so much that dawn had broken before he was fully in position. It was obvious that he had been more concerned with the situation he had left behind in Natal than on focusing on what he had been sent to do at the Cape front. Since the two generals, Botha and Andreas Cronjé, had joined his commando at Poplar Grove, on the evening of his previous retreat from Paardeberg, they had both complained incessantly about how idiotic they thought it was to reduce the size of their army in Natal in order to relieve a foolish old general who had got himself trapped by the English. They had not been happy that General Joubert had ordered them to take three thousand burghers out of Natal to aid Cronjé's escape. They had argued that the forces in Natal had been reduced too much and that the English would be able to seize the initiative, that even the bungling General Buller would be able to take advantage of the situation. And, they had continued to complain, that General Joubert's demand to know why the whole army had not risen to the call of the 'Lion of Potchefstroom' and gone to his aid had resulted in further commandos, in addition to theirs, making their way to Paardeberg, leaving yet more areas unprotected.

De Wet clucked to himself in disgust, for although he had waited a whole day for the 'additional' reinforcements, they had not arrived. Only small contingents under Commandants Helgaard Marthinus Theunissen and Stephanus Gerhardus Vilonel had turned up.

In total, he had almost four thousand men at his disposal, which de Wet admitted to himself, was a sizeable force by Boer standards. But it was insufficient to do anything meaningful with against an enemy of the size that he faced. And many of the burghers were disillusioned and had been pessimistic about the likely success of the attack on the kopjes. In hindsight, de Wet realised he should not have waited that additional day. He should have attacked earlier as the delay had allowed the pessimism of some of his burghers to ferment and affect other men. This had reduced the effectiveness of their assault. He would have achieved more with fewer men of conviction than he had been able to do with a larger but demoralised force. De Wet cursed himself for failing to take proper account of this fact. He shifted in his saddle as he took responsibility for the uncomfortable thought. Yes, it was true. He had to take the blame for not recognising the creeping dejection in his commando. Even the bravest burgher was unlikely to risk his life if he did not believe in the cause. And for many, the cause of rescuing General Cronjé was now pretty much played out; the only solution was for the stubborn old man to break out.

Of course he would not do it without persuasion, but surely even he must now see that the only solution was for him to escape. But he would need help. The English soldiers on the main Oskoppie would need to be distracted. De Wet mulled it over in his head. He would not split his commando next time. Instead, he would attack the main

Oskoppie with his entire force. He would mount his offensive on the opposite side of the kopje from the river. That would draw the English away from the route Cronjé would have to take to escape. The English would never expect another attack from the Boers after the dismal failure of the last one. The attack would be diversionary rather than a full offensive, so even his disillusioned forces should be able to pull it off. And this time he would make sure that General Cronjé knew what was going on. He would send Dannie Theron back to the Cronjé's laager to tell him about the plan.

De Wet straightened in his saddle as his mood began to improve. There was a solution, all was not lost. He drew on his reins, halted his horse and waited. In a few moments a pair of riders appeared through the deluge and brought their horses to a sudden stop at the unexpected appearance of the stationary de Wet.

"Hell, man, what are you playing at, you bloody fool?" one of the riders cursed. "Appearing out of the rain like that! You nearly gave me a heart attack!"

His companion considered the lone rider in front of them.

"Hello, Oom Christiaan. Has your horse gone lame?" he shouted above the drumming raindrops.

The other burgher instantly dropped his head and pulled his hat down low to hide his face under its wide brim. Muttering a self-deprecating expletive to himself, he rode on quickly in the hope that he had not been recognised by de Wet. The two remaining men watched him disappear through the curtain of rain. De Wet turned to the burgher.

"Have you seen Captain Theron?" he shouted.

The burgher leaned forward cupping his hand around his ear as he drew closer to de Wet.

"Have – you – seen – Theron?"

The man nodded. He held up his palm, signalling de Wet to wait. He guided his horse away from de Wet at a right angle to the route along which he and his comrade had just ridden. He stopped when he was just visible to de Wet, a grey smudge behind the dark waterfall of rain. Both men waited. Their demeanour was no longer hunched over their horses; they sat erect and alert, staring through the cascading water, watching for other grey shadows to emerge from the gloom. Then de Wet noticed the burger start to move and slowly disappear into the rain. After a moment a cluster of phantoms materialised and stopped in front of him. Then one of the riders moved closer and leaned forward, stretching out his hand. De Wet reached over and shook Theron's hand. Then he turned his horse to walk on. Theron fell into step beside him and the rest of the group followed at a distance. The discussion would begin once the storm had abated.

Twenty minutes later, the sun broke through the clouds, sending shafts of golden light across the veldt. The lightning and thunder rolled on across the countryside, the furious stabs and crashes in contradiction to the graceful curve of the rainbow that arched across the sky. The horses' hooves sploshed in the liquid mud, their heads bobbed up and down in rhythm to the sound and their ears flicked back and forth as though intrigued by the slopping sound. Their manes clung to their necks in wet, glossy streaks. Water dripped from the men's hats and ran in rivulets down the folds of their greatcoats. Delicate trails of steam rose from them as the soft afternoon sun drew the water from their clothes. The burghers, sitting erect to catch the last rays of the warming sun, rode on in silence, savouring the quiet that followed the passing of the storm. It was Theron who broke the moment and brought them back to the reality of their situation.

"You heard that we lost Commandant Theunissen and one hundred men?"

"I heard."

Silence.

"General Botha said he was reckless," Theron tried again.

De Wet grunted in response. The silence that followed was broken by de Wet.

"So what happened?"

"As Botha explained it to me, he was delayed and dawn arrived before they were in place. Theunissen initiated the attack on the main Oskoppie before Botha was ready. Botha ordered him back, but Theunissen was determined to drive the English from the kopje. However, there were too many English and he was forced back. He established himself on a small kopje and set up a good defensive position, holding off the initial English attack. But a second English assault was more organised and outnumbered Theunissen's commando. While he was withstanding the frontal attack, the English threw two flanking movements around the kopje. By the time he realised what was happening he was virtually surrounded. He and the commando made a desperate dash for freedom. A few men escaped, but most were captured."

"Well, Dannie, that's precisely our problem now. There are too many English soldiers. They outnumber us to such a degree that if we stand still they simply enclose us. The answer is to keep moving, to be mobile at all times, to pick our moment, rush in, strike and get out of trouble quickly."

"Can we win the war doing that?"

"Yes, if we have one thing."

"And what is that, Oom Christiaan?"

"Men of conviction. Men like you, Dannie, who believe beyond all doubt in the independence of our Republics and who are willing to give everything to preserve it. Do you know why we lost today?"

"I have an idea, but I would like to hear your view."

De Wet smiled at the young man.

"The reason we lost was because the men had no belief in themselves before they started. They are demoralised by the situation that General Cronjé has got himself into, and the fact that he is unable to get himself out of it. He could have escaped when you went to see him, but now, because of the increasing numbers of the enemy, it will be difficult. The English are everywhere."

De Wet fell silent, reflecting on his conclusion.

"They are everywhere," he continued. "Every kopje we tried to take today was covered with Khakis. We cannot defeat the English fighting their kind of war. Even if we shoot thousands of them, they would simply be replaced. If we stand our ground, they will simply surround us. No, we have to fight this war in a different way, in a way that suits us and plays to our strengths. We have to use our horses more and be more mobile. And we have to leave our wives and children and wagons at home. Only then can we take control of this war…, if we have enough burghers. To win we will need everyone who is willing to fight. So we cannot afford to lose a single burgher. We need Cronjé's men. We need to help them escape."

De Wet drew his horse up. The suddenness of his action took Theron by surprise and he had passed de Wet before he was able to rein in his own horse. De Wet looked at the young man as he turned his horse and walked it back to where he waited, but de Wet's gaze was distracted. His thoughts had brought him full circle. He would put his plan in place. He looked at Theron with fierce blue eyes.

"Dannie, I need you to return to General Cronjé and tell him that he *must* escape. Do not leave until you have convinced him to do so. He has to understand what a terrible effect his capture will have – *is* having – on the morale of our men. If we lose the Lion of Potchefstroom, then our cause will suffer a severe reverse. He *has* to escape, and he *has* to get every man out with him, even if he has to leave the women and children behind. He has no choice."

De Wet paused and then, leaning forward to emphasise his point, he said, "We *need* those men. We cannot afford to lose them to the enemy."

"Yes, Oom. I shall go tonight and tell him."

Saturday 24 February 1900

General Pieter Arnoldus Cronjé

General Pieter Arnoldus Cronjé sat wide-kneed on his low, three-legged trek stool, sipping from a tin mug of strong, hot coffee. He had completed his rounds, checking his situation and discussing with his officers where the English had probed at his defences or made advances during the night. On the whole he was satisfied, but the encroachment of the Canadians from Paardeberg Drift concerned him. They seemed to be different somehow and their tactics were more effective than those employed on his upstream flank. The Canadians were more creative in their approach and once more had caught the burghers by surprise last night, advancing another few hundred yards. Cronjé had ordered more men to defend the position and demanded that the officers be more vigilant and take more precautions to avoid any further surprises. If those Canadians carried on with similar success, he feared they would be in the main laager within a few days. But hopefully his reinforcements would have arrived before then.

He stared into his half-empty mug, deep in thought. The walls of the trench loomed over him as he sat alone, while around him the beleaguered Afrikander army gradually came to life. The burghers roused themselves from their fitful sleep to start preparing their meagre breakfasts. Hester had already made him breakfast and, once he was settled with a mug of coffee, she had left him to join the other women and girls to check on the wounded. It was now quiet from the direction of the field hospital. Even the desperate man whose distressed calls for his wife and daughters had gone on throughout the night had fallen silent. No doubt exhausted by long, sleepless hours of pain and the sodden discomfort of the torrential rain. In place of the anguished cries and sobs of the wounded and dying, it was the muted lows and whinnies of the livestock down in the lower parts of the valley that drifted up to Cronjé through the river mist. The damp air smelt fresh and clean. Last night's storm had washed it of the acrid smell of lyddite from the previous day's bombardment.

Cronjé sat quietly, drawing warmth from the small camp fire, trying to focus on how to deal with the advancing Canadians. But his moment of solitude and contemplation was blighted by a cloud of flies that already buzzed around his head. Normally he would be able to ignore them, but this morning they were particularly abundant and irritating. He frequently waved a hand in front of his face to discourage them. Through their annoying whine he determinedly recited words from the Book of Daniel: "*...so the king gave the order, and they brought Daniel and threw him into the lions' den. The king said to Daniel, 'May your God, whom you serve continually, rescue you!'*"

Cronjé watched the dancing flames of the fire, "So my Lord God," he murmured, "What plans do you have for me? Do you mean to rescue us?"

The mist that hung over the Boers was starting to thin as the sun lifted itself off the horizon. The muffled sounds of men drifted down the trench; their coughs and rasps, their low voices and the harsh clatter of metal plates and mugs. For some reason, the lack of native voices was noticeable this morning. Four days had passed since the servants and drivers had deserted the laager, at first in dribs and drabs and then *en masse*, melting away into the darkness. It was different today because Cronjé's driver, Jim Makokela, had also departed during the night. He was the last native to leave and, whereas his other servants had tended to go about their business quietly and unobtrusively, Jim had a presence that, when gone, was missed.

Cronjé stood up from his low trek stool and helped himself to more coffee from the pot suspended over the fire. He scowled at the inconvenience of having to do things for himself now that his servants had abandoned him. As he sat down, he thought again of Jim standing in front of him, announcing his departure. He had not just sneaked off like the rest of them. Cronjé cradled his tin mug in his hands as he pictured the scene.

Makokela had discarded his western clothes and stood tall and noble in his Zulu warrior's regalia. In his hand he carried the two fighting sticks, which never left his person, and his ox-hide shield. Then, in his own inimitable style, he had held his hand up in a respectful salute and declared, "Inkosi, the meat we have is now so bad that it is sapping my strength and my mind and also my spirit. How am I supposed to live without fresh meat from healthy cattle? It is not right that any man should live on meat that is like the bark of the buffalo thorn tree. And no man should have to live like a cow in his own mess as we do in these trenches. Inkosi, it is said that I am the best wagon driver in Southern Africa, and that is true, but what am I to do when the oxen and wagons are being destroyed by the Redcoats. There is no reason for me to stay. I have stayed thus far because I had hoped to be able to fight again in battle, as I did at Isandlwana, where we beat the Redcoats, and at Rorke's Drift and to avenge our defeat at oNdini."

At that, Cronjé held up a hand to indicate his desire to speak. Makokela stopped politely.

"Makokela," Cronjé spoke formally and in Zulu because standing before him was not his wagon driver but a noble and proud Zulu warrior. "You know that we have agreed with the English that this is a white man's war and that the Bantu peoples are not allowed to take up arms for either side, and yet you still wish to fight?"

"Inkosi, I am a warrior. I am a *Zulu* warrior. Do you expect anything else? Does the colour of my skin matter? Is it not my right to choose to fight when and where I wish? To do battle is in the blood of my nation and in my soul. But I no longer desire to fight in *this* war."

In response to Cronjé's quizzical look, Makokela continued. "What kind of war do you fight? This is no war! How can it be when the Afrikanders sit in their holes and the English stay away, and the only thing that happens is that the English throw explosions at us from breakfast to sun down?

"Inkosi, during the Zulu civil war that followed our defeat by the Redcoats, I chose the path of Zibhebhu kaMaphitha against the Royal House, but we were defeated and my kraal was attacked by the royalists. On that night, I did not hide in a hole. I fought and killed many of my enemies and escaped from my burning kraal. And so it should be here, Inkosi. I ask you, what are men coming to when they say they are at war, but all they do is sit around their camp fires and talk? What will the children say when they hear the tales of this battle of Paardeberg? If they were Zulu children, they would laugh and sneer! I must leave before the name of Makokela becomes associated with this 'battle'. You white people must fight your wars as you wish, but this is not my way. So I must leave!"

And with a final "Good-bye Inkosi" and salute he turned and left.

Cronjé grinned to himself as he recalled the dignity and solemnity with which the speech was delivered. He was not surprised. Jim had always had a certain way about him and a complete disrespect of all the other servants. He was a Zulu, and by being the last to leave the laager, he had shown that the Zulus were more courageous than all the other native peoples in the laager. Cronjé hoped that he would be able to find Jim after the war for there was no doubt that he was the best wagon driver in Southern Africa.

But Jim was right. The conditions in the trenches had become appalling. The rain had poured down continuously the previous afternoon and through the night and water had coursed through the trenches like small rivers. Now that the rain had stopped, the trenches were ankle-deep in slimy mud.

The Modder River had risen in a flash flood during the night and some of the horses and oxen, corralled under its high banks out of view of the English cannons, had been swept away. Mercifully, the piles of decaying corpses had also been washed downstream. With a bit of luck they would become beached near the English and stink them out instead. Cronjé hoped that the flies would follow them. He had never seen so many flies in his entire life. They had been a wretched nuisance at Magersfontein, but the swarms of flies at Paardeberg had become an indescribable irritation. They forced their way into your eyes, mouths and noses, and infested any food as soon as it appeared. Not that there was much food to attract them.

Many foodstuffs were now in short supply, especially flour, and therefore there were no biscuits, bread and cakes. Fortunately the surviving oxen meant there was a reasonable source of fresh meat, but the animals were in poor condition and they were losing so many every day it was impossible for the butchers to strip all the carcasses of their flesh before the meat started to go rancid. As a result, Cronjé had taken the precaution of ordering that food, especially meat, was to be rationed. Nothing was wasted from those animals that were butchered. The carcass was stripped of its hide and every bit of useable flesh was cut into strips, rationed out, and what remained was hung out to dry to make biltong, the biltong that Jim had refused to eat. He saw no point in eating meat which had been dried to the consistency of tree bark.

To ensure that there could be no claims of favouritism, the butcher had devised a system for handing out the rations of fresh meat. The meat would be cut into equally-sized pieces. The butcher would order the burghers to form a queue and he would then turn his back on the men and, without looking around, would hand out the meat. The burghers quickly got into the spirit of it. They joked and accused each other that they were passing secret signals to the butcher in order to get the best cuts, which only made the butcher explode with indignation. Brandishing his butcher's knife, he would turn on those nearest to him, filling the air with coarse expletives and causing the burghers to scatter. The procedure was a rare source of entertainment in the otherwise grim reality of life in the besieged laager.

And then Cronjé heard the first low thump of a canon. He took out his watch: nine o'clock. The bombardment had started on time. It was routine now. Every day at nine it would start, and continue through the day until sunset. The shelling would seem random and undirected at first, but it would soon settle into a pattern. Then it would be possible to work out where the main focus of the shelling was to be for the day. Soon the pure white mist would be replaced with a yellow miasma that would creep over the trenches and what remained of the wagons, smothering everything in acrid lyddite fumes.

Cronjé could hear the children, who had started to cry with the first explosions. Some were screaming hysterically. He tried to block out the tormenting sound but his shoulders slumped as he thought about the effect that the daily bombardment was having on the children. Even the women, and a more resilient and stubborn race of women did not exist, were becoming overwhelmed by the persistent shelling. Maybe he had been wrong to refuse the offer to evacuate the women and children. Then again, he doubted that they would have wanted to leave their menfolk. His Hester would have refused to go. And if they had agreed to leave the laager, there would have been no one to tend and care for the wounded. The right decision had been made at the time; he would not allow himself any regrets now.

Yet he could not stop being concerned about the plight of his people. Most of the men saw the constant shelling as little more than an inconvenience. Once they knew where the English were to focus their shelling, the burghers moved away from that part of the defences and couched in the safer trenches. They knew the enemy infantry would not attack during the initial bombardment of the day so they felt relatively confident that they were safe. They only had to deal with the mud and the stench of the trenches and the monotony of waiting until the ferocity of the bombardment slackened. The English soldiers would remain out of sight and out of danger during the shelling, but when it subsided they would move forward in short dashes until they became pinned down by the burghers. Then the shelling would increase again, the shells screaming over the prone Khakis to force the burghers back into their trenches. It was relentless, and while the trenches gave everyone physical protection, Cronjé had begun to notice the first signs of demoralisation creeping into some of the men. The one small positive point that Cronjé held onto was that the intensity of the bombing seemed to get less each day, but maybe he was just getting used to it. Whatever the reason he thanked God for small mercies as he took the final gulp of coffee from his mug.

As he did so, he noticed a change in the pattern of the shelling. As expected, the intensity of the shelling reduced. He stood up and strode along the trench where his battle-weary men were preparing themselves for the inevitable infantry assault. And then the barrage died down completely. The burghers looked at each other anxiously. They waited, their rifles pointing out onto the veldt, their fingers resting gently on the triggers. They searched the smothering yellow lyddite vapours for any movement.

After several minutes it was apparent that no attack was coming. Cronjé climbed out of his trench to investigate what was going on. A number of burghers followed suit, their Mausers at the ready to counter any surprise attack. The swirling, yellow fumes gave the silence an eerie quality.

"Have the English run out of shells?" whispered fifteen-year-old Pieter Krueler hopefully. Someone scoffed.

"It's possible," Krueler retorted, "considering how many they've used. They have to run out eventually."

"That's wishful thinking, neef. They're up to something," Cronjé enlightened him.

"There!"

Everyone looked in the direction of the shout and then towards where the man was pointing. Some distance away, a large, dark dome wavered and trembled like a monstrous, drunken elephant on the veldt. As they watched, it billowed and expanded into a great sphere.

"What is *that*?" asked Krueler.

"It's a balloon, dumb-head. They raise it above us to spy on us," explained 19 year old August Schulenburg knowledgably.

"Spy on us?"

"Yes," Schulenburg responded. "When they are up in the sky they will be able to see everywhere into the laager. And then they can tell the artillery where to direct their shells." He looked at Krueler with ghoulishly wide-eyes, the dark circles and his gaunt face exaggerating the effect. He leant over the boy with his arms raised fiendishly.

"There will be *nowhere* to hide," he moaned dramatically.

"No! What should we do?" said Krueler. Alarm showed in his thin, grimy face.

"Don't worry about them dropping bombs on you," Petrus le Roux said comfortingly. "Even with that contraption they won't be able to see into our trenches."

The boy looked relieved but Schulenburg continued. "Don't listen to him. There is nothing we can do. We just have to wait and let them drop bombs on us. Only now, when someone shouts 'Take cover' it will not matter. It is all up because the English will now be able to find every hole you crawl into and will pour a hell of shells onto you. You cannot hide from someone up there. There is no escape!"

Krueler stared from the haggard features of the youth to the tired face of the older man in horror, not knowing which one to believe. Finally, he came to a conclusion.

"Captain Theron was right. We must leave, before it's too late."

"Ignore him, neef," said le Roux. "He is only trying to scare you. When the English first used a balloon at Magersfontein it really put the shivers up us, but the solution was simple," le Roux chuckled. "We just shot it down."

Krueler relaxed. "Can we shoot it down again?"

"We can try, but they seem to have learned their lesson. They have positioned it further away this time."

"Come," Schulenburg grinned at Krueler. He slapped the boy playfully on the back to make amends for teasing him. "You're supposed to be one of the best shots in the country. Let's go shoot the balloon down."

Cronjé watched them leave, reflecting on the indiscipline in his army. His soldiers pretty much did as they pleased. The burghers were not unwilling; they were simply unaccustomed to being under orders. It was not uncommon for them to act without a specific order, but as long as it was useful, Cronjé did not mind. Maybe they would shoot down the balloon. He hoped so because the presence of the balloon did not bode well. The English would now be able to see any concentration of people and direct their fire towards them, or towards the horses or the cattle. The thought alarmed him, as did the sudden holler from the man running in his direction.

Cronjé watched as John Moody Lane, who called himself Jack, came rapidly towards him. He was one of the few Englishmen that Cronjé had taken a liking to, but that might be because he was actually Irish. He was a storekeeper in the tiny Transvaal town of Hartebeestfontein, where he had settled after coming to Southern Africa to seek his fortune. He had been given citizenship by the South African Republic, which was evidence, thought Cronjé, that the English argument that foreigners did not receive the franchise was unfounded, and that therefore their reason for declaring war was unjustified. As a citizen, Lane had an obligation to fight in a commando, but Cronjé soon discovered that Lane was uncomfortable about having to bear arms against his own countrymen. In fact, Lane had refused to do so. It was yet another example of the poor discipline in the Afrikander army. So Cronjé had given him responsibility for looking after the ammunition, a role that suited his storekeeper experience very well.

"General! General!"

"Yes, Private Lane," Cronjé replied as Lane pulled up before him, "I think I know what you are going to say."

Lane said it anyway, in his lilting Irish accent.

"General," he gasped, bending over, hands on knees, to catch his breath. "General," he panted. He had never got used to calling the old man 'Oom'. He tried again. "General, we need to move the ammunition wagons. So far the British have not seen them, but with that contraption," he pointed at the balloon slowly rising into the sky, "they will almost certainly do so and then 'Boom!' Every shell they possess will be directed at the wagons. We still have time to hide the ammunition before the balloon is airborne and they find their range."

"Ah, that is not quite what I expected you to say. I thought you were going to mention the horses." Cronjé scowled. Lane was right.

"Come," he yelled at those around him. "We need to save the horses and the ammunition. Follow me to the river so we can move the horses. Jack, find as many men as you can to help you unload the ammunition from the wagons. Hide it in the trenches. We need all hands to the plough before the English start the bombardment again."

The burghers hurried towards the river, while Lane led some thirty others to the terraces above the swirling Modder, where their ammunition wagons had been dragged. As they scrambled down the steep slope, the English cannons opened fire once more. The men worked like frantic ants, focusing on the first of the three wagons that had been parked in a line along the narrow terrace. As the wagon emptied, a few burghers started on the second wagon and others headed to the third to begin unpacking it.

As they approached the last wagon, which had sunk up to its axles in the soft sand, there was a monstrous explosion. The English shell had buried itself within the contents of the wagon as it exploded. A white dome of smoke erupted from the wagon, sending streams of debris from its midst like a multi-armed star. The front of the wagon was lifted from the clinging sand. The wheels tumbled from their axles and fell sideways onto their bulbous hubs where they trembled briefly like animals in the final throes of death. Barbs of wood and shards of metal struck out viciously at those nearest the wagon and embedded themselves in the flesh and bones of the men. As they fell screaming in agony, the other burghers automatically flung them-selves to the ground. As the contents of the wagon rained down on them, they covered their heads with their hands and prayed.

A thump near Lane made him look up. Inches in front of him lay half a wooden bullet case, the jagged edges driven into the soft sand. All around him bullets fell like metal hailstones. Above the patter of the falling bullets rose the pitiful cries of the injured men.

Lane leapt up and rushed towards the bodies sprawled beside the shattered wagon. The first burgher he reached was lying on his front writhing and frantically trying to turn over. Lane placed his hand on the man's shoulder and carefully rolled him over. As he did so, he recoiled in shock. The man looked at him in surprise, his eyes startled and imploring. He seemed to want to say something, but the lower half of his face was a gaping void edged with jagged flesh. Lane turned away and vomited.

Men rushed over desperately trying to help their stricken friends and relatives. Those coming to the rescue were soon consumed with grief at the sight of men with metal bars driven through their torsos and wooden splinters protruding from faces and bodies. Those who had died instantly had benefitted from the grace of God.

Shells continued to rain down on Lane and the men, many simply embedding themselves in the soft sand. Then shrapnel shells started to explode above them and the burghers scattered like autumn leaves blown in a gale. They carried and dragged their bloodied friends with them, determined not to leave any to a lonely and desolate death.

To those not helping the wounded, Lane yelled "It's too dangerous here. Let's help save the horses."

Even though the ammunition was Lane's prime responsibility, he recognised that the horses would ultimately be of more value to the Afrikanders. Ammunition could keep the enemy at bay, but horses offered the only opportunity of escaping to fight another day. Grateful for an excuse to be out of the immediate inferno of shrapnel scything through the air, the burghers ran away from the wagons and towards where the horses and cattle were hidden.

They were too late. The horses and cattle had been the first target of the English guns and a scene of carnage greeted their eyes. Those who had gone directly to save the horses were staring aghast at their destroyed animals, tears streaming down their faces. A few were among the shattered beasts, shooting those horses that were still writhing and shrieking in wild, uncomprehending anguish. Several horses and cattle had charged into the swirling river in panic and they now struggled hysterically in the surging, sucking waters, which indifferently washed them away. The new-comers turned away in horror and disgust. There was nothing they could do. As he turned to go, Lane bumped into Krueler. The youth glared up at Lane and snarled, "Do you call this fair play? How can they justify using that damnable thing to spy on our positions? And why this?" He swept his arm over the scene from hell. "We would not be so despicable to do something like this."

Sunday 25 February 1900

Captain Daniël Johannes Stephanus Theron

Captain Daniël Johannes Stephanus Theron was soaking wet, cold and exhausted. Gulping for air, he lay for a minute beside the Modder River, which he had just crossed. He had planned to make the trip to Cronjé on the previous Friday night, but the unrelenting rain had delayed him – he could not risk becoming disorientated in the downpour and getting lost while crossing enemy lines. The storm had caused the river to flood and, although Theron considered himself to be a strong swimmer, the swim across the river had been arduous and extremely alarming. But he could not delay any longer, so had no choice but to make the crossing regardless of the danger. The burghers on the opposite bank had informed him about a rope that was strung across the river and he had clung to it desperately during his crossing. Indeed, he had not really swum at all, but had hauled himself along the rope through the wild water. If it had not been for the rope, he believed, he would have been washed away by the power of the river. As it was, he still felt half-drowned.

Theron shivered. It might have been the cold, but it might also have been the ominous thought of getting the burghers across the river, swimming was not an activity in which Afrikanders excelled. And then there were the women, children, elderly and wounded; they would certainly not be able to get across, even with the aid of the rope. And what of the horses? They would have no chance of crossing the river in its present violent state. Theron frowned. That would mean that the Afrikander army would need to retreat on foot. That could only be done at night.

Theron felt the cold begin to penetrate to his bones so, still breathing heavily, he decided to move up the steep slope of the riverbank. He crept along silently and cautiously in the pre-dawn semi-darkness. Although he had passed through the front of Cronjé's lines, he had been warned that the General had also placed sentries at various stations along the river as an extra precaution now that the English had started to sneak forward during the night, making surprise attacks on his positions. Theron spotted a sentry sitting on a tree trunk that lay shattered on the ground. His shoulders drooped and his head was nodding forward and jerking back in the manner of someone mentally trying to stay awake and physically unable to do so. It would be very dangerous to approach the man without care. Theron had heard of an incident where a commandant had surprised one of his dozing sentries and has suffered a fatal wound when the man's rifle had gone off. He was taking no chances of that happening to him.

He carefully crept up on the dozing burgher and, when close enough, squatted behind a shrub, making sure that the sentry would not be able to see him when he awoke. Keeping his eye on the sentry, he ran his hand over the wet earth until he found a stone which he then threw, with some vigour, at the man. The well-aimed shot hit the burgher on a shoulder and the surprise made him yelp and leap to his feet. The rifle went off. The noise was startling in the silence, but the bullet went harmlessly through the jagged branches of the trees that scarred the pink pre-dawn sky. The barrel of the Mauser swept through the air as the man searched for the cause of his alarm. Theron crouched lower behind the shrub.

"Hey! It's me, Captain Dannie Theron."

"What? Who's there?" came the startled response, the Mauser swirling around dangerously.

"It's me, Captain – Dannie – Theron."

"God in heaven, Dannie! What's your game? You nearly made me shit myself!"

"You shouldn't have been asleep. What will Oom Piet say when I tell him?"

"Stop messing about and show yourself."

"Put up your Mauser. I'm not standing up with your twitchy finger on that trigger."

"How do I know you are Captain Theron and not some Khaki trying to fool me?"

"Now *you* stop messing. Who else could have snuck up on you like that? And anyway, if I was a Khaki, don't you think I would have killed you instead of throwing a stone?"

The burgher remained silent as he calculated the implications of what Theron had said. Eventually he lowered the barrel of his rifle.

"OK," he called sulkily, "but don't tell Oom Piet. He's already in a bad mood."

Theron

Theron stood up slowly and walked cautiously towards the burgher, who watched him warily, ready to raise his rifle if required. In the improving light, Theron noted the tattered, torn and dirt-smeared greatcoat draped over his drooping shoulders. His tough leather hat was still intact, but a white, salty sweat stain formed a band around it and a curtain of greasy hair, almost reaching his shoulders, hung lankly below it. Theron kept a cautious eye on the filthy hands that held the rifle, especially the one poised over the trigger. As he drew closer the burgher tilted his head to scrutinise Theron closely. Theron observed a disinterested flicker of recognition in his bloodshot eyes. Dark shadows showed on the tanned and dirty skin below his dull, blue eyes. Little else of his face was visible behind the expansive, unkempt beard. The sentry did not move and Theron stopped in front of him and smiled a greeting.

The burgher nodded curtly. He mumbled grumpily, "Follow me" and turned his back on Theron to walk up the slope. As he did so, an odour of stale humanity drifted towards Theron. Everyone Theron had come across in the last few days had an unwashed smell. He was aware that his own person had an unpleasant whiff, but the stink that rose from this man made Theron catch his breath and hold back a moment before he followed the shuffling figure away from the river.

They walked through the ruined willow woodland, the splintered branches standing stark and jagged against a blood-red dawn sky. The colour bled into the river mist that swirled around them and Theron thought the gait of the ghostly shadow in front of him was that of someone enduring life rather than living it. Theron shivered and drew his wet jacket more closely around him in a vain attempt to warm himself. Even without the dulling effect of the mist, Theron noted the silence. Not a single bird was singing on this cold, dead morning.

As they moved away from the river the mist thinned and fell away. An appalling smell of human and animal waste and death grew stronger with each step they took towards the trenches and dongas that lined the top of the riverbank and the people huddled within them. Theron attempted to moderate his breathing. He took shallow breaths to avoid the stink, but this only caused him to inhale more deeply and he gagged on the foul taste of the air. Eventually he gave up and resorted to holding his hand in front of his nose and mouth in a vain attempt to filter the noisome stench he was breathing in. Despite

363

the early hour, swarms of flies peppered the air with their erratic flight and their constant buzzing invaded the silence.

Theron's escort guided him though crowds of people in various stages of rousing. Some were lighting fires; many were simply sitting, morosely silent.

"Why has the General concentrated his forces like this?"

The man trudged on and spoke over his shoulder.

"The English have taken most of the trenches we dug at the beginning of the battle and have pushed in our flanks. We are all concentrated in this small area now. For a people who normally live miles from each other, it is a new experience." He gave a small, sardonic laugh.

As Theron passed by, the people stared dully at him from lifeless eyes, encircled with dark shadows. The gaunt faces of the men were disguised by their beards, but were clear to see on the unbearded youths and, particularly, on the women. There was none of the chat or joshing one would normally expect of an army after a good night's sleep and anticipating a hearty breakfast. The burghers sat quietly, either enveloped in their own thoughts or consulting their Bibles in the orange sunlight. The few women he passed were invariably cuddling a quiet, haunted-looking child, who snuggled close to its comforter. What a contrast to his last visit. These people seemed to be in despair, their spirit driven from them. Their lethargy was such that Theron doubted whether they even had the will to escape.

Beyond the ragged masses, on a terrace near the top of the ravine bank, Theron noted a dozen men standing in a circle among the splintered remains of willow trees. He was led in their direction. His escort tapped the shoulder of one of the War Council members who, recognising Theron created a gap for him to join. Silent greetings were nodded at Theron.

Colonel Albrecht was in the middle of expressing his views to the Council. He hesitated as Theron joined the group, gave him a curt Germanic nod of welcome and continued. His comments were accompanied with attentive and affirmative murmurs from his audience. When he finished speaking there was a polite pause to allow his arguments to register. Then Cronjé turned to their visitor.

Theron was suddenly conscious of how his own shabby attire compared rather favourably to the feral appearance of those around him. Cronjé had also noticed the contrast and quipped, "Welcome, Captain Theron. I must say you are looking well turned out this morning. You must give me the details of your tailor!"

The joke fell flat and only served to emphasise the dispirited mood of the Council. Cronjé grunted at the lack of humour among his officers and continued on a more serious note.

"So, Captain, what news of the reinforcements?"

Theron looked around the circle of men. He had the feeling that whatever news he gave them would be unwelcome. If there were reinforcements on their way, it would mean having to continue to fight, and the men did not look like they had much fight left in them. However, to be told there were no reinforcements did not change their current, objectionable situation. He delayed answering so that they knew there was no news about reinforcements and then avoided the question altogether.

"Oom, I have been asked by General de Wet to come to you again to advise you to withdraw your forces to Poplar Grove and to inform you that there is no alternative to this option. It is the view not only of General de Wet, but also of Generals Botha and Andreas Cronjé that your position here is untenable and that you should leave before you are forced to surrender." Theron noticed Cronjé bristle at the suggestion but continued. "Oom, should you be forced to surrender…"

This time Cronjé raised his hand to interject.

"My dear Captain, I have the greatest respect for you and I know you are simply the messenger, but if you use that word again I shall have to shoot you." He was only half joking. He continued. "When you joined us, we were discussing our ongoing strategy and the idea of surrendering had not arisen. I can assure you that surrendering has not crossed the minds of any of us here. Is that not so?"

The moment he finished speaking Cronjé realised his mistake. In articulating his thoughts in that way, he had offered the opportunity for those present to express their opinions about capitulating. He frowned at his own stupidity and prepared himself to have to counter those who spoke of capitulation with his own words of victory and glory. But the burghers remained silent. Cronjé gazed at each of them in turn. Although he felt sure that the thought of surrender *had* crossed the minds of some of them, no one spoke out to contradict him. He was genuinely touched by the realisation that it was their respect for him that kept them quiet. He turned back to Theron.

"Please continue, Captain," he said humbly.

"Yes Oom. Under those circumstances, it is the opinion of the generals that the loss of your men from the Republics' armies would be calamitous. It would amount to almost ten per cent of the entire Afrikander force. The demoralising effect on the rest of the army would be catastrophic. The surr… uhm … the … er … the loss of so many at Paardeberg would leave the road to Bloemfontein completely open for the English. It would be impossible to stop them."

Several of the listening officers nodded in agreement but before any could add their opinion to the discussion, a deep, monstrous roar rolled across the veldt towards them. Everyone turned in the direction from which it came. A murmur of consternation rippled around the Council. Some looked at their watches – it was only eight thirty – but that was definitely the sound of cannon, and it sounded huge. A few seconds later the shell hit the far end of the laager with an almighty explosion that threw a mountain of dirt, soil and rubble into the air.

"God in Heaven," someone burst out. "That must be as big as our own Long Tom. If they have guns that size we really are done for. It's surrender or get out! We need to decide and quickly."

The men leaned into the circle. The 'get out' plan was hurriedly discussed. The question was how to do it. Ideas came fast. The river was in flood. Many of the burghers could not swim. A bridge was required. There was plenty of wood around, most of it conveniently blasted to pieces by the English shelling. There was enough rope to lash it together. There was already one rope thrown across the river. Placing another next to it would help hold the bridge in place. With a bridge they could take the women and children as well.

Theron was averse to this idea, but did not raise an objection.

The bridge would have to be strong enough to bear the weight of the remaining horses and oxen so they could be rescued as well.

Theron did object to this and was supported in his arguments by Albrecht. To build a bridge strong enough to take livestock would take much longer. But they only had one night in which to build the bridge and during which to escape. This window of opportunity would not allow the construction of a bridge of sufficient strength to carry oxen and horses. But the burghers, having been reminded of their desire to save their horses, would not be shifted.

Theron suggested that the animals could be swum across. He knew it would not be possible, but he thought the burghers might not be aware of the strength of the raging waters. He hoped they would agree to the suggestion, realising the truth only when it was too late. It was a forlorn hope. He was informed about the poor wretches that had been swept away the day before, during the despicable shelling by the English. The horses would be needed, it was argued, to protect the flanks of the men who would have to march to safety. They could leave the oxen, but the horses would go. The decision was made.

It was arranged that wood, rope and other materials would be stockpiled along the riverbank during the day, and as soon as it was dark enough to hide the bridge-building activities, they would commence work. They would be across the river and well on their way across the veldt before daybreak. Theron would return to General de Wet during the night and ensure that his commando was in place to protect the retreating men. The War Council broke up, each man enthusiastically taking his orders to his commando to initiate the work. Theron watched them go. He was not sure whether their enthusiasm was the result of a belief that they would succeed or because they had something to distract them from the shells that were now raining down on the laager.

General Hector Archibald Macdonald

General Hector Archibald Macdonald limped up to Roberts' lean-to and stood outside the entrance. Inside Roberts sat at his desk, a lamp throwing a golden light on the paperwork over which his grey-haired head was bent in deep concentration. Chaprasi Chet Singh moved from behind him and stood smartly to attention. Roberts looked up.

"General Macdonald is here sir," Singh announced.

"Ah, General," Roberts smiled, "Come in, come in."

Macdonald hobbled into the canvas shelter, leaning heavily on his stick. Singh hovered, ready to offer support. Macdonald stopped in front of Roberts' desk, snapped to attention as best he could, encumbered as he was with his bandaged foot, and saluted.

Roberts leaned back in his canvas chair, his arms resting lightly on the table. He rolled his shoulders to release the tension that had built up from hours of pouring over his desk, reading and writing reports.

"It's good to see you out and about, General. How's the foot?"

"Fine, thank you, sir. It would be better if those damned doctors would leave it alone so that it could heal. Look at the size of my foot!" He pointed at it with his stick. "Virtually everything you see in that parcel is medical material. My foot is so suffocated that it might drop off from lack of air."

Roberts laughed. "You must sit down and rest your poor foot. Singh, please bring a chair for the General."

"That is very kind, sir. But I shall only stay if it is convenient and then only for a minute."

"Nonsense, Hector. I am delighted that you have visited. I need a break from all this anyway." He gestured at the papers scattered across his desk.

Roberts watched quietly as Macdonald was helped to another canvas chair which Singh had erected in front of the desk. Once he was settled, and as this was a social visit, Roberts asked Singh to pour each of them a glass of whisky. Scotch this time in honour of his guest. Singh also took and filled Macdonald's pipe. Then he got up and, taking his own chair, brought it around to the front of the desk and set it down before Macdonald. He eyed the other man's walking stick as he sat down.

368

"That is a fearsome-looking stick you have there," he commented.

"I believe it's called a knobkierrie, sir. It's a native war club." Macdonald held it up to show off the round, solid wooden head. "I wish I'd had one of these when I was a regimental sergeant major. I remember a few recruits who'd have benefited from having felt this on their skulls." The two men laughed.

"And your foot? How much longer do you have to suffer the attentions of our over-zealous doctors?"

"Not much longer, I hope, sir. The wound was remarkably clean. Bullet went straight through the top of my boot, my foot and the sole. Nice tidy little wound and only one broken bone. But the force of the bullet when it hit my foot nearly dislocated my blasted knee." Macdonald absent-mindedly rubbed his right knee in sympathy. "Those Boers have incredible weapons, sir. I have never faced the like of them before."

"Indeed, they do," agreed Roberts, "and unfortunately, they are superior to our own. And, though I hate to admit it, the men behind them are better marksmen than our soldiers."

Macdonald nodded ruefully. "Yes sir, but we should have expected that from last time."

"'81, you mean?"

"Yes sir, '81." A dark scowl crossed Macdonald's face. "That was a contemptible debacle. Those blasted politicians should have kept their damned noses out of our business. We could have won that war. We *would* have, if they'd given us time, if they'd given *you* time, sir."

Roberts nodded in agreement. "I like to think so, but it was not to be. I sailed all the way to Cape Town to take command and by the time I arrived the government had sued for peace. I disembarked from one ship and boarded the next one back to England – a ridiculous waste of my time. Still, it has been good to get a second chance."

The two men smiled at each other. Then Roberts continued, "So, General, I do not suppose you came here to complain about our politicians. To what do I owe the pleasure of your company? Is it solely sociable?"

"Not entirely, sir," Macdonald admitted. "I wish to discuss a matter which is a combination of professional consideration and personal revenge."

"*Revenge*, General?"

"Yes sir. Tuesday will be the 27th – the anniversary of the Battle of Majuba, or Majuba Day as the Boers call it. As you know, that is a very auspicious day for the Boer and a very inauspicious one for us."

"Truly inauspicious," Roberts concurred. He continued, with a twinkle in his eye, saying, "I heard you became a bit unruly that day, General."

Macdonald grinned back like the Cheshire Cat from *Alice in Wonderland*. "It was the only bright spot on a very dark day, sir."

"I suppose the Boers deserved what they got."

"Indeed they did, sir. They were over us like a rash and we, I am ashamed to say, were ill-prepared. I ran out of bullets and had to use my rifle like a club." He looked at his round-headed stick. "This would have served me well." He lifted it, feeling its weight as he executed a couple of mock blows with it. "Still, needs must. All I had was my rifle. I was knocking six bells out of them when, as I swung the rifle back over my head to bring it down on another beggar, this bear of a Boer grabbed the rifle from behind me and wrenched it from my hands. Well, as you can imagine, sir, I was incensed. I turned to face him and he glared at me. I'm pretty handy with my fists, so I let him have it. I felled him with a single blow. It was, and still is, the most marvellous punch I have ever thrown. He didn't crumple to the ground like a ragdoll, but toppled over straight as a Scots pine."

Macdonald drew a long drag on his pipe and slowly let the smoke drift from his lips as he savoured the memory.

"Like a Scots pine," he murmured. Then his eyes lit up, "But the thing I remember best of all was the look of utter surprise in his eyes as he slowly fell away from me." Macdonald let out a chuckle of pure delight as he recalled the scene. "It was magnificent, absolutely magnificent." A mischievous grin broke on his face and his eyes sparkled. "But his mates did not think so. They threw themselves at me and really roughed me over." Macdonald laughed. "I did deserve it, though. It was most un-officer-like behaviour," he concluded, with an embarrassed laugh. Then his embarrassment deepened and he flushed, "But you've heard that all before, sir, too many times, I fear."

Roberts smiled at his friend. He had led Macdonald along, knowing he would not be able to resist retelling the tale.

"My dear Hector," he laughed, "I shall never tire of hearing that story. It is one of the best antidotes to glumness I know. And hearing it from the horse's mouth, so to speak, makes it all the better."

Macdonald was caught up in the moment and joined Roberts, laughing heartily. Only when they stopped laughing did Roberts raise his glass of whisky. "To British pluck," he toasted.

"To British pluck!" responded Macdonald.

Roberts put down his glass and looked intently at Macdonald, whose eyes sparkled.

"So, General, you wish to avenge Majuba. And what is your recommendation on the matter?"

Macdonald was instantly serious. "They have to surrender tomorrow or, even better, on Majuba Day," he said bluntly.

Roberts was taken aback by Macdonald's sudden change in manner. "They do?"

"Yes sir. If Cronjé surrenders on Majuba Day, he will deprive the Boer of their most celebrated success against the British army. I would be satisfied if they surrendered tomorrow, but Majuba Day would be eminently better. The demoralising effect on the ordinary Boer will be significant. Imagine the message the news that 'the Lion of Potchefstroom' capitulated on Majuba Day would send to the Boer! And picture the jubilation back home. I can see the headlines in the *London Gazette*: 'Majuba Hill avenged!' After twenty years, a great wrong will finally be righted." Macdonald stared at Roberts expectantly.

"I admire your enthusiasm, General. However, I am doing all I possibly can. I have every cannon virtually melting from the number of shells we are pouring on the Boer. The balloon has improved the effectiveness of our bombardment." Roberts frowned, "I must say it is astonishing that the Boers have been able to withstand our bombardment thus far, but I think the Howitzers that arrived last night will change things. There's not much can survive shells that size."

"Sir, if I may, we should push the Canadians and Shropshires up faster. The Canadians in particular seem to have the measure of the Boers. They are already in a position which should allow them to get within the enemy defences with ease and we know how the Boer hates anything to do with close combat. The closer the Canadians get, the more likely the Boer are to surrender."

"I hear what you say, General. Indeed, I am already doing what you suggest. I am pushing forward as fast as I dare, but I shall not put men's lives at risk unnecessarily. You saw yourself the folly of advancing too quickly."

Macdonald looked disappointed.

"I tell you what, Hector, I will intensify the bombardment and instead of focusing on specific areas of the laager, I shall order the artillery to repeatedly sweep across the entire area. There will be nowhere for them to hide. I cannot force the situation any more quickly, but that approach should induce a quick surrender."

Macdonald nodded. He wanted to say more, to point out that guns alone had not succeeded so far and more was needed. He wanted to remind Roberts again of the dread that the Boers had of close combat with infantry. He wanted to emphasise to Roberts that the sight of a charging infantry brandishing cold steel bayonets was the sure fix to the present stalemate. Macdonald could see his desire to avenge the humiliation of Majuba Hill slipping away, but he held his tongue; Roberts was not for turning.

Monday 26 February 1900

General Pieter Arnoldus Cronjé

General Pieter Arnoldus Cronjé turned and pushed his way through the throng of silent burghers. Behind him, the men watched in horror as the shattered fragments of their bridge were swept away by the turbulent river. It was barely day-light and already the English balloon was airborne and directing shells into the laager. The nearly completed bridge had been their first target.

Cronjé tramped, heavy footed, back through the earthworks and trenches to his headquarters. He smirked to himself. His *headquarters* consisted of a stretch of trench, his trek stool, another for his Bible and a patch of earth into which was scraped a map of his defences and the main positions of the English and their guns. He sat down on his small trek stool, silent and moody as a grizzly bear. He stared distractedly at the rough earth map. A mug of steaming coffee appeared in front of his face and he looked up to see Hester offering him the hot, comforting drink, a tight-lipped smile barely perceptible on her fragile face. Fragile, thought Cronjé. He had never thought of Hester as fragile before, but now she looked like an aged child, her diminutive stature and vulnerability emphasised by her suddenly looking very old.

"Thank you, dear," he smiled at her. "Come, sit with me."

He took his Bible from the other stool, placed it in his lap, took the coffee from Hester and patted the seat, inviting her to sit. She joined him, folding her hands around her own coffee to draw heat into her cold fingers. He placed an arm around her and she burrowed into his coat, feeling the coldness of it against her cheek. She closed her eyes and tried to remember the times they had sat together on the steps of the stoep back home to watch the sunrise. How she loved those quiet times together, with the children still asleep and the huge ocean of the veldt stretching out in front of them. But even with her eyes shut and concentrating hard, she could not see it in her mind's eye. The constant noise of the shells and the smell of the trenches destroyed any memory of those beautiful African mornings.

"The bridge is gone?" she enquired quietly.

"Yes. The English have become very accurate with their guns."

"Could we have got away even if the bridge had been finished?"

"Only God knows the answer to that, my dear, and He did not want to give us the opportunity to find out."

"Maybe Dannie and Major Albrecht were right. Maybe we should have built a smaller bridge. Then we might have finished it and you and the men could have got away."

"Maybe. But I would not have left."

Hester sat up and looked him in the eye. "Piet," she said sharply, "if they had succeeded in building the bridge you *will* have gone."

"I would not have abandoned you, my dear."

"You would not have stayed on *my* account. I would not have allowed it. You know that."

"Of course, my dear, so I would have stayed for another reason – a military reason."

"Such as?"

"Oh, there are many. War is not black and white. I would have thought of one."

"I say, again, such as?"

"Hester, I am a general, I would have thought of a reason. The problem would have been to convince the others not to stay because I fear some of those idiots would have stayed with me. So we would not have been in a very much different situation."

"They do respect and admire you, Piet."

"Yes, so it would seem. Like I said, idiots."

"Pieter!" Hester scolded, "Enough of this nonsense. You are a great general. Look how you have taught the English not to mess with us – not to mess with the Lion of Potchefstroom. The English lion," she laughed mockingly, "is not a scratch on our Afrikander lion."

Cronjé drew his wife back to him enfolding her in his arms.

"You are very kind Hester and you are very dear to me. That is why I would not have left you."

"Piet ..." she started to object but he shushed her.

"It is no longer important. We are where we are. Now I need to stop the men from surrendering."

"Surrendering?" Hester broke from his embrace and sat up again. "Surrendering? Do you mean that?"

Cronjé sighed and he physically slumped, his shoulders falling like an undermined castle wall. "I did not tell you, but at the War Council yesterday there was a strong desire from many that we surrender. The commandants did not actually say it, out of respect for me, but it was obvious. They have lost heart and so have many of the burghers."

"But I thought you said many would have stayed and fought with you."

"Maybe not many, but some would have, the ones who still believe in our cause and who will fight to the bitter end. And to carry on fighting would have been possible if those who have lost heart had been able to leave, but with the bridge destroyed, those who want to surrender are still with us. Now they will complain about the conditions in which they are living and bemoan the fact that our position is impossible. Their discontent will spread like a contagion. An army cannot operate when there are those present who have given up on the cause. The rest will also lose heart."

"Are you saying we will surrender?"

"I hope not. I hope to be able to convince the commandants not to, especially now."

"Especially now?"

"Yes, Hester, especially now. I know you have had a terrible time these last few weeks, so you may have forgotten that tomorrow is Majuba Day."

Hester looked surprised and remained silent as she counted the days. "So it is," she said. "We must plan a celebration and a service of thanksgiving."

"That is a good idea. It will take the burghers' minds off surrendering. And I need to convince them not to surrender, or at least not today or tomorrow."

"So what did you say yesterday to convince them not to surrender?"

"Me? Oh, it was not anything I said. It was Dannie."

Hester's eyes sparkled. "What a wonderful man!" She smiled mischievously at Cronjé, "If only I was forty years younger."

"Ha!" came the grumpy response.

"And what did the delightful Dannie Theron say to change their minds?"

"First, he said there was no hope of reinforcements."

"He said *that*?"

"Did I not tell you?"

Hester shook her head.

"There will be no reinforcements. We are on our own. Then he said we had to escape, that the survival of the Republics depended upon it and that if we stayed here we would become prisoners and the Republic would lose one-tenth of its strength and we would lose the war. And then the English dropped their first big shell on us. Actually, it was that shell that really galvanised the burghers into deciding to escape – that and Dannie's words. It was decided we would build the bridge and escape from under the English noses. But now the English have blown up our bridge and we are back where we started, with surrender on everyone's mind."

"But to surrender to the English on *Majuba Day* would be insufferable. Surely they *will* see that?"

"I am not sure that they do," replied Cronjé. "Some of them really have had enough. And they worry about their wives and children."

"Wives and children! Pah! Such nonsense! *We* do not want to surrender. The children have been very badly affected, of course, but the women have no such notions of giving up, especially after all they have suffered. If they heard such nonsense from their husbands, or the other men, they would be *very* angry. They would take the rifles themselves and shoot at the English." Hester laughed. "Have you seen that Alletta Bezuidenhout? What a girl! She would lead the way. So brave and such a beauty. And *her* man was not so stupid as to stay behind," she added, looking pointedly at Cronjé. "No, he did not. A wise head on young shoulders there, hey old man?" she said grinning.

"Aagh!" Cronjé waved a dismissive hand. "He barely knew the girl. We have been together for more years than I can remember."

"Forty-two," Hester chided him.

"After all those years, I shall not let a few English soldiers force us apart." He drew her into him again and she did not resist. They remained silent for some time.

Hester eventually broke the quietness between them. "So now what, Piet?" she asked.

Cronjé drew in a long breath and let it out slowly. Hester waited.

"So now," he said, "I have to convince the War Council not to surrender today or tomorrow. I believe I can do that. I shall work on their pride. I shall remind them that the 27th of February is important to all Afrikanders. It is the day when we remember that no one can take our independence from us. We may be a small nation, but we have our pride and the victory at Majuba Hill is one of our proudest moments. Every year we give praise to God for what he did for us on that day. I shall tell them that if we surrender, we will not be able to celebrate our victory or give thanks to God for the English will not allow it. They will not allow it because they do not want to be reminded that we beat them in the past and we can beat them again. But most of all, they will not allow us to celebrate because, if we surrender, Majuba Day will be theirs. It will be *their* day of celebration. They will take our Majuba from us. Surely, we cannot allow that to happen?"

"No, Pieter, we cannot allow that to happen and neither can our friends." Hester hesitated and then asked in a quiet voice, "And after tomorrow, what then?"

Cronjé's entire body heaved as he drew another deep breath, which he held and then slowly exhaled. "And then," his shoulders drooped further, "and then, I think I shall be forced to surrender."

Tuesday 27 February 1900
Majuba Day

Lieutenant-Colonel William Dillon Otter

Lieutenant-Colonel William Dillon Otter stared into the African night. Somewhere out there, not much more than five hundred yards away, was the enemy. He tried to force his eyes to pierce the darkness so he could discern what they were up to, but it was no use – it was as though a black velvet curtain had been hung between them.

On either side of Otter, the soldiers of the Royal Canadian Regiment extended away along the trench. There were hundreds of them, but Otter was starting to doubt his own certainty about this fact. Even Captain Archibald Macdonell to his right and Captain Henry Bertram Stairs to his left were ghostly shadows and he could not see or hear any of the rest of his regiment. The order for complete silence was being strictly adhered to. At least, thought Otter, if he could not see or hear the Canadians, then neither could the Boers, which of course was the point. A stirring and rustle behind Otter made him turn around and squat down.

"Is it time, corporal?" he whispered.

From under a pile of groundsheets which hid the corporal, his pocket watch and his lamp, came a muffled voice.

"Yes sir. Three o'clock. It's time to start the advance."

"Thank you, corporal." Otter stood up and turned back to his place in the line of waiting men. He cleared his throat gently and spoke quietly to the captains who flanked him.

"Gentlemen, it is time to go. Captain Stairs, please return to the second line. Wait five minutes and then follow us. The Engineers are with you. They are to excavate scrapes in which we are to shelter should the Boers start shooting. So do not fall too far behind or the scrapes will be too far from us to allow us to reach them quickly. It will be difficult to see us. So stay close. Is that clear?"

"Yes sir."

"And, gentlemen, make sure everyone maintains complete silence. Good luck and God be with you."

"Thank you, sir," both captains whispered.

Stairs departed. Otter and Macdonell, touching the shoulders of the men standing next to them, said softly, "Get ready to move forward."

383

The order was passed down the line of tense soldiers. Otter listened as the whispered order faded into the distance. He waited until the message came back that everyone was ready.

"Let's go."

His voice came out louder than he intended. It resounded around his head like a clap of thunder. A sense of the protection afforded by the walls of the trench swept over him, which caused his sense of vulnerability to be all the greater as he scrambled out of the trench. He was followed by Macdonell and the others. There was a short period of confusion as they lined up in the dark. Each soldier placed his left hand on the right shoulder of the man to his left. Otter found his neighbour and felt Macdonell's hand rest on his own shoulder. He waited until it was confirmed by whispered messages that the entire company had linked up. Then he stepped slowly forward. The chain of men went with him.

Otter could just see the shadowy figure on whose shoulder his hand rested and he gripped the man's epaulette tightly. He took small, careful paces into the night towards the Boer lines. The weight of Macdonell's hand on his shoulder shifted as he moved, sometimes pulling back slightly as Otter went forward more quickly than Macdonell anticipated, and sometimes pushing when he hesitated too long. Otter counted every step he took. They were short strides, so he estimated that he would be on top of the Boer positions within six hundred to seven hundred paces, eight hundred at most.

Although he could not see the ground, he knew it was uneven and strewn with the debris of war. The willows that had once grown along the river now lay broken in pieces across their path. When someone stood on a brittle twig the snap seemed to reverberate through the stillness. The first time it happened Otter's head fizzed with a nerve-wracking sensation that his skull was too small to contain the dread that coursed through his brain about the consequences of the noise. Every man froze instantly, some in mid-step, their feet hovering in mid-air. They swayed gently like unstable statues, every muscle taut in anticipation of a red-hot projectile boring into their flesh. Their legs twitched in readiness to throw themselves to the ground. The second time sounded like an explosion and Otter's mind drained of any thoughts and emotions. He simply waited.

Otter felt Macdonell's hand push gently on his shoulder. Otter relaxed slightly. The immediate danger had passed. As he stepped forward Otter's tormented mind recalled the conversations he'd had with the officers of the Highlanders.

At Magersfontein they had also stolen towards the Boers in the pitch dark. They had described the same stomach-wrenching tension that he was feeling as he walked towards the enemy, not knowing how close he was to their trenches. Otter clenched his jaw. It was peculiarly comforting to know that the fear he was fighting to over-come had also been felt by the officers of the fearless Highlanders. But, that had not been the end of their story. Something had roused the Boers' suspicions. Nobody seemed to know what, for none had remembered hearing a noise that might have given them away, but the result had been devastating. The Boers had opened a vicious fusillade of rifle fire. And within five minutes the Highlanders had lost over seven hundred dead or wounded, including their commander, General Wauchope. The officers' descriptions of the confusion and terror among the men and of their anguished cries and terrified shouts had been both chilling and heart-wrenching. They had tried to move from closed order to open order, but there had been no escape from the deadly hail of bullets.

The officers had stressed to Otter that he and his men should fall to the ground immediately if the Boers opened fire because once they started to shoot, there would be no escaping their determination to kill British soldiers. Otter tried to swallow, but his mouth was as dry as the veld around him. Under the present circumstances, he thought, their advice was not a great comfort. He felt cold sweat trickle down his side from his arm pits. At Magersfontein, the Boers had fired when the Highlanders had been four hundred yards from their trenches; the Canadians were already within five hundred yards of the enemy when they had started their advance. Otter's greatest wish, at this particular point in time, was that he had never spoken with those Scottish officers. Fortunately for them, they had remained in the trenches to give the Canadians supporting fire should it be needed. And, thought Otter, that's where he should be. His natural leadership style was from the back, like Wellington or Napoleon, so that he could see what was going on and direct the attack as required. But this attack was different. It was at night and although progress was presently agonisingly slow, when the action started it would be fast and could be over in an instant, so he had to be in the thick of it – just like the unfortunate General Wauchope had been at Magersfontein!

Otter felt his stomach lurch and acid bile scalded the top of his throat as another cracking branch broke the silence. The hand on his shoulder closed tightly into a fist, tugging on his uniform, and Macdonell cursed vehemently under his breath. Otter froze. Sweet Jesus, how many times would they get away with it? He felt his knees giving beneath him, but steadied himself and looked behind him, towards the source of the noise. He could not see the second line of Canadians and Engineers that was following. He turned back and stared through the darkness towards the enemy.

Macdonell's hand relaxed and Otter shifted his weight to move forward. He went to count the step, but faltered. Damn, Otter cursed to himself. He had forgotten the number of paces he had taken. Was it 576? Or was it…? Bloody hell, he had no idea. He halted, his mind a jumble of numbers. He took a deep breath to calm himself down and exhaled slowly, but he could not even remember if the total was in the five hundreds or the six hundreds. If the latter, they were almost on the Boers. A few more steps, he thought. He walked forward counting his paces… ten, fifteen, twenty. He scrutinised the blackness. What was that? He stopped and stared. He was just about to have a word with Macdonell when an almighty clatter of metal rattled down the line to his right.

"Who's there!" came a shout in Dutch, followed almost instantly by the bark of a Mauser.

"Get down!" yelled Macdonell at the top of his voice. "Get down!"

But his second shout was drowned out by a storm of rifle fire. Bullets shrieked all around them. Otter hit the ground with such force that he almost winded himself. He let off three rounds, but the flicker of light from his barrel instantly drew more rounds upon him.

"Don't fire!" he shouted. "DO NOT FIRE!" He turned to Macdonell, "Pass the message down the line. The men are *not* to fire. It will make them an easy target for the Boers."

Shit, thought Otter, looking at the line of spitting flames in front of him. Their trench was less than fifty yards away. At that range they would pick us off to a man. The message not to fire travelled quickly and the Canadians lowered their rifles and pressed themselves into the cold dirt. Just inches above them the air swarmed with bullets.

Otter cautiously turned his head to look behind him. A long display of flickering flames flashed along the second line of Canadians. Beyond them, off to the left, another bank of flashes revealed that the Highlanders were giving the Boers the full benefit of their musketry to draw fire away from Otter and the front line. Soon the shooting from the second line died down and stopped. The Boers' shooting shifted to focus on the Highlanders. The air over Otter calmed down and he became aware of the sound, just audible above the snapping Mausers and the barking reply of Lee-Enfields, of the scrape of entrenching tools as the rear line of Canadians and the Engineers dug themselves into the soft earth as though their lives depended on it, which, Otter thought grimly, it did. Just as it did for him and his men, especially as daylight would soon be upon them. A faint glow had already appeared on the eastern horizon.

Otter turned to his right and whispered hoarsely, "Captain Macdonell?"

"Yes sir?"

"Pass on the order for everyone to crawl back towards the Engineers. They might have scraped something deep enough for us to shelter in by now. If not, we can help them. Be sure to instruct the men to move with absolute stealth."

"Yes sir."

Otter then turned to his left and reached out to the man next to him.

"Soldier?"

"Yes sir?"

Otter repeated the order, adding, "Do you understand? Absolute silence."

"Yes sir."

Otter lay still until he heard the sound of shuffling as the soldiers started to slither backwards towards the safety of the protective hollows they hoped had been prepared for them. He started to slide back himself. Progress seemed agonisingly slow. The shooting gradually stopped and, except for the occasional shot from a nervous Boer, a strained quietness fell over the veld. The eerie silence made Otter's skin crawl. Somewhere in that stillness hundreds of Mauser barrels were pointing in his direction, their owners' listening just as intently as he was, waiting for him to make a sound. Any snapping twigs would not be ignored this time.

In contrast to his slow retreat to the second line, the transition from inky-black night to daylight seemed to be progressing rapidly. As the eastern sky lightened to a pale pink, Otter knew the silence of their retreat would no longer protect his troops and soon they would be stuck in the open at the full mercy of the spiteful Mausers. A thin, wispy mist, glowing pink, was rising from the cold ground. Otter hoped it would thicken sufficiently to hide his men. Where the hell were those bloody Engineers and their trench? He was considering what to do for the best when, he heard a shouted order to fall back. Someone else apparently had the same concerns. The sudden holler from Macdonell nearly caused Otter to leap out of his skin.

"Do *not* fall back! Stay down," Macdonell yelled.

Otter turned and in the reddening half-light saw Macdonell in a semi-raised position looking anxiously around him. The Mausers burst into life. Macdonell flung himself down. A wave of death swept across the veld. A soldier leapt up and ran. He managed ten paces before he fell lifeless to the ground. Macdonell roared the order again and the men nearby flattened themselves into the earth.

Otter whipped his head around as he heard another cry of agony. The men on his far left flank were up and running, their dark forms bathed in a deep red glow by the rising sun. Otter watched in horror as some were flung to the ground by the force of the Mauser bullets smashing through their bodies.

Captain Stairs, crouching low over his entrenching tool and shovelling dirt with demonic frenzy, was suddenly aware of the rapid approach of several dark figures. Shit! The Boers were counter-attacking! Before he was able to pick up his rifle, the men were on him.

"Fall back!" came a shout, in a Canadian drawl, from one of the men as he dashed past.

The relief at hearing the Canadian accent was so great that Stairs did not take in what had been said. The first soldier had already passed, but Stairs leapt forward and grabbed the next infantryman running past him.

"What is going on?" he asked.

"We're falling back."

"What?"

"We've been ordered to fall back."

"That's crap! Pick up that tool and dig!"

He shoved the soldier into the shallow trench and chased after the other retreating Canadians. Bullets whizzed around him as he rushed across the veld yelling for them to stop and get back to the line of trenches being dug by the Engineers. As he neared one man, he heard a Scottish howl of anger from the Highlanders' trenches.

"The bastards are attacking!"

The soldier in front of Stairs was suddenly flung backwards and he crashed to the ground on his back. Bloody hell! Now the Scots are shooting at us as well. Stairs turned and sprinted back to the safety of his newly dug trench.

Macdonell looked at Otter, who was staring around him uncertainly. Macdonell crawled closer to him.

"Sir, we cannot stay here."

"I know captain! But we can't get up and run either. And that bloody sun is rising damned fast."

"Sir, we will have run for it."

"Are you mad captain? You saw what happened to those who tried that. We will be slaughtered. We will need to crawl… and crawl fast. Look, some are already doing it."

"Yes sir, but look at the amount of dust they are creating. Some are still getting hit."

"Hell! This is terrible!"

"Sir, we need to run for it. Some will be shot, but most should make it to the trench." Macdonell pointed, "Look, sir, it is only about thirty yards away."

Otter glanced over his shoulder at the fresh linear mound of sand that formed a scar across the veld.

"OK captain, give the order. Let's hope they can run bloody fast."

Macdonell yelled as loud as he could. "Fall back on the Engineers. I'll give every man who gets back before me a shilling."

He leapt up and sprinted towards the line of sand. Otter chased after him. The rest needed no encouragement. The race to the trench was on. Otter was delighted at how *fast* his men could run and he calculated that Macdonell was going to be considerably out of pocket by the time he threw himself into the trench that had been dug for their protection.

While his men laughed and joked at their relief at being safely hidden from the enemy by the protective mound of dirt, Otter crouched in the shallow trench and carefully studied his position and that of the Boers.

The vast African sun heaved itself off the horizon, throwing a long-shadowed, red veneer over the veld. Otter stared down his field glasses. The deep shadows, the broken remnants of trees and the thin red mist floating just above the ground made interpreting what he saw difficult, but he could make out a low ridge of freshly thrown up dirt less than one hundred yards from where he crouched. It ran more or less parallel to his own shallow trench and, like his, it started at the top of the river embankment, on his right, and extended at right angles into the veld. At numerous points along its length slouch hats would appear and then quickly disappear. There seemed to be a large number of them. Macdonell had informed him that his own force numbered only one hundred and forty men and twenty-five Engineers. He would not be making any stupid charges today. He noted that the line of his defences as they extended towards the river rose above the mist. He had to use that higher ground to his advantage.

"Captain."

"Yes sir?" Macdonell responded.

"Move the men into the trenches on that small rise to our right. Get the Engineers to improve that stretch of trench. It will give us a good position to make a stand for the day."

"Yes sir."

The Engineers, joined by the infantrymen, made short work of the soft soil and soon Otter had a respectable section of trench in which he and his senior officers could stand and survey the Boer lines.

"An opportune selection of defensive position, sir," commented Stairs.

"Indeed, we have been fortunate," replied Otter nonchalantly, but inwardly he was pleased with himself.

"Their main defensive trench is directly in front of us," he remarked, "running more or less parallel to our own. From the number of heads that keep popping up, there appears to be a lot of men hiding in there."

As he spoke, a slouch hat appeared above the lip of the enemy trench and disappeared instantly as the ground in front of the trench exploded in a haze of dust as it was peppered with Canadian bullets.

"Their defences are not as well prepared as before," observed Macdonell. "They have no parapet of soil to hide behind. We will be able to keep them nice and quiet today."

"And from our elevated position, we can partially see into their trench," added Stairs. "They will have to stay close to their front walls. That will reduce how freely they are able to move around."

"Very good," said Otter. "While it is light, there is no way for them to escape. There is also only one secondary trench that leads from the main one and back towards the main laager." Otter indicated the dark line of the trench. "If we put a rifleman – I suggest Corporal McHarg – near that stump," Otter pointed to it, "he will have a clear view down their auxiliary trench. No one will be able to retreat or approach without exposing themselves to being shot. Captain," Otter turned to Stairs, "can you make sure the Engineers establish a safe firing point for Corporal McHarg at that location? So, gentlemen, all we need to do now is sit and wait. Tonight that trench will be ours, *and* it will give us direct access into the main Boer camp."

"At last the table has turned. It does feel good to have the Boer under the cosh for a change," Stairs commented.

Otter watched Stairs and McHarg for a while as they supervised a couple of indignant Royal Engineers in the construction of his firing station. Trying to ignore the flies buzzing around his head, he took up his field glasses and scanned the Boer trenches. His binoculars passed over the black stain of the burnt Boer wagons and along the line of the trench in front of him. There was no activity in the trench. The Boers were sitting very tight. He dropped his line of sight down into the ravine towards the river.

"Well, I'll be…," he muttered to himself. Turning, he called over to a soldier.

"Get Corporal McHarg here instantly, private!"

"Yes sir," the man saluted and ran to fetch the corporal.

Otter returned the binoculars to his eyes and watched the shabby, slouch-hatted figure walk towards the river. McHarg appeared at his shoulder.

"Sir?"

Otter pointed out the Boer. "Someone to get your eye in, corporal."

The Boer stood with his feet shoulder-width apart and urinated into the river, gyrating his hips to sweep the arch of liquid from right to left and back over the water. McHarg raised his rifle and took aim, but Otter placed a restraining hand on the rifleman's shoulder.

"Let the man finish. We should all be allowed some dignity when we die."

McHarg nodded grimly and waited. As the man turned to retrace his steps to the Boer lines, McHarg slowly squeezed the trigger. The man crumpled backwards and splashed into the river. His hat floated slowly downstream.

The reaction from the Boer line was immediate. Their trench became alive with slouch hats and Mausers. The bullets sang through the air with such ferocity that all the Canadians could do was crouch behind their own defences and wait for the barrage to abate. When it did, the Canadians returned fire and it became obvious just how inadequate the Boer defences were. Several Boers were struck and their attack stopped quickly. It was apparent to Otter that there was considerable consternation among the enemy. He could hear raised voices and shouts coming from their trench. He ordered McHarg back to his post. The Boers' shouts died down, but Otter could hear snatches of a determined conversation. A plan was being hatched.

"Prepare the men for an attack," Otter said to his captains.

McHarg leaned into the wall of his firing station and stared down the barrel of his rifle. He squeezed the trigger back slightly and waited. A stillness descended over both armies. Otter tilted his ear, concentrating on every sound. Through narrowed eyes he searched the deep shadows for any movement that might hint at what the enemy were up to.

Suddenly a Boer appeared and sprinted down the auxiliary trench. His hat lifted from his head and tumbled to the ground behind him. Otter watched his arms and legs pumping as he sped away, his long strides looked clumsy on the uneven floor of the trench. The vicious bark of McHarg's Lee-Enfield made Otter jump. A puff of dust rose from the jacket between the man's shoulder blades and the Boer's lifeless body was thrown forward onto the ground just short of a bend that would have taken him to safety.

A primeval howl of grief rolled across the veld. It could have been a word or simply a meaningless sound, but it rose from deep within its owner's chest, bursting into the atmosphere. The silver mist seemed to shiver as the wretched moan rent the air, and then it died, as though slowly smothered. The sound startled the Canadians. Rifle barrels dipped and they craned their necks to locate the cause of the extraordinary noise. Then, for a brief instant, a white scrap flitted above the enemy trench. Otter thought he had imagined it. It reappeared, a stained scrap of white cloth, and then it was gone again.

"What the hell is going on?" asked Macdonell.

Men lowered their rifles but he barked at them. "Keep your rifles ready!"

A head appeared above the enemy trench but instantly ducked down under a shower of bullet-induced dust.

"Don't shoot," shouted Otter. "Just be ready."

"Who is going to win their little battle?" muttered Otter to himself. "Those who want to surrender or the nay sayers?"

The white scrap popped up and was instantly dragged down again. Angry voices erupted from the Boer lines. The white flag reappeared, followed by a head, shoulders and arms, as the man tried to scramble out of the trench, but other hands reached up and pulled him back. Otter could not understand what was being said, but there was obviously an exchange of curses and expletives.

He was not sure what to do. What would a British officer do? A full-out frontal attack? Kitchener might do that, but what about Roberts? Probably not. Wait for the Boers to surrender? That was the tactic they were working towards, but it seemed that the situation had now changed. The enemy were in disarray and decisive action was required to take advantage of the situation. Before he could stop himself, he heard his voice call out across the veld.

"Can you hear me?"

There was no answer. He felt a bit foolish. He could feel the eyes of his officers and men on him. He had started something so he could not back down now. Clearing his throat, he cupped his hands around his mouth and in a slow, clear and deliberate voice he called out again.

"Can – you – hear – me?"

"Yes. Who are you?" came a reply in Dutch.

Otter looked around. "Does anyone know what he said?"

There was a general shrugging of shoulders. He tried again.

"Do – you – speak – English?"

"No!" came back the emphatic response.

Again, Otter looked around. "Then how did he know what I said?" he asked in bemusement.

Again, there was a general shrugging of shoulders. Otter turned back towards the enemy lines just as someone clambered out of the trench with some difficulty. The man stood up and held his hands aloft. In one hand, he waved his hat, and in the other, a piece of dirty white cloth.

"Enough!" the man shouted. "Enough, enough!"

"Do not shoot!" Otter commanded, and then, to the man, he called "Come forward."

The man staggered forward and stopped. He looked bewildered. He turned his white-haired head this way and that as if looking for something, his long white beard sweeping to the left and right.

"Sweet Jesus," said Macdonell. "He's old enough to be my grandfather!"

"Hold your fire men," Otter ordered again. This was said more to reassure the confused old man standing before them than as an order to the Canadians, most of whom had already lowered their rifles. The Boer took another step and then collapsed onto his knees. He folded over and slumped forward, letting out a low, desolate moan. A youth jumped out of the Boer trench and ran towards the crumpled figure, crouching down and throwing a protective arm around him.

Otter heard Macdonell mutter to himself, "He's a boy. We're fighting granddads and their grandsons."

The youth spoke gently to the old man, who nodded, his whole body shaking with the vigour of his agreement. Then the boy looked up towards the Canadians and called out, "We have had enough. What must we do?"

Otter stood up in full view of the Boers. Macdonell and Stairs followed suit.

"Please step forward, sir," called Otter "and bring your comrade with you." He gesticulated vigorously for them to come closer.

The youth lowered his head to his elderly ward and spoke to him. Then he stood up and gently helped him to his feet. Behind them the Boer trench was lined with bearded faces under slouch hats, watching intently. The Canadians remained quiet as the two Boers staggered towards them.

"Captain, send two men to help our prisoners into the trench," ordered Otter.

As two soldiers supported the old man, the youth approached Otter, having already decided that he was the officer in charge. Angrily wiping away a tear, he stood to attention and saluted.

"Sir," he said, "my name is Pieter Krueler. This is my father and the last man you shot was my brother. We have had enough of this war. We have come to surrender."

Otter studied the gaunt-faced young man. "You speak English?"

The boy nodded.

"And the rest of you? What of them?"

"They are ready as well. You only need to call to them and tell them to surrender."

Otter nodded. To the two soldiers supporting the old man, he said, "Give that fellow something to eat and drink. You," he addressed the boy, "come with me."

Otter climbed out of the trench and gestured for the boy to follow. He rested a hand on Krueler's shoulder.

"Say to them, soldiers of the South African Republic, if you wish to surrender, we are ready to receive you honourably. Signal to us that you wish to do so and we will let you approach safely."

The boy cupped his hands around his mouth and translated for Otter. They stood and waited. Otter was about to tell the boy to repeat the message when a white handkerchief rose above the Boer trench, and then another and another, and two more and soon a ripple of scraps of white cloth rolled down the entire line of the Boer trench.

A chill ran down Otter's spine.

Captain Daniël Johannes Stephanus Theron

Captain Daniël Johannes Stephanus Theron lay on his stomach at the entrance to the shallow cave he had discovered on the upper slopes of Kitchener's Hill. With his upper body supported on his elbows, he surveyed the scene below him. The Modder River snaked across the veldt, its brown waters swirling in the late morning sun. Within one of its coils lay the black stain of the destroyed wagons, with its pearly-grey necklace of earthworks. In the centre of the dark smear a large white flag hung lifelessly from a tilting pole propped up against the burnt hulk of a wagon.

This was not how it was supposed to end. Theron had escaped from Cronjé's laager, as agreed, and had made his way back to Poplar Grove. He had even stolen an English horse to ride there. He had told de Wet of the plan to build a bridge and then returned to the battlefield that same night, creeping through the English lines and onto Kitchener's Hill. From there he was to give the signal, a few flashes of sunlight on a mirror, telling de Wet when Cronjé's army had broken free. De Wet would be poised to attack the kopje with his entire commando to distract the English, and the South African Republic Army would fight its way to freedom. *That* was how it was supposed to end.

But Cronjé had not appeared. Theron had stayed on the kopje, concealed at the entrance to his cave. De Wet's commando had remained hidden in the vastness of their veldt. They had waited all day and all night, until the dawn of Majuba Day. Majuba Day! Surely Cronjé would leave the laager on Majuba Day. And so he did, but not as Theron had been expecting.

Snaking from the devastated remnants of the laager was a dark line of people. Theron's vision blurred and he angrily blinked away the tears forming in his eyes. From a distance, the brown line looked like a small tributary of the Modder, but this was a river of humanity that crawled lethargically through the increasing heat haze. The army of heroic Afrikander soldiers had given up their weapons and were now restored to what they had been before the war – farmers, lawyers, teachers and clerks. The English soldiers gathered *en masse*, in two huge assemblies of spectators on either side of the line of prisoners.

Standing still and silent, at a respectable distance, they watched their conquered foe as they shuffled between their ranks. Theron wondered what the English thought of their bedraggled opponents now that they had come face to face. At regular intervals, Khaki guards patrolled the spaces between the two armies, bayoneted rifles at the ready, herding the Boers towards Paardeberg Drift.

So it was over. The English had prevailed. The English lion had overwhelmed the 'Lion of Potchefstroom'.

Theron felt a coldness creep over his body and a prickle ran through the muscles across his back. He felt his throat tighten and he fought the grief that threatened to overcome him. This was not the time for weakness. Cronjé's failure had opened the door for the enemy, he thought angrily, and the Afrikander nations now had to be even more determined if they were to stop the English invasion.

Why had he been so stubborn? Why would he not listen to the advice of others? How could he have believed he could have endured when he had so few against so many? It was pig-headedness. But even in his anger at the man, Theron could not completely relinquish his respect for the 'Lion of Potchefstroom'. He clucked with exasperation. There was no doubting the great man's patriotism and conviction that the English would not take another inch of Afrikander land. There were few men who could have given more of their lives to the Republic than Oom Piet had. And it was true that the Afrikander armies had failed in their duty to him in his time of need. He had not received the reinforcements he so desperately needed and which *might* have changed the situation in his favour. And now, on the veldt below him, the consequences were being played out. Theron said a quiet prayer to guide his people through this time of darkness.

He took up his field glasses to watch the serpentine line of people as it stumbled across the shimmering veldt. At its head rode the unmistakable bulk of Cronjé, astride a large, white charger. Theron assumed the beast must have been provided by the English especially for the occasion. However, the man Theron watched leading his people was not the proud, broad-shouldered Lion of Potchefstroom and destroyer of the English, but a stooping, vanquished figure whose body swayed uncomfortably with the rolling gait of his horse as it took him to his unwished-for destination. Beside him walked his clerk, his interpreter and the tiny form of Hester, her hand resting on the thigh of her man.

Behind them shuffled almost four thousand burghers and the few women and children of the laager. Theron saw a Khaki soldier walk forward and, taking something out of his pocket, crouch down and offer it to a child. The child cowered into the heavy skirts of her mother. A burly, bearded burgher stepped forward and gesticulated for the soldier to go away, but the mother put her hand on the burgher's arm and spoke to him. He responded furiously, pointing for her to carry on walking with the rest of the prisoners. She ignored him and, walking around him, she reached down and took the offering. Nodding curtly in thanks, she broke it in two and gave a piece to each of her children. The wretched girls did not savour the gift, which Theron assumed was chocolate; instead, they devoured it. Their hunger overwhelmed any pleasure they might have had from the treat. For a moment, the shared courtesy displayed between the soldier and the mother gave Theron hope. Maybe, he reflected, after the war, there would be a chance for the two nations to live in harmony.

But that was for the future.

Before then, the war still had to be won.

The people would need time to lick their wounds and mourn the fact that the English had taken Majuba Day from them. The English had avenged their humiliation and, in turn, had inflicted humiliation on the Afrikander nations. But all was not lost, General de Wet still stood between the English and Bloemfontein. And unlike Cronjé, de Wet was one of the new, young officers who understood that this was a different kind of war, a modern war, a war that required new tactics. And the responsibility for winning this war would now fall on the shoulders of the likes of de Wet, de la Rey, Botha and Smuts. They were untested and Theron wondered if they had the wisdom to win a war against the professional English army. And then there was the matter of the imbalance in numbers. How could they succeed against so many? One thing was certain, the young generals would have to change the way the war was fought. They would have to make use of every advantage they had over the English. They would have to use their knowledge of the land to defeat them. They would have to be completely mobile and not allow themselves to be caught like Cronjé was. And they would have to keep their men motivated to the cause.

The wives and daughters would be an enormous help in keeping the pressure on their menfolk to fight. Then there was the righteousness of their cause and the fact that God Himself would guide them to victory – of that there was no doubt.

"God give us the strength to recover from this disaster and fight another day," Theron prayed.

He rested his field glasses and let his eyes roam over the vast African panorama before him. He felt his heart swell at the beauty of what he saw. This was *his* land and he would not let anyone take it from him. Then he crawled into the cave and, sitting against the cool rock of the back wall, he waited for night to return. Under cover of darkness, he would make his way back to General de Wet at Poplar Grove. General de Wet would know how to get rid of the English.

Epilogue: Wednesday 21 January 1903

Alletta Susara Bezuidenhout

Alletta Susara Bezuidenhout shielded her eyes from the early evening sun and scrutinised the approaching horseman. Eventually, she called over her shoulder, "Ma, someone's coming."

From inside the house her mother replied, "Can you see who it is?"

"No, he's not from around here."

After a flurry of activity from within the house her mother emerged and stood next to her taller daughter, their poses identical, except for the old rifle carried by the older woman. The gaggle of younger members of the family congregated behind them. They all watched the slouch-hatted silhouette as it rode slowly towards them.

The young man was deep in thought. He did not guide his horse, but left her to plod up the track towards the farmstead. Gold-tinged dust puffed up around her hooves with each step and the youth rolled easily with the gait of the beast, his bowed head nodded to her movement. He might even have been asleep. When the animal stopped at the tethering rail he started and jerked his head up. She had come to a halt under an enormous fig tree. The man's gaze ran up the trunk of the old tree. He noted the scorch marks on the bark and the charred branches which hung limply over the shell of a burnt outhouse. Through the dark, door-less void with its fringe of smoke-blackened paint, he saw the collapsed corrugated roof resting on crumpled and burnt rafters. The white-washed outside wall, gilded by the evening sun, was blemished with patches of exposed brick where the intensity of the fire had blistered the plaster from its surface.

The scars of the war mesmerised him. He had seen many burnt-out dwellings during his journey from Cradock in the Cape to this isolated Transvaal farm, but this was the first time he had been so close that he could smell it. The dank odour of long-ago incinerated timbers still hung heavy in the air. His mare shook her head and nickered, impatient to have his weight off her back.

He turned towards the house and, spotting the family watching him from the stoep, he snatched off his hat and dismounted in some embarrassment. The women stared at him, their hands shielding their eyes from the low sun. The younger children murmured cautious questions and were shushed by their older siblings. Conscious of the untidy manner of his dismount, the youth made a show of rearranging his greatcoat, dusting off and replacing his hat, and searching in his saddle bag. Then he walked towards the house. As he came closer, silhouetted against the sun, he slowed and became more tentative.

A memory stirred in Alletta. She was not sure what it was, but there was something about way he moved and carried himself. He walked with his head lowered and his face hidden by the rim of his hat, as though he did not wish to face them.

At the bottom of the steps, the young man removed his hat and looked up. Alletta's heart leapt. She took an unconscious step forward and reached a hand towards him.

"Johan!" The instant the word left her lips, she knew she was wrong. Her mouth was suddenly dry, her throat tightened, she felt her heart constrict. Her hand flew to her lips and pressed hard on her soft flesh. Of course it was not Johan. He would be nearly twenty now. This was a boy of fifteen or sixteen.

"Johan?" her voice sounded small.

"No, sister. I am Hendrick, Janie's younger brother."

"He is all right, isn't he?" Her voice caught in her throat.

Hendrick Coetzee went to speak, but instead inhaled sharply and held his breath. He looked down and turned slightly away to hide his tears. Alletta saw the muscles in his jaw tighten as he struggled to compose himself. He raised an arm and brushed his sleeve across his eyes. His shoulders heaved as he exhaled. After a further hesitation he squared his shoulders, looked up and mounted the first step leading up to the stoep. He looked at Alletta's mother and stretched out his hand to her. He was holding a small, black object. She leant forward to accept the offering.

"This is for Alletta Bezuidenhout."

She paused, looked surprised and then turned to the tall woman standing next to her.

"It's for you, Lettie."

Coetzee turned his confused gaze on Lettie. He had been expecting a fresh, young girl with a smooth, youthful complexion and a smiling face. That's how Janie had described her. But this woman's face was bony and angular. The low sunlight cast deep, lined shadows across her face and emphasised the sharpness of her features which seemed to be set in a permanent frown. Her lips were tight and pensive, but their fullness hinted at her former beauty which had been eroded by nearly two years in an English concentration camp. She stared back at him with the fierce determination of someone who had endured much and had survived. He held the small, black Bible out to her.

"J–Janie asked me to return this to you," he stammered. "He said he was very sorry that he was not able to come himself."

"But he will still come? Won't he?" She asked the question automatically, out of hope.

Coetzee looked at her. Did she not understand?

"I'm sorry, sister. Janie was captured by the Khakis with Fredrick Marais in 1901. He – they were tried for treason. They were found guilty…," Coetzee faltered, "and … and Janie was…."

"Shush!" The sound was emphatic and harsh. Alletta knew what he was going to say and she did *not* want to hear it. But she instantly regretted the severity of her interruption as she looked down into his moist eyes. He was only a boy, she thought.

"I'm sorry, Hendrick, I did not mean to be abrupt."

With a shaking hand she took the Bible from him. She stared down at the small, black object in her hand. There followed an awkward silence, broken eventually by Coetzee.

"Janie wrote a note inside for you."

"A note?"

"Yes, to you. Inside the front cover."

"You read it?"

He could not hold her gaze. "I'm sorry."

She felt anger well up inside her. He read her note! Her note from Johan! She glowered at the top of his hat. The young man's shoulders shuddered and he sniffed abruptly. A tear splashed on the wooden step at his feet. She reached forward and touched his shoulder. He looked up and she smiled at him.

"Thank you Hendrick. Thank you very much for bringing the Bible back to me." She tried to continue. "It is very ki…," but her voice failed her.

She turned to her mother. She gave Alletta a tight-lipped smile.

"Ma," Alletta croaked. She took a deep breath, "I think I shall wait out here a while."

"Of course, darling." She reached up and touched her daughter's cheek. A tug on her skirt made her look down into the solemn face of a young child. Dear God, she wondered, when will the war be over for us? Forcing a smile and a cheerful voice, she turned to Coetzee, "Come, Hendrick, come inside. You must be starving. Come, have some coffee and something to eat."

As her mother shepherded everyone into the house, Alletta listened to her apologising to Coetzee.

"Sorry about the rifle, Hendrick, but my husband and my boys are still prisoners-of-war on St Helena. We have no idea when they might be back and there are some dangerous men roaming around these days. It will be good to have a man around the house again. I hope you will be able to stay for a while."

As the voices faded away into the house Alletta looked down at the little book in her hands. It surprised her that such a small thing could hold such profound messages, messages that had guided her throughout her life. And now, it seemed, her Bible contained a new message. Grasping the balustrade, she unsteadily sat down on the top step of the stoep. Hesitantly, and with trembling fingers, she opened the cover of her Bible. Inside she read:

My dearest Lettie, it seems our paths are destined not to cross again on God's earthly kingdom, but please do not mourn me. My death shall not be as I wished it to be, but it will be quick and my love for our People and my belief in our right to independence will remain unchanged. So, you see, I am fine. I will be with my Saviour in His blessed eternal home. Please do not let our parting cause you sadness. Rather, remember our time together. Although brief, it was the happiest time of my life. I wish you to have a good and full life and bear many children for the Republic. I ask you to hold me in your heart. I shall wait for you in the kingdom of Our Lord. God be with you always. Yours forever, Johan.

Alletta clutched the little book to her chest. Across the veldt, above the distant flat horizon, the huge African sun glowed crimson. She deliberately watched it sinking slowly towards the earth. Then she tilted her head back and closed her eyes tightly. A single tear escaped from the corner of her eye. The dying sun bathed the tear in its red glow and it ran down her cheek like a miniature river of blood.

THE END

Denouement

With Cronjé, four thousand Transvaal and Free State Boers surrendered to the British Army. After their defeat at Paardeberg, the Boers fell back, under the command of General de Wet, to Poplar Grove, the next defensible position on the Modder River. When French attempted a movement around the Boers' right flank, de Wet harassed him to such an extent that French complained to Roberts that he would be unable to complete the manoeuvre without additional forces. However, the defeat of Cronjé had such a demoralising effect on the Boers that many drifted away from their positions at Poplar Grove. The loss of burghers, through desertion, was so extensive that it forced de Wet to abandon Poplar Grove.

In Natal, on the day after the surrender of Cronjé at Paardeberg, Buller was finally able to relieve Ladysmith, effectively returning the Natal colony to the British.

With the collapse of the Boer defences at Poplar Grove, the route to Bloemfontein was opened and Roberts entered the capital of the Orange Free State unopposed on 13 March 1900. After a number of delays, due to disease among his troops and supply failures, Roberts marched north and captured Johannesburg on 31 May, and Pretoria, the Transvaal capital, on 5 June. With the capture of the capital cities and other main towns, Roberts believed the war to be over and he left South Africa to make a triumphant return the Britain. Kitchener was left behind to tidy up.

However, even before Roberts had departed, the war had entered a new phase, with the Boers changing tactics to a guerrilla campaign using mobile mounted commandos. Under the leadership of Generals Christiaan de Wet, Jacobus de la Rey, Louis Botha, Jan Smuts and others, the war continued for nearly two more years. It finally came to an end on 31 May 1902 with the signing of the Treaty of Vereeniging. It was the most costly war in which the British Government had engaged during the reign of Queen Victoria.

In 1909, the British Parliament passed the South Africa Act, through which the nation state of the Union of South Africa was created. In 1910 General Louis Botha became the first Prime Minister of the Union of South Africa. The Boers had regained control not only of their beloved Republics, but also of the Cape and Natal colonies.

Postscript: The Main Players

Major Friedrich Wilhelm Richard Albrecht was captured at Paardeberg and sent to the prisoner-of-war camp on St Helena.

Sergeant Alfred Atkinson died from his wounds on 21 February 1900. He was awarded the Victoria Cross for his acts of bravery during the Battle of Paardeberg. His medal is displayed at the Green Howards Museum, Richmond, Yorkshire, England. He is buried in Gruisbank British Cemetery, Paardeberg.

Johannes Petrus Coetzee was captured by British forces, together with Fredrick Abram Marais, at Wildefontein on the night of 16 June 1901. He was tried for treason and the attempted murder of a British soldier. Coetzee admitted joining the commando, but denied the charge of attempted murder. He was found guilty and returned to his hometown of Cradock. He was visited by his father, to whom he said: "Father, please tell mother and our family that they must not mourn me. I am fine. I am going to my Saviour and my blessed eternal home. I know you will mourn me and that is what is tormenting me." He was hanged on 13 July 1901. He was 16 years old.

Doctor Arthur Ignatius Conan Doyle DL left South Africa in August 1900 and later that year, believing the war to be over, published his history of the war, *The Great Boer War*. He continued to publish novels and played first-class cricket for the Marylebone Cricket Club, on one occasion taking the wicket of W.G. Grace. He was knighted in 1902. Conan Doyle died from a heart attack on 7 July 1930, aged 71. He is buried in the cemetery of All Saints Church, Minstead, Hampshire, England.

General Pieter Arnoldus Cronjé, accompanied by Hester, was sent to the prisoner-of-war camp on St Helena, where he remained until the end of the war. He was subjected to bitter recriminations by the Boers and ridiculed in the British press. He was shunned by other Boer generals and not invited to peace talks or asked to participate in post-war policy-making. In 1904 he took part in Anglo-Boer re-enactments, including the battle of Paardeberg, during the World Fair in St Louis, Missouri, and became dubbed 'the circus general' by the South African press. Under the circumstances, he did not return home from the USA, but instead joined a show on Coney Island, Brooklyn, New York. Cronjé did eventually return to South Africa and died in the Transvaal on 4 February 1911.

Lieutenant-General John Denton Pinkstone French was appointed Knight Commander of the Order of St Michael and St George (KCMG) in recognition of his services in South Africa. After the war, he returned to Aldershot and progressed rapidly through the ranks, becoming Field Marshal in June 1913. At the start of the First World War he was the natural choice as Commander-in-Chief of the British Expeditionary Force. However, disagreements over military tactics started almost immediately with Kitchener and Haig, and orders to retreat during the Battle of Mons were ignored by Smith-Dorrien, who instead mounted a vigorous defence of his position. In December 1915, French was returned to England as Commander-in-Chief of the British Home Forces, in which role he oversaw the defeat of the Irish uprising in 1916. In May 1918, he was appointed Supreme Commander of the British Army in Ireland; in December 1919, an Irish Republican Army unit attempted to ambush and kill him. French retired from the British Army in April 1921 and died from cancer of the bladder on 22 May 1925, aged 72. He is buried in the churchyard of St Mary the Virgin Church, Ripple, Kent, England. Ironically, French's sister, Charlotte Despard, was an anti-war campaigner, Irish nationalist and Sinn Féin member.

Colonel Ormelie Campbell Hannay was buried, where he fell, near Vendutie Drift. A wall plaque dedicated to his memory was placed in the Holy Trinity Scottish Episcopal Church in Stirling, Scotland.

Major-General Horatio Herbert Kitchener succeeded Roberts as Commander of British Forces in November 1900 and expanded the strategies devised by Roberts to force the Boer commandos to submit. These included a scorched-earth policy and the establishment of concentration camps to remove civilian support for the Boers from the contryside. Kitchener took a more conciliatory approach in the negotiations that brought the war to a close, compared to that of the Governor of the Cape Colony. The British government, wishing the war to come to an end, sided with Kitchener and the Treaty of Vereeniging was signed in 1902. Kitchener subsequently went to India as Commander-in-Chief and was promoted to the rank of Field Marshal in 1910. At the outset of the First World War he was appointed Secretary of State for War. Following his prediction of a long and costly war that would require huge armies to achieve victory, a recruitment campaign was initiated. The poster of Kitchener that was used in the campaign became one of the most enduring images of the war. Kitchener quickly fell out with French, the Commander of the British Expeditionary Force, over military tactics. The failure of the Gallipoli campaign, which Kitchener supported, and a negative press campaign engineered by French eroded Kitchener's political reputation and his influence in the British Government declined, although he remained a popular figure with the public. In 1916, he sailed to Russia on a diplomatic mission aboard the cruiser, *HMS Hampshire*. On 5 June the *Hampshire* struck a mine and sank. Kitchener's body was never recovered.

State President Stephanus Johannes Paulus Kruger attended the last session of the Volksraad on 7 May 1900 and fled from Pretoria on 29 May. For weeks he moved between safe houses in the Eastern Transvaal. In October 1900, he left South Africa for Mozambique and boarded the Dutch warship *Gelderland*, sent by Queen Wilhelmina of the Netherlands. His wife, who was ill, could not travel with him. She died in South Africa in July 1901. Kruger sailed to France and travelled to Germany, but the Kaiser refused to see him, so he settled in exile in The Netherlands before moving to Clarens, Switzerland, where he died on 14 July 1904. His body was embalmed and buried in The Hague. After permission was given by the British government, he was reburied on 16 December 1904 in the Heroes' Acre, Church Street Cemetery, Pretoria.

General Hector Archibald Macdonald continued to command the Highland Brigade during the war and he was knighted in 1901. In 1902, he was appointed Commander-in-Chief of British troops in Ceylon (Sri Lanka). While there he ruffled feathers by forcing the ill-disciplined local militia, most of whom were the sons of British planters, to show more 'spit and polish'. He also offended the Governor by yelling at him to get off his parade ground. His alienation was compounded through his preference of socialising with the locals, rather than the British community. Rumours began to circulate about him being homosexual, and when direct accusations were made (even though homosexuality was not illegal in Ceylon) he was advised by the Governor to return to London to avoid a scandal. Conversely, in London, Lord Roberts advised him to return to Ceylon to face a court martial and clear his name. Macdonald stopped over in Paris and, while there, he read in a newspaper the accusations made against him, which had been released to the press. Macdonald returned to his hotel room and shot himself. The suicide caused a public outcry. An attempt to hold a secret funeral at Dean Cemetery, Edinburgh, resulted in thirty thousand people attending to pay their last respects. The case file against Macdonald appears to have been destroyed after his suicide. In 1903, a Government Commission concluded: *we cannot but deplore the sad circumstances of the case that has fallen so disastrously on one whom we have found innocent of any crime attributed to him*. Memorials in his honour stand above Dingwall, Scotland, and at Mulbuie on the Black Isle, near his birthplace. Strangely, reports started to appear of Macdonald being alive and living in China. During the First World War the German High Command attempted to capitalise on his continued popularity in the British Army by fostering rumours that their own general, General August von Mackensen, was actually Hector Macdonald.

Fredrick Abram Marais was captured by British forces, together with Johannes Petrus Coetzee, at Wildefontein on the night of 16 June 1901. He was tried for treason, found guilty and returned to his home town for his execution. He was hanged in the public square on 10 July 1901. Before his execution, he called out to those watching: "My God! My God! See and behold these deeds that they are doing to me and my nation!" He was buried in a prison grave. In 1907 his body was exhumed and reburied in the Middleburg Cemetery. His name appears on the monument to the Boer fallen in the town square.

Lieutenant-Colonel William Dillon Otter continued as commander of the 2nd Battalion, Royal Canadian Regiment. After the war he became the first Canadian-born Chief of the General Staff for Canadian forces. He retired in 1910 as General Sir William Otter KCMG, CVO. During the First World War he came out of retirement to command operations for the internment of enemy nationals resident in Canada. He passed away on 6 May 1929.

Major Michael Frederic Rimington returned to the 6th Dragoons to take command of the regiment, as Lieutenant-Colonel, for the remainder of the war. He was mentioned in dispatches five times for his service in South Africa. In 1903, he took command of the 3rd Cavalry Brigade and in 1907 was posted to India, becoming Inspector-General of Cavalry. He remained in India until 1916 and was given command of a reserve centre in the United Kingdom until 1918. He retired from the British Army in 1919.

Field Marshal Frederick Sleigh Roberts handed command in South Africa to Lord Kitchener in December 1900 and returned to England as Commander-in-Chief of the Army in succession to Lord Wolseley. On his arrival at Southampton, he had an audience with Queen Victoria and the next day was welcomed home at Paddington Station by the Prince and Princess of Wales and driven in procession to Buckingham Palace. In 1905, he resigned his post and devoted himself to improving rifle skills and military training in the British Army. He was made Honorary Officer of many regiments. He died of pneumonia in France on 14 November 1914 while visiting Indian troops fighting in the First World War. After lying in state, he was given a state funeral and buried in St Paul's Cathedral.

Major-General Horace Smith-Dorrien was posted to India after the war and served under Kitchener. He returned to England in 1907 and played a key role as commanding officer in several of the major battles of the First World War. He retired in 1923 and published his autobiography, *Memories of Forty-Eight Years' Service*, in 1925. He died, aged 72, on 12 August 1930, following a car accident, and is buried in the cemetery of St Peter's Church, Berkhamsted, England.

Captain Daniël Johannes Stephanus Theron founded, in March 1900, a new scout corps called Theron se Verkenningskorps (TVK). He and the TVK achieved considerable notoriety for destroying railway bridges, releasing Boer prisoners and capturing British officers, rations and arms. Lord Roberts labelled him "the chief thorn in the side of the British" and a bounty of £1,000 was offered for his capture. In September 1900, Theron was cornered by British mounted infantry and killed by a salvo of cannon fire. On learning of his death, General de Wet said: "Men as lovable or as valiant there might be, but where shall I find a man who combined so many virtues and good qualities in one person?" Theron is honoured on a number of monuments, including one in Pretoria, inaugurated, in 2002, by the former South African President, Nelson Mandela. His great-great-niece is the noted actress, Charlize Theron.

Lieutenant James Vipan Maitland Watermeyer died in 1939.

General Christiaan Rudolf de Wet was to become one of the most renowned Boer generals of the war. Developing and implementing guerrilla tactics that suited the mobile Boer army, he successfully campaigned against the British forces until the end of the war. De Wet took an active part in the peace negotiations that were to end the war and was a signatory of the Treaty of Vereeniging. He was briefly, during the negotiations, Acting State President of the Orange Free State, when President Steyn was struck down by illness. After the war, de Wet and other Boer generals visited Europe to raise funds to rebuild the Free State and Transvaal colonies and to attempt to modify the terms of the peace agreement. Huge crowds welcomed the generals across Europe. In 1902, de Wet published his memoirs, *De Stryd tusschen Boer en Brit* (*Three Years War*). In 1907, he was elected to the Orange River Colony parliament and appointed Minister of Agriculture. He was an active campaigner for the closer union of the Southern African colonies, which happened in 1910 with the formation of the Union of South Africa. With the outbreak of the First World War, de Wet was instrumental in leading a rebellion against the South Africa Government, because of its support of the British against the Germans. During a brief civil war, his commando was defeated and he was taken prisoner and sentenced to six years' imprisonment and fined £2,000. The fine was paid by sympathisers and he was released after one year, having given a written promise to take no further part in politics. De Wet withdrew from public life and died, some say a broken man, on 3 February 1922. He was given a state funeral and is buried at the foot of the Women's Monument in Bloemfontein.

Postscript: Supporting Cast

Captain Henry Mittleberger Arnold was shot on 18 February when he stood up to survey the Boer lines. He died five days later.

Private Jonathan Brown was killed in action during the Boer War.

Private A. Bruce died as a result of wounds he sustained on 18 February.

Private Jimmy Carpenter died of disease while on active service on South Africa.

General Andries P.J. Cronjé surrendered in June 1900 and later jointly led the National Scouts, a force of 1,360 surrendered Transvaal burghers who took up scouting service with the British Army.

Mrs Hester Susanna Cronjé (née Visser) accompanied her husband, General Pieter Cronjé, to the prisoner-of-war camp on St Helena until their return in 1902. She died in 1903.

Private G. Dibble died of typhoid fever while serving in South Africa.

Private James Halkett Findlay was killed in action on 18 February.

Major Douglas Haig was given, in January 1901, command of a column of two thousand five hundred men to patrol Cape Colony. His duties included the burning of farms and rounding up of Boer women and children into camps. In May 1901 he was given command of the 17th Lancers. Haig was mentioned in dispatches four times during his service in South Africa. Between 1902 and 1914 he served variously in India and England, mainly in non-combat roles, including organising the British Expeditionary Force (BEF). At the start of the First World War he commanded half of the BEF, under the overall command of Field Marshal Sir John French. As a consequence, he was a commanding officer for some of the key opening battles of the war. He succeeded French as Commander-in-Chief of the BEF in December 1915 and then presided over the disastrous Battle of the Somme, for which he was later dubbed 'Butcher Haig' because of the huge loss of life that resulted. In 1917, he was promoted to Field Marshal. Haig retired in January 1920 and devoted the rest of his life to the welfare of ex-servicemen. He was a co-founder of the British Legion in 1921. Haig died from a heart attack, aged 66, on 29 January 1928 and was given a state funeral. He is buried at Dryburgh Abbey, Dryburgh, Scotland, his grave marked by a simple Commonwealth War Graves Commission headstone. In 1937, an equestrian memorial statue was erected in his honour in Whitehall, London.

Band Sergeant William Hall died of typhoid fever in late 1900, while serving in South Africa. He left a wife and seven children, the oldest aged 11.

Colonel Charles Gore Hay, 20th Earl of Erroll, was given command of the Yeomanry Brigade in South Africa. After the war, he held the office of Lord-in-Waiting to King Edward VII and took part in the First World War. He died on 8 July 1927, aged 75.

Lieutenant General Thomas Kelly-Kenny and his 6th Division distinguished themselves at Poplar Grove, after a six-hour march under a scorching sun. In October 1901, through the influence of King Edward VII, a close personal friend, Kelly-Kenny was appointed Adjutant-General to the Forces. Lord Roberts was opposed to the appointment as he considered Kelly-Kenny too conservative about reforming the army, but, supported by the King, Kelly-Kenny retained the post until 1904, the year in which he was knighted. In 1905 he was decorated by the Kaiser with the order of the Grand Cross of the Red Eagle and in 1906 took part in a royal mission to Japan to present the Order of the Garter to the Emperor, where Kelly-Kenny received the Grand Cross of the Rising Sun. After that Kelly-Kenny resided mainly in the UK, living the life of a socialite and mixing regularly with the royal family. He retired in 1907 and in 1909 he sold his Irish estates to his tenants. He died on 26 December 1914 and is buried in Hove Cemetery, Sussex. He left strict instructions that he was not to have a military funeral.

Pieter Krueler and his father were taken to the prisoner-of-war camp on St Helena. His father died while a prisoner. His younger brother, mother and sister all perished in a British concentration camp. During the First World War Krueler enlisted with the German army and took part in their Eastern African campaigns. He fought for the Nationalists in the Spanish Civil War. He died in 1986 at the age of 101.

John (Jack) Moody Lane was captured and sent to St Helena.

"Jim" Makokela continued as a wagon driver for many years. He was employed for a while by Percy Fitzpatrick and their time together is described in Fitzpatrick's auto-biography, *Jock of the Bushveld*.

August Schulenburg was sent to Bermuda as a prisoner of war. After his release, he took advantage of his proximity to North America to visit German relatives who had settled in the US Midwest. He studied at the Washington University Medical Department in St Louis, Missouri. In 1904, he was invited to join a reception of Boer veterans who were taking part in re-enactments of battles from the war as part of the 1904 St Louis World Fair. He graduated in 1906 and returned to South Africa in late 1907. The British colonial government did not recognise his American qualification so he travelled to London and enrolled at Guy's Hospital Medical College to attain the appropriate qualification. As a general practitioner, Schulenburg spent most of his career in Ventersdorp and Potchefstroom. He died in 1964.

General Spruit undertook the escort of the Executive Council (Republic Governments) during the time it was attempting to avoid capture by the British. He was killed on 6 February 1901 in an action against Smith-Dorrien.

Count Adalbert Sternberg was one of the last Boer sympathisers to leave Jacobsdal as the British were capturing the town. He fled with the intention of joining up with Cronjé, but was captured, trying to cross the Modder River, on the night of 14 February. He was able to convince the British authorities that he was a war correspondent and was allowed to go to London. However, he caused a furore by claiming to have been acting as a military adviser to the Boers. As a result, he was forced to leave for France.

Colonel George Henri Anne-Marie Victor de Villebois-Mareuil was promoted to the rank of Major-General and given command of all foreign volunteers in March 1900. He died on 6 April 1900 in a skirmish against Methuen near Boshof, Transvaal, having refused to surrender and while waiting for nightfall to make good his escape. He was given a full military burial at Boshof, paid for personally by Methuen. His body was exhumed and reburied in the Heroes' Acre in Magersfontein in 1971. A memorial to Villebois-Mareuil was erected in Nantes, France. De Villebois-Mareuil's horse was taken to Britain by Lord Chesham, where it lived until February 1911. Its heart and ceremonial trappings were buried on the village green in Latimer, England, next to the South African war memorial.

Pieter Daniël de Wet fought beside his brother in a series of successful operations against the British. However, with the fall of Pretoria, Piet de Wet became disillusioned with the conduct of the war and the physical devastation being caused by it. He became increasingly pessimistic about the outcome of the war and surrendered to the British in July 1900. In early 1901, he appealed to his brother to give up the struggle. In response, Christiaan threatened to shoot him like a dog if they ever met. De Wet became involved in the peace committee movement, trying to convince active Boers to surrender. In early 1902, de Wet took command of a unit of the Orange River Colony Volunteers, which undertook scouting activities for the British. De Wet suffered condemnation after the war as a "hands-upper" and was never forgiven by his brother.

Author's Note

Although this novel is based on historical events, it is above all a story. The names used for many of the characters are those of people who took part in the events described, however the descriptions of their personalities, behaviours, thoughts, beliefs and decisions are entirely fictional.

Although I have remained, to a large extent, true to the main events leading up to and during the Battle of Paardeberg, I have taken substantial liberties in the detail for the purpose of allowing the narrative to flow. Also, I have been liberal with the presence of some characters. For example, although Arthur Conan Doyle was present in South Africa during the Boer War, he arrived in the country after the Battle of Paardeberg took place.

It is noteworthy that the names of British combatants are generally well recorded whereas those of Boer combatants are not. I have therefore been particularly inventive with the use of Boer characters in this novel. A number are entirely fictitious and others, although they took part in the war, played no part at Paardeberg. I have taken the liberty of placing them at Paardeberg purely in order to balance the use of historical characters in the narrative.

I have also shortened some timescales to allow certain events to occur within the period during which the story takes place. Most particularly, I have curtailed the time it would take for the symptoms of enteric fever to develop.

Finally, although greatly interested in history, I am not an historian. As a consequence, I have no doubt made many historical *faux pas*, for which I ask your indulgence.

Sarie Marais – Boer War Song

My Sarie Marais is so ver van my hart,
Maar 'k hoop om haar weer te sien.
Sy het in die wyk van die Mooirivier gewoon,
Nog voor die oorlog het begin.

O bring my trug na die ou Transvaal,
Daar waar my Sarie woon:
Daar onder in die mielies by die groen doringboom
Daar woon my Sarie Marais,
Daar onder in die mielies by die groen doringboom
Daar woon my Sarie Marais.

Ek was so bang, dat die kakies my sou vang,
En ver oor die see wegstuur;
Toe vlug ek na die kant van die Upington se sand
Daar onder langs die Grootrivier.

Die kakies is mos net soos 'n krokodillepes
Hul sleep hou altyd water toe.
Hulle gooi jou op 'n skip vir ''n lange lange trip
Die josie weet waarna toe.

Verlossing het gekom, en die huistoe gaan was daar,
Trug na die ou Transvaal,
My liewelingspersoon sal seker ook daar wees
Om my met 'n kus te beloon.

Sarie Marais – English Translation

My Sarie Marais is so far away from my heart,
But I hope to see her again.
She lives in the district of Mooi River,
Since before the war began.

Oh, bring me back to the old Transvaal,
To where my Sarie lives:
There by the corn fields near the green thorn tree,
There lives my Sarie Marais.
There by the corn fields near the green thorn tree,
There lives my Sarie Marais.

I feared so that the English would get me,
And send me away across the sea;
So I fled to the sand banks of the Upington,
There down by the Great (Orange) River

The English are just like crocodiles,
They always drag you down to the water.
They throw you on a ship for a long long trip,
Only the Lord knows to where.

Liberation came, and it was time to go home,
Back to my dear Transvaal.
The person I love will certainly be there,
To reward me with a kiss.

Sources

Of course the internet served as an invaluable source of information for this novel, but I have restricted my list of sources to the key books I consulted. Several of the books listed below are available as ebooks from the Gutenberg website (www.gutenberg.org).

Conan Doyle, Sir Arthur (1900) *The Great Boer War*. Smith, Elder & Co., London.

Farwell, Bryon (1976) *The Great Boer War*. Harper & Row, New York.

Jones, Spencer (2009) *The Influence of the Boer War (1899–1900) on the Tactical Development of the Regular British Army 1902–1914*. PhD thesis, University of Wolverhampton, UK.

Kruger, Rayne (1959) *Goodbye Dolly Gray*. Cassell & Co, London.

Miller, Carman (1993) *Painting the Map Red: Canada and the South African War, 1899–1902*. McGill-Queen's University Press, Montreal, Canada.

Packenham, Thomas (1982) *The Boer War*. Futura, London.

Pulser, Cameron and Wright, Harold (2000) "It's just like the resurrection": The Boer Surrender to the Canadians at Paardeberg. *Canadian Military History*, 9: 47–54.

Smith-Dorrien, Horace (2009) *Isandlwana to the Great War*. (first published as *Memories of Forty-Eight Years' Service*), Leonaur.

Sternberg, Count (1901) *My Experiences of the Boer War*. Longmans, Green and Co, London.

Wessels André (2000) *Lord Roberts and the war in South Africa 1899–1902*. Army Records Society, Sutton Publishing, Stroud.

De Wet, Christiaan Rudolf (1902) *Three Years' War*. Charles Scribner's Sons, New York.

Wilson, Herbert Wrigley (1900) *With the Flag to Pretoria: A History of the Boer War of 1899–1900* (Volumes I and II). Harmsworth Brothers, London.

Dear reader,

Reviews from readers like you play a very important role in encouraging others to consider reading new authors. If you enjoyed this book, please consider writing a short review on the website where you purchased it and also on https://www.goodreads.com/ and sharing the review with your friends on your social networking sites. It would really mean a lot!

Thank you,

Martin Marais

www.ingramcontent.com/pod-product-compliance
Lightning Source LLC
Chambersburg PA
CBHW030936150426

42812CB00064B/2926/J